THE DAYS OF ROGER FEDERER

THE DAYS OF ROGER FEDERER

RANDY WALKER

New Chapter Press

"The Days of Roger Federer" is published by New Chapter Press (www.NewChapterMedia.com) and is distributed by the Independent Publishers Group (www.IPGBook.com).

The cover photos are courtesy of Chris Nicholson. Special thanks to Wojtek "Voo" Dzidowski for his assistance with research.

For more information on this title or New Chapter Press contact:
Randy Walker
Managing Partner
New Chapter Press
1175 York Ave
Suite #3s
New York, NY 10065
Rwalker@NewChapterMedia.com

Contents

From The Author

How did this book come about? Those who know me know my penchant for compiling "On This Day" type information. It started during my early days while working for the U.S. Tennis Association when I put together "On This Day In U.S. Open History" that media and fans still enjoy to this day. During my days as the press officer for the U.S. Davis Cup team, I put together "On This Day In U.S. Davis Cup History." Soon all of this information was morphed together, built upon and published in my book "On This Day In Tennis History" – that soon became a mobile app (available at www.TennisHistoryApp.com). In 2007, when I published Rene Stauffer's book *"Roger Federer: Quest for Perfection"* (www.RogerFedererBook.com), I included a section that was called the "Roger Federer career time-line." This document, through the years, was added to and expanded and used in promoting Stauffer's book and eventually became this book. Roger Federer is one of the most important figures in the history of tennis so, as a tennis historian, I felt it important to document his career in this manner for people of the present and future to enjoy. Feel free to engage with us on Twitter via our @FedererBook handle and via the Facebook page for the Stauffer "Quest for Perfection" book.

Thanks for your interest and I hope you enjoy the project.

Randy Walker
New York, N.Y., 2014

JANUARY

January 1

2014 – Roger Federer plays his first singles match of his 2014 season, beating fellow 32-year-old Jarkko Nieminen 6-4, 6-2 in his opening match at the Brisbane International in Australia. Federer plays the match with a new 98-square inch oversized racquet, newly-designed with his racquet company Wilson after tinkering with larger racquet frame months earlier after Wimbledon. "I had a much longer time to get ready for this swing than I had last time around, after Wimbledon, before the American summer so I'm not thinking about it when I'm going out there, which is a great thing," Federer says of his new racquet. The 69-minute match increases Federer's career head-to-head against the Fin to 14-0, after first playing him at the 2002 Kremlin Cup in Moscow.

2002 – Roger Federer and his future wife Mirka Vavrinec complete play representing Switzerland at the Hopman Cup, the official mixed team competition of the International Tennis Federation, as the Spanish team of Arantxa Sanchez Vicario and Tommy Robredo eliminate

Switzerland from contention with a 3-0 victory in Perth, Australia. Vavrinec, who marries Federer in 2009, loses the opening women's singles match to Sanchez-Vicario 6-2, 6-0. "I am really gutted," says Vavrinec after the 50-minute match. "On the WTA circuit, my defeats only harm me, but here in Perth, I have now twice put Roger in a difficult position." Robredo then clinches the Spanish victory with a 7-6 (7), 6-2 win over the twenty-year-old Federer. Says Robredo of his singles win, "To start the year like this is unbelievable...to beat Roger, I mean he is a really great player. I managed to win the tiebreak and then just played great in the second set. In the meaningless mixed doubles match, Robredo and Sanchez-Vicario beat Federer and Vavrinec 6-2, 6-3.

2010 – Roger Federer loses to Robin Soderling, the same man he beat the previous June to win the French Open, by a 6-7 (6), 7-6 (1), 6-2 in the semifinals of the season-opening Capitala World Tennis Championship exhibition tournament at Abu Dhabi, United Arab Emirates.

2011 – Top-ranked Rafael Nadal defends his title at the Capitala World Tennis Championship exhibition tournament in Abu Dhabi, United Arab Emirates with a 7-6 (4), 7-6 (3) victory over Roger Federer in a match that does not feature a service break. Federer leads 3-0 in the first-set tie-breaker before Nadal wins the next five points and holds on to win it 7-4. In the second tie breaker, Nadal takes a quick 3-1 lead and holds on to win four of the next six points.

2003 – Roger Federer beats fellow Swiss Michel Kratochvil 6-4, 6-4 to reach the quarterfinals of the Doha Open in Qatar. "I am happy with my form here in Doha," Federer says following the match. "Initially I had some problems with the balls which I think become quite heavy because of the weather conditions here in Doha. I couldn't serve well enough in the first match, but I feel my serve is coming back. I wanted to make a good start here and I am glad I have reached the quarterfinals of the Qatar Open. This is a good start for me."

January 2

2011 – Rafael Nadal and Roger Federer, the world's No. 1 and No. 2-ranked players and the top two seeds at the Qatar ExxonMobil Open respectively, kick off the 2011 ATP World Tour season in Doha by hitting tennis balls on a court laid over the water of Doha Bay. "It was a fantastic experience," says Nadal. "For the past three years we have done a few different things, and this one was a very nice experience. It's going to be a very exciting season for me, I think. I would love to play against Roger a few more times this year, because when we play each other it's in the final." Says Federer of the experience, "It was good fun. It was so different. You're always excited and nervous to see how it will turn out. It is always nice promoting an event and an entire tour with Rafa. I am of course very excited about playing another season."

2003 – Jan-Michael Gambill upsets top-seeded Roger Federer 6-4, 7-5 in the quarterfinals of the Qatar Open in

Doha. Gambill gets "last laughs" on Federer, losing his first four matches against the future world No. 1 before winning in Qatar in their fifth and final meeting. Federer hits only one ace, connects on only 58 percent of his first serves and wins 67 percent of the points when he got those first serves in.

2009 – Andy Murray edges Roger Federer 4-6, 6-2, 7-6 (6) in the semifinals of the Capitala World Tennis Championship tennis exhibition in Abu Dhabi, United Arab Emirates.

2010 – Roger Federer defeats David Ferrer of Spain 6-1, 7-5 for third place in the Capitala World Tennis Championship tennis exhibition in Abu Dhabi, United Arab Emirates. Rafael Nadal wins the title with a 7-6(3), 7-5 win over Robin Soderling, who defeated Federer in the semifinals.

2001 – Roger Federer and Martina Hingis combine to lose only 11 total games as they lead Switzerland to a 3-0 win over Australia at the Hopman Cup in Perth. World No. 1 Hingis beats No. 56-ranked Nicole Pratt 6-1, 6-1 in 48 minutes, while Federer, age 19, gives Switzerland the unassailable 2-0 lead beating Richard Fromberg 6-3, 6-2. Federer and Hingis then pair in mixed doubles, beating Fromberg and Pratt 6-1, 6-3.

2014 – Roger Federer and his French partner Nicolas Mahut win a thrilling quarterfinal doubles match at the Brisbane International, defeating the Bulgarian-French combination of Grigor Dimitrov and Jeremy Chardy 7-6, 6-7, (11-9) in an hour and 40 minutes.

January 3

2005 – Roger Federer needs less than an hour in his opening match of the 2005 season beating David Ferrer 6-1, 6-1 in the first round of the Qatar Open in Doha. The match is the second career meeting between Federer and the future top five player from Spain, whom Federer beats all 14 times they play through July of 2013.

2006 – Top-ranked Roger Federer opens his 2006 tennis season by defeating Czech Ivo Minar 6-1, 6-3 in the first round of the Qatar Open at Doha. Federer needs only 18 minutes to secure the first set, despite wearing a brace around his right ankle from an injury late in the 2005 season. "The last thing you want to do is start with a loss," says Federer. "I was happy with my movement and that's obviously important after the injury. And I'm pleased with the way I was hitting the ball. I felt very composed. I was confident because I was playing well in practice, but it's still a new year and you want to make sure you will do well again."

2012 – In a rematch of the tournament final from a year ago, Roger Federer kicks off his 2012 season with an easy 6-2, 6-2 win over Nikolay Davydenko in the first round of the Qatar Open in Doha. "I'm very happy," Federer proclaims in his post-match press conference. "It was a good first match for me into the new season, and I think it was a combination between me playing actually really well in the first match and Nikolay just not finding his range, what we're used to seeing from him in the past." The win improves Federer's record over Davydenko to

16-2, including his 6-3, 6-4 victory on the same court 12 months earlier.

2014 – Hitting nine aces and breaking serve five times, Roger Federer advances into the semifinals of the Brisbane International with a 6-1, 6-1 victory over Marinko Matosevic 6-1, 6-1 in just 58 minutes. "Tonight I felt very good against Matosevic who can play very dangerous," says Federer. "He's got a good enough serve and return as well. But I was able to control most of the match except the very beginning. For that, I'm very happy."

January 4

2011 – Roger Federer continues to enhance his reputation of being the master of the "tweener" shot as he hits a dramatic through-the-legs winner en route to beating Dutch qualifier Thomas Schoorel 7-6 (3), 6-3 in the first round of the Qatar Open in Doha in his first official match of the season. Leading 5-2 and faced with a ball that changed direction after clipping the top of the net, Federer slams the ball through his legs for a clean winner into the corner. "It's one of the best shots again of my career, one I'm going to look back on and smile, of course," Federer says. "It was quite fantastic."

2006 – Roger Federer needs two tiebreakers to beat Fabrice Santoro 7-6 (2), 7-6 (5) in one hour, 25 minutes and reach the quarterfinals of the Qatar Open in Doha.

2012 – Playing in cool and windy conditions in a second-round night match at the Qatar Open in Doha, Roger Federer defeats Slovenia's Grega Zemlja 6-2, 6-3 in his second match of the season. "Obviously it's very cold for all of us, but it's how it goes, especially with the wind," Federer says. "If the wind wasn't there, things would change quite a bit. But like this, you're not only focusing on playing your opponent, playing point-by-point tactics, but also thinking of the conditions and just getting through the match unhurt. So that's all going through your head."

2014 – Roger Federer advances into his 114th ATP singles final with a 6-3, 6-7 (3), 6-3 win over Jeremy Chardy of France in the semifinals of the Brisbane International. The win moves Federer into the final against fellow 32-year-old Lleyton Hewitt, one of his biggest rivals. "We go back 17 years, our coaches back in the day were best friends," Federer says. "I struggled a lot against him in the early stages of my career." Federer, however, is defeated in the doubles semifinals, losing with partner Nicolas Mahut to Juan Sebastian Cabal and Robert Farah of Colombia 7-6 (5), 6-3.

January 5

2014 – Chasing his 78th career ATP title, that would move him third place alone in the all-time title leaders list, Roger Federer falls to fellow 32-year-old Lleyton Hewitt 6-1, 4-6, 6-3 in the final of the Brisbane International. Federer, tied with John McEnroe with 77 career ATP singles titles, had his serve broken three times and committed 22 unforced errors in the first set alone. "The way you tough it out ... congratulations," Federer says in a court-side interview. "I would have loved to have won the title, but Lleyton was better than me today." The No. 61-ranked Hewitt won for a ninth time in 27 career meetings against the 17-time Grand Slam tournament champion, who is ranked No. 6.

2011 – Twelve years after first practicing and competing against each other as eight-year-old olds Roger Federer beats his longtime childhood friend Marco Chiudinelli 7-6 (5), 7-5 in one hour, 48 minutes to advance into the quarterfinals of the Qatar Open in Doha. The meeting is the second at an ATP event between the two childhood friends, who first played each other in an "official tournament" in 1989 at a 10-and-under tournament called "The Bambino Cup" in Arlesheim, Switzerland. Their previous meeting in ATP Tour play came, appropriately, at their hometown tournament in Basel, Federer winning 7-6 (7), 6-3 in the semifinals.

2010 – Nine years after facing off against each other for the first time as pros in the first round of Wimbledon in 2001, Roger Federer and Christophe Rochus of Belgium, face off in the first round of the Doha Open. As he did when he defeated Rochus in three straight sets for his first-ever Wimbledon match victory in 2001, Federer also dominates Rochus 6-1, 6-2 in Doha, hitting an incredible 47 winners and 12 aces.

2001 – After beating Amanda Coetzer 6-1, 6-0, Martina Hingis pairs with Roger Federer to win the decisive mixed doubles against Coetzer and Wayne Ferreira 6-2, 6-3 to move Switzerland into the final of the Hopman Cup with a 2-1 victory over South Africa. Federer had a chance to clinch victory for Switzerland against Ferreira, but falls by a 6-3, 3-6, 6-3 scoreline, setting up the decisive mixed doubles match.

2012 – Roger Federer edges Andreas Seppi of Italy 6-3, 5-7, 6-4 to advance in to the semifinals of the Qatar Open in Doha. When asked what the difference was in the match at the end, Federer says, "Just I guess the head-to-head. I guess my variation and my power just was maybe a bit too much at the end. I don't know. Little things."

2005 – Roger Federer defeats Greg Rusedski 6-3, 6-4 in one hour, one minute to advance to the quarterfinals of the Qatar Open at Doha.

2006 – Roger Federer advances into the semifinals of the Qatar Open in Doha with a 6-4, 6-3 victory over Marcos Baghdatis. The two players will famously play each other again later in the month when Baghdatis is an expected finalist at the Australian Open, giving Federer a run in a four-set loss.

January 6

2001 – Roger Federer and partner Martina Hingis win the Hopman Cup, the official mixed team competition of the International Tennis Federation, for their native Switzerland with a 2-1 victory over the United States. After Hingis defeats Monica Seles 7-5, 6-4, Federer clinches the victory for his country defeating Jan-Michael Gambill 6-4, 6-3. "I handled the pressure well and played well," says Federer after clinching the victory for Switzerland. In the meaningless mixed doubles match following the singles, Seles and Gambill beat Hingis and Federer 2-6, 6-4, 7-6 (7-5) to make the final score 2-1.

2006 – Roger Federer defeats Tommy Haas 6-3, 6-3 to advance to the final of the Qatar Open in Doha against Gael Monfils. "It was difficult to get winners because of the slow nature of the court, but I am happy to be in the final here again," Federer says of his win over Haas, his third straight over the German to increase his head-to-head lead against him to 4-2. "The crowd really got behind me, they really get emotionally involved when I am playing." Monfils gushes in excitement and awe of meeting Federer in the final, saying, "Roger is such a great player and I can't say how excited I am to be playing the final against him. Hopefully, I'll be able to maintain my focus and not get overawed by the occasion."

2005 – Roger Federer advances to the semifinals of the Qatar Open in Doha with a 6-1, 6-2 victory over Feliciano Lopez. Says Federer. "I was able to put pressure on him from the first serve and I am happy that I am playing so well."

2003 – Defending champion Roger Federer loses for the opening round of the Sydney International, falling to Argentinean left-hander Franco Squillari 6-2, 6-3. Coupled with his win over Federer in the first round of Hamburg in 2001, Squillari boasts a career head-to-head advantage of 2-0 against Federer, a distinction he retires with in 2006. In his post-match press conference, Federer cites a leg and groin injury sustained the previous week in Doha that slows him in the match. "I couldn't serve 100 percent," says Federer. "I felt it was hurting already. Because it went away for the days I haven't been practicing so much between my loss in Doha and here. I thought it went away, but it came back now again during the match. So I have to make sure I get treatment now on it, and hopefully it won't bother me at the Australian Open. Like this, it's not so fun to play."

2009 – Roger Federer needs only 49 minutes to beat Potito Starace 6-2, 6-2 in his opening match of the 2009 season at the Qatar Open in Doha. Federer loses only three points on his first serve the entire match and converts on four of his five break points.

2010 – With three service breaks in the first set and one in the second set, top-ranked Roger Federer advances into the quarterfinals at the Qatar Open defeating Evgeny Korolev of Russia 6-2, 6-4."I know how he plays, so I had the match under control," Federer says of the No. 53-ranked Korolev. "He plays a lot of balls on the forehand, so I was able to stay ahead in the match. There were long rallies in the second set, but I am pleased to have reached the quarterfinals."

2011 – In a rare match that does not feature one ace from Roger Federer, the world No. 2 easily beats Viktor Troicki of Serbia 6-2, 6-2 in 65 minutes to advance into the semifinals of the Qatar Open in Doha. "I am happy with my form here and in this match," Federer says. "It wasn't a tough match and I was quite comfortable. I was in control of my shots and created many opportunities. This was easy compared to the first two matches."

2012 – Citing a back injury, Roger Federer is forced to withdraw from his semifinal match with Jo-Wilfried Tsonga at the Qatar Open in Doha. It marks only the second time in Federer's career where he is not able to compete, the other being in a quarterfinal match against James Blake at the 2008 Paris Indoors "Sorry for holding a press conference before the match has even been played, but I hurt my back in my second-round match against (Grega) Zemlja and just got a little bit better for the match against (Andreas) Seppi," Federer says to reporters. "I don't feel a whole lot of improvement for today, and I just don't think it's the right time to risk anything more right now. I still have pain, and that's why it was the only right decision, a difficult one for me. It's a sad moment for me and for the tournament and for the fans, but health goes first." In 996 career matches, Federer has never been forced to retire from a match because of injury in mid-match.

January 7

2011 – Roger Federer beats Jo-Wilfried Tsonga 6-3, 7-6 (7-2) to advance to the final of the Qatar Open in Doha, improving his record to 22-3 in Doha. "I have played good tennis this week," says Federer, the 2005 and 2006 Doha champion. "Obviously, I am excited to have reached another final. This sure has been a great week and I am looking forward to my next match." Federer says that breaking Tsonga's serve in the second game of the match set the tone for the match. "It was a crucial service break for me," he says. "That set me up nicely for the remainder of the match. The second set was more competitive as I was serving really well." Federer wins the final five points of the match at 2-2 in the second-set tiebreaker.

2005 – Roger Federer requires only 64 minutes to defeat Nikolay Davydenko 6-3, 6-4 to advance to the final of the Qatar Open at Doha.

2006 – Roger Federer defeats Gael Monfils of France 6-3, 7-6 (5) to win the Exxon Mobil Open in Doha, Qatar for second straight year. The title is his 34th career singles title and his fifth straight title in the Middle East. Says Federer of his success in the Middle East, "It's almost like Wimbledon. I play and I win." Federer becomes the first player to win consecutive titles in Doha since Stefan Edberg in 1994 and 1995.

2009 – Roger Federer defeats Andreas Seppi of Italy 6-3, 6-3 to advance into the quarterfinals of the Qatar Open in Doha.

2010 – Roger Federer finishes his 6-2, 4-6, 6-4 win over Ernests Gulbis of Latvia what tennis commentator Jason Goodall calls "considerable aplomb" – an ace out wide – in the quarterfinal of the Qatar Open in Doha. Federer kicks the other ball from his pocket into the stands after staving off the young Latvian in their first career meeting.

Later in the year, Federer is not so lucky against Gulbis, losing in his opening round match in Rome 2-6, 6-1, 7-5.

January 8

2014 – At a fundraising event for his foundation billed as "An Evening with Roger Federer and Friends," Roger Federer warms up with 75-year-old Rod Laver in the Australian Open center court that bears his name prior to his exhibition match with Jo-Wilfried Tsonga. "Hitting with Rod Laver for me clearly is an absolute dream come true. It's in his arena as well, it's named after him and he deserves it so much," the 32-year-old Federer says. "While I was playing my racket was feeling extremely heavy. That means I was very nervous, which I really was." Laver stays to watch Federer beat Tsonga 6-7 (5), 6-3, 7-5 in the main exhibition match. Organizers announce that more than $1 million was raised before and during the event.

2011 – Roger Federer becomes the first player to win the Qatar Open in Doha three times as he defeats Nikolay Davydenko 6-3, 6-4 to claim the 67th title of his career. The 29-year-old Swiss gains revenge for his defeat by Davydenko in the semifinals of the same event the year before. "It does feel great," says Federer, the 2005 and 2006 Doha champion. "I can't believe the season is under way and I'm already on the board with a title." Federer rolls to the title without the loss of the set, but was wary of Davydenko entering the final. "When he's (Davydenko) on, he's easily top 10 if not top five potentially, and that's why this is obviously a huge win, because I thought he was playing well," Federer says. "I thought the level of play was extremely high. I was almost flawless, and I was able to play offensively when I needed to, and when I wanted to it all worked out. So I'm really pleased with such a great final."

2005 – World No. 1 Roger Federer begins his 2005 season with a tournament victory defeating Ivan Ljubicic of Croatia 6-3, 6-1 in the final of the Qatar Open in Doha for his 21st straight match win. The Swiss star wins his 14th tournament final in a row (dating to October of 2003) wins every service game he plays during the week and loses only 23 games in five matches during the event. "At the moment I think Federer is playing better than Sampras did," says Ljubicic after the match. "It's just that Pete went on for seven years. We will have to see through the years how Roger copes."

2009 – Roger Federer saves three set points coming back from deficits of 1-5 and 3-6 in the second-set tie-breaker and defeats Philipp Kohlschreiber of Germany 6-2, 7-6 (6) to advance to the semifinals of the Qatar Open in Doha. "I had a strong finish," Federer says of winning the last five points of the match. "I am not thinking ahead. I want to win the title."

2010 – Top-ranked Roger Federer is upset by Nikolay Davydenko, 6-4, 6-4 in the semifinals of the Qatar Open at Doha. The win was only the Russian's second win over Federer in their 14th career meeting, also having beaten Federer at the year-ending championships in London in November. The upset prevents yet another final-round match-up between Federer and main rival Rafael Nadal. The second-ranked Nadal defeated Viktor Troicki of Serbia 6-1, 6-3 in the other semifinal.

January 9

2009 – Andy Murray defeats Roger Federer for a fourth straight time to increase his series lead against the Swiss to 5-2 with a 6-7 (6), 6-2, 6-2 win the semifinals of the Qatar Open in Doha. In the post-match press conference, Federer throws out a backhanded compliment to Murray, suggesting that he can one day reach the No. 1 ranking, but points out that the Scot had yet to break through and win a major title. "If he carries on playing the way he is he will have his shot [at the top ranking]," Federer says. "I would hope, though, that if he were to become world No 1 he would win a Grand Slam first, not like on the women's side. No disrespect to Jelena Jankovic [who claimed world No 1 status without winning a single grand slam title]. Especially after the No 1s we have had in the last few years. It took Rafa Nadal five Grand Slams before he became No 1. The question is whether he [Murray] is going to win a Grand Slam, well 'yes.' He has got a chance in the next few years and as the years go by I guess his chances increase because he is becoming a better player. But there are a few other guys out there who want their first slam, not only him." When presented with Federer's comments, Murray does his best to deflect the issue. "I would like to win a Slam but I think anybody who gets to world No. 1 will have shown great consistency and deserves to be there," he says. "I would love to win a Slam but if you can get to

No. 1 in the world at anything you do it is something to be proud of." When asked to comment on his five wins over Federer in their seven career matches, Murray answers, "To have won that many matches against somebody as good as him is awesome. But I would still exchange all my wins against him for the one in the U.S. Open."

January 10

2007 – Roger Federer plays his first competitive match of the season, albeit in a non-sanctioned unofficial pre-Australian Open exhibition event at the Kooyong Tennis Club in Melbourne, and defeats Radek Stepanek 7-6 (7-2), 6-7 (7-4), 7-6 (7-5). Stepanek, who curiously wore an ambish style camouflage tennis outfit, lead 5-2 in the final-set tiebreaker but lost the last five points of the match. "Playing such a long match gives me a lot of information for what I could do better, and what's already in place," Federer says. "Concentration is the biggest factor. It's kind of tough to get into things entirely." Federer also says he is happy with his decision not to play a sanctioned ATP event prior to the Australian Open for only the second time. "You have to look at the big picture — I needed a break," he says. "I wasn't really in the mood to play a tournament the first week of the year. I also wanted to have a life — have Christmas and New Years' and take it easy a little bit. For me, it was most important to come to Melbourne in the mood to win the Australian Open, not feel like it's a pain."

2004 – Reigning French Open champion Juan Carlos Ferrero defeats Roger Federer, the reigning Wimbledon champion, 6-4, 6-4 to win the Champions Challenge exhibition event at Hong Kong.

January 11

2002 – Twenty-year-old Roger Federer and 21-year old Andy Roddick meet for the second time in their professional careers in the semifinals of the Adidas International in Sydney, Australia, Federer registering the 7-6(3), 6-4 victory. The two go on to play 24 career matches, including three Wimbledon finals and one U.S. Open final.

At the 2011 U.S. Open, Roger Federer was asked how much tennis he watches when he is not playing. Said Federer, "When I'm on vacation, none. When I'm at home, none. When I'm at tournaments, I watch a lot. That's kind of how it is."

January 12

2002 – Roger Federer wins his second career singles title, completing a Swiss sweep of the Adidas International in Sydney, defeating Juan Ignacio Chela 6-3, 6-3 in the final. Federer's fellow Swiss Martina Hingis wins the women's singles title defeating Meghann Shaughnessy 6-2, 6-3. Federer's win over Chela lasted only 50 minutes and he lost only one set en route to the championship. "I'm happy to start a year like this," says Federer, who finished the 2001 tennis season ranked No. 12, highlighted by his

Wimbledon fourth-round victory over Pete Sampras. "I really didn't expect to win this tournament."

2013 – Saying "Today I take much more pleasure out of doing the gym work than I ever have," 31-year-old Roger Federer, speaking at a press conference prior to competing in the Australian Open for a 14th year, says he still loves the competing in tennis as he did year before. "I think as long as that's the case, that means I love it very much so," says Federer of training and going to the gym. "I used to honestly not really like it at all until I was maybe 22, 24 maybe at times. I know why I'm doing them. I know they're necessary. Sometimes it's not the thing you want to do every day of the year, but I know it's only a handful of weeks, then obviously you give everything you have. I think it's always a bit of a test for me going into the practice season. Am I hungry and motivated to wake up, go on the practice courts for hours? There was not one problem."

January 13

2013 – Twenty-year-old Australian upstart Bernard Tomic is asked in a pre-Australian Open press conference about a possible third-round confrontation against 17-time major champion Roger Federer. The cocky Tomic responds, "If he gets that far. He has to get there first." The comments reverberate through the tennis community as a grand sign of disrespect to Federer. Both players eventually win two matches to set up the third-round match, which Federer wins 6-4, 7-6 (5), 6-1

2013 – "The numbers are mind boggling" says Pete Sampras to Greg Garber in an article published on ESPN. com of the Roger Federer career record in advance of the 2013 Australian Open, including victories in 16 of 27 major singles championships between Wimbledon in 2003 and the 2010 Australian Open. "If there was an event he and I were born to win, it was Wimbledon," Sampras tells Garber of he and Federer. "He has a great belief in himself. It's a good lesson for kids out there. The great ones struggle, but they keep working at it. Roger and I, we had the ability. You just have to realize you still have it."

2008 – Roger Federer meets with the press prior to the Australian Open and declares himself 100 percent fit after what he describes as a stomach virus that forces him to pull out of the Kooyong Classic preparatory exhibition in Melbourne. "I'm not sick very often," Federer says. "It just took me five days, a week, I don't know. It was just a tough thing to get over with. It wasn't just the flu for two, three days, then it sort of gets better. It took me longer than that. I didn't panic necessarily because I knew I had enough time before the tournament started. But it was just a bit different. I didn't mind having more time off. Just resting all day, maybe getting a little session in at 6:00 in the evening. It was also some sort of a different experience. But it's never nice to be ill. It's something I don't enjoy." It is later revealed in March that Federer actually suffered from glandular fever that slows his performance.

January 14

2014 – Roger Federer begins play in his 57th straight major tournament, setting a new standard in men's tennis, defeating Australian wild card James Duckworth 6-4, 6-4, 6-2 in the first round of the Australian Open. Federer breaks the record set by Wayne Ferreira of South Africa, who played 56 straight major singles titles from the 1991 Australian Open to 2004 U.S. Open. The match also is the first for Federer with Hall of Famer Stefan Edberg as his coach. "It's obviously great fun playing in front of him," Federer say of Edberg. "It's in a way a dream come true for me. I used to watch his matches and get inspired to play this great game, so it's very special."

2003 – Still suffering from a nagging groin injury that affected him in early tournament loses in Doha and Sydney, No. 6 seed Roger Federer squeaks into the second round of the Australian Open defeating Flavio Saretta of Brazil 7-6 (7-4), 7-5, 6-3. "I'm happy I won in three today because it could have easily gone four or five or even lost it," says the 21-year-old Federer. "I'm happy that I sneaked out of this one." Federer's match is the first scheduled match on Rod Laver Arena on the second day of play. "If you win the match, when you play at 11, you have still a little bit left of the day," says Federer of the benefits of playing early. "It's a very nice atmosphere out on that center court. The Aussie people are really nice. It's special anyway to go on court in a Grand Slam on center court. I'm happy I went through."

2007 – "Hello again," says Roger Federer to the media corps as he opens his pre-tournament press conference at the Australian Open and discusses his unexpected loss to Andy Roddick in the preparatory exhibition event the Kooyong Tennis Club. "Last year I lost a match, too (heading into the Australian Open) just it was earlier so you guys had more time to write about it," Federer says to the press. Despite the loss, Federer says he feels confident heading into the tournament after his three exhibition matches, "I think I played a good match against Marat (Safin) and had good moments against Andy, as well. Against (Radek) Stepanek, that was the first match I played all season. It was just important to kind of get a feel for playing points again. I think for me it worked well. I came out of the tournament feeling like, 'Okay, I'm playing well. Now I'm ready for the Australian Open' as much as I can. It's always very early in the season. It's for everybody the same. You can't expect yourself to be already peaking like crazy. You're in an exhibition tournament."

2012 – In his pre-Australian Open press conference, Roger Federer discusses the rumors of his potential Olympic mixed doubles pairing with the retired Swiss tennis legend Martina Hingis for the London 2012 Games later in the year. After Hingis flirts with the idea of making a comeback to compete in the Games, where mixed doubles would be played for the first time since 1924, the potential blockbuster mixed doubles pairing does not materialize. "Yeah, uhm, I mean, I called her up," says Federer of his phone call with Hingis the previous month. "I was like, I think we need to talk about this whole mixed situation. She was asked a lot in the press 'cause she mentioned that my team contacted her. I was on vacation. She was playing World TeamTennis. She had to answer all the questions. It was a bit unfortunate for her really because all of a sudden she was in this pressure situation wanting to get more information that she didn't have. I just let it run its course. I didn't know how far it was going to go anyway, but the conclusion to it was she's a wonderful person. I've looked up to her in a big way because she's only a year older but made the breakthrough so much earlier. I remember seeing her play very often. I always was a big fans of hers. For me, it was the only player I could imagine playing mixed together with at the Olympics. At first I didn't even know there was a mixed at the Olympics. I just thought it could be a nice opportunity to get an Olympic medal for Switzerland. I knew it was going to be difficult for me in terms of playing so many matches, then her coming back out of retirement. I just wanted to see what was her feeling. She was the one to basically also tell me I should focus on winning singles and defending my doubles. She's very happy staying in retirement. She thinks it's the only right thing for me to do. She basically took the decision for me, which was very nice of her. We were very happy I think at the end of the phone call and didn't have any hard feelings. She was very nice."

January 15

2008 – Top-ranked Roger Federer begins his quest for a third straight Australian Open title with a 6-0, 6-3, 6-0 thrashing of Diego Hartfield in the opening round of the Australian Open. Federer shows little signs of what he says was a stomach bug that affected him leading into the year's first major title. Federer's chief rival, Rafael Nadal, who also advances into the second round with an easy straight set victory, says he is impressed with Federer's debut match at the 2008 tournament. "I saw last four games in the match," Nadal says of Federer. "The result says a lot. Well, I can't say too much because in the last four or three games when you are winning 6-0, 6-3, 6-0, it's tough to say anything, no?"

2013 – Roger Federer opens his 2013 Australian campaign on Rod Laver Arena against Benoit Paire beating the Frenchman 6-2, 6-4, 6-1 in 83 minutes. Federer enters the Australian Open without playing a warm-up tournament, but shows no signs of any rusty play. Says Federer, "Benoît's a good player, a good talent. I haven't played a match this season yet. You're not sure [how you're going to play] and that's why you're relieved when you get through the first one."

2007 – Roger Federer has a topsy-turvy straight-set first-round victory at the Australian Open, losing serve three times in the first set before reeling off nine straight games in his 7-5, 6-0, 6-4 victory over Bjorn Phau of Germany. The German, who actually had beaten Federer the last and only other time they played back in 1999, breaks the Federer serve three times taking a 5-3 lead in the first set. Federer, however, turns up his game to another level and wins nine straight games that includes winning the second set with the loss of only six points. "I got broken in the first set three times, and that makes you a little bit nervous," says Federer. "You try to stay cool, but I got a little bit nervous."

2012 – Rafael Nadal attacks Roger Federer on the day before the Australian Open claiming he does not make public statements that are critical of certain issues in men's tennis so as not to hurt his public reputation, while, behind closed doors in ATP meetings, he is quite critical. As reported by Australia's *Herald Sun* newspaper, quoted local Spanish media, Nadal says "For him it's good to say nothing. Everything positive. 'It's all well and good for me, I look like a gentleman,' and the rest can burn themselves. Everyone is entitled to have their own opinions." Nadal says Federer's opinions were not in line with those of most of his fellow professionals. "The tour is fine, but there are some things that are bad. That's all we're saying," Nadal says. "And the vast majority of players have this same opinion. [Federer's] got a different opinion. The vast majority have one opinion, and a small minority think differently. Maybe it's them who are wrong."

January 16

2014 – For the first time in a decade, Roger Federer plays a match at the Australian Open outside of Rod Laver Arena, taking to Hisense Arena, the No. 2 court at Melbourne Park and beats Blaz Kavic 6-2, 6-1, 7-6 (4) in the second round. Federer had played his previous 63 Australian Open matches on Laver Arena. "I was excited to be playing here," Federer says during his on-court post-match interview. "This ain't just some little side court."

Federer later quips, "I came out early to make sure I didn't get lost, so I was here on time."

2012 – After fighting through a tough first set against No. 172-ranked Alex Kudryavtsev of Russia, Roger Federer cruises to a straight-set 7-5, 6-2, 6-2 victory in the opening round of the Australian Open. Federer tells reporters that his injured back, that caused him to withdraw from the pre-Australian Open event in Doha, is not an issue, despite struggling in the opening set. "I've been feeling fine for three, four days now and been able to practice full out. Today was fine," Federer says. "It was just tough against a guy who hits big and flat from both sides and takes a lot of chances. In some ways, for the first match, it was a bit more - how do you say - intense, where I felt a lot of pressure…. I really tried to put in an effort to every point play as hard as I could first to see how the back felt, try to get into it, hopefully win, and then see how I feel tomorrow."

2003 – Roger Federer beats Lars Burgmuller of Germany 6-3, 6-0, 6-3 in the second round of the Australian Open.

2005 – One year removed from winning the Australian Open for the first time, Roger Federer discusses the differences between his feeling entering the 2004 Australian Open, without a full-time coach, and his current situation that now features Australian legend Tony Roche as his new coach. "I'm feeling better this year than last year really, because last year I had to fight with the expectations and the comments of people telling me that I don't have a coach, that that was a totally wrong decision, and those things put the pressure on me," says Federer. "Now one year without a coach, I feel very confident. I know that I can handle it myself. I know I can do it. Plus now with the help of Tony, the group is still the same around me. It couldn't be any better. Of course, the pressure's here to defend the title, but that is for me almost now a normal thing, so we'll see."

2010 – In his pre-Australian Open news conference, Roger Federer updates the media on the status of his game, his career and traveling to Australia as a family for the first time after his marriage to long-time girlfriend Mirka Vavrinec and the birth of their twin daughters the previous summer. "I feel great," Federer says. "A new start to the season is in a way always refreshing and exciting. Everything sort of starts at zero except the rankings, which is a good thing, thank God. Most importantly obviously I'm focused on my game. I think I put in a lot of work last year trying to get back to No. 1. Also in the off-season I try to work extremely hard because the year before I think I lacked that a bit through illness and everything. So I think I'm back where I want to be. Also my game's following. I maybe wasn't as successful as I wanted to be the last few tournaments, but I was able to reach No. 1 in the world but obviously the back-to-back with the French and Wimbledon was an amazing accomplishment for me. On top of that, on the personal note, that I was able to sort of handle everything at the same time was quite fascinating actually for me as well. I'm excited now traveling the world as a family. It's a first for me, as well. Like I said before, it's going really well. It's really inspiring."

January 17

2008 – Nine years after they first played against each other, Roger Federer and Fabrice Santoro play for an 11th and final time, the No. 1 ranked Federer crushing the double-handed stroking "Magician" 6-1, 6-2, 6-0 in the second round of the Australian Open. "He's still working hard," says Santoro of the player he beat two times in his career. "He's still improving. It's tough to say, because he was a tremendous player the past four years, and I think he's a better player today. He's a better athlete, too. He's moving unbelievably well."

2005 – Roger Federer slams an incredible 54 winners in his 6-1, 6-1, 6-2 first-round win over Fabrice Santoro at the Australian Open. Federer wins all 12 points in the first three games and loses just three points as he raced to a 5-0 lead in the first set. "I think the start was important for me," Federer says. "That set the tone for the rest of the match. I never really gave him a chance."

2007 – Roger Federer makes short work of Jonas Bjorkman in the second round of the Australian Open, defeating the Swede 6-2, 6-3, 6-2 in what is the final meeting between the two players. The two play five times with Federer winning all five times in straight sets, including the semifinals of Wimbledon in 2006 and the third round at the All England Club in 2001, one round before Federer upset seven-time champion Pete Sampras.

2009 – Roger Federer dominates his Olympic gold-medal-winning doubles partner Stan Wawrinka 6-1, 6-3 in 57 minutes to win the Kooyong Invitational exhibition tournament, an Australian Open tune-up event at the Kooyong Tennis Club in Melbourne.

2011 – Roger Federer opens up the defense of his Australian Open title with a 6-1, 6-1, 6-3 throttling of Lukas Lacko of Slovakia. The Associated Press writes, "Federer was in such a rush to get through to the second round that he barely waited for the ball boys to get back into place between points." Says Federer, "I'm really enjoying myself playing really well at the moment. Very happy how things are going."

2006 – "Getting used to the conditions," is the response from Roger Federer when asked what is most satisfying part of his 6-2, 6-3, 6-2 Australian Open first round win over 19-year-old wild-card entry Denis Istomin from Uzkekistan. The only surprise of the match comes when Federer has his serve broken by the No. 195-ranked Istomin when he serves for the second set, but is otherwise never threatened in the opening day match on Rod Laver Arena. `It's never really easy, first round in a Grand Slam," says Federer. "As long as I win, I'm happy. It was a good start." Says Istomin of playing the world No. 1. "I played good today, but had too many unforced errors (39). It was very good for my career... he gave me seven games."

2010 – Rafael Nadal, Andy Roddick, Kim Clijsters, Lleyton Hewitt and others join Roger Federer in participating in a charity exhibition match on Rod Laver Arena organized by Federer to raise money for victims of the devastating earthquake that struck Haiti three days before the start of the Australian Open killing more than 150,000 people. The fund-raiser raises more than $600,000. "I had the idea that we could do something to help Haiti after the tragic earthquake so I spoke to some other top players and they all said, 'Yes, we should do something,'" Federer tells reporters in his pre-event news conference. "I think it's something as a tennis family we're very happy to do."

January 18

2014 – Roger Federer advances into the fourth round of the Australian Open for a 13th straight year with a 6-2, 6-2, 6-3 win over Teymuraz Gabashvili of Russia. Says the 32-year-old Federer after the match, "I'm just happy to be waking up in the morning and not feeling like an old man."

2000 – Future world No. 1 Roger Federer plays and wins his first main draw match at the Australian Open, defeating Michael Chang 6-4, 6-4, 7-6 (5) in the first round in Melbourne. Federer goes on to reach the third round, losing to Arnaud Clement 6-1, 6-4, 6-3.

2006 – Roger Federer hits 38 winners, including an ace on match point, and advances into the third round of the Australian Open with 6-1, 6-4, 6-0 demolition of Florian Mayer in 72 minutes. "It's so nice to get quick matches in the heat," says Federer. "I thought I handled it well in the heat -- I'm very happy with my performance."

2003 – With a 6-3, 6-4, 6-2 win over Sweden's Andreas Vinciguerra, Roger Federer advances into the fourth round of the Australian Open for the second straight year. Says Federer of his progression into the round of 16, "My first match here was tough. He made me work really hard. I was a little tense. The second-round match was easy, you know. So now today I had to work hard again but I just wanted to stay aggressive on my own serve, not to have to run too much because he makes you run a lot. So today was a real good test. I played well. I'm happy with today's performance."

2012 – Roger Federer advances into the third round of the Australian Open by walk-over as his opponent, Andreas Beck of Germany, chooses not to play due to pain in his back. "I saw him in the locker room, and he came up to me," Federer says. "I was like, Hey, what's going on? Good to see you again, because he's a good friend. I've practiced with him in the past in Switzerland. He said, I'm not so good actually. I have a bad back. It came as a surprise. He said he had a lot painkillers and pain during the last match. I think it happened four, five days ago. He doesn't want to risk it early in the season, best five sets against me. Nothing he could have done, even though he would love to play against me. I guess it's the only smart decision for him to take." Ironically, the match is scheduled to be played on the Vodafone Arena, the No. 2 court at the Australian Open, that would have ended a streak of 52 straight matches for Federer played at the Australian Open on the Rod Laver Arena center court.

January 19

2013 – Roger Federer straight-sets brash 20-year-old Bernie Tomic 6-4, 7-6 (5), 6-1 in a highly anticipated third-round match at the Australian Open. Federer, 31, does most of his talking with his racquet, which is the only true form of communication in highest levels of professional tennis. Tomic speaks brazenly of it being his time to beat Federer leading into the hyped third-round meeting, even suggesting when the draw came out that the player many regard as the greatest ever may not even reach a third-round match with him. However, despite the straight-set score, Tomic competes with fire and vigor and displayed signs of his talent that many have touted will lift him to a top 10 ranking at some point in the future. He leads 4-1 and 5-3 in the second-set tie-breaker, but was unable to close, falling victim to a series of brilliant Federer shots. After Federer wins the last four points of the second-set tie-breaker to take the two-sets-to-love lead, Federer sets the tone early in the match, breaking the No. 43rd-ranked Tomic's serve in the opening game of the match, the first time the young Aussie had lost his serve in the tournament and the first time he has lost his serve in 76 previous service games dating back to winning the Sydney International title the previous week. The win is also a milestone for Federer, marking his 250th career singles victory at a major tournament, extending yet another record in his unmatched career.

2008 – World No. 1 Roger Federer plays an epic match of survival, fending off the upset challenge of No. 49-ranked Janko Tipsarevic of Serbia 6-7 (5), 7-6 (1), 5-7, 6-1, 10-8 in the third round. Federer serves a personal record of 39 aces at the time to win the match in four hours, 27 minutes. Says Federer, "I don't often get to play five-setters unless they're against (Rafael) Nadal at Wimbledon. It was good to be part of something like this." Federer converts on only five of 21 break points in the match but converts on the most crucial break late in the fifth set. "I create myself so many opportunities and then it's just you don't make them," says Federer of his missed opportunities. "He played great. Give him credit for playing as well in the big points. I missed so many opportunities in the first three sets, which I think I should have won them all. I'm down two sets to one, and I feel like, 'Why is this happening this way?' but he was hanging in there. I missed my opportunities and just I couldn't play the way I normally play maybe on those big points. It was one of those days. I just maybe didn't feel that great, but I fought hard and it's just a good feeling, coming back from two sets to one and winning like that in the fifth."

2007 – Roger Federer wins his 33rd straight match with a 6-3, 6-3, 7-6 (5) win over Mikhail Youzhny to set up a fourth-round match-up with No. 14 seed Novak Djokovic, the man who he would beat later in the year in the final of the U.S. Open. "It's Djokovic, yeah," says Federer to reporters when asked to summarize his potentially challenging third-round match. "Played him twice last year: Davis Cup and at Monaco. Beat him both times. He's definitely improved since. Time has gone by. Youngsters always improve quickly. Yeah, he's came through his rounds fairly comfortably…It's a dangerous match for me, that's for sure. Of course, I'm the big favorite. This is maybe his big moment where he can maybe make a name for himself no doubt but he already missed that opportunity twice. Usually when I beat a guy twice, I know how to play him. I hope I can take advantage of that."

2005 – Roger Federer wins his 23rd consecutive match – equaling his career-best streak at the time – beating Japanese qualifier Takao Suzuki 6-3, 6-4, 6-4 in the second round of the Australian Open.

2009 – Roger Federer, seeded No. 2 at the Australian Open behind Rafael Nadal, opens up his campaign in Melbourne with a 6-1, 7-6 (7-4), 7-5 win over No. 35th-ranked Andreas Seppi of Italy. Federer, not seeded No. 1 at the Australian Open for the first time since 2004, tells reporters in his post-match press conference of his refreshed attitude entering the 2009 season after a 2008 season where he struggled with glandular fever, losing his No. 1 ranking, but also winning Olympic gold in men's doubles and winning the U.S. Open for a fifth straight year. "I do take vacation every year, two weeks, two and a half weeks, where I go on vacation to the beach and take it easy," Federer says to reporters. "I've been doing it for the last six or seven years now. I always take at least two weeks. It was needed. The season was long and tough, but it was a good one. I finished strong at the Olympics, at the U.S. Open. I like to just get away from everything, get away from people, just be alone for a while with my girlfriend. We had a lovely time. Then you're also hungry again to practice. You're happy to come back on tour. That's always what I look for when I have a schedule, is that I enjoy the tournaments but then also I enjoy being away so that I'm happy to be back again, have new stories, happy to talk to guys, happy to meet the fans, sign autographs like crazy, go out on court and leave it all out there. I like to have these extreme ways."

2010 – "Scared is a bad word; I don't like that word," says Roger Federer to reporters after surviving a 4-6, 6-2, 7-6 (2), 6-0 first-round Australian Open challenge from Russia's Igor Andreev. "Ask a boxer if he's scared of the other guy. I don't think he's going to say yes," Federer says. When questioned about his motivation in tennis after winning his record-breaking 14th major singles title at Wimbledon, completing a career Grand Slam at the French Open and the birth of his twin daughters within the last year. "I maybe wasn't as successful as I wanted to be, you know, the last few tournaments, but I was able to reach No. 1 in the world," Federer says. "But, obviously, the back to back with the French and Wimbledon was an amazing accomplishment for me."

2011 – Roger Federer says he is "happy I survived a scare" as he withstands a tense five-set challenge from Gilles Simon, ending a two-match losing streak to the Frenchman with a 6-2, 6-3, 4-6, 4-6, 6-3 win in the second round of the Australian Open. "You just try to stay calm even though I'm not playing for much," Federer says. "He's playing for the huge upset, and I'm just trying to get through." Simon, ranked as high as No. 6 in the world and having beaten Federer in their only two previous meetings back in 2008, was fresh off winning the pre-Australian Open warm-up event in Sydney after recovering from knee problems that kept him off the tour for long stretches, causing his ranking to drop to No. 34. "I'm just sad that I had to play Roger this soon in the tournament," he says. "Even with a very good match from me, it was not enough."

2006 – The importance of saving energy in early-round matches at Grand Slams is a discussion Roger Federer has with reporters after defeating Germany's Florian Mayer in the second round of the Australian Open 6-1, 6-4, 6-0 in only 72 minutes. "It might come down to, you know, this one match where you're going to be tangled up in the fifth set and you need some reserves," Federer says. "I definitely feel like if I keep on playing the way I am, not losing too much energy out on the court I can -- maybe it's going to pay back eventually. Again, if I lose in straight sets, didn't really matter, did it? I prefer obviously always to win in straight sets. When I feel like I can, I'll try, you know, as hard as I can. So for this reason I'm very pleased with my first two matches here." When asked if he can actually be a better tennis player than he is at this moment, the world No. 1 says he can definitely can tweak his return of serve, volley and serve among other areas as his career moves along. "There's still potential left," he says. "But, again, I'm very pleased the way I'm playing. There's not really a need to change the game. Maybe further down the road in my career in a couple years when I'm maybe not that fast any more around the court, then maybe it would be good to maybe come to the net a little bit more often. I feel I can play this game for many years to come because I feel like I don't use too much energy out on the court because I play very relaxed."

2002 – Seeded No. 11, Roger Federer beats Germany's Rainer Schuettler 7-6 (8-6), 7-6 (7-5), 6-4 to reach the fourth round of the Australian Open for the first time in his career.

1966 – Stefan Edberg, one of Roger Federer's childhood heroes who goes on to become his coach, is born in Vastervik, Sweden.

January 20

2014 – Advancing into the quarterfinals of a major tournament for the 41st time, Roger Federer defeats Jo-Wilfried Tsonga 6-3, 7-5, 6-4. Federer approaches the net 41 times in the match, winning 34 of those points. "I thought I played really well tonight," says Federer, advancing into the Australian Open quarterfinals for the 11th straight year. "You've got to bring your best game [against Tsonga], because he dictates play a lot. I think I did a good job dictating play. Jo does that to you, he makes you play aggressive, because if you don't he will. I thought the tactics worked well tonight. We spoke about it before the match. I don't go to matches unprepared before like I used to."

2003 – David Nalbandian, seeded No. 10, defeats No. 6-seeded Roger Federer 6-4, 3-6, 6-1, 1-6, 6-3 in the fourth round of the Australian Open – his third match win against Federer in as many matches. Rene Stauffer, in the book *Roger Federer: Quest for Perfection* writes that "Federer seemed dazed against Nalbandian and struggled with the Argentinean's backhand and strong counter-attack."

2004 – Second-seeded Roger Federer beats Alex Bogomolov Jr., 6-3, 6-4, 6-0 in the opening match of the Australian Open on Rod Laver Arena. Federer wins seven consecutive games at the end of the match, winning it in 1 hour 29 minutes. "I'm happy to have started well, straight sets in the first round is a good start," says Federer. "The beginning was a little bit tentative, the way I played. But after I started to go more for my shots, and I also volleyed well today, served well. So overall, I'm really happy the way it started."

2012 –Roger Federer plays his 14th tiebreaker in his 11th career match with six-foot-10 Ivo Karlovic and beats the big-serving Croatian 7-6(6), 7-5, 6-3 in the third round of the Australian Open. "I thought it was going to be at least one tiebreak, if not two, so one is good. It's okay," says Federer. "He's a tough man to play against really. I'm happy I found a way today. The first set was crucial."

January 21

2002 – Roger Federer blows a match point and loses an epic round of 16 match with Tommy Haas at the Australian Open 7-6 (7-3), 4-6, 3-6, 6-4, 8-6. Federer, seeded No. 11, holds a match point against the No. 7-seeded Haas at 6-5 with Haas serving at 30-40, but nets a backhand. Federer then makes another four consecutive errors as Haas holds serve, breaks Federer and serves out the victory.

2007 – In the third career meeting between Roger Federer and Novak Djokovic, Federer remains undefeated against the 19-year-old Serbian with a 6-2, 7-5, 6-3 win in the round of 16 of the Australian Open. "I'm very happy with how everything went," says Federer of the win over the No. 14-seeded Djokovic. "He's a good up-and-coming junior. He's really made his marks now, the last six months especially, also in the beginning of the year. We've both been on some winning streak. I was hoping for a good start and I got that. I thought I was pretty much in control all the time today." Federer says he was a bit more motivated to play well against the future world No. 1, based on his recent strong play, winning nine straight matches including the title in Adelaide and the media hype that came into the match. "I think it's more the media that hypes up all those things, asking a thousand questions about the next opponent. That kind of gets you going and fired up already," says Federer. "I felt that was the case for the Djokovic match, whereas I didn't have those questions leading up to the other matches. I feel like I'm being asked to kind of perform. I'm happy when I do, it's a good feeling to come out and play well."

2008 – "Many times you see routine scores but actually matches were hard-fought," says top-seed Roger Federer of his 6-4, 7-6 (7), 6-3 victory over No. 13 Tomas Berdych in the fourth round of the Australian Open. "This was a tough match today," Federer says, one round removed from an epic 10-8-in-the-fifth-set third-round win over Janko Tipsarevic. "I thought Tomas is always a dangerous player. Every time I play against him it's never easy. He's a great ball striker, got a great serve. You've got to be very careful." Federer trails 3-1 in the second set and fights off two set points at 6-5 and 7-6 in the second-set tie-breaker,

Berdych losing them missing a drop shot into the net and missing a routine forehand long. "Thank God he didn't win that second set because you never know what's going to happen, because I think he was the better player in that set," says Federer. "So for me, that was a huge set to win and I benefited off it in the third set."

2009 – No. 2 seeded Roger Federer has little trouble advancing into the third round of the Australian Open defeating No. 118-ranked Evgeny Korolev 6-2, 6-3, 6-1 in just 86 minutes. Federer's win sets up a third round encounter with former champion Marat Safin. "It's going to be a nice match for sure," Federer says of his 2004 Australian Open final re-match. "We have a history. We have played a few times. We've played in majors before and played some good matches before. Played in Davis Cup before. So yeah, we go way back. Him, of course, being a former No. 1, same for me, former Grand Slam champion, it's an intriguing matchup. Back when he was really at his very best -- we had different personalities growing up. I sort of chilled out and he kept on going. It was just always, I thought, a good matchup. So I was actually happy. I think it was last year at Wimbledon I played him. We had a good match there. Yeah, I expect it to be tougher here on the hard courts, which should suit his game more."

2010 – Playing in front of British Prince William, Roger Federer beats Victor Hanescu 6-2, 6-3, 6-2 in 99 minutes the second round of the Australian Open. Following the match, on-court television presenter Jim Courier asks Federer to say a few words to the Prince and says "Your Royal Highness, welcome to the world of tennis. Thanks for coming." Just prior to his press conference, Federer meets with the Prince, whose great grandfather King George VI, then the Duke of York, actually played at Wimbledon in the men's doubles competition in 1926. "He was happy he could make it," Federer says to reporters when asked of his conversation with the Prince. "I'm not gonna tell you everything he just said to me. You've got to have a little bit of a secret. He looked really happy coming to a sports venue. I think he's had a very busy schedule the last few days. He shook a lot of hands, and I knew mine was one more."

2011 – Roger Federer is described as being at his "vintage best" as he defeats Xavier Malisse 6-3, 6-3, 6-1 in the third round of the Australian Open. The one hour, 45 minute match marks an Open Era-record 57th career match win at the Australian Open for Federer. Federer is asked in his post-match press conference with all of the wins he has in his career, what gets him excited on the court. "Playing exciting tennis like I was able to do today," answers Federer. "Coming to the net, trying out a few different things, hitting dropshots, big forehands, playing tactically the right way. I enjoy that. Obviously playing on Rod laver Arena or any center court around the world where usually I am put on to play is obviously a lot fun. It takes a lot of hard work to get there because in the beginning you need some great results to get to the show courts. Maybe sometimes when you're there you want to stay there. You can really cement your place on the big show courts, which I've been able to do. That's obviously now a dream come true playing all around the world on all the great courts we have."

2006 – Advancing into the fourth round of the Australian Open without the loss of a set, Roger Federer tells reporters that there is indeed a danger of being complacent when cruising through easy rounds at Grand Slam tournaments. "I think the danger is the long tournament, tough conditions, the five-setters, dangerous players are always around in a draw like this," says Federer after defeating Max Mirnyi 6-3, 6-4, 6-3 in the third round. "I cannot take anybody lightly. I got to focus on playing well and playing good tennis. So far I've been able to do that. Obviously, it looks like it's going to be a walk in the park, but it's definitely not going to be that. Players change, they adapt, they try other things. Like this match tonight, I thought that was a dangerous match. I got through it quite comfortably. I hope I can keep it up."

2005 – Roger Federer needs less than two sets to advance into the fourth round of the Australian Open when Jarkko Nieminen retires against Federer with an abdominal injury, trailing 6-3, 5-2.

January 22

2000 – Playing in a third-round match at a major tournament for the first time in his career, eighteen-year-old Roger Federer loses meekly to Arnaud Clement of France 6-1, 6-4, 6-3 at the Australian Open. Federer commits an incredible 77 unforced errors in the one-sided loss.

2014 – Described as a "master class performance" Roger Federer advances into the semifinals of the Australian

Open for an 11th straight year with a 6-3, 6-4, 6-7 (6), 6-3 win over Andy Murray, playing his second tournament since coming back from back surgery. "Andy played well and put the pressure on me so I'm happy to get the win," Federer says. "I probably miss more break points than other guys but I kept my composure and kept the poker face and tonight it worked."

2004 – Following his 6-2, 6-3, 6-4 second-round victory over No. 156-ranked Jeff Morrison of the United States, Roger Federer tells reporters that, after winning his first major title at Wimbledon the previous year, anything less than winning the Australian Open will not be satisfying. "I guess I expect more of myself," says Federer. "I know I can win this tournament. Before, I would have been happy maybe with the quarters or the semis. Now it's an okay result, but it's not satisfying. I guess I'm more hungry for more. I know now what it takes to win a Slam -- how to prepare, how to do it all the way because two weeks tend to get very long in a Grand Slam."

2012 – Roger Federer needs only 104 minutes to dismantle 19-year-old Australian upstart Bernard Tomic in the fourth round of the Australian Open, then tells reporters that the results was as expected, despite the media hype surrounding the young Aussie. "Pretty much as expected," Federer says of the match. "I played him before, so it wasn't like I played him for the very first time. Maybe the score suggested differently, but I thought we had a lot of long games, tough points, and I thought he did actually really well."

January 23

2005 – Roger Federer hits 36 winners and slams nine aces and beats Marcos Baghdatis 6-2, 6-2, 7-6(4) in the round of 16 of the Australian Open. The win sets up a quarterfinal match with Andre Agassi who withstands 51 aces by Joachim Johansson in a five-set win. "Who's Roger?" jokes Agassi in his post-match on-court interview when asked of his next opponent, the top seed and defending champion. In his post-match press conference, Federer takes offense when he is asked whether he is good enough form to beat someone of the level of Agassi. "I don't know why you ask me a question like this," he says. "I think I've proven myself in the past, and I know my game's good enough. Also on my day where I'm not playing perfect I know I can beat him. He's not as good as he was when he was at the top of the rankings, otherwise he would be there. Fortunately, I'm there. I think he has to raise his game, not me."

2011 – Equaling the mark set by Jimmy Connors, Roger Federer advances into the quarterfinals of a major tournament for a 27th straight time beating Tommy Robredo 6-3, 3-6, 6-3, 6-2 at the Australian Open. "I'm happy I'm still alive and going strong in the tournament," Federer says following the win. "It's a tough match. I knew Robredo was going to come out and hit a lot loopy shots and make me earn it. He wasn't going to just give it to me. I thought he was really able to play strong midway through the second set. I really had not many chances on his own serve, like he didn't have on my serve in the first set. But I found a way. I was able to play a bit more aggressive and sort of not make some stupid mistakes I did at the end of second set, which really cost me the set, I thought. I was able to battle through."

2007 – In a windy quarterfinal match on Rod Laver Arena, Roger Federer loses his serve four times in a 6-3, 7-6 (2), 7-5 victory over No. 7-seed Tommy Robredo at the Australian Open. "The break of serves, they're due to the wind I assume," Federer says "I had to kind of change my game around a little bit. I think my attacking style really worked out well -- I'm really happy to have come through."

2009 – Roger Federer beats Marat Safin 6-3, 6-2, 7-6 (5) in the third round of the Australian Open in what is Safin's final career match at the major tournament he won in 2005. Safin tells reporters following the match that the 2009 season is his last on tour. "I love playing against the guy," says Federer of playing Safin. "He brings something different to the tennis world with his character, the way he is on the court and the way he is off the court. He's larger than life. I respect him for what a competitor he is. I hope it's not the last one tonight. If it were to be the last one at the Australian Open, I think we both kind of feel good about having played each other at the highest level."

2013 – Roger Federer edges Jo Wilfried Tsonga 7-6 (4), 4-6, 7-6 (4), 3-6, 6-3 in three hours and 34 minutes in the quarterfinals of the Australian Open to set up a rematch of the previous year's Wimbledon and Olympic final with Andy Murray. "I thought he played very aggressive,"

Federer says of Tsonga. "I love those four-set or five-set thrillers and I was part of one tonight."

2008 –World No. 1 Roger Federer beats No. 12 James Blake 7-5, 7-6 (5), 6-4 to advance into the semifinals of the Australian Open and extend his career record against the American to 8-0. Blake gushes of Federer and his kindness and demeanor following the loss, "A lot of the veterans or retired players are kind of shocked that he is as nice as he is," Blake says. "Honestly, I saw him at dinner last night. We said, 'How's it going?' The waitress came over and said, 'Do we need to move you guys apart?' No, we don't care. We can be friendly. "So he doesn't try to make himself somewhat unknown or mysterious to the rest of us. He seems to be like one of the guys in the locker room. Then you go out there and he beats the . . . out of you. You come back in the locker room and he's one of the guys."

2010 – Roger Federer wins his 50th career match at the Australian Open defeating No. 31 Albert Montanes of Spain 6-3, 6-4, 6-4, in the third round to set up a fourth-round match against long-time rival Lleyton Hewitt. "It was important to come through the first week," Federer says. "I feel good, I feel confident. Physically I'm fine and mentally fresh and that's the way you want to go into the second week." Says Hewitt of playing Federer, "The bloke I play next is human, and I'd like to get one back on him. He doesn't lose too many matches, especially big matches, and especially Grand Slams,"

January 24

2014 – In the 33rd career meeting between Roger Federer and Rafael Nadal, the left-handed Spaniard wins his 23rd career match against Federer 7-6 (4), 6-3, 6-3 in the semifinals of the Australian Open. Despite Federer's newly-found confidence, his larger-faced racquet and new coach Stefan Edberg in his box, Federer is not able to exorcise the hex that Nadal has over him, Nadal winning his eighth match with Federer in his their last 10 matches and all confrontations at Grand Slam events outside of two matches at Wimbledon in 2006 and 2007. Federer wins only 23 of 42 points when he comes to the net, frequently seeing Nadal blast passing shots or force volley errors. "I tried a few things ... then again, Rafa does a good job of neutralizing you," Federer says after the match. "So I guess at times I couldn't quite do what I wanted to do, but that's because of Rafa."

2004 – Roger Federer dominates Australian wild card Todd Reid 6-3, 6-0, 6-1 to advance into the round of 16 of the Australian Open. After he drops serve in the fifth game of the first set, the No. 2 seeded Federer, 22, reels off 14 consecutive games to win the first two sets and take a 4-0 lead in the third. Federer hits 31 winners in the 74-minute win. "I played well, had my difficulties in the start, but it went better in the end," says Federer "I'm just happy to be again through to the fourth round. I hope I can go better this time."

2006 – A post-midnight rally from Roger Federer enables the world No. 1 to close out a five-set victory over Tommy

Haas in the fourth round of the Australian Open. Federer calls winning the first two sets of his 6-4, 6-0, 3-6, 4-6, 6-2 victory "perfect tennis" before he staves off a furious rally from Haas in two hours, 58 minutes. "I was never really too nervous, to be honest," Federer says of the Haas comeback. "I just tried to focus on my own service games because he was the guy who had to react and do the whole work. So I was up two-sets-to-love so I was never really close of losing this match. I mean, he would need 25 points in a row in the end, so that's still a long way to go. I just thought if I can get one break, that would totally change the match and change the momentum. That's exactly what I got in the fifth set." Haas uses his post-match press conference to criticize two-time Australian Open champion and Australian TV commentator Jim Courier saying, "When you actually listen to him commentating or listen to him talk about Roger Federer, sometimes it makes me sick almost," Haas says. "I love Jim Courier, but it's unbelievable. Maybe in six years, I'm going to shake Jim's hand and say, 'Listen, you're right.' Maybe this guy wins 15 Grand Slams. Who knows? This guy right now is pretty much the guy to beat. If somebody can do it this week, great."

2012 – Roger Federer plays his 1,000 career pro singles match defeating Juan Martin del Potro 6-4, 6-3, 6-2 to advance into the semifinals of the Australian Open for a ninth straight year. "I'm happy with 1000 matches in total," says Federer. "It's nice to win this one. Eventually I will forget which was one was my 1000th match and someone will remind me again. I do not remember my 500, and that was the U.S. Open final against (Andre) Agassi. No bigger matches than those ones. It's a big milestone, I agree. It's a lot of matches and a lot tennis. Either I have been around for a long time or I'm extremely fit. You decide which way you want to describe it. I don't know. But I'm happy."

January 25

2005 – Roger Federer plays near perfect tennis in dominating Andre Agassi 6-3, 6-4, 6-4 in the Australian Open quarterfinals, slamming 22 aces to extend his winning streak to 26 matches and to 24 against opponents ranked in the top 10. "He just outplayed me," Agassi says. "He was too good. I would suggest to his next opponent that he doesn't look to me for advice." The match, ultimately, becomes Agassi's Australian Open swan song.

2006 – Roger Federer saves six set points in the third set and survives against No. 5 Nikolay Davydenko of Russia 6-4, 3-6, 7-6 (7), 7-6 (5) in three hours 13 minutes in the quarterfinals of the Australian Open. Davydenko leads 4-1 and 6-3 in the third-set tiebreaker before Federer is able to hold off the Davydenko threat. "You haven't seen me scrambling too much, especially back-to- back matches," says Federer, who beat Tommy Haas in five set in the fourth round. "For some, it might be a surprise…."If you look down the results I've had with Davydenko, many of them have been tough. Same thing with Haas. So this for me is no surprise. Maybe it is for you. I'm not surprised. Don't be surprised if it's going to be tough again on Friday (in the semifinals against Nicolas Kiefer), because I've had some tough matches with Kiefer. He's beaten me a couple of times, so I'm ready for a tough one at least."

2008 – Roger Federer's streak of consecutive major singles finals is snapped at 10 as Novak Djokovic of Serbia upsets the world No. 1 7-5, 6-3, 7-6 (5) in the semifinals of the Australian Open. Federer, the two-time defending champion and the owner of 12 major singles titles, fails to reach the singles final at a major event for the first time since the 2005 French Open. Says Federer, "I've created a monster that I need to win every tournament." Says the 20-year-old No.-3 seeded Djokovic, "I am just very amazed I coped with the pressure today. In the most important moments, I played my best tennis. It's just amazing, indescribable, to beat the No. 1 player of the world, one of the best players this sport has ever had, in straight sets."

2009 – Roger Federer rallies from two-sets-to-love down to overcome Czech Tomas Berdych 4-6, 6-7(4), 6-4, 6-4, 6-2 to reach the quarterfinals of the Australian Open. "I wasn't thinking of losing, that's for sure," Federer says of his thoughts while down 0-2. "The finish line was still very far for Tomas. I knew that. He pushed me to the limit. You've got to hang in there, there's no other solution." The momentum in the match turns when Federer breaks the 23-year-old Berdych's serve in the seventh game of the third set, when Berdych misses three volleys and blows five game points. "In the end it becomes very mental, and I know that this is where my biggest strengths always come into play," Federer says. "That's why I'm always going to favor myself in a fifth set." After hitting 13 unforced errors in the first set and 11 in the second set, the world

No. 2 hit only four and three in the third and fourth sets, respectively. It marked his fourth career comeback from two sets down and third in a major -- the previous being in 2001.

2007 – Roger Federer crushes Andy Roddick 6-4, 6-0, 6-2 in the semifinals of the Australian Open in one of the most devastating displays of top-level tennis ever seen. After Roddick leads 4-3 in the first set, Federer reels off 15 of the next 17 games with incredible shot-making that leaves Roddick mesmerized. Says Federer, "I had one of those days where everything worked and I was unbeatable. It's just unreal. I'm shocked myself. I've played good matches here, but never really almost destroyed somebody. That's a highlight of my career."

2013 – Andy Murray beats Roger Federer for the first time at a major tournament, defeating the Swiss 6-4, 6-7 (5-7), 6-3, 6-7 (2-7), 6-2 in the semifinals of the Australian Open. "I've obviously lost some tough matches against him in the slams, so to win one, especially the way that it went tonight, was obviously nice," says Murray, 0-3 against Federer in his career at major tournaments entering the match.

2010 – Roger Federer registers his 15th consecutive win over former world No. 1 Lleyton Hewitt with a 6-2, 6-3, 6-4 win in the fourth round of the Australian Open. Federer is asked in his post-match press conference if playing Hewitt brings out the best in him. "Well, now it does," Federer responds. "It used to not be the case, but we had some really good matches back when I lost, but I always think they're extremely tough, physically and mentally very challenging. You know you're gonna be caught up in quite a tough match always against him. Even though the scoreline predicts something else tonight, I had to really dig deep and come up with some amazing shots to beat him tonight."

2011 – In a match described by media as having the intensity of a practice session, defending champion Roger Federer dominates his countryman and gold-medal winning Olympic doubles partner Stan Wawrinka 6-1, 6-3, 6-3 to reach the semifinals of the Australian Open. Federer, playing in his record-tying 27th consecutive Grand Slam tournament quarterfinals, faces only one break point in the match. "I obviously played Stan many times in practice and in matches ... maybe a bit of a battle for him to get used to the conditions," says Federer. "I had to fight extremely hard and I thought Stan played an amazing tournament." Wawrinka had advanced into the quarterfinals with a straight-set win over Andy Roddick in the fourth round in what was ultimately the swan-song Australian Open match for the American.

January 26

2012 – Roger Federer loses his fifth straight match to Rafael Nadal and his 18th in their 27 meetings 6-7 (5), 6-2, 7-6 (5) 6-4 in the semifinals of the Australian Open, their first semifinal meeting at a major tournament since the 2005 French Open. "I haven't lost in five months or something so it's not that bad," says Federer. "Don't feel too sorry for me. Obviously I would have loved to have come through and gotten a crack, a chance at winning the title here again. I thought Rafa played well from start to finish. It was a tough match physically as well. I'm disappointed, but it's only the beginning of the season. I'm feeling all right so it's ok." With Nadal leading 5-2 in the second set, the match is suspended for 10 minutes for the local Australia Day firework celebrations. On the resumption of play, Federer loses 11 points in a row.

2004 – Roger Federer ruins the Australia Day spirits of Aussie fans and of native son Lleyton Hewitt, beating the No. 15-seeded Australian 4-6, 6-3, 6-1, 6-4. The match comes four months after Hewitt beats Federer in five sets to clinch Australia's Davis Cup victory over Switzerland in the previous year's Davis Cup semifinals. "I'm very, very happy to have taken my revenge," says Federer after the win "It hurt me big-time that match."

January 27

2005 – Roger Federer lets a match point slip away in his titanic 5-7, 6-4, 5-7, 7-6 (6), 9-7 loss to Marat Safin in the semifinals of the Australian Open. Federer fails in his attempt to become the first man since Pete Sampras in 1994 to capture three consecutive major titles. The four-and-a-half-hour defeat – in which Federer holds a match point in the fourth-set tie-break – is Federer's first loss in 30 matches since the previous year's Athens Olympics and first loss against a top 10 rival in 24 matches stretching back to October 2003. It is also the first time the runaway world No.1 drops a set – let alone the match – in five major semifinals, and only the third occasion from 62 matches that the brilliant Swiss loses after winning the first set in a major match. Says Federer, "It's a real pity. I mean, I had my chances but he didn't allow me to take them. It's really unfortunate. I thought I played, under the circumstances, really well."

2006 – Roger Federer, seeded No. 1, beats Nicolas Kiefer, seeded No. 21, 6-3, 5-7, 6-0, 6-2 in the semifinals of the Australian Open. "I'm very happy, because even though people take it as normal when I win, a Grand Slam semifinal is a huge match," Federer says. "Even though I don't show it, inside I'm very relieved and delighted." Kiefer appearance is his first semifinal at a Grand Slam tournament in his 35 major tournament appearance.

2010 – Trailing by a set and 1-3 in the second set, Roger Federer reels off 13 games in a row and survives a late challenge to fend off Nikolay Davydenko 2-6, 6-3, 6-0, 7-5 in the quarterfinals of the Australian Open. "I've played him (Davydenko) many times and I know he goes through many phases," Federer says. "Some of those phases are a notch under what he can be, so I was hoping for that." Federer wins the third set 6-0 despite hitting only two winners in the set. Davydenko enters the match having won his last 13 matches, including two wins over Federer at the year-end championships in London and in the semifinals of Doha. The win moves Federer into his 23rd consecutive Grand Slam tournament semifinal and he describes his achievement as "definitely one of the most incredible things I have in my resume."

2009 – In devastating fashion, Roger Federer routs Juan Martin del Potro of Argentina 6-3, 6-0, 6-0 in the quarterfinals of the Australian Open. "The last couple games are not that much fun, let's put it that way, "a humble Federer says of the one-sided match. "You want to almost put him out of his misery because you know how tough it is for him."

2011 – Novak Djokovic ensures that for the first time since 2003, Roger Federer will not be a reigning champion of any of the four major tournaments as he defeats the defending champion 7-6 (3), 7-5, 6-4 in the Australian Open semifinal. "Novak was the better player tonight. You got to accept that and move on from here," says Federer. "It's not the end in any way. It's a start for many other tournaments after this. Sure, it's disappointing and it hurts in the moment itself. I wish I could have won here again for the fifth time, but wasn't possible tonight." The loss for Federer also guarantees that for the first time in three years neither Federer or Rafael Nadal will play in a Grand Slam final after David Ferrer's upset of No. 1 seed Nadal in the quarterfinals. Federer is asked to comment on former Australian star Todd Woodbridge's saying that the tournament marks the changing of the guard on top men's tennis. "Yeah, I mean, they say that very quickly," Federer says in his post-match press conference. "Let's talk in six months again."

January 28

2004 – Despite 55 unforced errors, No. 2 seed Roger Federer advances into the semifinals of the Australian Open – and one match from taking over the world No. 1 ranking – with a 7-5, 6-4, 5-7, 6-3 win over nemesis David Nalbandian of Argentina. Entering the match, Federer had only won once against Nalbandian in six total matches, including the previous year's Australian and U.S. Opens. "It's really nice to beat him in a Slam," says Federer of avenging his Grand Slam losses to Nalbandian. "It always hurts double if you lose in a Slam. To get him back at least once, because he also beat me at the U.S. Open, it's nice. I'm happy to have beaten (Lleyton) Hewitt and Nalbandian on the way to the semis. It's only my second (Grand Slam) semifinals in my career. It's a very big satisfaction I have right now."

2007 – Roger Federer wins his 10th major singles title, defeating Fernando Gonzalez of Chile 7-5, 6-4, 6-4 in the final of the Australian Open. Federer becomes only the fourth man in the Open era to win a major title without the loss of a set – the last being Bjorn Borg at Roland Garros in 1980. "Equaling records, doing something that hasn't been done for a long time, it's really nice, there's no doubt," says Federer of winning a major without losing a set. "It wasn't ever a goal for me up to win a Slam without dropping a set. All I care in the end is to hopefully hold that trophy, even though it might be 20-18 in the fifth set. I don't mind, as long as I win. Of course, now that it's all over, it's great to think, Wow, not having dropped a set. It's quite amazing." The championship match is umpired by Frenchwoman Sandra De Jenken – the first time in tennis history a woman umpired a men's Grand Slam singles final

January 29

2006 – Roger Federer gets emotional, cries and hugs all-time great Rod Laver during the post-match ceremony following his 5-7, 7-5, 6-0, 6-2 win over upstart Cypriot Marcos Baghdatis in the final of the Australian Open. Federer has difficulty putting to words the emotions he feels during the post-match ceremony and sobs after receiving the trophy from Laver. "I hope you know how much this means to me," he says as he wipes away tears. Federer becomes the first player to win three consecutive major tournaments since Pete Sampras wins at the 1994 Australian Open. The title is his seventh career major title, tying him with John McEnroe, John Newcombe and Mats Wilander and moving him ahead of two of his boyhood idols Boris Becker and Stefan Edberg, who each won six major singles titles. "I left my idols behind me now. That means something. I'm very pleased," says Federer of passing Becker and Edberg. "I'm definitely on a great roll at the moment. I don't forget that it's been a tough road for me. I amaze myself every time I do well. It's been so consistent, too winning so many slams, seven out of the last eleven. It's quite incredible. I try to keep it up, stay healthy and keep enjoying it, because that's what I'm doing, and I think that's what makes me play well."

2009 – Roger Federer straight-sets Andy Roddick 6-3, 7-5, 7-5 to reach the final of the Australian Open and place himself one match shy of equaling the Pete Sampras record of most men's major singles tournament victories of 14. "When Pete did it in 2002, everyone was saying how kind of lofty of an achievement it was. I don't know if we thought we would see it again anytime soon," says Roddick of the men's record of 14 majors. "I guess Roger is a contemporary of mine, which doesn't lessen the effect. I see Pete and Andre [Agassi] and I still get a little jittery. But it's crazy to think it's come full circle and the magnitude of the numbers Roger has acquired. It's pretty scary if you sit down and look at them and know what it takes to accomplish that."

2010 – Roger Federer crushes Jo-Wilfried Tsonga 6-2, 6-3, 6-2 to advance into the Australian Open final against Britain's Andy Murray and wastes little time before poking fun at the British drought of men's major champions. "I know he'd like to win the first for British tennis since, what is it, 150,000 years?" Federer cracks of Murray in his courtside interview with Jim Courier. "The poor guy who has to go through those moments over and over again." Courier then reminds Federer that the drought is actually only 74 years when Fred Perry last won a major title in 1936. "Oh," Federer then responds. "I missed it by a little bit." Federer then elaborates, stating, "He's got a lot of expectations…The pressure's going to be tough, so we'll see how he handles it. I'll make sure I'll make it as tough as possible."

January 30

2003 – In a victory that clinches the No. 1 ranking and places him in his second career Grand Slam tournament final, Roger Federer dismantles No. 3 seeded Juan Carlos Ferrero of Spain 6-4, 6-1, 6-4 in the semifinals of the Australian Open. After being one match away from the No. 1 ranking in the semifinals of Montreal the previous year – losing his chance in a loss to Andy Roddick – Federer is asked by reporters if he is now relieved to finally move to the No. 1 ranking. "Relief"? Kind of," Federer responds. "Relief for me was Wimbledon. No. 1, obviously it's something I've been close to the last few months. I could never take my chance. I tried everything at The Masters but wasn't good enough. But I put myself in a good spot for the Australian Open. I'm happy to have had a great start now to the season, and to finally be No. 1."

1999 – Laurence Tieleman of Italy, a journeyman professional who achieves a career-high ranking of No. 76 in the world, plays a match he can tell his grandchildren about as the 26-year-old beats a 17-year-old Roger Federer 7-5, 6-1 in the semifinals of the Heilbronn Challenger in Germany. The round before, in the quarterfinals, Federer escapes with a 6-7, 7-6, 7-5 victory over American journeyman pro Justin Gimelstob. Tweets Gimelstob 14 years after his loss to Federer, "2 match points serving for the match at 5-4 in the third set. Still haunts me! Would have loved that win for my résumé!"

2014 – "It's Stan's week, that's clear," says Roger Federer to Swiss journalists at the Davis Cup draw ceremony in

THE DAYS OF ROGER FEDERER

Novi Sad, Serbia as he discusses returning to the Swiss Davis Cup team that will face Serbia after countryman Stan Wawrinka wins the Australian Open four days earlier for this first major title. "And I hope to be able to support him a bit here because I know what he's going through."

January 31

2010 – Roger Federer win his 16th major singles title—and his fourth Australian Open men's singles title—defeating Andy Murray 6-3, 6-4, 7-6 (11). The major title is the first for Federer as a father as he becomes the first dad to win a major singles title since 2003. Says Federer, "I'm over the moon winning this again. I played some of my best tennis in my life these last two weeks. It's also very special—the first Grand Slam as a father." Murray, despite holding a 6-4 career head-to-head advantage over Federer fails in his second major final to beat Federer and win his first Grand Slam title. Referencing Federer's teary runner-up speech from the year before when Federer lost a five-set final to Rafael Nadal, a teary-eyed Murray says in his runner-up speech, "'I can cry like Roger, it's just a shame I can't play like him.'"

2014 – Playing Davis Cup for Switzerland for the first time since 2012, Roger Federer beats Ilija Bozoljac 6-4, 7-5, 6-2 as Switzerland takes a 2-0 lead over Serbia in the Davis Cup first round in Novi Sad, Serbia. Bozoljac holds a set point while leading 5-2 in the second set, but Federer wins five games in a row to take a two-sets-to-love lead before closing out the straight-sets win. "Ilija was playing well, especially in the second set," Federer says. "It was a tough game, it could have been one set all." Federer originally announced that he would skip this first-round match, but changes his mind after his fellow Swiss Stan Wawrinka wins the Australian Open over Rafa Nadal after Federer loses to Nadal in the semifinals. Michael Lammer and Marco Chiudinelli clinch the match for Switzerland the next day with a victory in the doubles rubber

FEBRUARY

February 1

2009 – Roger Federer is reduced to tears of disappointment after losing to Rafael Nadal 7-5, 3-6, 7-6 (3), 3-6, 6-2 in four hours, 22 minute in the final of the Australian Open. Nadal's win over Federer – his fifth 13th win in the last 19 matches between the two tennis titans – prevents Federer from equaling Pete Sampras' record of 14 Grand Slam tournament titles. In the on-court trophy ceremony, Federer tries to speak of the match, but tears well up in his eyes and he says "Maybe I'll try later. God, it's killing me," before bursting in full sobs of disappointment. After being presented the champions trophy by Australian tennis legend Rod Laver, Nadal then hugs and consoles Federer and says to him, "Roger, sorry for today. I really know how you feel right now. Remember, you're a great champion. You're one of the best in history. You're going to improve on the 14 of Sampras."

2004 – Roger Federer wins his first Australian Open crown, his second career major singles title and clinches the world's No. 1 ranking with a 7-6 (3), 6-4, 6-2 win over

Marat Safin in the men's singles final at the Australian Open. "What a great start to the year for me, to win the Australian Open and become No. 1 in the world," Federer says. "To fulfill my dreams, it really means very much to me." In his post-match press conference, he is asked how his second major title in Australia compares to winning his first major at Wimbledon the previous year. "Totally different really," says Federer, "because, like I've always said, that Wimbledon victory for me was such a dream and such a relief. I cannot really describe what I felt right then, right there. But now I kind of know how it feels. It's still really nice. It just gets me all emotional inside. Yeah, it's just unbelievable. You come here, you prepare, you leave after three weeks basically, and you're finally the winner after such a long time. It just really feels good."

February 2

2004 – Roger Federer becomes the No. 1 player in the world for the first time in his career, replacing Andy Roddick in the top ranking on the ATP computer. Federer holds the ranking for the next 237 weeks, an ATP World Tour record, relinquishing the top spot to Rafael Nadal on August 17, 2008. Federer regains the No. 1 ranking on July 6, 2009 after he defeats Andy Roddick in the Wimbledon final. He holds the top ranking another 48 weeks until the end of the 2010 French Open. Federer again holds the No. 1 ranking for 17 weeks following his seventh Wimbledon title in 2007.

1999 – Playing in only his fourth ATP-level tournament, 17-year-old Roger Federer, ranked No. 243, defeats world No. 5 and reigning French Open champion Carlos Moya of Spain 7-6 (7-1), 3-6, 6-3 in the first round of the Marseille Open in France.

2001 – Roger Federer beats Goran Ivanisevic 6-4, 6-4 in 57 minutes to reach the semifinals of the Milan Indoor championships in Italy. Federer, ranked No. 27, out aces Ivanisevic, ranked No. 123, 8-7 while the Croatian throws in nine double-faults in the 57-minute match. The meeting is the second and final meeting between the two players – Federer also winning at the AXA Cup indoor ATP event in London in 2000. Five months later, both players have hallmark tournaments at Wimbledon, Federer upsetting seven-time champion Pete Sampras in the fourth round for his first major victory at a Grand Slam event, while Ivanisevic, a wild-card entry ranked No. 125, benefits from Federer's upset of Sampras and is the surprise winner, beating Patrick Rafter in the final.

February 3

2001 – After three previous defeats, Roger Federer beats Yevgeny Kafelnikov for the first time in his career, registering a 6-2, 6-7 (7-4), 6-3 decision in a semifinal of the Milan indoor tournament.

2002 – Davide Sanguinetti becomes the first Italian in 10 years to win the Milan Indoor Championships, his first ATP title, upsetting defending champion Roger Federer

7-6 (2), 4-6, 6-1 in the final. After losing the first-set tie-breaker, Federer breaks Sanguinetti twice in the second set to even the match. Sanguinetti then breaks Federer in the fourth game of the third set and, after Federer was unable to capitalize on three break points to go down 4-1, he fades and is broken again to falter in the third.

2008 – Roger Federer is among 70,000 fans who attend the Super Bowl in Glendale, Arizona where the New York Giants upset the New England Patriots 17-14 in Super Bowl XLII. The Patriots were looking to become the first team in National Football League history to finish the season with a perfect 19-0 record. However, Plaxico Burress catches a 13-yard touchdown pass from Eli Manning with 35 seconds left hand Tom Brady and the Patriots their only loss of the season.

February 4

2001 – Roger Federer, at age 19, wins the first ATP title of his career, defeating Julien Boutter of France 6-4, 6-7, 6-4 in Milan, Italy. "What a relief," he says after the match. "I'm really happy to have won my first title here in Milan. As a kid you always dream of winning your first title." The day is entirely a happy day as Rene Stauffer writes in his book *Roger Federer: Quest for Perfection.* "But the excursion to Milan didn't end very happily for Roger's father," Stauffer writes. "In his excitement, he locked his car keys inside the car and had to smash in the car window to retrieve them."

1999 – Following up his first-round win over No. 5-ranked Carlos Moya, Roger Federer, ranked 243, beats No. 63-ranked Jerome Golmard of France 6-7 (6-8), 7-6 (7-5), 7-6 (7-5) to reach the Marseille Open in France.

2000 – Ranked No. 61, Roger Federer registers one of his first wins over a big server as he defeats No. 17-ranked Mark Philippoussis 6-4, 7-6(3), 4-6, 6-4 leveling the Davis Cup tie between Switzerland and Australia at 1-1 on a carper surface in Zurich. The 18-year-old Federer seals the victory on a double fault from Philippoussis.

February 5

1999 – Roger Federer's run in his fourth career ATP tournament comes to an end as Arnaud Clement of France reaches the semifinals of a pro tournament for the first time, beating the No. 243-ranked Roger Federer 6-3, 6-3 at the Marseille Open in France. Yves Allegro, Federer's friend and fellow player, tells Rene Stauffer in the book *Roger Federer: Quest for Perfection* that during this time, he was sure that Federer would be an elite player in professional tennis. "I said back then that he would make it into the top 10 or maybe even to No. 1, but many people laughed at me," Allegro says to Stauffer.

2000. Roger Federer and Lorenzo Manta rally from a first-set setback to shock Wayne Arthurs and Sandon Stolle 3-6, 6-3, 6-4, 7-6(4) and give Switzerland a 2-1 lead in the Davis Cup first round in Zurich. "I'm surprised," says Federer, a day after beating Mark Philippoussis in singles "I didn't think we could win both these matches. I was hoping but I wasn't at all positive, particularly about the doubles." The Swiss pair save two set points in the fourth set forcing the tie-break. Says Australian captain John Newcombe, "In the end it was Federer who hit three points in a row in the tiebreak and they were crucial – the killing blows."

February 6

2004 – Just five days after winning the Australian Open and just four days after securing the world No. 1 ranking for the first time, Roger Federer struggles out of the gate in a transition from summer hard court conditions in Australian to indoor clay conditions in wintry Bucharest, Romania but beats No. 72-ranked Victor Hanescu 7-6 (4), 6-3, 6-1 to give Switzerland a 1-1 tie with Romania in the Davis Cup first round. Before arriving in Bucharest, Federer stops off in his hometown of Basel, Switzerland, where he is greeted by fans with cowbells and flags and signs welcoming the new world No. 1. He then is jetted off to Romania on via private air charter, courtesy of a wealthy dual Swiss-Romanian citizen.

2000 – In a two-and-a-half-hour duel between the top two teenagers on the ATP Tour, Lleyton Hewitt, ranked No. 15, defeats Roger Federer, ranked No. 61, 6-3, 3-6, 7-6(2), 6-1 to draw Australia even with Switzerland 2-2 in the Davis Cup first round in Zurich. It was the second meeting between the two 18-year-olds, Hewitt improving to 2-0 after beating Federer 7-6 (4), 2-6, 6-4 in the first round of Lyon the previous year. After Federer's loss to

Hewitt, Federer would lose just three matches in the next 33 in Davis Cup play. In the fifth and decisive match of the series, Mark Philippoussis lifts Australia to the 3-2 victory by beating George Bastl

At the 2013 U.S. Open, Roger Federer was asked about the influence that Arthur Ashe, the man whose name is fitted on the U.S. Open's stadium court, who passed away due to AIDS on Feb. 8, 1993. "It was before my time, so not that much, honestly," Federer answered. "I wish more so, so for me I feel mostly connected through the center court, just that it's named after him and then hearing later on all the great things he did for the sport really. Unfortunately like (Bjorn) Borg or maybe before that, it's just a little bit before my time. I don't remember seeing him play, only highlights when he won Wimbledon and so forth, but just hearing what a great human being he was and how inspirational and influential he was. It's a pity he's not with us anymore. I would have loved to meet him, no doubt about it."

February 7

2003 – Roger Federer, ranked No. 6 in the world, registers his third consecutive Davis Cup singles win in which he drops just six games, defeating No. 77-ranked Raemon Sluiter of the Netherlands 6-2 6-1 6-3 in Arnheim, Netherlands.

2004 – In a match lasting three hours, 45 minutes, the Swiss pair of Roger Federer and Davis Cup debutant Yves Allegro register a 6-4, 1-6, 6-3, 3-6, 10-8 win over Andrei

Pavel and Gabriel Trifu to give Switzerland a 2-1 lead over Romania in the Davis Cup first round in Bucharest.

"Roger's got too many shots, too much talent in one body. It's hardly fair that one person can do all this – his backhands, his forehands, volleys, serving, his court position ... the way he moves around the court, you feel like he's barely touching the ground, and that's the sign of a great champion. And his anticipation, I guess, is the one thing that we all admire." —Rod Laver on Roger Federer in 2007

February 8

2002 – Roger Federer, ranked No. 13, beats Marat Safin, ranked No. 7, 7-5, 6-1, 6-2 on indoor red clay as Switzerland and Russia draw even 1-1 after the first day of the Davis Cup first round. Federer, ironically, drops just eight games to Safin on clay when they meet a few months later in the Hamburg final, Federer winning 6-1, 6-3, 6-4.

2004 – Roger Federer beat No. 53-ranked Andrei Pavel 6-3, 6-2, 7-5 to secure Switzerland a place in the quarterfinals of the Davis Cup with the match-clinching victory over Romania. "It was not an easy match, despite the score," Federer says. "I think I was lucky because I won the first two sets a little sooner [than expected], just before Pavel regained his determination and rediscovered his dangerous backhands." Federer comes back from a 1-4 deficit in the third set to close out the straight-set win.

2003 – Roger Federer and George Bastl are defeated by the Dutch pairing of Paul Haarhuis and Martin Verkerk

3-6, 6-3, 6-4, 7-5 as the Netherlands take a 2-1 lead over Switzerland in the Davis Cup first round in Arnheim, Switzerland.

February 9

2001 – Playing Davis Cup for Switzerland in his hometown of Basel, Roger Federer puts his country up 1-0 against the United States with a 6-4, 7-6(3), 4-6, 6-1 victory over Todd Martin. "It's for sure one of the top victories I have now," says the 19-year-old Federer. "I mean to play in Basel, in Davis Cup and everything together, it just gives it a great mixture." Playing just five days after winning his first ATP singles title in Milan the previous Sunday, Federer rates his Davis Cup success on par with his breakthrough tournament victory. "It's tough to say," Federer says. "In Milan I won five matches in a row. Here now it's one match, but it's something very special. As I told you, Davis Cup here in Basel, and a lot of fans watching also. My family's here. I don't know, it just is nice."

2002 – Paired with Marc Rosset, Roger Federer is defeated by Marat Safin and Yevgeny Kafelnikov 6-2, 7-6 (6), 6-7 (9), 6-2 as Russia takes a 2-1 lead over Switzerland in the Davis Cup first round in Moscow.

2003 – Roger Federer sets up a decisive Davis Cup match victory for his teammate Michel Kratochvil as he defeats No. 19-ranked Sjeng Schalken of the Netherlands 7-6(2), 6-4, 7-5 to draw Switzerland even at 2-2 against the Netherlands in the first round in Arnheim, Netherlands.

Kratochvil then beats Martin Verkerk 1-6, 7-6 (5), 7-5 (6), 6-1 in the decisive fifth match to give the Swiss the 3-2 victory. Says Schalken of his match with Federer, "This is what I'm worth – I can't play any better." Says Federer, "I kept serving well, and that made the difference."

February 10

2001 – Fueled by confidence after his first ATP tournament victory and a first-day singles victory over Todd Martin, Roger Federer dominates the doubles court alongside Lorenzo Manta, leading Switzerland to a 2-1 lead over the United States in the Davis Cup first round in Basel, Switzerland defeating the American pair of Justin Gimelstob and Jan-Michael Gambill 6-4, 6-2, 7-5. "The confidence is here," says Federer. "Somehow, for me, I feel where the other guy is serving more on big points, I'm more confident. I don't know, it's just a different situation when you come out of a few bad tournaments. You have to -- it's like when you ski, you stay away from the gates, your mind falls out of the race. You can take more risk when you have more confidence."

2012 – Playing in his first Davis Cup World Group match in eight years, Roger Federer is shocked by No. 17-ranked John Isner of the United States as the six-foot-10 inch American uses his big serve and pounding forehand to beat Federer 4-6, 6-3, 7-6 (4), 6-2 to give the U.S. a 2-0 lead against Switzerland in the first round of the Davis Cup on an indoor clay court in Fribourg, Switzerland. The loss is Federer first in singles in Davis Cup play also in eight years.

"I thought he played great," Federer says. "He played it tough and served great when he had to. I just missed a couple more opportunities than he did and that's what cost me the match." The 26-year-old Isner calls victory the "biggest win of my career thus far." Says U.S. Davis Cup captain Jim Courier of Isner, "I don't know I have ever seen anyone finish a match against Roger Federer the way he did today. That was pretty amazing."

2002 – Roger Federer, ranked No. 13, crushes No. 4-ranked Yevgeny Kafelnikov 7-6 (6), 6-1, 6-1 on indoor red clay to draw Switzerland even at 2-2 against Russia in the Davis Cup first round in Moscow. In the first set tie-break, Kafelnikov comes back from a 2-6 deficit only to double fault and subsequently lose the tie-breaker the then the next two sets decisively. However, Federer's efforts are in vain as Switzerland loses the series 3-2 when Michel Kratochvil is defeated by Marat Safin in the fifth and decisive match 6-1, 7-6 (6), 6-4. "For me personally, it was great tennis this weekend," Federer says of beating two Top 10 players in his singles matches. "I hope, next year we will reach semifinals or even finals."

February 11

2001 – Roger Federer clinches a near single-handed victory for Switzerland over the United States in the first round of Davis Cup, defeating Jan-Michael Gambill 7-5, 6-2, 4-6, 6-2 in the 3-2 win in Federer's hometown of Basel. Federer, who beat Todd Martin in the opening singles and paired with Lorenzo Manta to beat Gambill and Justin Gimelstob in the doubles rubber, becomes one of seven players to win three live matches against a U.S. Davis Cup team, joining Laurie Doherty of Britain, Henri Cochet of France, Frank Sedgman and Neale Fraser of Australia, Nicola Pietrangeli of Italy and Raul Ramirez of Mexico. Says Federer, the future world No. 1, "My total game was good the whole weekend. I can't complain. I was serving well, feeling well from the baseline... Usually when I get tired I let go a little bit mentally, but that was absolutely not the case. It was just total relief, total happiness at one time. I was so happy for the team, happy for Switzerland -- to beat such a big country." Says Gambill of Federer, "You'd have to be blind not to see that he's got a great future in store for him."

2012 – Paired with his Olympic gold medal-winning partner Stan Wawrinka, Roger Federer's worst Davis Cup series of his career ends as he and Wawrinka are beaten by the ad-hoc pairing of Mike Bryan and Mardy Fish 4-6, 6-3, 6-3, 6-3 as the United States clinches a shocking 3-0 victory over the Swiss on indoor red clay in Fribourg, Switzerland. "I played well enough in doubles, but Stanislas not so much," Federer says, with some controversy, after the match. Federer adds that Wawrinka "didn't have his best match in singles; it's a shame, because of that defeat, we weren't able to put the U.S. under pressure." On the opening day of play Wawrinka is defeated by Mardy Fish in the opening rubber of the series, while Federer is defeated by John Isner, to put Switzerland in a nearly insurmountable 0-2 hole after the first day of play. Fish was substituting for Bryan's twin brother Bob, who skipped the series after the birth of his daughter Micaela.

February 12

2013 – Roger Federer holds a media day on the Monday of the ABN AMRO Championships in Rotterdam, Netherlands dubbed "Manic Monday" by the ATP. Federer begins the day visiting the Giant Tennis Racquet in Rotterdam's city centre with tournament director and former Wimbledon champion Richard Krajicek, where he unveils and raises his own 2012 champion's flag during a flag parade at Boompjes along with the mayor of Rotterdam in celebration of the tournament's 40th anniversary. Federer then returns to the tournament site, conducts his pre-tournament press conference, four television interviews, a practice session with David Goffin and an autograph opportunity for fans. In the evening, Federer dresses up in a suit and visits with sponsors and then takes part in the tournament's opening ceremony on centre court with Krajicek and wheelchair tennis star Esther Vergeer. "They asked me if I could do most of the things today, and I said that's no problem for me," says Federer. "Sometimes, it's easier for me to do it all in the same day. I'm happy to help get the tournament promoted."

2000 – Eighteen-year-old Roger Federer defeats defending champion Fabrice Santoro 7-6 (4), 7-5 to reach his first ATP singles final at the Marseille Open in France.

February 13

2000 – Roger Federer plays his first ATP Tour singles final, but loses to countryman Marc Rosset 2-6, 6-3, 7-6 (5) in the final of the Marseille Open in France. The match between to the Swiss players marks the first time in the history of the ATP where two players from Switzerland compete in a singles final.

2003 – Roger Federer advances to the quarterfinals of the Open 13 in Marseille, France, defeating Jarkko Nieminen of Finland 6-2, 6-3.

2013 – Roger Federer defeats Grega Zemlja of Slovenia 6-3, 6-1 in 58 minutes to improve to a 22-5 career mark at the ABN AMRO Indoors in Rotterdam, Netherlands.

"Every time I hit it, I am amazed that it actually stays in," Roger Federer told Brad Gilbert on ESPN2 during the 2012 French Open of his "squash shot" slice forehand.

February 14

2003 – Roger Federer advances into the semifinals of the Open 13 tournament in Marseille, France with a 6-4, 4-6, 6-4 win over Raemon Sluiter.

2013 – Roger Federer advances into the quarterfinals of the ABN AMRO Indoors in Rotterdam defeating 123-ranked Thiemo de Bakker 6-3, 6-4. "I'm happy. Things are obviously pretty quick indoors," Federer says after winning in just over an hour.

"The best way to beat him would be to hit him over the head with a racquet. Roger could win the Grand Slam if he keeps playing

the way he is and, if he does that, it will equate to the two Grand Slams that I won because standards are much higher these days."
—Rod Laver on Roger Federer after the 2007 Australian Open

February 15

2001 – Future all-time men's major title holder Roger Federer beats Bob Bryan, the future all-time men's doubles major title holder with his twin brother Mike, by a 7-6(1), 6-3 margin in second round of the Open 13 in Marseille, France.

2003 – Roger Federer defeats Karol Kucera of Slovakia 7-6 (5), 6-3 in 86 minutes to advance to the final of the Open 13 in Marseille, France. The match is the fourth and final meeting between Federer and Kucera, Federer winning three of the four career match-ups.

2013 – Roger Federer, ranked No. 2 in the world, loses to No. 39, Julien Benneteau 6-3, 7-5 in the quarterfinals of ABN AMRO tournament in Rotterdam. Says Benneteau after his second career victory over Federer, "Afterwards I told Roger I was sorry, but he said: 'It's okay. That's sports.'" Says Federer following the loss, "I don't want to leave, I want to play. I feel bad for the fans who don't get to see me now. Hopefully this wasn't my last time here."

February 16

2003 – Roger Federer beats Jonas Bjorkman 6-2, 7-6 (6) in the final of the Open 13 in Marseille, France, for his fifth career ATP title. Federer rallies from being down 0-3 in the second set to force the second-set tie-breaker that he wins on his third match point. "To me, it's a dream to win here," says Federer. "In 2000, I lost the final in the third set tie-break against Marc Rosset, so I was very nervous today."

2005 – Roger Fedrerer fires seven aces and beats Czech Bohdan Ulihrach 6-3, 6-4 in 73 minutes in the first round of the ABN AMRO Indoors in Rotterdam, Netherlands.

"He's the most gifted player that I've ever seen in my life. I've seen a lot of people play. I've seen the Lavers, I played against some of the great players—the Samprases, Beckers, Connors, Borgs, you name it. This guy could be the greatest of all time. That, to me, says it all. He's probably the greatest player that ever lived. He can beat half the guys with his eyes closed!" —John McEnroe, born on Februrary 16, 1959, on Roger Federer in 2004.

February 17

2005 – Roger Federer defeats practice partner and fellow Swiss Stanislas Wawrinka 6-1, 6-4 to reach the quarterfinals of the ABN AMRO tournament in Rotterdam, Netherlands. Teenage qualifier Wawrinka, who carves the biggest win of his career in the previous round when he upset France's Sebastien Grosjean, barely knows what hit him in the first set as he loses it in 25 minutes. The second set looks to head in a similar way when he is again broken at the beginning but, cheered on by a boisterous crowd, Wawrinka finds his footing and even earns a break point when his illustrious opponent serves for the match.

2009 – Roger Federer announces that due to back problems he is pulling out of the Dubai Championships in the United Arab Emirates and Switzerland's first round Davis Cup series against the United States in March. Switzerland, deprived of Federer, loses to the Andy Roddick-led United States in Birmingham, Alabama 4-1.

February 18

2005 – Roger Federer advances to the semifinals of the ABN AMRO Championships in Rotterdam defeating Nikolay Davydenko 7-5, 7-5. Davydenko has his chances to take the match into a third set, earning two break points in 11th game of the second but Federer safely negotiates the danger. "It was fun on one side but it was a very tough battle and I'm happy to be through to the semis," says Federer after his win.

2012 – Nikolay Davydenko leads Roger Federer 6-4, 3-1, but falters and loses 4-6, 6-3, 6-4 in the semifinals of the ABN AMRO tournament in Rotterdam. "These are the kinds of matches you need to help your confidence," says Federer, who also saves a triple break point at 4-all in the third set. He closes out the 20th encounter between the two veteran players on his first match point to advance in two hours and 16 minutes after winning 13 of the last 14 points of the match. "I think my mindset was there," Federer says. "Even though I was down 0-40, I knew it wasn't over and that I still had a shot. I had a winner's mindset. Sometimes you don't have those days, but [today], I believed I could still win and I think that got me over the finish line."

February 19

1999 – Playing in only his fifth career ATP level pro tournament, Roger Federer, age 18 and ranked No. 178, leads world No. 2 Yevgeny Kafelnikov of Russia 3-1 in the third set, but falters and loses 6-1, 5-7, 6-4 in the quarterfinals of the ABN AMRO Championships in Rotterdam.

2004 – Roger Federer wins his 16th straight match defeating Andrei Pavel, 7-6 (2), 7-5 in the second round of the ABN AMRO Championships in Rotterdam, the Netherlands. Federer squanders a 5-2 lead in the first set, and breaks once in the second set in the 11th game.

2005 – Roger Federer beats Mario Ancic 7-5, 6-3 to reach the final of the ABN AMRO Championships in Rotterdam, Netherlands. Federer breaks Ancic late in the opening set as he gets accustomed to the Croatian's huge serving style. The Swiss surges into the lead in the second set, assuring victory and his third final of the season with breaks in the third and final games of the set to wrap up the one-hour, 21-minute victory.

2007 – Roger Federer ties Jimmy Connors' record of 160 consecutive weeks as the top-ranked player in men's tennis. Federer, the winner of 10 major singles titles, first attained the No. 1 ranking on February 2, 2004 and is assured of breaking the Connors record the following week. Connors was ranked No.1 from July 1974 to August 1977.

2012 – Roger Federer wins his first tournament of the 2012 season, defeating Juan Martin del Potro 6-1, 6-4 in the ABN AMRO World Tennis Tournament final in Rotterdam. "In the first set, I was rock solid. I played great from start to finish," says Federer. "In the second set, it got tighter. I'm happy I was able to sneak it out." With the win, Federer extends his streak of winning at least one ATP World Tour title each season to 12 years in a row.

February 20

2004 – Tim Henman upsets world No. 1 Roger Federer 6-3, 7-6 (9) at the ABN AMRO quarterfinals in Rotterdam, Netherlands, improving his head-to-head record against the Swiss to 6-1. Henman also ends Federer's 16-match winning streak that included his first Australian Open title and his nascent ascent to the No. 1 ranking. In the second set, Federer leads in the tie-break 5-1, 6-3, 7-6 and 9-8, wasting six set points. "I knew it was going to be a tough math, it's really what I expected," Federer says. "It was tough. I think he was playing really well. I couldn't play like I maybe usually do, but that definitely has something to do with his game as well."

2005 – Roger Federer wins his 24th career singles titles, defeating Ivan Ljubicic 5-7, 7-5, 7-6 (5) in the final of the ABN AMRO Championships in Rotterdam in two hours, 42 minutes. Federer strikes 12 aces and 28 total winners against 42 unforced errors as he defeats Ljubicic for the fifth time in eight meetings. "Today was very close, it could have gone either way," says Federer, who was 2-4 down in the deciding tie-break.

February 21

2010 – Roger Federer announces his withdrawal from the Dubai Championships due to a lung infection. A four-time winner in Dubai, Federer says he expects to recover in time to compete in Indian Wells in two weeks.

"He captured five Wimbledon crowns in a row from 2003-2007 and was victorious five consecutive times at the U.S. Open as well (2004-2008). He also has won a men's record seventeen major singles titles. Moreover, Federer advanced at least to an unimaginable twenty-three straight semifinals at the majors. He stands alone at the top of my list at the best ever because of his unfailingly high standards, unassailable record and the extraordinary versatility of his court craft." —Steve Flink in rating Roger Federer as the greatest men's tennis player of all time in his book "The Greatest Tennis Matches of All-Time"

February 22

2000 – Roger Federer, 18, upsets No. 2 seed Nicolas Kiefer of Germany 6-2, 6-3 in the first round of the AXA Cup in London. At the time, Kiefer, ranked No. 4, is the highest ranked player Federer has beaten at this stage in his career.

2005 – To promote the upcoming Dubai Duty Free Championships, Andre Agassi and world No. 1 Roger Federer conduct a "practice session" on top of the helipad of the Helipad of the Burj Ar Arab hotel, the world's most luxurious hotel. The hotel stretches 321 meters above the water on a man made island, and is the world's most recognizable hotel. The hotel's helipad stands 211 meters above the ground. "The view is absolutely amazing here, and it was very different when I was asked to do this as I didn't know what to expect," Federer says to ATPtennis. com. Later in the week – and at ground level – Federer defeats Agassi 6-3, 6-1 in the semifinals of the event.

February 23

2001 – Roger Federer hits seven aces and defeats Alex Corretja 6-4, 6-2 in 73 minutes in the quarterfinals of the ABN AMRO tournament in Rotterdam. The win is the first for Federer against Corretja in three total meetings. Later in the year, Corretja beats Federer in the quarterfinals of the French Open.

2005 – Two-time defending champion Roger Federer trails Czech qualifier Ivo Minar by 3-1 in the third set and by 4-3 in the final-set tiebreaker, but escapes by a 6-7 (5), 6-3, 7-6 (5) margin in the first round of the Dubai Open. The No. 119-ranked Minar, who had a break point to take a 4-1 lead in the final set, but proceeds to lose four games in a row as Federer takes a 5-3 final-set lead. The two-time Wimbledon champion, however, is unable to serve out the match and the two players engage in a final-set tie-breaker. Minar leads by a mini break at 4-3 in the final-set tiebreaker, but Federer holds on to clinch victory 7-5. "He had already won three matches here in the qualifying competition, which gave him a longer and better preparation," Federer says. "It can become dangerous against any player in the Top 200. Two or three times I thought the match might slip away, especially when I nearly went a double break down (in the third). I didn't have enough rhythm and I wasn't as aggressive as I would like to be. But he played as aggressively as I would have like to, and was in a very dominant position, so in the end for me it turned out to be a fine win."

Februrary 24

2000 – Big-serving Croatian left-hander Goran Ivanisevic is upset by a 18-year-old Roger Federer 7-5, 6-3 in 65 minutes to reach the quarterfinals at the AXA Cup in London. Federer, who ousts No. 2 seeded Nicolas Kiefer in the first round, advances to face another Swiss Marc Roset in the quarterfinals. Federer and Ivanisevic face each other only two times in their careers, Federer also winning in the quarterfinals of Milan in 2001. Ivanisevic has Federer to thank for eliminating seven-time champion Pete Sampras in the round of 16 at Wimbledon, helping to pave the way for Ivanisevic to win his one and only major at the All England Club that year.

2001 – Roger Federer defeats Andrei Pavel of Romania 6-7 (4), 6-4, 6-0 to reach the final of the ABN AMRO tournament at Rotterdam. Federer wastes a set point leading 5-4 in the first set then reels off eight consecutive games to win the contest in 110 minutes.

2005 – Top-ranked Roger Federer saves two consecutive match points in the final-set tie-break and beats Juan Carlos Ferrero 4-6, 6-3, 7-6 (6) to reach the quarterfinals of the Dubai Open in the United Arab Emirates. Ferrero leads 2-0 in the second and 4-2 in the third set. For Federer, it's the third straight match that he wins a final-set tiebreaker – adding in his final-round win over Ivan Ljubicic in Rotterdam the previous week and his first-round win over Ivo Minar – that sets an ATP record, broken by John Isner who wins five straight matches in final-set tie-breakers in 2007 in Washington, D.C.

2014 – Federer excites fans with another of his famous "tweener" shots, hit during his 6-1, 6-4 opening round win over Benjamin Becker at the Dubai Championships. Says Federer of his between-the-legs lob winner shot, "Two shots before that, the dig I had on the volley, I didn't think I was going to make that. And then the second one was just a reflex. I thought he was going to go to the forehand, went to the backhand. I got it over somehow, and then I thought that was maybe actually going to win, and then he got to it quite comfortably and he had to hit the lob because I was so close to the net. Then because he was coming in already, I thought maybe he was going to be pretty close to the net so let me try the lob instead of just the hit just like I usually play it. It worked perfectly, so I'm happy I didn't miss it wide and even better that he got it back so he created even more to it." Continues Federer on his shot, "Yeah, it's rare for me to win that point with the lob in that circumstance. I know I can hit it, but it's always exciting, it's so rare to get that opportunity to line it up because it's a safe shot for me almost to a degree. It was exciting, and the fans enjoyed it, which is almost as important as winning the point."

February 25

2000 – Marc Rosset comes back from a set down to beat an 18-year-old Roger Federer 3-6, 6-4, 6-4 in the quarterfinals of the AXA Cup in London. Federer is defeated by his 11 years older compatriot for the second straight tournament, as Rosset also beats Federer in the Marseille final two weeks earlier, Federer also winning the first set in that encounter.

2013 – Roger Federer suffers a first-set hiccup, but then rolls over No. 129-ranked Malek Jaziri of Tunisia 5-7, 6-0, 6-2 in one hour, 30 minutes in the first round of the Dubai Duty Free Championships in Dubai. "We were both not playing really well in the beginning. We were both missing a lot of first serves, or him in particular," says Federer, who serves 10 aces in the match. "I think because I couldn't take advantage, I went from 'not so good' to really 'not so good.'"

February 26

2007 – Roger Federer begins his 161st straight week as the No. 1 player in the ATP rankings, breaking the ATP record of 160 consecutive weeks set by Jimmy Connors in 1977. Says Federer, "I have been counting the days…This record is something special to me. Even if I lost it tomorrow it would still take somebody more than three years to beat it." Federer ushers in his record week at No. 1 with a victory over Kristian Pless 7-6 (2), 3-6, 6-3 in the opening round of the Dubai Open.

2005 – Just five days after facing each other in a photo shoot on top of the helipad of the Burj Ar Arab hotel, the world's most luxurious hotel, Roger Federer routs Andre Agassi 6-3, 6-1 in the semifinals of the Dubai Duty Free Championships in the United Arab Emirates. Federer's win places him into the final to face Croatia's Ivan Ljubicic in a title match for the third time in the first two months of 2005 season.

2014 – In a two-hour-and-nine-minute struggle, Roger Federer beats Radek Stepanek to reach the third round of the Dubai Championships. Federer trails 0-2 in the third set, but rallies to win five games in a row to take the match 6-2, 6-7(4), 6-3. "I started to understand what I was doing wrong which made me maybe play a little bit tentatively from the baseline, what made me not make enough shots

[and] why I wasn't playing as aggressively as I wanted to," Federer says after the match. "I couldn't find the right balance between offense and defense. It was almost a bit too late for everything, but I kind of hung around and I took the positives out of the match."

February 27

2005 – Roger Federer wins his 25th career singles title defeating Ivan Ljubicic 6-1, 6-7 (6), 6-3 in the final of Dubai Open in the United Arab Emirates. The title is Federer's third in a row in the oil-rich middle eastern city. Says Federer, "To win three times here is fantastic. It's the first time to have achieved that anywhere." The win also marks the third time in the young tennis season that Federer beats Ljubicic in a tournament final, also beating the Croatian the previous weekend in Rotterdam and the previous month in Qatar. "I hope we can keep this rivalry going," Federer says of playing Ljubicic. "It is good for Ivan, good to see a different face on the other side of the net."

2013 – Roger Federer advances into the quarterfinals of the Dubai Duty Free Championships for an eighth time in 10 visits, defeating Marcel Granollers of Spain 6-3, 6-4. Federer extends his career head-to-head lead on Spain's Marcel Granollers to 2-0 – both matches being played in Dubai, in the round of 16 and being by 6-3, 6-4 margins.

2003 – Top-seeded Roger Federer defeats Hicham Arazi 7-5, 6-3 to reach the semifinals of the Dubai Champsionships. The 21-year-old Federer better manages the gusty winds to defeat Arazi for the third time in four meetings. "I think I was playing too passive at the start because I just wanted to keep the ball in play," says Federer.

2014 – Winning 12 of the last 14 games. Roger Federer defeats Lukas Rosol of the Czech Republic 6-2, 6-2 in 58 minutes in the quarterfinals of the Dubai Championships.

February 28

2013 – The number "8" is Roger Federer's favorite and lucky number and which makes his 6-2, 6-2 win over Nikolay Davydenko in the quarterfinals of the Dubai Duty Free Open that much more special as it marks his 888th career ATP singles match victory. Federer wins 888th career match Thirteen years after first facing each other at the Italian Indoor Championships in Milan, Roger Federer and Nikolay Davydenko face off for the 21st time on the ATP World Tour in the quarterfinals of the Dubai Duty Free Championships in the United Arab Emirates, Federer winning by a 6-2, 6-2 margin. "I was very happy, it was a good match for me. I served well from the start. Then, also, I thought I had good timing on the return in particular after missing a lot of returns in the first match [versus Malek Jaziri]. And the second match, obviously, he was serving bigger, [Marcel] Granollers. Today, I thought I was really striking it well, and then [the] virtue of that, was [that I] getting the first strike in and then I was able to control the baseline more."

2007 – Highlighted by a winning passing shot between the legs from about 10 feet behind the baseline, Roger Federer extends his career-best winning streak to 38 matches defeating Daniele Bracciali 7-5, 6-3, to reach the quarterfinals of the Dubai Open in the United Arab Emirates. Says Federer of his "tweener" winner, "It was a shot which I have not hit for a long time."

2014 – Roger Federer beats Novak Djokovic for the first time in 18 months, defeating the world No. 2 3-6, 6-3, 6-2 in the semifinals of the Dubai Championships. It marks Federer's first win over Djokovic in four attempts, dating back to Federer's last win over the Serb in the final of Cincinnati in 2012. "I think I was able to play a bit more aggressively as the match went on," Federer says after the match. "I knew I was in a bit of trouble (after the first set) and not looking good at all, because he has a tendency to really run with it and play more freely on your serve. It was just a matter of trying to play consistent but remain aggressive – sometimes being overly aggressive to see if it works. Then I started to serve very well, something I haven't been able to do really this week yet. I knew to have a chance (against Djokovic), I needed to serve well, so I'm just very happy I was able to deliver that."

2006 – Roger Federer begins the defense of Dubai Open title with a 7-6, 6-3 victory over fellow Swiss Stanislas Wawrinka, his first match since winning the Australian Open. "I am quite pleased with the way I played," Federer says. "I really don't care about the bad shots as long as the end result is fine."

2012 – Roger Federer opens up play at the Dubai Duty Free Championships with a 6-0 set, advancing past Michael Llodra 6-0, 7-6 (6) in the first round. Federer wins the first 11 points of the match and wins the first set in just 18 minutes. "It's always great to start off a tournament winning the first set 6-Love," says Federer. "I don't know when that's the last time it's happened to me. After that, I really had to sort of make sure I controlled Michael as much as I could because I know he's a dangerous player. He likes to move forward, and he obviously started to serve a bit better."

February 29

2013 – On leap day, Roger Federer defeats No. 15-ranked Feliciano Lopez 7-5, 6-3 in the second round of the Dubai Duty Free Championships, increasing his career record against the Spaniard to 10-0. "It was difficult," says Federer. "I obviously played Feliciano many, many times way back when - and now on tour as well - but I've never played him when he was ranked so high and potentially so confident."

MARCH

March 1

2014 – Roger Federer wins his 78th career ATP World Tour singles title, moving out of a third-place tie with John McEnroe on the all-time list, defeating Tomas Berdych 3-6, 6-4, 6-3 in the Dubai Championships in the United Arab Emirates. The 78 singles titles for Federer is only bettered by Jimmy Connors (109) and Ivan Lendl (94). The tournament win, his sixth in Dubai, also gives him at least one title for 14 years in a row, equaling Lendl's record. The 32-year-old Federer trails Berdych by a set and a service break before rallying for victory. "It was a tough match," Federer says in a courtside interview. "Tomas had the advantage and could have, should have, brought it home, but maybe I got a little lucky."

2006 – World No. 488-ranked Mohammed Al Ghareeb of Kuwait holds 5-3 first-set lead against world No. 1 Roger Federer, but is unable to close out the set and loses 7-6 (5), 6-4 in the second round of the Dubai Open in the United Arab Emirates.

2003 – Roger Federer needs less than an hour to defeat Ivan Ljubicic of Croatia 6-3, 6-2 and reach the final of the Dubai Open. "I felt I was returning his serve really well and his second serve was not as tough to return as I thought it was going to be because he was struggling with his toss in the wind," says Federer of the 55-minute victory.

2013 – Roger Federer lets three match points slip away in the second set and falls to Tomas Berdych 3-6, 7-6 (8), 6-4 in the semifinals of the Dubai Duty Free Championships in the United Arab Emirates. Federer holds a 6-4 lead in the second set tiebreaker and a third match point at 8-7 before Berdych is able to hang on and force the third set on his third set-point opportunity. Berdych breaks Federer at 2-2 in the final set and holds on win the match in two hours and 19 minutes. "I leave this match with a lot of regrets," Federer tells reporters. "The match was in my racket. You do all the right things for so long and then at the end you've got to explain why you didn't hit two shots decent."

2007 – Roger Federer and Novak Djokovic play their fourth career match with the 25-year-old Federer beating the 19-year-old Djokovic 6-3, 6-7 (6), 6-3 in the quarterfinals of the Dubai Open.

2012 – For the 12th time in 12 career meetings, Roger Federer defeats Mikhail Youzhny, beating the Russian 6-3, 6-4 in the quarterfinals of the Dubai Duty Free Championships. Says Federer, "I sort of get on a roll once you're a set and a break up and then that comes into playing because he might know how difficult it is to come back because he has never come back against me in a situation like this

this is maybe where the head to head plays a little bit of a role. Other than that, early on you just go out there and try to play another good match, and that's what I did today."

March 2

2003 – Roger Federer wins his sixth career ATP singles title, beating Jiri Novak 6-1, 7-6 (2) in the final of the Dubai Open in the United Arab Emirates. The match features four straight breaks of serve in the middle of the second set, Federer firing three aces in the 76-minute match.

2006 – Roger Federer advances into the semifinals of the Dubai Open in United Arab Emirates with a 6-3, 6-2 win against Robin Vik of the Czech Republic. At 2-0 (15-40) in the second set, Federer fires four consecutive aces to hold serve. "I'm not sure if I played much better than before, but it's just the feeling I have now, it's more relaxed," says Federer of the 58-minute match.

2007 – Roger Federer beats No. 9-ranked Tommy Haas 6-4, 7-5 to reach his fifth straight Dubai Open final in the United Arab Emirates. The win also marks Federer's 40th straight victory. Federer doesn't lose serve in the match and saves a set point at 4-5 in the second set. Says Federer after the match, "It was extremely physical out there tonight. Lots of tough points and it was very tough to get the breaks. I know he didn't face any breaks (in Memphis) all of last week."

2012 – In a match featuring no service breaks, Roger Federer defeats Juan Martin del Potro 7-6 (5), 7-6 (6) to reach the final of the Dubai Duty Free Championships for a seventh time. Federer trails 6-2, facing quadruple set point, but wins the last six points of the match to close out the straight-set victory. "It was a good comeback, especially on a quick court," says Federer of his end-of-the-match rally. "I didn't believe I was going to come back, but at least sort of make him a bit nervous. Next thing I know, I had a great point at 6-All and I was able to come through. So it was a great match for me. We both served well, which was then difficult to get some rhythm off the baseline. But overall I thought it was a tough match."

2005 – The Swiss News Agency runs a short news story describing Roger Federer's trip to the New Brighton Township in South Africa as part of his newly-formed Roger Federer Foundation. Federer spends the day playing visiting schools, infirmaries and homes of locals, plays soccer and basketball with children, plants a tree gives out t-shirts. Writes Rene Stauffer in his book *Roger Federer: Quest for Perfection* of the trip, "His communications advisor at the time, Thomas Werder, suggested he allow several media representatives to travel with them to events in the township and generate major publicity hits in numerous media outlets. Federer, however, refused. It wasn't a matter of achieving the greatest possible media coverage under the motto of "do good works and talk about them." The news of his visit to the township came as a surprise to most of the Swiss media."

March 3

2007 – Roger Federer wins his 41st straight match, tying Bjorn Borg for the fourth-longest streak in the history of men's tennis, defeating Mikhail Youzhny of Russia 6-4, 6-3 to win the Dubai Open for a fourth time. "It's nice to be playing against the history books," Federer says after the match. "I never thought I would ever do such a thing." The 41-match win streak ties Bjorn Borg for the fourth-longest men's streak in the Open era. He is five short of Guillermo Vilas' 1977 record. Ivan Lendl (44 in 1981-82) and John McEnroe (42 in 1984) also stand in front of Federer. "I am on a nice roll right now and I am playing in Indian Wells next," Federer said. "I have won there the last three years, so hopefully I can win again. But if I don't, it's all right. I will start all over again."

2008 – World No. 1 Roger Federer is dismissed in the first round of the Dubai Open in the United Arab Emirates, losing to Great Britain's Andy Murray 6-7 (6), 6-3, 6-4. Murray, who beat Federer in the first round of Cincinnati in 2006, moves to a 2-1 record in three career meetings with the world No. 1. Murray does not face a break point during the match. "My expectations are not sky high at this point," said Federer, playing for the first time since losing to Novak Djokovic in the Australian Open semifinals on Jan. 25. "Obviously, I haven't played much so you don't go in with any expectations, actually. You hope to get past the first round, no matter if it's a guy with no ranking or a guy ranked basically in the top 10."

2012 – Roger Federer defeats Andy Murray 7-5, 6-4 to win the Dubai Duty Free Championships for a fifth time and pocket his 72nd career ATP singles title e. Federer does not drop a set in the event and improves his head-to-head record with Murray to 7-8. "This is perfect. This is great. Any title is a good one, I'll tell you that," Federer says. "I have a losing record against Murray."

2006 – Roger Federer reaches the final of the Dubai Open beating Mikhail Youzhny 6-2, 6-3 to set up a match-up with Rafael Nadal, who defeats Rainer Schuettler, 6-4, 6-2.

March 4

2006 – In a battle of the No. 1 and No. 2 players in the world, No. 2-ranked Rafael Nadal defeats world No. 1 Federer 2-6, 6-4, 6-4 in the final of the Dubai Open in the United Arab Emirates. Nadal's win ends Federer's 56-match hard court winning streak. Says Nadal, "I think it is unbelievable to win against the best player in the world — perhaps the best in history of the game." Federer had won the event the last three years and his other two tournaments in 2006, Doha and the Australian Open. Says Federer, "I think Nadal deserved to win because he played so consistent. I started off really well, but sprayed a little toward the end. But I am very happy with my game right now. And hopefully, I will pay him back soon."

2000 – Magnus Larsson of Sweden hits one ace, nine double faults and connects on only 47 percent of his first serves but still beats 18-year-old Roger Federer 6-3, 7-6 (6) in the semifinals of the Copenhagen Open in Denmark.

2004 – Roger Federer beats Tommy Robredo for the fifth time in five meetings with a 6-3, 6-4 win to reach quarterfinals of the Dubai Open in the United Arab Emirates.

March 5

2004 – Top-seeded Roger Federer improves his career head-to-head with Romania's Andrei Pavel to 4-0 with a 6-3, 6-3 win in the quarterfinals of the Dubai Open in the United Arab Emirates.

2012 – Playing for the second time at New York's Madison Square Garden, Roger Federer loses to Andy Roddick's 7-5, 7-6 (9-7) in the BNP Paribas Showdown exhibition match. In his post-match interview, Roddick, ranked No. 31 in the world in what would eventually be his final year of pro tennis, makes fun of his 2-21 career record against Federer saying, "I'm obviously in Roger's head. He had no idea how to play me and I capitalized on that..." Says Federer, "I loved my time [at Madison Square Garden] with [Pete Sampras] and to do it here with Andy, one of my greatest rivals, was great. We've had some great battles in great stadiums, and this is one of them."

March 6

2004 – Roger Federer defeats Jarkko Nieminen of Finland 7-6 (7), 6-2, to advance to the final of the Dubai Open in the United Arab Emirates. Nieminen leads in the tie-break 6-4 and 7-6, but is not able to break through and win the set from the world No. 1.

2014 – Roger Federer meets with the press in advance of the BNP Paribas Open in Indian Wells and discusses his solid start to his 2014 season that includes a final-round showing in Brisbane, a semifinal finish at the Australian Open and winning his 78th career ATP singles title in Dubai."I'm happy to see the hard work is paying off and the decisions I took," says Federer. "I've been pain-free for a long period of time now, which is the goal. It feels great, for three to four months now, I'm solid. Winning is a good feeling and I'm a lot more eager to play." Of his motivations to continue to play at age 32, Federer says, "If I can't play for No. 1, I'll play for winning titles. It's nice to do it again. (Winning in Dubai) was a big win for me."

March 7

2004 – Roger Federer rallies to beat first-time ATP Tour singles finalist Feliciano Lopez of Spain 4-6, 6-1, 6-2 to win the Dubai Open in the United Arab Emirates. Federer becomes the first player to successfully defend his Dubai Open title and extends his record for the year to 16-1.

2014 – In front of a standing room only crowd at the new Court No. 2 at the Indian Wells Tennis Garden at the BNP Paribas Open, Roger Federer pairs with newly-minted Australian Open champion and former Olympic gold-medal winning doubles partner Stan Wawrinka for an attractive opening round doubles match against Rohan Bopanna and Aisam-Ul-Haq Qureshi. Playing as a team for the first time in 18 months, Federer and Wawrinka defeat the No. 6-seeded team 6-2, 6-7(4), 10-6. The pair last match together as a team came in Davis Cup versus the Netherlands in September 2012.

March 8

2008 – In an article published in the *New York Times,* Roger Federer reveals to the world that he had been suffering from mono-nucleus, with is blamed on a recent run of poor play for the previously dominant Federer. "They weren't sure I was over it, but now I'm creating antibodies, and this really shows you are over it," he is quoted as saying. "But I lost a lot of fitness. I was feeling so great in December up until the moment I got sick, so this has been my problem the last couple weeks: really getting back on track. I haven't practiced and couldn't really work out the way I wanted to, because you have to be very careful with mono….I finally have the green light and finally I can give 100 percent in practice again, because it wasn't fun sort of being there sort of halfway. I didn't enjoy that too much. But again, it was interesting, and you've got to go through those moments, as well. I know that. Through a career, a long career maybe as No. 1, you have to go through injuries and sicknesses. For me, it was only a matter of time before the younger guys were going to come up. Now that they're here, they're good and everything, but I'm still No. 1 in the world."

2014 – With coaching consultant Stefan Edberg and good friend and rock singer Gavin Rossdale watching on from his player box, Roger Federer opens up his singles campaign at the BNP Paribas Open beating Paul-Henri Mathieu 6-2, 7-6 (5). After his win, Federer is asked by media if he feels "old" playing the tour at age 32. "You always had some niggling injuries or some pain that goes with being a professional tennis player," says Federer. "It's not like I played pain-free up until last year or anything. So that's an illusion. From that standpoint, I don't feel old either because there are many guys playing who are my age now. I feel there are many guys from the junior times my age still playing, and there's not that many 18 years olds, who I'm playing against actually. The youngest guys are usually 21, 22 years old."

March 9

2013 – Roger Federer loses one point on his first serve in his 6-2, 6-3 win over Denis Istomin to open the defense of his title at the BNP Paribas Open in Indian Wells, Calif. In winning his 889th career ATP match win, Federer hits 72 percent of his first serves in and hits 31 winners against 15 errors in the 58 minute match. The win is also Federer's 40th career match win in Indian Wells.

2007 – In his pre-event press conference in Indian Wells, Calif., Roger Federer reveals that he recently practiced with fellow tennis legend Pete Sampras at his Los Angeles home. "I'm thinking who's around in L.A.?" Federer says to the press. "So I rang up Pete and said, 'Any chance?' He was like, 'Yeah, sure.' I'm totally excited. He was one of my favorite players when I was growing up, and beating him in his backyard in Wimbledon was so special to me. So I wanted to try to beat him in his house." Federer tells the press that the two players, who only played once in their ATP careers – Federer's five-set win in the Wimbledon fourth round in 2001 – played some games, sets and tiebreakers. However, the 26-year-old Federer refuses, while smiling, to report any scores but does let people know of Sampras' current form. "Very good, surprisingly," he says of Sampras, 36. "Very good, you know. Not good enough to beat me."

March 10

2008 – A sell-out crowd of 19,690 that includes golf legend Tiger Woods pack Madison Square Garden in New York City for the NetJets Showdown exhibition match between Roger Federer and Pete Sampras. Federer, an owner of 12 major singles titles, edges 14-time major singles titlist Sampras in a third-set tie-breaker 6-3, 6-7 (4), 7-6 (6) in the sometimes competitive celebration of tennis. Says Sampras, "It was a great night for tennis." Writes the Associated Press of the match, "There were moments when, if you squinted a bit, you would have sworn that was the Sampras of old, rather than an old Sampras. There were moments when, if you listened to the whip of the racket through the air, you would have been absolutely sure Federer was giving it his all. And then there were moments when, as you watched Sampras throw his racket to the ground in mock disgust or saw Federer raise an index finger to celebrate four aces in a single game, it didn't really matter whether this match counted or not." Says Federer after the match, "I don't think winning or losing was really the issue tonight. I think we both tried to do our best and have a fun night, and that's what it turned out to be."

2006 – Addressing the media in advance of the Pacific Life Open in Indian Wells, Calif., Roger Federer is asked to assess whether he and Rafael Nadal are officially in a rivalry, just six days after losing to the world No. 2 Nadal in the final of the Dubai Open, their fourth career meeting. "I've played only four times, but obviously we've been No. 1 and No. 2 for a little bit now and I guess we'll have to see how it progresses," Federer says. "But I always said, you know, there's more players than just Nadal, and I still believe that. And I think, you know, the other players will play well, too, here in Indian Wells, and the game coming up. We'll see if Nadal can back it up at the French, at the clay court season and everything. But I don't think we can call it yet a rivalry. There's just too many other great players round."

2014 – Roger Federer plays four tie-breakers in singles and doubles play and win them all at the BNP Paribas Open in Indian Wells, Calif. In singles, he beats Dmitry Tursunov 7-6(7), 7-6(2) in the third round of singles, then, with Stan Wawrinka beats Ernests Gulbis and Milos Raonic 7-6 (3), 7-6 (4) in the second round of doubles.

March 11

2005 – Roger Federer spearheads "The ATP All-Star Rally for Relief" exhibition at the Pacific Life Open in Indian Wells, Calif., to raise funds to assist in relief of those affected by the devastating tsunami in Asia. Nine top players compete in the exhibition, including Federer, Andre Agassi, Andy Roddick, Kim Clijsters, Lleyton Hewitt, Elena Dementieva, Marat Safin, Amelie Mauresmo and others. Players walked through the stands with cans to solicit cash contributions, that raised $18,282.76 alone. Federer also donates money and memorabilia for fund-raising auctions. Writes Rene Stauffer of Federer in his book *Roger Federer: Quest for Perfection*, "What differentiates Federer from many other athletes who are willing to give back to people who are in need is the personal devotion. It's not enough for him just to send money. He is, as the campaign in Indian Wells demonstrated, also willing to get himself personally involved and invest his precious time to the project."

2007 – Roger Federer's bid to break Guillermo Vilas's ATP record of 46 straight wins in men's tennis ends in his opening round match at the Pacific Life Open in Indian Wells, Calif. Federer, the No. 1 player in the world, is stunned by No. 60 Guillermo Canas of Argentina 7-5, 6-2, ending his match win streak at 41. "He just kept the ball in play and moving me around," Federer says. "He put me away when he had to. He played the perfect match. The right guy won." Canas, recently reinstated into professional tennis after serving a 15-month suspension due to breaking the ATP's banned drug policy, is a "lucky loser" entrant into the event after losing in the qualifying rounds of the tournament. Says Canas, "It's my first Masters Series after I start again and to beat the world No. 1 and to play like this is great for me." Says Federer of the blown match win streak, "Sooner or later it had to happen, so it's OK. It's no problem."

2013 – On a day in which a magnitude 4.7 morning earthquake shakes the California desert, Roger Federer advances to the quarterfinals of the BNP Paribas Open in Indian Wells with a 6-3, 6-1 win over Ivan Dodig in exactly one hour. "For the first few seconds, I wasn't sure what was happening," says Federer of the earthquake. "I ran outside. It was a very strange feeling to have because you see the windows shaking. It was quite scary for a second there."

2012 – Roger Federer beats 19-year-old American Denis Kudla 6-4, 6-1 in his opening round match at the BNP Paribas Open in Indian Wells, Calif. "I'm always relieved and happy when I am able to find my way into a tournament, see some of the matches, so it's a good start for me," Federer says. "I didn't know Kudla very much, or at all, really, so it was a good win for me."

March 12

2006 – Top-ranked Roger Federer defeats Nicolas Massu 6-3, 7-6 (4) in the opening round of the Pacific Life Open in Indian Wells, Calif. Writes Bill Dwyre in the *Los Angeles Times* of the encounter, "His best chance was when he was receiving at 5-6 in the second. But Federer casually hit two baseline bombs into the same deep corner that were so good, all Massu could do was watch and smile. In the tiebreaker, Federer was Federer, same as he was in the news conference afterward: poised, even-tempered, amazed that others are amazed. "I always worry about crashing out in the early rounds," he said, "and then having to sit here and explain why.""

2010 – The "Hit for Haiti" tennis exhibition fundraiser is held at the BNP Paribas Open in Indian Wells featuring a blockbuster doubles match of Roger Federer and Pete Sampras against Andre Agassi and Rafael Nadal. Sampras and Federer win the pro-set 8-6 in a match that was rarely serious. Wrote Diane Pucin of the *Los Angeles Times*, "Sometimes the tennis got a little serious. Sampras crushed a forehand winner, then shared a fist bump with his partner. "You always have to get serious, huh Pete" Agassi said. It seemed to get very serious when Agassi made a comment about Sampras' supposed penchant for being a bad tipper. Sampras stopped smiling and then crushed an overhead. At the end he told the crowd, "I tip very well, trust me," Sampras said at the end. Everyone laughed." Said Federer of his participation in the famous foursome, "My heroes were [Boris] Becker and [Stefan] Edberg growing up. As they retired, Pete was the obvious choice. I loved watching him play. It feels very special to share the court with him. I've never played doubles with him. This is a big moment in my career."

2014 – Thirty-two-year old Roger Federer defeats 35-year-old Tommy Haas 6-4, 6-4 in the fourth round of the BNP Paribas Open in Indian Wells, Calif. The match is the 16th meeting between the two veterans, Federer extending his series lead over his German rival to 13-3. Federer then teams with Stan Wawrinka to beat reigning U.S. Open champions Leander Paes and Radek Stepanek 6-3, 6-7 (6), 7-6 in the doubles quarterfinals.

March 13

2005 – Roger Federer opens up the defense of his title in Indian Wells, Calif., with a 6-3, 6-3 win over Mardy Fish, Federer's fifth win in five matches against the American. Federer remained on target despite a temperate drop and brisk wind kicking up in the second set. "It was tough from then on to really get some good rallies going," Federer said. "But I was always ahead. Made it easy."

2013 – Roger Federer wins a lively fourth-round match with Olympic doubles partner Stan Wawrinka 6-3, 6-7(4), 7-5 in two hours and 20 minutes at the BNP Paribas Open in Indian Wells. Federer serves for the match at 5-4 in the second set, but is broken at love. After winning the second-set tiebreaker, Wawrinka leads 2-1 with a break in the third set, but is broken the next game and is broken again in the 12th game of the set. Federer improves his record over Wawrinka to 13-1. "Today it was extremely close again," says Federer. "I should have maybe closed it out in the second set, but he did well to stay in it."

2009 – Twenty-seven-year-old Roger Federer announces on his RogerFederer.com website that he and his longtime girlfriend Mirka Vavrinec are expecting their first child, which comes to be twin girls.

2012 – Saying "I guess my experience helped me to stay calm and just weather the storm," 30-year-old Roger Federer beats hard-serving 21-year-old Milos Raonic of Canada 6-7 (4), 6-2, 6-4 to reach the round of 16 of the BNP Paribas Open in Indian Wells, Calif. "Maybe if I was younger I'd be more panicky about him hitting aces left and right and making me feel uncomfortable," says Federer of his first career meeting with Raonic. "I have been there so many times before against some of the all-time great servers that it was obviously not going to happen tonight. I just hoped to stay calm."

2011 – Roger Federer beats Igor Andreev 7-5, 7-6 (4) in his opening round match at the BNP Paribas Open in Indian Wells. The win increases Federer's career record against Andreev to 4-0 and marks the first time Federer fails to give up a set against the Russian after a four-set wins at the Australian Open the previous year and in the Gstaad final in 2004 and their epic five-setter in the fourth round of the U.S. Open in 2008. "I thought it was another tough match against him," says Federer.

2014 – Roger Federer needs only 69 minutes to tame the hard-serving Kevin Anderson 7-5, 6-1 in the quarterfinals of the BNP Paribas Open in Indian Wells, Calif. Federer breaks the 6-foot, 8-inch South African at love to win the first set, then breaks serve twice again in the second set to close out the straight-set win. "You know, I gave myself chances and started with a few more returns in play at five-all," Federer says to reporters after the match. "I was just also now in the match at that point, feeling good movement-wise, feeling good absorbing his pace. Then also being aggressive myself. I think the combination there in those 10 minutes, they all worked out for me. So it was big to win the set and then to go on to break early in the second. Then double break was like a bonus. From then on I was home basically. It was a really good match for me."

March 14

2006 – No. 1 and two-time defending champion Roger Federer defeats his junior doubles partner Olivier Rochus 3-6, 6-2, 7-5 in the third round of Indian Wells. "I think I've never been so close to beating him," says Rochus, who beat Federer once in the juniors, but never since the age of 14. "On the big points, he always serves aces or makes the great forehand. He's not No. 1 for nothing." A couple months later, Federer will win an even tougher match against Rochus, saving four match points in beating him in Halle, Germany.

2009 – Playing in his first match since publicly announcing that he and girlfriend Mirka Vavrinec are going to be parents, Roger Federer defeats world No. 52 Marc Gicquel of France 7-6 (4), 6-4 in his opening round match in Indian Wells. "I think in a way I always had the dream that once I became No. 1 in the world that if I have a child I hope I have it early enough so he can see me playing," Federer tells reporters of his pending parenthood after the match. "So this is very exciting. I think it's not going to really disturb my mindset on tennis a whole lot. I've always made sure that my schedule is, you know, get away from tennis a little bit and then come back when I'm ready to play again. That's why I didn't play for the last five to six weeks. I think it's going to be pretty much the same. I don't really have to adjust a whole lot. If it does something to me, I think it's going to motivate me to play for a long time."

2010 – Roger Federer surrenders a set to Victor Hanescu of Romania for the first time in five meetings, but wins a one-sided third set in his 6-3, 6-7 (5), 6-1 opening match at the BNP Paribas Open in Indian Wells, Calif. Federer returns to competitive tournament tennis for the first time since winning the Australian Open on January 31.

2013 – Rafael Nadal, playing his first hard-court tournament after missing seven months because of a left knee injury, routs Roger Federer in barely one hour 6-4, 6-2 in the quarterfinals of the BNP Paribas Open in Indian Wells. Federer, the defending champion, drops his 19th match to Nadal in their 29 meetings, this the first ever match in a tournament quarterfinal. "I mean, I could play," Federer says after the match of his health, the Swiss visibly impaired with a bad back at times in the match. "I'm happy to be out there and able to compete, you know? But it's obviously a small issue. That doesn't work against guys like Rafa, obviously." Says Nadal, "I played a fantastic first set. The second set was strange. Roger didn't fight as usual. Probably he had some problems and he didn't feel enough comfortable to keep fighting." The win for Nadal avenges a 6-3, 6-4 loss that Nadal suffered to Federer on the same court in the semifinals the previous year. Says Nadal of his series advantage over Federer, "If I think that I am better than him because I beat him 19 against 10, I will be very stupid and very arrogant. This is not the case."

2012 – Roger Federer overcomes a first-set hiccup and beats Thomaz Bellucci 3-6, 6-3, 6-4 to advance to the quarterfinals of the BNP Paribas Open in Indian Wells, Calif. The win his Federer's 73rd straight win against an opponent ranked outside the Top 20 in the ATP Rankings. "I was quite surprised, but at the end I found a way, dug deep and came through," Federer say. "At the end of the day, these are the wins that sort of almost feel better, to be quite honest, because when you're playi0ng great, it's simple, and it's easy."

2014 – Dubbed "Federinka" by tennis fans and media, Roger Federer and Stan Wawrinka fall in the doubles semifinals of the BNP Paribas Open in Indian Wells, Calif., losing to No. 2 seeds Alexander Peya and Bruno Soares 6-4, 6-1.

March 15

2014 – Guaranteeing him a return visit to the top five in the ATP rankings, Roger Federer easily defeats Alexandr Dolgopolov 6-3, 6-1 in the semifinals of the BNP Paribas Open in Indian Wells, Calif., to set up a final-round match-up Novak Djokovic "I'm just playing more freely overall and with more confidence because I can get to more balls without thinking," Federer says of his current form and 11-match win streak.

2005 – Roger Federer beats Gilles Muller of Luxembourg 6-3, 6-2 advancing to the fourth round in Indian Wells. "When I go into a match, that's what I think about, even though maybe I'm the big favorite and my opponent hasn't played many of the big matches on big courts around the world," Federer says.

2006 – Roger Federer beats French teenager Richard Gasquet 6-3, 6-4 in the fourth round of the Indian Wells Masters not facing a break point over the course of the 57-minute match.

2011 – Giving up only two games and needing only 58 minutes, Roger Federer defeats Juan Ignacio Chela 6-0, 6-2 to advance to the fourth round of the BNP Paribas Open in Indian Wells. The meeting increases Federer's match record to 6-0 against Chela in their final career meeting. Says Federer, with a smile of the match, "It was a great match. For me, anyway…"

March 16

2014 – Novak Djokovic beats Roger Federer in tensely-fought final at the BNP Paribas Open in Indian Wells, Calif., decided by a final-set tie-breaker. After failing to serve out the match at 5-4 in the third set, Djokovic rallies to win five of the first six points of the decisive tie-breaker and holds on for a 3-6, 6-3, 7-6(3) win in their 33rd career meeting. "As

I said before the match today, very few points will decide a winner, and that's what happened," says Djokovic, trailing in the career head-to-head against Federer 17-16. "Roger is playing in a very high level.... He just played better than he did in the last 13, 14 months. I needed to really be in the top of my game and very concentrated the last moment in order to win. That's what I've done. Very proud of my achievements during this tournament." Says Federer of the loss, "It was an interesting end to the match, no doubt, but I think he played well. At the end he made sure he kept the ball in play and I might have made a few too many errors when it really mattered. But I think he made a crucial sort of 20 minutes, half an hour midway through the second set and third set where things could have gone either way. But credit to him for toughening it out and winning that second set and getting the breaker in the third."

2004 – Roger Federer increases his record to 19-1 for the year beating Mardy Fish 6-4, 6-1 to advance into the quarterfinals at the Pacific Life Openi in Indian Wells. "I think he's got an unbelievable serve, especially his first serve," says Federer of Fish, lavishing praise on the developing American. "It's very tough to read. He hits a lot of aces. He's got great speed on that, too. I think he's got a very all-around game, all-surface game, as well. You know, I just think he needs a little bit more time."

2005 – For the third tournament in a row, and for the fourth time in five tournaments played in 2005, Roger Federer faces Ivan Ljubicic and again beats the Croatian 7-6 (3), 7-6(4) to reach the quarterfinals of the Pacific Life

Open in Indian Wells, Calif. "I am so motivated for the tournament," Federer says. "I really want to defend this title and I feel I am able to dig much deeper than I used to." Despite the close scoreline, Federer holds a decent disparity in points won in the match, winning 83 to 66 from Ljubicic.

2006 – World No. 1 Roger Federer needs only 67 minutes to defeat No. 6 ivan Ljubicic 6-2, 6-3 in the quarterfinals of the Pacific Life Open in Indian Wells. "This was an excellent match for me – maybe the best of the season," says Federer, who breaks the hard-serving Croatian three times in the match versus only having one break point against Ljubicic on the same court a year before.

2008 – Ending a rare two-match losing streak, world No. 1 Roger Federer scores a routine 6-3, 6-2 opening round victory over Guillermo Garcia-Lopez at the Pacific Life Open in Indian Wells, Calif. "It just sort of takes you back to reality," says Federer of his consecutive losses to Novak Djokovic in the Australian Open semifinals and to Andy Murray in the opening round of Dubai. "But in some ways it was good for me too. I guess because I was winning so much."

2009 – "It's always a bit of a success story to get his serve back," says Roger Federer of six-foot-10 Ivo Karlovic, whom he beats 7-6 (4), 6-3 in the third round of BNP Paribas Open in Indian Wells."Ivo has really improved a lot over the past few years so it's always nice to get through a tough match like this." Federer gets the only break of the match in the sixth game of the second set, while Karlovic fails to manufacture a break point against the world No. 2.

2010 – For the first time in his career Roger Federer loses a best-of-three-set match after holding a match point, losing to Marcos Baghdatis 5-7, 7-5, 7-6 (4) in two hours 22 minutes in the third round at the BNP Paribas Open in Indian Wells. Federer leads 5-4 (40-15) in the second set and 6-5 (40-30) in the third set – all match points he squanders as a receiver. Federer also leads 4-1 in the deciding set but is unable to close out the Cypriot. "I was doing many things right," Federer says, "but then the next thing you know, I'm stuck in a third set and you never know what's going to happen. It was a decent match but maybe wrong choices at the wrong time for me."

2012 – Roger Federer defeats Juan Martin del Potro 6-3, 6-2 in the quarterfinals of the BNP Paribas Open in Indian Wells, Calif. Federer breaks Del Potro three times while not losing his serve in the 69-minute match.

2011 – In a night session at the BNP Paribas Open in Indian Wells, Calif., that also features world No. 1 Rafael Nadal, world No. 2 Roger Federer plays young upstart American Ryan Harrison for the first time in his career and beats the 18-year-old 7-6 (4), 6-3 to reach the tournament quarterfinals. Earlier in the session, Nadal beats India's Somdev Devvarman 7-5, 6-4. Writes Bill Dwyre of the *Los Angeles Times* if the Federer-Nadal double-header night session, "These two superstars share the same session about as often as kings share thrones."

March 17

2012 – Playing Rafael Nadal for the first time at the BNP Paribas Open, Roger Federer reaches the Indian Wells final for the fourth time with a 6-3, 6-4 win over his rival from Spain. The match is played in heavy overcast conditions and a light rain halts play for a few minutes after Nadal nets a return that gives Federer a match point. After the lines on the court are dried of the light moisture, Federer fires an ace to close out the the win in one hour, 31 minutes victory. "He played a great game to come back into the match and he played also a good game at 5-4," Federer says. "I knew it was going to be tough serving it out. Obviously there is a bit more relief on top of that with the wait, having to wait at 30-40. That was special in itself. I know how well I played tonight, so I'm just really pleased with my performance." The win is Federer's 10th in 28 career matches with Nadal and avenges his loss to the Spaniard in the semifinals of the Australian Open.

2005 – Roger Federer needs just 67 minutes to beat Nicolas Kiefer 6-4, 6-1 to advance into the semifinals of the Pacific Life Open in Indian Wells. Federer fires four aces and wins 57 of the 94 total points played to even his career series with the German at 3-3. "I haven't lost a set. I have been playing really well," Federer says. "Sometimes you win matches and if you are No. 1 in the world you still don't feel very happy. But this week has been good." Maria Sharapova, who plays on the Stadium Court before Federer, says of the world No. 1, "It's like he's Mr. Perfect and nothing's going wrong for him at this point."

March 18

2006 – Roger Federer cruises to a 6-2, 6-3 victory in exactly one hour over Paradorn Srichaphan of Thailand in the semifinals of the Indian Wells Masters. "He really mixes up the game not like any other player," Srichaphan says of Federer. "A normal player will play the same way the whole match, but Roger, he's really good with mixing up the ball, with the spin, with the slice and the serve."

2012 – Roger Federer defeats John Isner 7-6 (7), 6-3 to win his record fourth BNP Paribas Open title, winning $1 million, avenging his loss to the American in the Davis Cup first round in February. Federer struggled with a cold for most of the two-week tournament, but was able to prevail. "I was able to come through and so convincingly at the end is amazing," he said. "I've really played amazing these last three matches in particular. I couldn't be more happy. They were really great wins." Federer was cheered on by friends that included musicians Gwen Stefani and her husband Gavin Rossdale, and Vogue editor in chief Anna Wintour. Federer won three straight titles in Indian Wells from 2004-06 and his fourth snapped a tie with Jimmy Connors and Michael Chang. "What surprises me is that I've actually won this again after all this time," Federer said, "and particularly this year where I was struggling and hurting a lot at the beginning of the year."

2004 – Roger Federer defeats Juan Ignacio Chela 6-2, 6-1 to advance to the semifinals of the Pacific Life Open in Indian Wells, Calif., to set up an anticipated semifinal with Andre Agassi. "That would be a great match again," says Federer. "Especially now, these last two years, I enjoy playing Agassi because I thought I can finally compete with him. Because before he was just too good. Gave me a hiding at the U.S. Open one time, and also before when I just came on tour. Now that I also beat him, I think he would like to have that rematch, get a chance for revenge. So it will be a nice match for the fans and for everybody -- also for us especially." Despite his 20-1 record on the season, Federer tells reporters after the match that he does not feel unbeatable, despite what many pundits and observers say. "No, because I know there's very dangerous players out there," he said. "Just because I've won a lot of matches this year and I only lost one, that doesn't make me feel like I'm unbeatable." Says Agassi of Federer, "The guy has been playing spectacular tennis, especially this year, even toward the end of last year. His game has a lot of weapons. I'm just going to have to hit my shots."

2008 – Roger Federer extended his winning streak to 19 consecutive matches against Frenchmen, beating Nicolas Mahut 6-1, 6-1 in the third round of the Pacific Life Open. "Look, I've always enjoyed playing against the Frenchmen," says Federer. "They have good techniques, playing style, unbelievable shot-making. It sometimes tends to be easier playing against them. They make you play better tennis than, for instance, the Spaniards, who are just going to throw the ball into play." Says Mahut, who only manages to win only one point off Federer's serve in the first set, "I was feeling like a junior today." Federer extends his win streak over French players to 24, before losing later in the year to Gilles Simon in the first round of Toronto.

2009 – Roger Federer beats Fernando Gonzalez 6-3, 5-7, 6-2, increasing his career record against the Chilean to 12-1 to advance into the quarterfinals of the BNP Paribas Open in Indian Wells. The second set loss is only the sixth dropped set for Federer in 37 total against Gonzalez, the man whom he beats in the final of the Australian Open in 2007. "I enjoy playing Fernando because it's so tactical, but then at the same time it's so brutal, so aggressive," says Federer of the hard-hitting Chilean. "It's pretty interesting with him. When he is 30-Love up (for example), he doesn't care if it's a forehand or backhand coming his way, he's just going to rip it anyway, so there is lack of rhythm at times. He can serve extremely well, as well, even though he's not that tall. We know each other since a long time. We've played on many occasions so we know each other's games very well. I think that's always fun to play somebody like that."

2011 – In a day of high-profile singles and doubles matches, Roger Federer beats fellow Swiss Stan Wawrinka 6-3, 6-4 in the quarterfinals of the BNP Paribas Open in Indian Wells, Calif., and then pairs with him to beat Rafael Nadal and Marc Lopez 7-5, 6-3 in a doubles semifinal. "There are no secrets out there with Stan," Federer says of his singles match. "It makes it really difficult playing a good friend like him."

March 19

2006 – Roger Federer becomes the first player to win the men's singles title at the Pacific Life Open in Indian Wells, Calif., for a third straight year when he defeats James Blake 7-5, 6-3, 6-0 in the final. "I hope I get the [big] whale," says Federer just after his victory, referencing the tournament sponsor's unique trophy, a huge whale that is the center of Pacific Life's marketing program. Federer trails 1-4 in the first set, before reeling off 18 of the next 22 games. Writes Lisa Dillman in the *Los Angeles Times* of Federer, "The way he pulled Blake around the court, Federer might as well have been at the control of a video game." Says Federer of his performance, "I felt very, very confident on the court. At some moments obviously I knew this is almost impossible that I'm going to lose this final."

2005 – Saying "If I play my best, he will do it better. He is not at the same level as the rest of us" Guillermo Canas of Argentina is defeated by Roger Federer 6-3, 6-1 in the semifinals of the Pacific Life Open in Indian Wells. "I had to actually fight to actually really play well today," says Federer. "He was giving me a hard time. I had a few tough couple of games. Once I got through that, my rhythm started to pick up and I started to play better. I'm happy the way the match ended. That's very promising for tomorrow." Federer's win avenges his previous loss to Canas in the second round of Toronto in 2002, their only previous meeting. The two won meet again for another two years when Canas snaps Federer's longest match-winning streak – 41 matches – on the same court.

2009 – Three-time champion Roger Federer beats Fernando Verdasco 6-3, 7-6 (5) to move into the semifinals of the BNP Paribas Open in Indian Wells. Verdasco, fresh after reaching the Australian Open semifinals, where he lost an epic struggle to Rafael Nadal, had two set points serving at 6-5 in the second set. "I don't think I played the best match of my life, but I think it was solid." Says Federer, "When it got tough I couldn't come up with the backhands I wanted to, so I think those kind of let me down. I got lucky to get back into the match. I played a good breaker, so good luck I snuck out of it. It was difficult. I wasn't quite happy with the match today, but for a while there I actually was playing okay."

2011 – Roger Federer loses in the singles semifinals and doubles final at the BNP Paribas Open, falling 6-3, 3-6, 6-2 to Novak Djokovic in singles and, with Stan Wawrinka, losing to Alexandr Dolgopolov and Xavier Malisse 6–4, 6–7(5–7), [10–7]. Says Federer of his day to reporters following the doubles final, "I thought I played actually well today, in singles and in doubles. Sure, it's a bit of a pity that I couldn't get either one of them, but that's how it goes when you sign up for doubles. That's what can happen. It's no problem. I thought I played good in the singles. I also thought the week with Stan in doubles was a lot of fun and I really enjoyed it. I just thought Dolgopolov and Malisse played really well today in the final."

March 20

2004 – Playing in desert temperatures of 100 degrees, Roger Federer wins the last eight points of the match and defeats Andre Agassi 4-6, 6-3, 6-4 in the semifinals of the Pacific Life Open in Indian Wells, played mostly from the baseline in the 38-degree C (100-degree F) heat. One break of serve in each set proves crucial. In the third set at 4-all, Agassi leads 40-15 on serve when Federer wins a spectacular point which turns the match in his favor. "It looks even better on TV," says Federer, watching the replay of the point during his on-court television interview. "That's the one thing that makes him a great player, is that he sort of strikes so quickly, you never know," Agassi says of Federer's final stretch of brilliant play. "He can play just a few minutes of great tennis and that's enough to get himself over the hurdle."

2005 – In the final of the Pacific Life Open between the two best players in the world, Roger Federer defeats Lleyton Hewitt 6-2, 6-4, 6-4, marking Federer's seventh consecutive win over his Australian rival and his 17th straight victory in a tournament final. "It's always been my dream to be the best. Now I am and I am enjoying it," says Federer, a winner of 42 of his last 43 matches. "The more victories you get, the better you feel." The final is highlighted by an amazing 45-shot rally, when Federer holds break point in the second game of the second set. Hewitt wins the point with a dive volley. "One of my best in my life," Federer says of the rally. "During a final against Lleyton, that was fantastic, and that it didn't finish in an error. We were both tired after that rally."

March 21

2004 – Committing only five unforced errors, Roger Federer wins for the first time against nemesis Tim Henman in a completed match defeating the No. 9-ranked player 6-3, 6-3 in the final of the Pacific Life Open on an uncomfortably hot 100-degree day at Indian Wells Tennis Garden. Entering the final, Henman held a curious 6-1 head-to-head advantage over the world No. 1, his lone loss coming when he had to retire with a neck injury in the fourth round of Miami in 2002. Federer's lone blemish on his 22-1 record for the year came courtesy of Henman in the third round of Rotterdam. "I didn't think I served any different to the last few times against him, but the difference was I didn't double-fault today," says Federer of his victory. "I told myself, it's important, I'd rather make him hit some good approach shots and good returns than just to get away from him, then he would feel the pressure just by his presence, knowing he would come to the net. I think then I started to feel good in the middle of the game. Then, you know, the confidence was my way."

2014 – Losing only three points on his serve the entire match, Roger Federer defeats Ivo Karlovic 6-4, 7-6 (4) in his opening round match at the Sony Open in Key Biscayne, Fla. Federer breaks Karlovic in the fifth game of the first set and loses his only point in the 29-minute opening stanza at 5-4, 40-0. Federer loses only one point on serve entering the second-set tie-breaker. Later, Roger Federer attends the Miami Heat basketball game and meets star Heat player Dwyane Wade who posts photos of himself and Federer with the caption,

"Hanging with the great @roger_federer_ after the game 2nite in our locker room. We have something in common. We're both 32 and they love to call us old.#Champions #EnuffSaid #StillGettingitdone"

2007 – While in Miami to compete in the Sony Ericsson Open, Roger Federer visits his fellow sports super star Tiger Woods, who is playing a practice round at the PGA Tour event at the Doral Country Club. Woods sees Federer in his gallery and pulls him within the ropes and onto the fairway so they could visit between practice shots. Says Woods with a smile, "They don't want to have people inside the ropes…I'm sure I'll get fined for it. I don't mind paying, because he was starting to get hassled pretty good and I didn't think that's why he came out here. He came out here to enjoy himself and watch me slap it around a little bit." Woods and Federer also dine on Woods's yacht the previous night. "I think he's a wonderful supporter of golf, and I think it's pretty neat when you have probably the most dominant athlete on the planet out there in your gallery," Woods says of Federer. Says Federer of watching golf, "I had never really seen live golf from professionals up until the last year. It's different from sitting in a stadium watching soccer or a tennis match. You've got to know where to stand to see the ball. For me, it was hard to follow the ball. I lost it just because he hits it so hard and so far… With us, they scream after every point. With him, it's not every shot."

2008 – Federer reaches the Indian Wells semifinals in a walkover over Tommy Haas, who withdraws from the tournament with a sinus infection. Federer also gets a walkover victory over Haas in the fourth round of Wimbledon in 2007.

2009 – Andy Murray beats Roger Federer for the fourth straight time, winning 6-3, 4-6, 6-1 to advance to the BNP Paribas Open final in Indian Wells. "He's a great counterpuncher and reads the game really well," Federer says of Murray. "He has great feel. So he's very confident at the moment. You can tell, the way he plays. He knows he doesn't have to play close to the lines because he can cover the court really well."

March 22

2008 – Mardy Fish dominates world No. 1 Roger Federer 6-3, 6-2 in 63 minutes in the semifinals of the Pacific Life Open in Indian Wells, Calif. Says the 98th-ranked Fish, "This wasn't, obviously, Roger's best day. But hopefully I had a little something to do with that." Says Federer, "He was just trying to go for everything, and it worked. I didn't even play particularly bad on the break points...Every time he read the right side on the serve, and he kept the ball in play. When he wanted to attack, everything worked. That was just impressive by his side, and I couldn't do much to control it. I didn't even think he served particularly well. It was just impossible to return his first serve, which it normally is anyway. But I couldn't get into his second serves, and that was the disappointing part about today." In the other men's semifinal, Australian Open champion Novak Djokovic defeats defending champion Rafael

Nadal 6-3, 6-2. The following day, Djokovic beats Fish for the title 6-2, 5-7, 6-3.

2003 – Roger Federer fends off a tough second-set challenge from Luis Horna and beats the Peruvian 6-2, 7-5 in his opening round match at the NASDAQ-100 Open in Key Biscayne, Fla. In his post-match press conference, Federer is asked by reporters of his feelings to now be in the top five in the ATP world rankings. "I think it's a great feeling to be in the Top 5 and to have achieved good things so far," says Federer. "So I think it was a struggle for me last year, after I won Hamburg and made my first step into the Top 10. That was more difficult because I was so happy maybe and so relieved and reached my goal, my dream goal. Of course Top 5 and No. 1 in the world is always dreams for any player. But Top 10 is another milestone. I don't know if it was because of that that I didn't play as well after. But, you know, now that I finished the year in the Top 10 and had some time to think about all this, now I got used to it and nothing really changed if I'm No. 12, 6 or 4 or 20."

March 23

2000 – Roger Federer beats Justin Gimelstob 7-5, 6-3 in the first round of the Ericsson Open in Key Biscayne, Fla. The meeting between the 23-year-old Gimelstob and the 19-year-old Federer marks the only singles meeting between the two players on the ATP Tour. The two also played in the quarterfinals of the Heilbronn Challenger in 1999, Federer winning 6-7(3) 7-6(3) 7-5.

2014 – Losing just seven points on his serve, Roger Federer defeats Thiemo de Bakker 6-3, 6-3 in 63 minutes to reach the round of 16 at the Sony Open in Key Biscayne, Fla. The win comes one round after Federer loses just three points on serve in a 6-4, 7-6 (4) opening round win over Ivo Karlovic.

After beating Ryan Harrison at the BNP Paribas Open in Indian Wells in 2011, Roger Federer was asked what it is like to play against American players in front of American audiences and cites one of his most memorable matches of his career, the 2005 U.S. Open final against Andre Agassi. "The toughest situation I've ever been in was when I played Agassi in the finals of the U.S. Open, which I really felt was most extreme," Federer said. "It was just nice to be part of such a, for me a historic match, really, and thinking maybe it was going to be Andre's last match of his life. Then he still came back obviously for another year and played a few tournaments. But people kind of expected that if he won maybe he could retire and all those things. Crowds were just absolutely amazing. I have always enjoyed playing over here against Americans. They've always respected me and even been behind me at times, you know, which has been nice to see. They're good tennis fans, and I enjoy playing in this country."

March 24

2007 – Tiger Woods waits through a rainstorm to watch Roger Federer win his opening match at the Sony Ericsson Open, a 6-4, 6-3 decision over 19-year-old American Sam Querrey. "It's great Tiger watches tennis – a great honor for our sport," Federer says. The match is delayed more than two hours due to the rain, beginning at 10:18 p.m. and ending at 11:20. The match was his first for Federer since his 41-match winning streak ended with a loss to Guillermo Canas at Indian Wells on March 11.

2003 – In a three-set match that lasts only 75 minutes, Roger Federer advances into the round of 16 at the NASDAQ-100 Open in Key Biscayne, Fla., defeating Juan Ignacio Chela of Argentina 6-1, 3-6, 6-1. "I thought the match was quite short for a three-setter," says Federer. "It was not like one of these three-setters where you come off the court and you're totally exhausted. It felt good out there today, was very nice temperature for both players. I think I played well. Even though I lost the second, I still felt like I was hitting the ball well, and good attitude."

2012 – Despite being tricked by a fan calling a ball out while serving for the match, Roger Federer wins his opening round match at the Sony Open in Key Biscayne, Fla. with a 6-2, 7-6 (3) win over American Ryan Harrison. With Federer serving for the match at 6-2, 5-3, Federer is tricked by a fan calling a ball "out" from the stands when facing break point at 15-40. As Federer's forehand floats near the baseline, a fan yells "out" and Federer slaps his next shot with two hands off to the side of the court, only to learn that the ball was actually called good by the linesperson. Federer, however, regroups and wins the second set – and the match – in a tie-breaker. "It completely threw me off," Federer says of the fake call from the stands. "It's the first time it has ever happened in my career."

March 25

2003 – Roger Federer, seeded No. 4, defeats No. 14 Sjeng Schalken of the Netherlands 6-3, 6-2 in the fourth round of the NASDAQ-100 Open in Key Biscayne, Fla. Schlaken and Federer would meet again later in the year in the quarterfinals of Wimbledon, Federer winning 6-3, 6-4, 6-4 en route to his first major singles championship.

2006 – Defending men's champion Roger Federer loses seven consecutive points in the second-set tiebreaker but overcomes the lapse to win six straight games in the final set and beats Arnaud Clement, 6-2, 6-7 (4), 6-0 in the second round of the NASDAQ-100 Open in Key Biscayne, Fla.

2014 – In only 49 minutes, Roger Federer defeats Richard Gasquet 6-1, 6-2 to reach the quarterfinals of the Sony Open in Key Biscayne, Fla. Federer hits 25 winners, converts five of six break points, hits 68 percent first serves and wins 88 percent of those points in the one-sided win. "Look, things went well out on the court today," an understated Federer says after the match.

March 26

2005 – Roger Federer wins his 17th match in a row defeating Olivier Rochus 6-3, 6-1 in the opening round of NASDAQ-100 Open in Key Biscayne. "It's always hard to start a tournament,' Federer says. "But I actually felt quite comfortable and quite confident going into today's match." The win also gives Federer a 43-1 record since the start of the 2004 U.S. Open the previous August.

2012 – Andy Roddick, playing in the hometown of the event of his recently-passed agent Ken Meyerson, stuns Roger Federer with inspired and powerful play in an improbable 7-6 (4), 1-6, 6-4 win in the third round of the Sony Ericsson Open. After closing out the victory, Roddick pointed to the sky in a salute Meyerson, who died of a heart attack the previous October. "My agent was from here and his wife was here," Roddick says after the match. "I felt like I was a crazy person, because I think I was having full dialogues with him the last 30 minutes of the match." Roddick, only ranked No. 31 after flirting with Federer at No. 2 in the world during part of Federer's reign as world No. 1, had only beaten the Swiss twice in 23 previous meetings. "You know, he's still very good," Federer says. "I'm happy to see him play really well."

2007 – Top-ranked Roger Federer beats Nicolas Almagro 7-5, 6-3 to advance to the fourth round of the Sony Ericsson Open. "I had to be very concentrated today, because I knew from the start he's a really big hitter," Federer says of the match in which dropped just five points on first serve.

2001 – In a preview of the Wimbledon final of 2003, Roger Federer defeats Mark Philippoussis 3-6, 7-6(4), 6-2 in the third round of the Ericsson Open in Key Biscayne, Fla. "I think obviously against Philippoussis it's not easy to get the rhythm because he's serving at 130 nonstop," says Federer. "You don't get a lot of rallies, and when you serve, he misses quite a bit or the rallies don't take look. I wasn't really happy about my game today, but somehow I got through and that's what's most important."

2011 – Roger Federer wins career ATP match No. 762 - tying him with former great Pete Sampras for seventh place all-time - with a 6-4, 6-3 win over Radek Stepanek in his opening round match at the Sony Ericsson Open in Key Biscayne, Fla. "Look, sure, yes, it's nice tying Pete, but he could have played for many more years," Federer says of the record to reporters following his victory. "He could still win some matches on tour now if he wanted to. Yeah, it's a funny stat, but it shows how long I have been around already, how much I've won all around the world and all the different surfaces and that I have played whatever, over 10, 12 solid seasons. I've never missed big chunks of seasons. That's how you end up with so many wins, I guess."

2014 – Despite leading by a set and twice up a service break in the second set, Roger Federer is upset in the quarterfinals of the Sony Open in Key Biscayne, Fla., falling to No. 21-ranked Kei Nishikori 3-6, 7-5, 6-4 in the quarterfinals of the Sony Open in Miami. Federer enters the match having lost only 18 points on serve in his previous three matches but struggles with his serve in his first night match of the tournament. He wins the first set despite connecting on only 38 percent of his first serves – eventually raising it to 53 percent for the match, and is not able to hold on despite leading by a service break at 2-1 and 4-3 in the second set. "Just couldn't find my rhythm on my serve, which was surprising especially after how well I played and served especially this week," Federer says. "It didn't take off the same way it did during the day time. You can expect that with the temperature drop." Federer hits 29 winners and 39 unforced errors in the match against Nishikori's 25 winners and 42 unforced errors. The win improves Nishikori's record to 2-1 against Federer, making him just the third player (along with Rafael Nadal and Andy Murray) to play the 17-time Grand Slam champion at least three times and ave a winning record.

March 27

2001 – Roger Federer edges Thomas Johansson 7-6 (7-3), 5-7, 7-6 (9-7) in the round of 16 of the Ericsson Open in Key Biscayne, Fla. The two future major tournament winners would play again a month later at the Italian Open with Federer once again winning by the closest of margins 7-6(3), 4-6, 7-6(5) in the first round. Johansson would go on to win the Australian Open, his first and only major in 2002, while Federer would not break through for another two years at Wimbledon in 2003.

2004 – Roger Federer wins the final three games and the last six points of the match to edge No. 54-ranked Nikolay Davydenko 6-2, 3-6, 7-5 in the second round of the NASDAQ-100 Open in Key Biscayne, Fla. Federer hits 36 unforced errors battling the windy conditions and fails to convert on five consecutive break-point opportunities in the final set. "Today wasn't my best," Federer says. "It was a tough one and I didn't think I was going to turn it around." Davydenko leads 3-1 on serve in the deciding set, but is not able to hold his lead and upset the world

No. 1. The match is the second career meeting between the two players, Federer winning their first meeting also by 7-5 in the third set two years earlier in Milan.

2007 – For the second time in a month, Roger Federer loses to Guillermo Canas of Argentina, falling by a 7-6 (2), 2-6, 7-6 (5) margin in the fourth round of the Sony Ericsson Open in Key Biscayne, Fla. Canas ends Federer's 41-match win streak in the first round of the Indian Wells two weeks earlier and in Key Biscayne, ends the Swiss maestro's chance at winning his third straight title in the island paradise. Says Federer. "It's one of those matches I never should have lost." Says Canas, "I'm surprised because I beat two times the No. 1 in the world. Really, I don't know what is my secret I'm just trying to enjoy the moment. For me it's like a dream."

2009 – Roger Federer wins his opening match at the Sony Ericsson Open in Key Biscayne, Fla., beating Kevin Kim, 6-3, 6-2. "I felt good," says Federer, without a Masters Series title in his last 12 attempts. "I've never played him before but I realised very quickly what his pattern was, especially on the serve."

2010 – With famed *Vogue* magazine editor Anna Wintour sitting in his player box, top-ranked Roger Federer wins his opening match at the Sony Ericsson Open in Key Biscayne, Fla., beating Nicolas Lapentti 6-3, 6-3 in Miami. "It's a friendship. I don't know. Very simple," says Federer of Wintour to reporters in his post-match press conference. "She's a good friend of ours. We know her since a long time. She's a great fan of tennis. She comes out to, not only watch me but also she went to go see other matches today. We're very friendly and we stay in touch. It's nice she came."

March 28

2004 – A hard-hitting 17-year-old from Spain named Rafael Nadal, ranked No. 34 in the world, stages a shocking upset of world No. 1 Roger Federer, claiming a 6-3, 6-3 win in the third round of the Sony Ericsson Open. Federer, the reigning Wimbledon and Australian Open champion, had won 28 of 29 matches dating back to the previous November, but the Swiss struggles with illness from the previous few days and Nadal plays impeccable tennis, never facing a break point, executing 81 percent of his first serves and winning 13 of 14 points at the net. "I'm very happy because I played one of the best matches in my life," Nadal says. "Obviously, he didn't play his best. If he had played his best tennis, I would have had no chance. I probably never served like this in my life, and that was the key." Says Federer of the debut match his future main rival, "I think it's always difficult to play someone for the first time, first of all, but I think overall he played a very good match. He was the better player today. It was tough for me. I had time to get the rhythm, but he played very aggressive and I couldn't quite play maybe the way I wanted to." When asked if he was surprised by the result, Federer says, "No, no, I'm not surprised. I've heard a lot about him and saw some matches of him. I think this is not a big surprise for everybody."

2003 – In the conclusion of a match where he leads 5-3 in the third set, 21-year-old Roger Federer blows three match points and falls to Albert Costa in a rain-delayed quarterfinal match at the Sony Ericsson Open. Costa needs only 13 minutes upon the resumption of play with him leading 6-5 (deuce) in the final set, finishing off the No. 4-seeded Federer, 7-6 (4), 4-6, 7-6 (7). Federer holds two match points serving for the match at 5-4 from the previous day and another at 6-5 in the final-set tie-breaker.

2005 – Improving his record to 44-1 since the start of the U.S. Open the previous year, Roger Federer edges Mariano Zabaleta 6-2, 5-7, 6-3 in the third round of the Sony Ericsson Open, extending his win streak to 18 matches. Federer serves for the match at 5-3 in the second set, but double-faults on break point, then loses his next service game en route to losing the second set. In the final set, Federer breaks the Argentine for a 5-3 lead and safely serves out the victory. "I thought he played a pretty good game to break me," Federer says. "Maybe I wasn't serving my best any more at the end of that second set, but he did well to stay in the match and break me a second time. I was not playing very well at that point and he took advantage of it."

2006 – No. 1 Roger Federer needs only 58 minutes to beat Dmitry Tursunov of Russia 6-3, 6-3 to advance into the quarterfinals of the NASDAQ-100 Open. "It's always more difficult to play a guy for the first time," Federer says after securing his 25th victory of the season against just one loss.

2011 – Winning a match on the ATP Tour for a 763rd time, Roger Federer advances into the round of 16 of the Sony Ericsson Open in Key Biscayne, Fla., with a 7-6 (4), 6-4 win over Juan Monaco of Argentina. The win moves Federer out of a seventh-place tie with Pete Sampras for most singles match wins on the ATP Tour.

March 29

2001 – Patrick Rafter has little trouble defeating a 19-year-old Roger Federer 6-3, 6-1 in 56 minutes in the quarterfinals of the Ericsson Open in Key Biscayne, Fla. "It was a big match for me to play Pat here, probably the conditions favor him; the surface and everything," says Federer, ranked No. 24. "I tried my best today, but I never really found my game. I had some chances in the beginning, but he served well and after that I didn't have any chance at all on his serve, especially, and also in the rest of the game I just -- he made me play bad and he could -- really I would say I made him play well. I don't know. I've got to work on my serve the next few weeks because it has been a disappointment all week long. No second serve, you cannot beat Pat Rafter." Federer lost to Rafter in his Grand Slam tournament debut at the 1999 French Open. The two play for a third and final time in their careers later in the year in Halle, Germany, Rafter making it a career three-peat against Federer with a 4-6, 7-6(6), 7-6(4) victory.

2002 – Roger Federer defeats a world No. 1 player for the first time when he defeats top-ranked Lleyton Hewitt 6-3, 6-4 in the semifinals of the NASDAQ-100 Open in Key

Biscayne, Fla. The win moves Federer, seeded No. 12, into the final of the Masters Series event for the first time and ends Hewitt's 15-match win streak. "It's something special," says Federer of his victory. "I've never beaten a No. 1 player before. I've beaten players who were No. 1, but not exactly the time. Plus, I've broken his winning streak and all this. So it's quite a special moment for me, obviously. First Masters Series final, gives me a chance of winning it. So, I mean, it's very nice."

2005 – A day after edging Mariano Zabaleta of Argentina in three sets, Roger Federer is again pushed to the limit beating Croatia's Mario Ancic 6-3, 4-6, 6-4 to reach the quarterfinals of the Sony Ericsson Open. "I'm definitely stronger mentally than in the past," says Federer. "I just have the feeling I can rely on many strengths in my game which carry me through sometimes, even though maybe I'm not playing great. Like it happened especially tonight, I never really felt I got the rhythm, but still came through. It was obvious it's going to be hard to find the rhythm against Ancic because he serves so big, but still I would have liked just to feel better from the baseline."

2008 – Erasing all seven break points he faces on the day, Roger Federer beats Gael Monfils 6-3, 6-4 in the second round of the Sony Ericsson Open in Key Biscayne, Fla. "I tried to play in an aggressive way," says Federer, who breaks Monfils serve in the eighth game of the first set and the third game of the second set.

2009 – Saying "It doesn't matter who's in front of me. I just like the thrill of winning and playing well," Roger Federer beats Nicolas Kiefer 6-4, 6-1 at the Sony Ericsson Open to book a fourth-round match against American Taylor Dent. The match ends up being the 15th and final meeting between the two players, Federer winning 12 of their matches, including the semifinals of the 2006 Australian Open.

2010 – An unusually inconsistent Roger Federer edges Florent Serra 7-6 (2), 7-6 (3), in the third round of the Sony Ericsson Open in Key Biscayne, Fla. The top-ranked Federer loses serve three times and commits 35 unforced errors, versus 32 from the No. 61-ranked Serra. "It's nice to having won two breakers, because that doesn't happen every match you play," says Federer. "Sure, I still have to tidy up my game a bit, having had one break up in the first and two breaks up in the second, it's normally something that doesn't get away from me, but I thought he came up with some good stuff, and that made it difficult for me to close it out. That's why I'm happy to still be through."

March 30

2006 – One week after beating him in the final of the Pacific Life Open in Indian Wells, Roger Federer rallies from a break down in the opening set and again beats James Blake 7-6 (2), 6-4 in the quarterfinals of the Sony Ericsson Open in Miami. The win is Federer's 46th straight victory on U.S. soil and his 25th consecutive victory against an American player. "It was a good match. I thought it was a tough match, as expected really," says Federer. "He's really tough out of the blocks really, tough to get a hold of him because he really takes a lot of chances and usually also serves well in the beginning and everything. So had a real feeling like it was tough all the way till the end. I thought at one stage maybe I could have taken advantage more of my chances early on in the second, but anyway I'm happy with the result because two sets, straight sets against James, I think that's always a good result."

2011 – Starting his match with Olivier Rochus at 12:37 am – the latest match start of his career – Roger Federer mercifully needs only 51 minutes to advance into the quarterfinals of the Sony Ericsson Open in Key Biscayne, Fla., with a 6-3, 6-1 victory. The match is late to start due to a backlog of matches due to rain.

During the 2011 Sony Ericsson Open in Miami, Federer was asked in a post-match press conference of his overall impression of the city, "I like it a lot," he said. "I've always enjoyed coming over here. It's not one of those tournaments that needed a lot of time to warm up to. I have come here as a junior, I guess, you know, jeez, back in when I was 14. I played at the Biltmore Hotel and then at Flamingo Park down on South Beach, and then I played the first Orange Bowl that was held here on Key Biscayne. I won on this center court and became world No. 1 beating (David) Nalbandian and (Guillermo) Coria in the semis and finals. So I've felt really very much comfortable in the surroundings here, and then when the tournament came around, I kind of knew my way around. I knew Coconut Grove, South Beach, Key Biscayne, so I felt always very welcomed here and I always played good tennis here. Then you get to know the nightlife, get to know the good restaurants, get to know a lot of friends around here because you always come back here every year. And, yeah, on top of that you play well, it's even nicer. It's always been a place I enjoyed coming to and playing.

March 31

2010 – At 16 minutes after midnight, Roger Federer pushes a forehand long, giving Tomas Berdych a 6-4, 6-7 (3), 7-6 (6) win in the round of 16 of the Sony Ericsson Open in Key Biscayne, Fla. Federer squanders a match point serving at 6-5 in the final-set tiebreaker, but Berdych hits a forehand winner into the corner, then wags his tongue in relief. He then wins the next two points to close out the upset victory. "I fought as much as I could," Federer says. "My game has issues at the moment. I'm definitely lacking timing. I don't know where that comes from." Says Berdych, "After a match like that, the feeling is great. I'm really happy the way I finish it." Federer and Berdych each win 119 points in the match. Says Federer of the loss, "It fuels my desire to go to the practice courts, because I don't like to lose these type of matches." The loss marks Federer's second straight event in which he loses after holding a match point, squandering a match point in a loss to Marcos Baghdatis in Indian Wells.

2011 – After only six minutes of play, Gilles Simon throws in the towel and retires with a stiff neck down 0-3 in the first set in the quarterfinals of the Sony Ericsson Open. Federer, ranked No. 3, breaks Simon's serve two times when Simon asks for a medical break that results in the retirement. The crowd boos Simon as he walks off the court. "It's not a whole lot fun honestly because you see the guy being booed off the court, which he clearly doesn't deserve," says Federer. "I understand the frustration from the people paying a lot of money to come see us play for multiple hours potentially, and then it's over within ten minutes. It's not great."

2002 – Thirty-one-year-old Andre Agassi wins his 700th career match, defeating 20-year-old Roger Federer 6-3, 6-3, 3-6, 6-4 in the final of the NASDAQ-100 Open in Key Biscayne. The match is Federer's first in a Masters Series event, but the loss prevents the No. 12-ranked Federer from entering the top 10 in the rankings as he only moves up to No. 11. "I'm disappointed I didn't make it to Top 10 this week because I had a chance," says Federer. "But I feel progress in my game again. This week from the baseline I was actually playing really well. I beat Lleyton (Hewitt) from the baseline, so I think that says a lot already, and I was for a while dominating Andre a little bit today in the third and in the beginning of the fourth. This week has been great tennis. I really hope to take it over to the clay court season, because I know also there I have the potential to play well."

2005 – World No. 1 Roger Federer closes the gap in his career series with Tim Henman, beating the world No. 6 6-4, 6-2 in the quarterfinals of the NASDAQ-100 Open. The win for Federer is his fourth in 10 career meetings with Henman. "He's one of the guys I've got a bad record against, so it's always good to beat him," says Federer.

2006 – In only 59 minutes, Roger Federer beats David Ferrer 6-1, 6-4 to reach the final of the NASDAQ-100 Open at Key Biscayne, Fla. Federer trails 3-0 in the second set but rallies to win six of the last seven games. "The second set was tighter, but his game suits me on hardcourt," Federer says. "I'm playing so well that it was tough for him from the start."

2008 – No. 1 Roger Federer advances to the fourth round of the Sony Ericsson Open when Robin Soderling retires from illness down 6-4, 3-0. "There is a big difference between not playing at all and playing a set and a half. I prefer today," Federer says. "I get the feel of the tournament playing a match and I'm able to handle the conditions."

2009 – Roger Federer overcomes eight break points in a remarkable stretch and beats American wild card Taylor Dent, ranked No. 467, 6-3, 6-2 in the round of 16 of the Sony Ericsson Open in Key Biscayne, Fla. The match is the first professional meeting between the two 28-year-olds, Dent beating Federer in the semifinal of the grasscourt junior event in Roehampton, England in 1998 7-6, 4-6, 6-3.

APRIL

April 1

1978 – Mirka Vavrinec, Roger Federer's wife, is born in Bojnice, Slovak Republic.

2011 – In a raucous atmosphere, despite the one-sided nature of the match, Roger Federer is beaten handily by chief rival and world No. 1 Rafael Nadal 6-3, 6-2 in the semifinals of the Sony Ericsson Open in Key Biscayne, Fla. The win, the most decisive win for Nadal over Federer at the time, increases his record over his Swiss rival to 15-8. "I think I played a very, very good match, very solid and serious," says Nadal. "In the first set especially I think I played very, very well. In the second set I think he played worse. He had more mistakes than usual. He tried to play shorter points, so I think second set he didn't play well." The sell-out crowd of 14,500 becomes very vocal in support of both players, chanting each player's name, started by Federer fans trying to urge their player to get back into the one-sided match. "It's definitely a very nice feeling to get the support from the crowd, especially against Rafa, obviously," says Federer. "I think definitely had something to do with the score. I'm not sure I wanted it or not because it meant I was down in the score. It's definitely nice hearing my name go through the stadium. I've had some great times here in Miami. Definitely nice feeling to have to play out there and hear that."

2005 – Hitting an impressive 30 winners in front of partisan pro-Agassi crowd, Roger Federer defeats six-time champion Andre Agassi 6-4, 6-3 in the semifinals of the NASDAQ-100 Open in what ultimately becomes Agassi final appearance in the event. "I played great off the baseline, great focus," says Federer. "I didn't only play against him, but against the fans tonight. They were really backing him up. I remember it was very similar to the year when I played the finals here against him. Maybe not as extreme because this time he was losing and then he was winning, so it was a tough match tonight. I'm extremely happy with the level of play." The win extends Federer's win streak to 21 and improves his record on the season to 31-1.

2008 – "Is that who I play?" Andy Roddick asks facetiously after beating Julien Benneteau 4-6, 6-3, 6-2 to set up a Sony Ericsson Open quarterfinal showdown with Roger Federer, the man whose beaten him in 11 straight times and has a 1-15 career record against. The top-ranked Federer advances into the match-up by beating Jose Acasuso of Argentina 7-6 (6), 6-2.

2009 – A passing shot that clips the net and hops over the racquet of Andy Roddick on the second-to-last point of the match proves to be the decisive shot for

Roger Federer in his 6-3, 4-6, 6-4 semifinal at the Sony Ericsson Open in Key Biscayne, Fla. Federer's net-cord shot gives him a match point on Roddick's serve, which he successfully wins to close out the match and increase his head-to-head record against Roddick to 17-2. Says Federer to reporters of his "lucky" shot, "I thought I hit a good pass. I mean, it was. The thing is, with this net, it's super tight this week, whereas last week it would have been a different net cord. I remember having a lot a lot of unlucky bounces over the years here with the let cords because those things fly off that net cords like crazy. It could have landed in the back fence. I was happy it stayed in. I hung in there. You got to create yourself chances. If you do get lucky on a big point, it just happens, but you got to put yourself in that position, and that's what I was able to do."

April 2

2006 – Roger Federer wins three straight tie-breaker sets and wins the NASDAQ-100 Open in Key Biscayne, Fla., beating Ivan Ljubicic of Croatia 7-6 (5), 7-6 (4), 7-6 (6), winning the last point of the match off a net-cord winner off a backhand return-of-serve. "I guess I had to work extremely hard to get that lucky over the years," says Federer of his fortunate shot on match point. "Obviously, it's funny, when it happens on match point for a tournament victory. I think it happened to me once before in the finals in – I thought it was Vienna against Novak. I didn't know what to do either. I guess it just happens. I really didn't need it that net cord, that's for sure." The tournament title is the 37th of Federer's career and the fourth in 2006. Only three total points separate the two players – Federer winning 124 total points to 121 for Ljubicic. Says Federer, "This is very nice to have such a close match and come through it and show once again I really belong in the number one position and deserve all of these trophies I win." With the win, Federer also becomes the first player ever to win the "Coast-to-Coast Double" – the American hard court titles in Indian Wells and Key Biscayne – back to back in consecutive years.

1999 – In the 100th year of Davis Cup play, Roger Federer makes his Davis Cup debut, defeating Davide Sanguinetti 6-4, 6-7 (3), 6-3, 6-4 in the opening day of play in Switzerland's defeat of Italy in Neuchatel, Switzerland. The match was the first for the 17-year-old Federer in a best-of-five-set match. "At first I was nervous but then I calmed down," says Federer, ranked No. 123. "I didn't do very well in the tie-break and took too many risks. But I think in the end taking a lot of risks combined with the public's support helped me win." Writes Rene Stauffer in the book *Roger Federer: Quest for Perfection,* "Federer's Davis Cup debut could not have been better. He decisively beat Italian No. 1 Davide Sanguinetti, ranked No. 48 in the world, 6-4, 6-7 (3), 6-3, 6-4 in his first match in the 3-2 win for the Swiss. 'It was unfortunate that Federer was playing for the opponent,' Italy's team captain, Paolo Bertolucci, said afterwards, 'but it was fun to watch him. There are not many people in the world who can play tennis so well.'"

April 3

2005 – Two points from defeat in the third-set tie-break, Federer rallies from two-sets-to-love down to defeat Spain's Rafael Nadal 2-6, 6-7 (4), 7-6 (5), 6-3, 6-1 in three hours and 43 minutes to win the NASDAQ-100 Open in Key Biscayne, Fla. Federer trails 4-2 in the third set and 5-3 in the third set tie-break before rallying to win his 22nd consecutive match and his 18th consecutive final. "It was uphill. I tried to force Rafael too much, but I finally got myself to relax," Federer says. "I thought I'd be all right if I could get him into a fifth set." Federer hits 74 unforced errors to Nadal's 54, but he also hit 51 winners to Nadal's 32. Says the 18-year-old Nadal, ranked No. 31, "He hits balls on lines. He is No. 1, no?" Writes Bud Collins in the *Los Angeles Times*, "The kid from Spain was on a fantastic joy ride. It was a thief's dream. He had stolen the first two sets Sunday and was driving toward the men's title here in the Nasdaq-100 Open. Then the Swiss guy who had been run over for two hours pulled himself together, caught the teenager and claimed the prize as the rightful owner after a 3-hour 43-minute marathon."

2009 – Roger Federer shocks the tennis world not with his brilliant play but with a rare display of his temper as he smashes his racquet against the court in disgust in the latter stages of his 3-6, 6-2, 6-3 semifinal loss to Novak Djokovic at the Sony Ericsson Open in Key Biscayne, Fla. Falling behind 2-0 in the final set, Federer nets an easy shot at the start of the next game, then raises his racquet over his head and smashes it the court. "I didn't lose it, I was just frustrated," says Federer of the racquet smashing episode. "Just because I smashed the racket, it doesn't mean I lost it. It didn't feel great, it was just a natural thing that I did." Mike Dickson from the *Daily Mail* writes of Federer, "Wimbledon's self-appointed King of Cool acted more like a raging John McEnroe in Miami when he smashed his racket in frustration at losing" and that "Long-term Federer observers could not remember such a tantrum since his junior."

2008 – With new fiancé and *Sports Illustrated* swimsuit model Brooklyn Decker in attendance, Andy Roddick ends his personal 11-match losing streak to Roger Federer, defeating the world No. 1 7-6 (4), 4-6, 6-3 in a highly-entertaining quarterfinal match at the Sony Ericsson Open in Key Biscayne, Fla. Says Roddick to the crowd following the match, "I came in knowing that nobody has beaten me 12 times in a row. So I had that on my side." Roddick, who last beat Federer in the semifinals of the 2003 Canadian Championships, improves his record to 2-15 against the five-time Wimbledon champion. "I figure I was due," Roddick says. "He hadn't missed a ball in a crucial moment for about six years against me. I figured the law of statistics had to come my way eventually." Says Federer of the loss, "I am just sort of disappointed not to see my name playing in the finals. I think I have the game to obviously be there."

2006 – Roger Federer is officially unveiled as a Goodwill Ambassador for UNICEF in a presentation in New York. "We have no doubt that his status as a tennis superstar provides an excellent platform for him to be an effective advocate on behalf of children," says UNICEF Executive

Director Ann Veneman. "But talent is not the only thing that sets Roger Federer apart from the rest of the sports world. Our interest in appointing him as a Goodwill Ambassador was inspired by his personal story, and the commitment he has demonstrated to using his fame to benefit children." Says Federer, "I may have achieved a lot on the court, but I would also like to try to achieve more now off the court. That's one of my big goals in the future...I have been lucky in life and able to pursue my passion for tennis. It's important to me to help the many children throughout the world who do not have the basic resources they need."

April 4

1999 – In a dead-rubber fifth-match in the Switzerland vs. Italy Davis Cup first round in Neuchatel, Switzerland, Roger Federer loses to Gianlucca Pozzi 6-4, 7-6 (4). Pozzi, born in 1965, is the oldest player Federer faces in his ATP Tour career.

2014 – Roger Federer defeats Mikhail Kukushkin 6-4, 6-4, 6-2 to draw Switzerland even at 1-1 with Kazakhstan in the Davis Cup quarterfinals in Geneva. Federer's win comes after his teammate, No. 3-ranked Stan Wawrinka, is upset in the opening rubber to Andrey Golubev. Federer says following the win that he is happy to finish the match in straight sets to rest up for the important doubles match with Wawrinka the next day. "Definitely it's an advantage and good for me not to waste any energy because I do see myself playing all three days, even though I play second on Sunday," Federer says. "Clearly I trust Stan that he's going to be fit and healthy and fighting till the very end. It was unfortunate today for his match but I think Golubev played really a smart and a good match in good indoor conditions for him.Now we're just going to start all over again, really. That's what I told Stan. The weekend has only just started. There's no drama and that's how I saw it going into my singles match."

2003 – Roger Federer, ranked No. 5, avenges three consecutive losses to Nicolas Escude, defeating the No. 62-ranked player 6-4, 7-5, 6-2 to draw Switzerland even with France at 1-1 after the first day of the Davis Cup quarterfinal in Toulouse, France.

April 5

2014 – Roger Federer and Stan Wawrinka lose their fourth straight Davis Cup doubles match as a team, falling to Andrey Golubev and Aleksandr Nedovyesov 6-4, 7-6 (5), 4-6, 7-6 (6) as Kazakhstan takes a surprising 2-1 lead over Switzerland in the quarterfinals in Geneva. Says Doskarayev of beating the 2008 Olympic doubles gold medalists, "It's like a dream. I told the guys before the match: Miracles may happen, but you have to believe in miracles."

2003 – Swiss Davis Cup captain Marc Rosset substitutes himself in the line-up for the Swiss Davis Cup team to partner Roger Federer against the French pair of Nicolas Escude and Fabrice Santoro in the Davis Cup quarterfinals in Toulouse, France. Rosset's decision proves pivotal as he and Federer win 6-4, 3-6, 6-3, 7-6 (4) to give the Swiss a key 2-1 lead.

"I was impressed by how much we had in common," Roger Federer said of golfing legend Tiger Woods when they first met when Federer won the 2006 U.S. Open. "He knew exactly what I was going through and I see what he has to go through. I've never spoken with anybody who was so familiar with the feeling of being invincible." Continued Federer of seeing Woods sitting in his player's box when he played the U.S. Open men's singles final against Andy Roddick, "It was terrific for me to see him go into my player's box, shake his fist, and enjoy himself. He was the loudest one in my box. I was surprised how loose he was about it. He was happy as a kid to be able to watch the final. I think we'll do things together more often."

April 6

2014 – Playing in a fifth and decisive Davis Cup match for the first time in his career, Roger Federer defeats Andrey Golubev 7-6(0), 6-2, 6-3 to lift Switzerland into in the Davis Cup semifials for the first time since 2003. Federer's victory caps a final-day sweep for the Swiss in Geneva as Stan Wawrinka evens the score at 2-2 after rallying to beat past Mikhail Kukushkin 6-7(4), 6-4, 6-4, 6-4. "I was hoping so much I was going to get a chance to play and not just watch Stan play," says Federer following his win. "I got the opportunity and I'm happy I lived up to the hype and the expectations, and I was able to get the boys through so very happy for them."

2003 – With groundstrokes and passing shots described as "dazzling" by the Associated Press, Roger Federer devastates Fabrice Santoro 6-1, 6-0, 6-2 to clinch Switzerland's Davis Cup quarterfinal victory over France in Toulouse. Santoro is a late replacement for Sebastien Grosjean, who is not able to play due to a thigh injury. Federer's win gives the Swiss the 3-1 lead in their eventual 3-2 victory. "I would have liked to have stood up to Federer," Santoro says following the loss. "But I have to admit there are several degrees of class between Federer and me." Adds French Davis Cup captain Guy Forget if Grosjean would have put up a better fight than Santoro, "I don't know if Grosjean could have beaten Federer the way he played today." Federer wins 90 percent of the points on his first serve.

2001 – Roger Federer loses to Nicolas Escude 6-4, 6-7 (1), 6-3, 6-4 to put Switzerland down 0-2 after the first day of play of the Switzerland vs. France Davis Cup quarterfinal in Neuchatel, Switzerland. Federer's loss comes after his teammate Marc Rosset loses an epic five-hour, 56-minute 6-3, 3-6, 7-6 (4), 6-7 (6), 15-13 match to Arnaud Clement. In a midnight press conference after his loss, Federer tells Swiss reporters of his dissatisfaction with Swiss Davis Cup captain Jakob Hlasek. Writes Rene Stauffer in his book *Roger Federer: Quest for Perfection*, "Federer's emotional outburst revealed the less familiar, uncompromising side of his personality—like a proud lion reacting passionately when things were not going his way."

April 7

2001 – Roger Federer pairs with Lorenzo Manta and works to try and bring Switzerland back from an 0-2 deficit for the first time ever in Davis Cup, cutting France's lead to 2-1 with a 5-7, 6-3, 7-6(4), 6-7(3), 9-7 win over Fabrice Santoro and Cedric Pioline. The match is the longest doubles match of Federer's career at four hours and 26 minutes. The Swiss team save a break point at 1-2 in the final set, and need one break point to take the 8-7 lead before closing out the victory.

One of the scenes that is often seen at Roger Federer matches is the "Shhhh Genius at Work" banners that his fans frequently hang at matches he plays. At the 2007 Australian Open, Federer was asked if he is aware of these signs. "Yeah, of course," he said with a smile. "It's really nice. I have so many fans, especially on my website as well. We cracked the 100,000 members actually this week during the Australian Open. I've met many of them. Always writing me mail, you know, kind of getting in touch with me, showing it when they're in the stadium. I've seen that banner many, many times. It's always kind of nice to see them again. Maybe it's not the same person, but the same banners out. Yeah, it gives me a good feeling." When then asked what the word "genius" means to him, Federer said, "I mean, look, I guess I'm the best tennis player in the world. You can call me a genius because I'm outplaying many of my opponents, kind of maybe playing a bit different, winning when I'm not playing my best. All of that maybe means a little bit of that. So it's nice."

April 8

2001 – After defeating Arnaud Clement 6-4, 3-6, 7-6(5), 6-4 to draw Switzerland even with France at 2-2, Federer plays the role of spirited cheerleader in the fifth and final match between George Bastl and Nicolas Escude. Bastl nearly enables Switzerland to come back from a 0-2 deficit for the first time ever, holding match point, but falls by a 1-6, 7-5, 6-7 (3-7), 6-4, 8-6 scoreline. At the Monte Carlo Open weeks later, Federer is asked to reflect on the emotional weekend. "The next couple of days after Sunday was tough because I screamed so much for George and was tough, tough weekend," Federer says. "I felt little bit sick after next few days, but I think that's normal. I think the screaming for George took more energy out of me than my own match." In the three-day series, Federer is on court for a total of 10 hours, 41 minutes.

"I've heard comparisons between what Federer is doing and what Tiger Woods is doing these days. But, here's the thing: Tiger doesn't do anything to you. Obviously, he's intimidating, but Tiger is playing the course, just like you. But Federer is playing you. And when he takes away the thing you do best, it just cripples you. He does what it takes to beat you, regardless of what kind of player you are."
— Patrick McEnroe to the St. Petersburg Times, 2007

April 9

2004 – Roger Federer beats Nicolas Escude 6-2, 6-4, 6-4 to open up the Switzerland vs. France Davis Cup quarterfinal in Lausanne, Switzerland. "I was really happy to play in the opening rubber as usually I have to wait for the second game," says Federer. "I started off by serving badly in the last game and it was tight, but I got my serve going and it got me through." Arnaud Clement draws the series even with Switzerland beating Ivo Heuberger 6-3, 6-3, 6-2.

After winning the title in Toronto in 2006, Roger Federer is asked if he ever guards against overconfidence in his matches. Says Federer. "I used to underestimate many opponents coming on the tour. I remember in juniors it happened to me. On the ATP Tour level I would think this guy has a weird technique, he can't beat me. I have a beautiful technique. The next thing I know I lose 1-2 because I totally lost it on the court. I paid many times very hard for not really respecting my opponent enough, I would think. Not in a bad way, but just his game. I've totally stopped doing that. That's what's actually now in a kind of way paying off for me now that I don't underestimate anybody anymore."

April 10

2004 – Roger Federer pairs with Yves Allegro in Davis Cup play against France in the quarterfinals in Lausanne, Switzerland, but falls to Nicolas Escude and Michael Llodra 6-7 (4), 6-3, 7-6 (5), 6-3 in exactly three hours to give France the 2-1 lead.

In 2007, Roger Federer reflected on first visit to Wimbledon in 1998. "I was very nervous going into my junior first round," Federer says at Wimbledon in 2007. "I remember after the warmup I was going up to the umpire telling him, I think the net is too high, because I was so nervous. I felt like the net was double the height. He actually went down and checked it. The net was, of course, accurate, so I kept on playing and won my match."

April 11

2009 – Roger Federer and girlfriend Mirka Vavrinec are married in Basel, Switzerland in a modest ceremony attended by a small group of close friends and family. Federer announces the wedding on his website RogerFederer.com saying, "Earlier today, in my hometown of Basel, surrounded by a small group of close friends and family, Mirka and I got married. It was a beautiful spring day and an incredibly joyous occasion. Mr. and Mrs. Roger Federer wish all of you a Happy Easter weekend."

2004 – Roger Federer beats Arnaud Clement 6-2, 7-5, 6-4 to draw Switzerland event with France at 2-2 in the Davis Cup quarterfinal in Lausanne, Switzerland. Federer's teammate Michel Kratochvil, however, loses the fifth and decisive match 7-6(3), 6-4, 7-6 (6) to Nicolas Escude. Federer does not play another Davis Cup World Group match for Switzerland again until 2012.

April 12

2005 – Roger Federer beats Greg Rusedski 6-3, 6-1 in the first round of the Monte Carlo Open in the fifth and final meeting between the two players. Rusedski, the left-handed Canadian-born Brit, wins the first meeting with an 18-year-old Federer in the semifinals of Vienna in 1999, but loses the next four meetings with the future world No. 1 all in straight sets.

2011 – Roger Federer needs only 50 minutes to win his opening match of his clay court season, beating Philipp Kohlschreiber 6-2, 6-1 at the Monte Carlo Open. "Look, I think clearly a good start for me into the clay-court season. Not much I can take out of this match, I think, except maybe I varied it well that he couldn't play his game," Federer tells reporters after the match. "He wasn't able to or he couldn't really play aggressive the way maybe he was hoping to do today. I was able to do all the things I was hoping to. I was consistent, consistently dangerous, too. I felt well in the offense, and in the defense I was fine. But then at the end, it's a quick match."

April 13

2005 – Roger Federer wins his 24th straight match defeating Albert Montanes of Spain 6-3, 6-4 in the second round of the Monte Carlo Open.

1998 – Roger Federer wins his third ITF junior singles title at the City of Florence International Championships in Italy, defeating Filippo Volandri 7-6, 6-3 in the final.

At the 2001 Monte Carlo Open, Roger Federer is asked if he actually learned to play tennis on clay when he was growing up. Answers Federer, "Well, I used to -- in the winter, I used to even practice indoors on clay in a balloon. I used to play more on clay than anything else. In the summer, on clay. In the winter, on clay. And I was 14 when I went to the Swiss National Tennis Center, and in the winter I used to play on fast indoors. So I don't know why my clay court career started so badly."

April 14

2005 – Roger Federer wins his 25th straight match, defeating Fernando Gonzalez 6-2, 6-7 (3), 6-4 to advance into the quarterfinals of the Monte Carlo Masters in Monaco.

2008 – Roger Federer announces on his RogerFederer.com website that he will start to work with coach Jose Higueras immediately at the Estoril Open in Portugal. "I am excited as I have asked Jose Higueras, one of the most respected and accomplished coaches in the world of tennis, to join me," Federer says. "We are going to spend the week together to see if we could make a good team." Federer enters his first clay-court tournament of the year having not reached a final in the four tournaments he has played in the 2008 season.

2011 – Roger Federer needs 72 minutes to defeat Marin Cilic 6-4, 6-3 in the second round of the Monte Carlo Open. Federer calls the victory "another solid performance."

April 15

2004 – Richard Gasquet, an 18-year-old qualifier ranked No. 101 in the world and playing in his first ATP tournament of the year, upsets world No. 1 Roger Federer 6-7 (1), 6-2, 7-6 (8) in the quarterfinals of the Monte Carlo Open. The Frenchmen fights off three match points in the final-set tie-break to end Federer's 25-match winning streak. The loss is Federer's first since he loses in the semifinals of the Australian Open in January to Marat Safin.

2008 – Roger Federer rallies from a set down to defeat No. 80-ranked Olivier Rochus of Belgium 4-6, 6-3, 6-2 in the first round of the Estoril Open in Portugal.

2009 – Playing just four days after his marriage to long-time girlfriend Mirka Vavrinec, Roger Federer defeats Andreas Seppi, 6-4, 6-4 in the opening round of the Monte Carlo Open. Federer originally decides to skip the important clay-court tournament, but surprisingly accepts a late wild-card into the tournament.

2011 – In a shock upset, Roger Federer falls in the quarterfinals of Monte Carlo Open to No. 9-ranked Jurgen Melzer by a 6-4, 6-4 margin. Federer entered the match having not previously lost a set to his Austrian opponent in three previous matches. Reporters after the match ask

Federer if it makes a difference to lose to a player who is not Rafael Nadal or Novak Djokovic. "Not really," Federer says. "Look, I don't think I've lost against a left-hander other than Nadal in, I don't know, seven or eight years. I'm happy to have done something like that. Then again, you know, it's always disappointing regardless against who you lose. As long as you keep trying, test all the things out there, you feel like you gave it all the chances, that's really what matters to me. Look, I wish I could have gone further in the tournament. It was okay. I got three matches. I'm pretty happy."

April 16

2001 – Nineteen-year-old Roger Federer defeats 29-year-old Michael Chang 6-4, 6-3 in the first round of the Monte Carlo Open for his first career victory in Monaco. Following the match, Federer discusses his comfort-level and results on clay with reporters. "I mean let's put it that way, my results are way better on other surfaces, but my best Grand Slam result came at the French last year, so I was and I still think am a good clay courter," says Federer. "I'm not that worried about my career on the clay. I mean, today was a tough opening first set for me. There was a lot of fighting, because I really didn't feel good on the court. So that's a match I have to go through. It's really good to win matches like this on clay. I'm really happy to be through to the second round, because I can win confidence very quickly on clay. It's good to start off the clay court season with a win, definitely."

2009 – Stan Wawrinka gives his Olympic gold medal-winning doubles partner Roger Federer a terrible wedding gift, beating the Roger Federer 6-4, 7-5 in the third round of the Monte Carlo Open, Federer's first tournament since getting married to longtime girlfriend Mirka Vavrinec. Federer, who practiced only 10 days on clay prior to the event, faced 14 break points in the match. "Like I told him, the loss doesn't hurt as much just because I know it's against a good guy," says the No. 2 ranked Federer, who had lost to Rafael Nadal in the previous three Monte Carlo Open finals. Says the No. 13-seeded Wawrinka, "Maybe not the most spectacular tennis, but it's my most beautiful victory."

April 17

2006 – Roger Federer faces Novak Djokovic for the first time his career and, despite 37 unforced errors, beats the 18-year-old 6-3, 2-6, 6-3 in the first round of the Monte Carlo Open. Federer's play is described as "sluggish" by media outlets as the world No. 1 commits 37 unforced errors against Djokovic, who advances into the tournament's main draw via the qualifying tournament. "I'm satisfied to have won and relieved it's over," says Federer. "It was not easy. I didn't play great but you need time to adapt to the surface."

2007 – Roger Federer struggles to beat qualifier Andreas Seppi of Italy 7-6 (4), 7-6 (6) in his opening round match at the Monte Carlo Open. "It was tough," Federer says.

"Conditions were quick. A lot of bad bounces. He already had three matches in his legs and it was my first."

April 18

2008 – Top-ranked Roger Federer beats No. 146th-ranked local favorite Frederico Gil of Portugal 6-4, 6-1 in the quarterfinals of the Estoril Open at Oeiras, Portugal.

2013 – Andy Murray loses to Stan Wawrinka 6-1, 6-2 in the round of 16 of the Monte Carlo Masters, ensuring that Roger Federer will return to the No. 2 ranking.

In Montreal in 2009, Roger Federer is asked, having been on the ATP Tour for a decade, if he has a photographic or encyclopedic memory of all of the matches he has played in his career. Answers Federer, "I think I know a lot about my history, the matches I've played, the points I've played and stuff. I guess in today's game we get reminded so many more times, you see it and you have pictures and film and everything, but I'm getting to the point where I start forgetting matches now, because I just have played so many. I think it's past 700 or 800 now. That's not counting doubles and qualifying and Challengers and Satellites and Juniors and everything. I'm getting up there. And it hit me when I played Gilles Muller at the U.S. Open last year, and for two days I said I never played the guy and I'm excited to play him for the first time, and then even when I was walking into the tunnel going into the match, I never thought I played him before. And then I think (John) McEnroe was making fun of me saying, 'I can't believe

Roger makes a mistake, because the guy has played him twice before, once in Bangkok and once in Indian Wells.' But I completely forgot those matches. That was the first time of me starting to forget matches, I think."

April 19

2008 – After over four months of play for the year, Roger Federer finally reaches his first final of the 2008 season by defeating No. 104-ranked Denis Gremelmayr of Germany 2-6, 7-5, 6-1 in the semifinals of the Estoril Open in Portugal. Federer, who admitted earlier in the year that he was recovering from mono, advances into the final match against No. 4 ranked Nikolay Davydenko having not faced a player ranked higher than No. 68 in the clay-court tournament.

2006 – Roger Federer needs only 46 minutes to beat Alberto Martin of Spain 6-1, 6-0 to advance into the third round of the Monte Carlo Open.

2007 – Top-seeded Roger Federer defeats Hyung-Taik Lee of Korea 6-4, 6-3 to reach the quarterfinals of the Monte Carlo Open. The match is the final meeting between Federer and Lee – their only previous meeting being a 6-3, 6-3, 7-6 (2) win for Federer in the first round of Wimbledon in 2003.

2001 – Roger Federer defeats Arnaud DiPasquale, the man who beat Federer for the Olympic bronze medal in 2000, by a decisive 6-1, 6-2 margin to reach the quarterfinals of the

Monte Carlo Open. "My objective for the clay court season was to reach at least once the quarterfinals, so it's really nice that it happened in the first tournament because we never know what will happen afterwards," says Federer. "The first two tennis matches were okay, but today it was really a lot better. I felt better, I was missing less, and it worked out well. Although, Arnaud wasn't feeling very good, I played a very good match."

April 20

2007 – Roger Federer wins his 500th career ATP tour match defeating David Ferrer 6-4, 6-0 in the quarterfinals of the Monte Carlo Open. "I am very happy to have done it here," says Federer of his milestone win. "That is a lot of games. I'm glad they are victories."

2008 – Roger Federer wins his first ATP singles title in five months winning the Estoril Open in Portugal when No. 2-seeded Nikolay Davydenko retires with a left leg injury while trailing, 7-6 (5), 1-2. The event is Federer's fifth tournament of the season and his first title since he won the 2007 ATP World Tour year-end championships. It had been eight years since Federer had needed so many events to even reach a final. The tournament win is the 54th of Federer's career.

2001 – Sebastien Grosjean of France defeats Roger Federer 6-4, 6-3 in the quarterfinals of the Monte Carlo Open, his second win over the future world No. 1. In his post-match press conference, the first question posed to Federer is

"Sebastien was simply too good for you today?" which draws a sharp response. "No, I don't believe it. Not at all," says Federer. "I was not at the best of my tennis. I was even far from it. I am sad that I played a good match yesterday and that I missed this one. It's difficult, but my level couldn't come back today. I tried, but also Sebastien played well. I also had the impression that I was unlucky now and then. He was touching the lines. That's it; it happens."

2006 – Top-ranked Roger Federer beats hometown boy Benjamin Balleret 6-3, 6-2 in the third-round of the Monte Carlo Open.

April 21

2006 – Roger Federer needs 61 minutes to beat David Ferrer 6-1, 6-3 to reach the semifinals of the Monte Carlo Open.

2007 – Roger Federer sets up a Monte Carlo Open final against Rafael Nadal with a 6-3, 6-4 win over Juan Carlos Ferrero. Federer trails 1-3 in the first set and saves two break points to go down two breaks at 1-4, but rallies to win five games in a row to win the first set before winning the match in 85 minutes. "It's always fun to see the No. 1 and No. 2 playing against each other," says the world No. 1 Federer of the final-round match-up with Nadal.

Roger Federer is one of the most popular tennis players in the history of the sport. Part of the reason for this is the amount of time he spends signing autographs for fans after matches and practice. "I like signing autographs a lot because I think it's something where the players and the fans get together," Federer said. "They see me from far away, behind -- it's just too much space in between us. When they can come close to the players, I think that is some special moment for everybody. If they can take pictures, maybe touch me, whatever, for them it's a highlight of the day. If I can give them that, I think that's a lot of satisfaction for me, too."

April 22

2006 – Top-ranked Roger Federer and world No. 2 Rafael Nadal both advance into the final of the Monte Carlo Open – marking the first time that the top two seeds have met in the final of the Mediterranean principality's ATP event since Ivan Lendl defeated Mats Wilander in 1985. Federer defeated No. 12 seed Fernando Gonzalez 6-2, 6-4 while Nadal beat Gaston Gaudio 5-7, 6-1, 6-1.

2007 – Roger Federer loses his fifth straight match to Rafael Nadal on clay, falling 6-4, 6-4 to his Spanish rival in the final of the Monte Carlo Open. Despite the loss, Federer is upbeat in his post-match press conferences on future matches against Nadal on clay. "I feel this match gave me some information," Federer says. "I'm absolutely in the mix with him on clay. I feel like I'm in good shape for the rest of clay-court season, and it's going to come down to the French Open to see who wins."

April 23

2006 – Rafael Nadal beats Roger Federer for the fourth time in five meetings, defeating the seven-time Grand Slam tournament champion 6-2, 6-7 (2), 6-3, 7-6 (5) in the final of the Monte Carlo Open. "I was beating him easier today than in Paris," says Nadal, who beat Federer in a four-set French Open semifinal 11 months prior. "To begin the clay season like this, for me, is unbelievable." Federer, who was appearing in his 12th consecutive final, makes 78 unforced errors in the loss that drops his record on the year to 28-2.

2008 – Roger Federer escapes from what would have been one of his most embarrassing losses of his career when he rallies from 5-1 down in the third set to defeat No. 137-ranked Ruben Ramirez Hidalgo of Spain 6-1, 3-6, 7-6 (1) in the second round of the Monte Carlo Open. Ramirez-Hidalgo, a qualifier who had not won an ATP Tour match on the year, serves for the match two times in the final set, but is not able to punch through. "In the end at least it was fine," Federer says after his escape. "But for one and a half sets, I was quite disappointed. Rarely am I in a situation like this, 5-1 down in the third, and I still manage to come back."

2000 – Roger Federer announces on Easter Sunday, via a faxed press release, that he is breaking away from the Swiss Tennis Federation and his longtime coach Peter Carter to work exclusively with Peter Lundgren starting October 1, 2000. Writes Rene Stauffer in the book *Roger Federer: Quest for Perfection*, "The official separation from the guidance of the Swiss Tennis Federation made sense for Federer because it provided him with a more flexible environment that was adjusted to his own needs. However, the fact that Federer decided to work with Lundgren and not Carter, whom he knew better and with whom he had worked together much longer, came as a surprise to most. Federer could not really explain the reasons for the choice." Stauffer writes that Federer says his inner gut feelings makes him choose Lundgren as his exclusive coach. "It was a toss-up," Federer tells Stauffer.

April 24

2008 – One day after nearly losing in the first round to unheralded Ruben Ramirez Hidalgo, Roger Federer returns to "normal" and easily defeats Gael Monfils 6-3, 6-4 to advance into the quarterfinals of the Monte Carlo Open. "My forehand worked well today," Federer says. "And I was just happy, after yesterday, (to be) playing so well. Today was fine again. It's good I reacted so well after yesterday's tough match."

When asked who he would play against if there was such thing as a time machine and he could travel back to play against the greatest players in history, Roger Federer said Rod Laver and Bjorn Borg.

April 25

2008 – Roger Federer pulls ahead of nemesis David Nalbandian 9-8 in their career head-to-head with a hard-fought 5-7, 6-2, 6-2 victory in the quarterfinals of the Monte Carlo Open. "The level of play was excellent today," Federer says of the match. "Tough rallies. I think I definitely played my best match of the tournament, no doubt." Says Nalbandian, "I think we both played (at) a great level. I got a little tired in the second set and third set." Nalbandian wins the first five head-to-head matches against Federer starting with a second round match in Monte Carlo in 2002. "It's always nice playing against him," Federer says. "Because of the great player he is. He's (a) wonderful ball striker."

At the 2006 Australian Open, Roger Federer is asked what would be the best single bit of tennis advice he would give to a beginner of intermediate tennis players. Answers Federer, "Well, you go through up and downs in tennis. It's a very mentally tough game emotionally, I think because you win a lot and you lose a lot, too. You lose usually more than you win in the beginning. You have to stay positive and enjoy it and get good support from family and coaches. Then, you know, be tough. When the days come, your chance comes along, you want to take your chance and don't choke on it "

April 26

2008 – Roger Federer advances into the final of the Monte Carlo Open when Novak Djokovic retires with breathing problems with Federer leading 6-3, 3-2. A curious highlight of the match comes with Federer leading 3-2 in the first set and the five-time Wimbledon champion turns to the Djokovic camp and tells them to "be quiet" after a close call on the baseline.

2010 – Roger Federer plays his first doubles match of the 2010 season, pairing with fellow Swiss Yves Allegro to defeat Johan Brunstrom of Sweden and Jean-Julien Roger of the Netherlands 6-4, 7-6 at the Italian Championships in Rome. Federer and Allegro go on to reach the event's quarterfinals – bettering Federer's singles appearance at the event after an opening round loss to Ernests Gulbis – before losing to Sam Querry and John Isner 6-4, 6-4.

April 27

2008 – Rafael Nadal improves his clay-court record against Roger Federer to 7-1, winning his first title of the year with a 7-5, 7-5 win over the world No. 1 in the final of the Monte Carlo Open. The tournament win for Nadal is his fourth straight in Monte Carlo and earns him his 98th win on clay in his last 99 matches, losing only to Federer in the 2007 Hamburg final. Federer leads Nadal 4-3 in the first set and 4-0 in the second set, but commits too many unforced errors to consolidate his leads.

2010 – Roger Federer is shocked in his opening match of the clay-court season, falling by a 2-6, 6-1, 7-5 scoreline to No. 40th-ranked Ernests Gulbis of Latvia at the Italian Championships in Rome. "I hope I can come back from this," Federer says, alluding to the upcoming French Open. "That's usually what I do after a loss like this. Sometimes it takes a loss to wake up and shake you up for your approach the next week. When you always win, sometimes you forget how hard it is."

April 28

2003 – The BMW Open in Munich begins play with Roger Federer as the No. 1 seed, the first, and only time Federer competes in the event in Germany, despite it being less than 200 miles from his home in Basel, Switzerland

In 2002, Roger Federer was asked how he transformed himself from being a fiery, ill-tempered junior player to being a model of calm and sportsmanship as a professional. "When I was very young, when I started playing tennis I started very early, when I was three years old, but I was always swearing around the court and throwing my racquet – but really bad," Federer said. "So, my parents felt embarrassed and they would tell me to stop because they said they wouldn't come with me to tournaments anymore. So I had to kind of settle down. But this actually took me until I was maybe 19, maybe one or two years ago, which I really started to make improvements. Before I would still, like, complain on every point I would lose and all this stuff. So I don't know how I got over it. I kind of thought like I'm losing too much energy by always getting upset with myself, and now I'm totally calm. I got very good press at the French and Wimbledon for my behavior on the court. Yeah, but now I have to almost watch out that I'm not too calm sometimes on the court."

April 29

2009 – Roger Federer is out-aced 15-1 but beats Ivo Karlovic 6-4, 6-4 to advance into the third round of the Italian Championships in Rome. "I got off to a good start in both sets, which is always good, kind of comforting against Ivo," says Federer. "He found his groove later on, on his serve but I already had the break in the second, which is perfect. It was just important to be really solid on my serve. I had two close service games in the beginning. From then on, I was pretty much cruising." Karlovic commits 38 total unforced errors – 22 in the first set – against only 16 for Federer in the 69-minute match.

2003 – Top-seeded Roger Federer of Switzerland opens up play for the first time in the BMW Open in Munich, defeating Zeljko Krajan of Croatia 6-4, 6-3.

April 30

2009 – Roger Federer avenges his 2008 quarterfinal loss in Rome to Radek Stepanek by defeating the Czech 6-4, 6-1 to advance into the quarterfinals of the Italian Championships. Federer breaks serve four times and wins the re-match in 66 minutes, incredibly dropping just three points on his first serve. "This year was very different," says Federer of the re-match. "I could read his first serve. His second serve was not a problem either. I didn't have a problem even to attack his second serve, whereas last year I was just trying to get the ball into play, and then obviously he was able to mix it up and make me doubt

THE DAYS OF ROGER FEDERER

much more. This year was good. I had the control from the baseline, and he didn't have the opportunities like he did have last year. I played well really when I had to, so I'm really happy with the performance today....When you walk on the court you still have sort of the highlights from that match. But you try to give it another shot. It's a different match. I'm still always going to be the favorite against him. I just tried to get off to a good start and I did, which is perfect."

2005 – Roger Federer announces his withdrawal from the Italian Championships due to what he says is inflammation in both feet. Federer's withdrawal leaves Andy Roddick as the No. 1 seed in the event.

MAY

May 1

2003 – Roger Federer advances into the quarterfinals of the BMW Open in Munich with a 6-4, 6-3 win in 59 minutes over Raemon Sluiter of the Netherlands. The match is the final career meeting between Federer and Sluiter, Federer winning all four matches.

2009 – Roger Federer withstands the net-rushing onslaught of Mischa Zverev, defeating the German qualifier 7-6 (3), 6-2 in the quarterfinals of the Italian Championships. The win sets up a semifinal match-up with Novak Djokovic, whom Federer has beaten seven of 10 previous times, but Djokovic winning the last meeting weeks earlier in Miami.

With the all-time record for most men's singles titles at Grand Slam tournaments, a family and millions of dollars, Roger Federer was asked at the 2010 Australian Open on what his motivations are in tennis and in life. "Love for the game, like it's always been," said Federer. "There's always ways to motivate and challenge you. Never really been in it for the money anyway. It's always been my dream to play on the biggest stages around

*the world, especially Wimbledon. I've lived through many more
things than I ever thought I would, so I feel very fortunate. I'm
looking forward to many more years hopefully on tour."*

May 2

2003 – In their third career meeting, Roger Federer defeats
Mikhail Youzhny 6-2, 6-3 to reach the quarterfinals of the
BMW Open in Munich.

2007 – In one of the most bizarre exhibitions in the history
of the sport, clay-court maestro Rafael Nadal defeats grass
court king Roger Federer 7-5, 4-6, 7-6 (10) in Palma de
Mallorca, Spain in an exhibition played on a court where
one side of the net is a grass surface and the other half is a
clay surface. Says Nadal, a native of Mallorca and the two-
time reigning French Open champion, of his win over the
four-time reigning Wimbledon champion, "It was a long
match, with many changes of pace and with little time to
adapt. My feet are suffering as a price of having to adapt
to the grass." The special court takes 19 days to install
and costs $1.63 million to construct. Nadal has a record 72
straight clay wins. Federer has a 48-match grass run that
includes four Wimbledon titles. .

2009 – Defending champion Novak Djokovic rallies
after a rain delay to beat Roger Federer 4-6, 6-3, 6-3 in
the semifinals of the Italian Championships in Rome,
extending Federer's title drought to seven months.
Federer, who hadn't won a tournament since the previous

October in his hometown of Basel, Switzerland, leads by a service break in the second and third sets before faltering.

May 3

2003 – Roger Federer advances into the final of the Munich Open, defeating Stefan Koubek of Austria 6-2, 6-1. Jarkko Nieminen of Finland advances into the final to face Federer when Yevgeny Kafelnikov of Russia withdraws due to a neck injury, Kafelnikov trailing, 6-4, 1-0

Has Roger Federer ever used a sports psychologist? He was asked this question while competing in the Italian Open in 2003. "No," *he said. "I had that once when I was playing Juniors because I* *was getting too upset, so I needed some help how to think about* *different stuff and how to get rid of that. Then I kind of worked* *on myself, also, the way I wanted to present myself on the court* *and the way that made me feel natural and good. Finally, now I* *can really say today that I feel good out there, and I don't have* *-- I'm over-motivated or under-motivated now. I have the right* *line, and this makes me feel good out on the court."*

May 4

2003 – Roger Federer wins his seventh career ATP singles title defeating Finland's Jarkko Nieminen 6-1, 6-4 in the final of the BMW Open in Munich. The top-seeded Federer, playing in Munich for the first time in his career, needs only 56 minutes to win the final of the clay-court event.

2004 – Roger Federer plays his first clay-court match of the 2004 season defeating Jonas Bjorkman, 7-6 (4) 6-3 in the first round of the Italian Championships in Rome. "I thought it was a pretty good, actually, draw for me, not to play a clay courter in the first round, but you never know what's gonna happen in the first round anyway, so it doesn't really matter who you play," Federer says. "I had the chance early to break and I didn't. That kind of just made me play more defensive. I didn't believe too much in my shots. You could see I was shanking a lot of balls and getting worried and upset. That's what happens – especially on clay. You can get very quickly frustrated, and that's what happened. I'm very happy I won the first set, because the second set at least I could take some chances because in the beginning I was just playing safe."

May 5

2004 – Albert Costa, ranked No. 39 but only two years removed from his French Open singles championship, upsets No. 1 ranked Roger Federer in the second round of the Italian Open 3-6, 6-3, 6-2. "I played more aggressively, that was the key," says Costa of the difference between the first set and the second and third sets. Federer commits 44 unforced errors – twice as many as Costa – in the loss. "Definitely I didn't play my best, but my opponent did play well," Federer says following the loss. "For me it's not a disaster because I knew how tough the clay-court season is for me."

2010 – Roger Federer wins his first match on clay in the 2010 season beating Bjorn Phau of Germany 6-3, 6-4 in the opening round of the Estoril Open in Portugal. Federer loses 17 points on his serve in rebounding from a first-round loss in Rome the previous week.

May 6

2008 – Roger Federer evens his career head-to-head series with Guillermo Canas at 3-3 with a 6-3, 6-3 victory over the Argentine in his opening round match at the Italian Championships in Rome. Canas famously beats Federer in back-to-back tournaments in 2007 in Indian Wells and Miami, combined with an opening round win over the Swiss at the 2002 Canadian Championships. The match, ultimately, becomes the final meeting the two and Canas becomes one of the few players to boast to not have a losing record against the Swiss maestro.

2003 – Roger Federer beats Paul-Henri Mathieu of France 6-3, 7-5 in the opening round of the Italian Championships in Rome and discusses with reporters the perception that he is the most naturally talented player in the game. "Everybody was talking about, 'How talented you are,' and, 'How easy it looks' and you feel like you kind of have to live up to this and play the miracle shots, the crowd-pleaser stuff, but I kind of stopped with that," Federer says. "All I want in the end is to win the match and not hit the best shot of the tournament, of the match. I kind of feel now that I know in what moment to play which shot. I think this is very important for my game. This is also why

I can – I'm for over six months now in the Top 5. I think this is a big step for me mentally."

May 7

2003 – Roger Federer out-aces Mariano Zabaleta 14-0 in his opening-round 7-6 (4), 6-2 win over the Argentine at the Italian Championships in Rome. Following his victory, Federer is asked, since Italian is one of the languages of his native Switzerland, what his proficiency is in Italian. "I understand a little bit because it's not too far away from French, but I don't know, never had really the chance to learn Italian," he says. "In school we had English and French. Then I went to the French-speaking part of Switzerland so I learned the French because I couldn't speak at all. Italian never really got close to me, so... But I really think it's one of the most beautiful languages in the world. It's one I really would like to learn. So maybe one day, you know, I come back to Rome or maybe after my career I'll be able to speak to the Italian media and fans and whoever..."

2007 – Roger Federer and Rafael Nadal face off against each other on the doubles court as Federer and Swiss partner Stan Wawrinka fall to Nadal and Carlos Moya 6-4, 7-6 (7-5) in the first round of the Italian Championships in Rome. "I'm getting to know him pretty well," Federer says of Nadal. "It was fun."

2013 – Playing his first match in eight weeks, Roger Federer begins the defense of his Madrid Open championship with a 6-3, 6-3 win over Radek Stepanek. "I didn't think I played incredible, but that's not what I was expecting myself to do here, but I didn't play bad either," says the 31-year-old Federer. "Overall, I'm very happy, because he (Stepanek) has caused me difficulties in the past. Today that wasn't the case and I thought I was pretty much in control." Federer increases his career head-to-head record to 12-2 against the 34-year-old Czech, who beat Federer in 2002 in Gstaad and in 2008 in Rome.

May 8

2006 – Top-ranked Roger Federer defeats Juan Ignacio Chela of Argentina 6-2, 6-1 in the first round of the Italian Open in the only meeting between to the two players on clay.

2007 – One year after squeaking out a 7-5 in the third set victory over Nicolas Almagro in the quarterfinals of the Italian Championships, top-ranked Roger Federer again beats the Spaniard in Rome, this time by a 6-3, 6-4 in the second round. "I wasn't too happy when I saw the draw come out because he's a great clay-courter and a very dangerous player on any surface," Federer says of Almagro. "So to come through convincingly in two sets, not being broken and both times racing away with the lead with an early break, was perfect."

2008 – Top-ranked Roger Federer withstands 12 aces from 6-foot-10 Ivo Karlovic and defeats the Croatian 7-6 (4), 6-3 in the round of 16 of the Italian Championships in Rome.

"It's difficult to judge against him. Ivo has an unbelievable serve, probably the best we have in the game," says Federer of the Karlovic serve, consistently clocked over 130 mph. "And he comes to the net too, so there's always a lot of pressure."

2010 – Roger Federer crashes out of the semifinals of the semifinals of the Estoril Open, falling to defending champion Albert Montanes of Spain by a 6-2, 7-6 (5) margin. Federer hits 48 unforced errors, mostly off his backhand side.

2003 – In 49 minutes, Roger Federer crushes No. 19-ranked Tommy Robredo 6-1, 6-1 to advance into the quarterfinals of the Italian Championships in Rome. "Who expected this? To beat Tommy Robredo 1-1 on clay?" says Federer to reporters following the match. "I'm very, very pleased. The match went well from the start. I felt good on the returns, tried to keep the rallies short on my own service games. It worked perfectly so I didn't have to change anything. I had the perfect game plan and I'm very happy."

May 9

2001 – Reigning U.S. Open champion Marat Safin leads Roger Federer by a set and a break, but falters and loses to the 19-year-old Swiss 4-6, 6-4, 7-6 (6) in the second round of the Italian Championships in Rome. Federer closes out the match with an ace, one of his 43 winners in the match against 64 unforced errors. Safin blamed his loss on a lack of practice since he suffered a back injury in March.

He says he had only began to practice late the previous week. Federer compares himself with the fiery Russian to reporters following the victory, saying he too can be as unpredictable. "I think we are very similar," Federer says. "We get cross on the court if we're not happy with our games. We are disappointed when it's not going well. We are happy when it works well. I think we can both hit shots, like, you don't expect. So I think we have something similar. Of course Marat is, ranking-wise and result-wise, in a different league, but I hope I can catch up with him."

2003 – Playing in front of a spirited Italian crowd, Roger Federer defeats Filippo Volandri 6-3, 5-7, 6-2 in the quarterfinals of the Italian Open, preventing Volandri from becoming the first home country Italian Open semifinalist in 25 years. Following the win, Federer speaks to reporters about the difficulties of playing an Italian in Rome. "It's little bit strange· because I really like the Italians when they have no favorite basically, but when you play against Italian, they can be very mean to you," says Federer of the Italian Open crowds. "I felt sometimes little treated unfair out there but I try not to show anything. I was a little bit disappointed sometimes, just the way people were talking to me. You know, you hear it. It's just sometimes, I thought, it was just a little bit overboard. You can do it once, but they did it like 20 times. Always to hear what you say sometimes during a match, I'm really not a guy that shows too much emotions, they kind of use this. It was a little bit something I didn't quite like, but I guess and I hope that the crowd's gonna be a little bit more behind me next match. You know, just to add, I have no problem, I actually quite like this. I understand that they're supporting the

Italian. This is what they should do. But if they go against the other guy – and this was only let's say five guys in the crowd – and this was a little bit the people who I had problems with. But the rest were good but it's just a few which didn't act the way they should. Support their player is fine, but not go against their opponent. That's just my way of looking at fair play."

2005 – Returning to play after a three-week layoff due to feet inflammation, world No. 1 Roger Federer defeats Fernando Verdasco 6-4, 6-3 in his opening round match at the Italian Open.

2008 – The backhand Roger Federer completely breaks down as the world No. 1 is stunned in the quarterfinals of the Italian Championships, falling to No. 27-ranked Radek Stepanek of the Czech Republic 7-6 (4), 7-6 (7). Says Federer of the erratic backhand, "You've seen me many times, it happens all the time. It's something I've been trying to get rid of for 10 years but still not today...I don't know if it was just the backhand. I think I missed plenty of opportunities throughout the match. He's difficult to play. He gives you little rhythm and he always changes his game up a lot." Says Stepanek of Federer, "He definitely doesn't have the results he was used to in previous years, but the other players are getting better."

2013 – No. 2-ranked Roger Federer, playing in his first event after a two-month layoff, suffers a shock upset loss to No. 16-ranked Kei Nishikori of Japan 6-4, 1-6, 6-2 in the third round of the Madrid Open. "I was lacking control from the baseline, and that pretty much carried through from start to finish," Federer says. "Overall, I'm pretty disappointed with my play. I'm not sure how well Kei thought he played. I didn't think he had to play his very best either, which is even more disappointing. It doesn't change my mindset going forward. I'm going to go back to the practice court, train hard, and make sure I don't have these kind of days anymore."

May 10

2001 – One day after upsetting reigning U.S. Open champion Marat Safin, Roger Federer is defeated 7-6 (4), 6-2 on a rain-soaked day by Wayne Ferreira in the third round of the Italian Championships in Rome.

2003 – Roger Federer advances into the Italian Open final in Rome for the first time when No. 2-seeded Juan Carlos Ferrero retires due to an arm injury trailing 6-4, 4-2. Federer advances to face another Spaniard Felix Mantilla, who rallies past Yevgeny Kafelnikov 4-6, 7-6 (3), 6-4. Federer says in his post-match press conference that he is "not far away" from breaking through and winning a major singles title and becoming the No. 1 player in the world. "My ranking shows it, the way I'm playing, the people who I beat, but it takes more," Federer says. "It takes one year around to play very solid tennis and play well in the big events and to get a chance to be No. 1 or to win a Grand Slam. So I'm not thinking about No. 1 right now. It's more match per match and to try to be as consistent as possible. When I see that I have a chance to be No. 1, then I'll try my best to get there, but right now, I'm just too far away from (Andre) Agassi and (Lleyton) Hewitt in the points-wise, I think. You would need over more than one Grand Slam win to get close to them. So I'll just try to play well in the small tournaments and hopefully use my chance in the Slams in the future."

2006 – Inspired by a morning meeting with the Pope, Roger Federer advances into the third round of the Italian Championships defeating Potito Starace of Italy 6-3, 7-6 (2). Says Federer of meeting the Holy Father, "Yes. It was an emotional day today. In the morning, meeting the Pope was very, very nice and a big honor of course. Got to shake his hand, exchange a few words in German, and that's it. But of course, it was very special for me. I'm Catholic after all, so it was very nice. Then, after on, the great match here. It was a perfect day."

2007 – In one of the most surprising upsets ever at the Italian Championships, world No. 1 Roger Federer is defeated by No. 53-ranked Filippo Volandri of Italy 6-2, 6-4 in the third round. Says Federer, "I just couldn't get into the game. I was serving horrendous, and you don't get any free points on clay if you are not serving well. It is very disappointing to go out at this stage of the tournament, but it does happen in tennis." Federer, the runner-up in Rome in 2003 and 2006, is put in the unusual position of going four straight events without winning a title – his longest stretch without winning a tournament becoming world No. 1 in February 2004.

May 11

2003 – Felix Mantilla of Spain upends Roger Federer 7-5, 6-2, 7-6 (8) to become an unlikely singles champion at the Italian Open in Rome. The 28-year-old Mantilla, who says that his game does not have "the serve of Pete Sampras, the volley of Pat Rafter, nor the talent of Andre Agassi" capitalizes on 69 unforced errors from Federer to win the biggest title of his career. Says Mantilla following the victory, "I felt like I have found my inner self." Says Federer of the loss, "The whole match was extremely disappointing for me. He (Mantilla) plays patient and it's a little bit boring. Whatever shot you play, good or bad, it comes back the same way. It just became frustrating, and after making such a dreadful start I had the feeling that his victory was meant to be."

1997 – At the age of 15, Federer wins his first ITF world junior tournament in Prato, Italy, defeating Luka Kutanjac of Croatia 6-4, 6-0 in the final.

2004 – Roger Federer survives a difficult first-round match in Hamburg, defeating Gaston Gaudio of Argentina 6-1, 5-7, 6-4. Four weeks after the loss to Federer, Gaudio goes on to become the unlikely winner at the French Open.

2005 – In a match that lasts only 53 minutes, Roger Federer dominates Tomas Berdych 6-2, 6-1 in the second round of the Hamburg Masters in Germany. Federer slams 25 winners against only six from his Czech opponent.

2010 – Roger Federer withstands a tough second-set challenge from Benjamin Becker, but advances in to the third round of the Madrid Masters with a 6-2, 7-6 (4) win over the German.

2006 – Roger Federer defeats Radek Stepanek 6-1, 6-4 in 56 minutes to advance into the quarterfinals of the Italian Championships in Rome.

May 12

2007 – Roger Federer announces his split with his coach of more than three years Tony Roche. Federer announces the change via his web site RogerFederer.com calling the decision mutual. Federer's most recent result was a third-round loss in Rome, his fourth consecutive tournament without a title, his longest such drought since he rose to No. 1 in the rankings in February of 2004.

2004 – Roger Federer improves his record to 28-3 on the season with a 6-3, 6-3 win over Nicolas Lapentti of Ecuador to move into the third round of the Hamburg Masters in Germany.

2005 – Roger Federer beats Tommy Robredo 6-2, 6-3 to reach the quarterfinals of the Hamburg Masters in Germany.

2006 – Top-ranked Roger Federer needs five match points, and two hours and 33 minutes, to beat Spanish qualifier

Nicolas Almagro, 6-3, 6-7 (2), 7-5 in the quarterfinals of the Italian Championships.

2009 – Roger Federer opens up play in his final tournament before the French Open by defeating Robin Soderling of Sweden 6-1, 7-6 at the Madrid Masters, hitting 24 winners against 25 unforced errors from Soderling. Three weeks later in Paris, Federer unexpectedly meets Soderling again in the final of the French Open, again beating the Swede 6-1, 7-6(1), 6-4 to win at Roland Garros for the first time.

May 13

2012 – Roger Federer wins 74th title of his career, edging Tomas Berdych 3-6, 7-5, 7-5 to win the Madrid Open, played on a controversial blue-colored clay. The win moves Federer ahead of Rafael Nadal into the No. 2 ranking. "It is amazing to win here again," says Federer of winning in Madrid for a third time. "It has been a tough tournament. Tough to move, but you've got to try to make the most of it. Here there was some good tennis and some bad tennis, but you see that in all tournaments."

2006 – Roger Federer escapes the upset bid by David Nalbandian in a final-set tie-breaker as the world No. 1 advanced into his 13th consecutive final with a 6-3, 3-6, 7-6 (5) victory in the semifinals of the Italian Championships. Federer survives against the No. 3 ranked Nalbandian despite finishing with 50 unforced errors against 53 by Nalbandian.

2004 – Roger Federer advances into the quarterfinals of the Tennis Masters Hamburg defeating Fernando Gonzalez, 7-5, 6-1 in 74 minutes in the second career meeting between the two players.

2005 – Roger Federer beats 2004 French Open runner-up Guillermo Coria 6-4, 7-6 (3) to reach the semifinals of the Tennis Masters Series Hamburg.

2010 – Roger Federer advances to the quarterfinals of the Madrid Masters beating fellow Swiss and Olympic doubles partner Stanislas Wawrinka 6-3, 6-1,

May 14

2006 – In an epic match that officially cements the rivalry between Roger Federer and Rafael Nadal as one of the greatest in the sport, Nadal defeats Federer 6-7 (0), 7-6 (5), 6-4, 2-6, 7-6 (5) in five hours and six minutes in the final of the Italian Open in Rome. Federer leads by 4-1 in the fifth set and holds two match points at 5-6 in the fifth set, before he lets the 19-year-old from Mallorca back into the match to successfully defend his Italian title. Says Federer, "I'm on the right track, a step closer with this guy, just got caught at the finish line, but I should have won." The win for Nadal is his 53rd straight win on clay, tying the Open era record of Guillermo Vilas and also marks his 16th career singles title, tying Bjorn Borg for the most titles won as a teenager.

2005 – Top-ranked Roger Federer beats Nikolay Davydenko of Russia 6-3, 6-4 to reach the final of the Tennis Masters Series Hamburg and set up a re-match with Frenchman Richard Gasquet, one of only two men to beat him in the last eight months. "I am definitely looking forward to a second chance to get him," Federer says of Gasquet, who beat him at the Monte Carlo Open the previous month. "I have more ideas now how to approach the match."

2004 – Roger Federer beats Carlos Moya 6-4, 6-3 to reach the semifinals of the Hamburg Masters in Germany in his first-ever clay court meeting with the 1998 French Open champion. Federer also won all three previous meetings on other surfaces against the Spaniard.

2008 – Top-ranked Roger Federer needs only 58 minutes to register his ninth consecutive straight-set victory over Jarkko Nieminen, beating the Finnish player 6-1, 6-3 to advance into the third round of the Tennis Masters Series – Hamburg.

2009 – Roger Federer advances to the quarterfinals of the Madrid Open defeating James Blake 6-2, 6-4.

2010 – Roger Federer rallies from a set and a break down to defeat Ernests Gulbis 3-6, 6-1, 6-4 in the quarterfinals of the Madrid Open. Federer avenges his loss to Gulbis from two weeks earlier in Rome. "I think it's one of the toughest things in tennis if you lose against a player and you have to play against him in the next couple of weeks," Federer says. "I was very happy with the way I was able to return and mix up the game a bit and at the end I thought it was a really great performance." Gulbis breaks Federer to start to the second set, but immediately breaks back en route to losing six games in a row to lose the second set. He breaks for a 2-1 lead in the third set and never is again threatened on his serve.

May 15

2003 – Roger Federer loses to Mark Philippoussis 6-3, 2-6, 6-3 in third round of the Hamburg Masters Series – the first, and only time, the Australian would beat Federer in his career. The two would next face each other six weeks later in the singles final at Wimbledon, where Federer is able to win his first major singles title with a 7-6 (5), 6-2, 7-6 (3) victory.

2005 – Roger Federer defeats Richard Gasquet of France 6-3, 7-5, 7-6 (4) to win the Tennis Masters Series – Hamburg in Germany for his 28th career singles title. Federer's win avenges his loss to the 18-year-old Gasquet in the quarterfinals of the Monte Carlo Open the previous month – one of only two losses Federer suffers in his last 59 matches. With the win over Gasquet, Federer increases his record on the year to 41-2 and to 57-2 dating back to the U.S. Open. "Once you've won once or twice here, you come into the tournament with confidence," says Federer, who wins the title without losing a set.

2004 – Roger Federer and Lleyton Hewitt face off against each other for the first time on clay as Federer dominates Hewitt 6-0, 6-4 to reach the Hamburg Masters final in

Germany for the second time in his career. "I guess I could have served better, but apart from that, he was just too good," says Hewitt, who had won seven of the 10 previous meetings with Federer.

2008 – Roger Federer wins his sixth career match with Robin Soderling – against no losses – beating the Swede 6-3, 6-2 to advance into the quarterfinals of the Tennis Masters Series Hamburg.

2009 – In the only clay-court meeting between Roger Federer and Andy Roddick, Federer defeats Roddick 7-5, 6-7 (5), 6-1 to reach the semifinals of the Madrid Open. Federer improves his head-head record against Roddick to 18-2 with the victory.

2010 – Roger Federer increases his record to 10-0 against David Ferrer, beating his Spanish opponent 7-5, 3-6, 6-3 in the semifinals of the Madrid Open. The win sets up a final-round match with Rafael Nadal, whom he had not played since the 2009 Madrid final, won by Federer.

May 16

2004 – Roger Federer ends the 31-match clay court winning streak of Guillermo Coria, defeating the Argentine 4-6, 6-4, 6-2, 6-3 to win the Tennis Masters Series Hamburg singles title in Germany for the second time. "I have the experience of big finals now, and I also know that I've played well in them and won them," says the No. 1-ranked Federer after the victory. "It was a very important win for me. I am more relaxed now before the French." The loss is the first on clay for Coria since the previous year's French Open semifinals.

2009 – Rafael Nadal saves three match points in an epic four hour, 3 minute 3-6, 7-6 (5), 7-6 (9) semifinal win over Novak Djokovic at the Madrid Open to set up a final-round meeting with Roger Federer, who easily defeats Juan Martin del Potro 6-3, 6-4 in the other semifinal. "What's important for me is to get past that semifinal hurdle that I haven't been able to get past in the last couple of months," says Federer.

2007 – In his first match since his split with his coach Tony Roche, Roger Federer struggles to beat Juan Monaco of Argentina 6-3, 2-6, 6-4 in his opening match at the Tennis Masters Series – Hamburg. The match is the first career meeting between the two players.

2008 – Roger Federer has little trouble with Fernando Verdasco in the quarterfinals of the Tennis Masters Series – Hamburg, defeating the Spaniard 6-3, 6-3.

2010 – Rafael Nadal defeats top-ranked Roger Federer 6-4, 7-6 (5) in the final of the Madrid Open, reversing the result of the 2009 final – the last time the two legends faced off against each other in their epic rivalry. Nadal improves his head-to-head record against Federer to 14-7. "The clay-court season will not be judged here but in Paris," Federer says after the loss. "We will see what happens in three weeks. I feel I'm ready for Paris. I felt a major improvement in my game compared to last week when I came here from Estoril. It's been a wonderful event for me."

May 17

2002 – Roger Federer, seeded No. 11, beats No. 2 seeded Gustavo Kuerten 6-0, 1-6, 6-2 in the quarterfinals of the Tennis Masters Hamburg. Federer benefits from 17 unforced errors from Kuerten in the first set, before the Brazilian settles his game in the second set. Federer breaks Kuerten for an early 2-0 lead in the third set, before Kuerten breaks back, ties the score at 2-2, before Federer takes the final four games of the match.

2007 – Top-ranked Roger Federer needs only 65 minutes to advance into the quarterfinals of the Tennis Masters Series Hamburg with a 6-2, 6-3 win over Juan Carlos Ferrero of Spain. The win is Federer's fifth straight over Ferrero, the former world No. 1 and French Open champion, who won the first two – and three of the first five – career meetings with Federer.

2008 – While Roger Federer easily defeats Andreas Seppi of Italy 6-3, 6-1 in one semifinal of the Tennis Masters Series Hamburg, Federer's main rival Rafael Nadal wins an epic match with Novak Djokovic 7-5, 2-6, 6-2 in a match that determines the No. 2 ranking. With his win over Djokovic, Nadal keeps the No. 2 ranking for a 148th straight week – a record streak at that ranking.

2009 – Roger Federer beats top-ranked Rafael Nadal in his home country on a clay court, beating his Spanish rival 6-4, 6-4 in the final of the Madrid Open, his first title of the 2009 season. "There are no positives; there is little to analyze," says Nadal following the match. "He broke and broke and I went home." The win marks only the second time Federer had beaten Nadal on clay to go with his win over his chief rival in the final of Hamburg in 2007. The win also ends Federer's five-match losing streak to Nadal, a stretch that included losses in the finals of the 2008 French Open and Wimbledon and the 2009 Australian Open.

May 18

2013 – Roger Federer finishes off his first career meeting with Poland's Jerzy Janowicz after midnight in Rome 6-4, 7-6 (2) in the quarterfinals of the Italian Championships. Janowicz serves for the second set at 5-4, but hits crucial double faults and is broken back before Federer closes out the straight-set win in 85 minutes.

2002 – Roger Federer advances into the final of the Tennis Masters Series Hamburg – his second career final at a Masters Series event – defeating Max Mirnyi 6-4, 6-4.

2008 – One year after having his 81-match clay court winning streak snapped on the same court, Rafael Nadal exacts revenge on Roger Federer, beating the world No. 1 7-5, 6-7 (3), 6-3 in the final of the Hamburg Masters in Germany. The title is Nadal's first in Hamburg and completes a career sweep of the major clay court titles, joining former world No. 1 players Marcelo Rios and Gustavo Kuerten as only the third man to sweep Monte Carlo, Rome and Hamburg. "It was a strange match," Nadal says. "Roger made some mistakes in the first set that helped me…It was important to win because it was the last big clay-court tournament I never won." Nadal raises his record against Federer to 8-1 on clay and 10-6 overall. "I could have served a little better; it wasn't my best performance, maybe. I have to go for big serves -- he is a good return player," says Federer, who had won the previous 41 matches he played in Germany, dating back to 2003.

2007 – Top-ranked Roger Federer struggles to subdue No. 12 seeded David Ferrer 6-3, 4-6, 6-3 in the quarterfinals of the Tennis Masters Series – Hamburg. The match marks the first time Federer loses a set to Ferrer but increases his head-to-head record against the Spaniard to 7-0.

May 19

2002 – Roger Federer dominates Marat Safin to win his first Tennis Masters Series title at the German Open in Hamburg, defeating the Russian 6-1, 6-3, 6-4 in the singles final. Federer calls the win, at the time, "probably the best match of my career." Says Federer, "I played really well. It has been a wonderful tournament for me, really incredible. I have played well all week and it gives me great confidence going into the French Open." Says Safin, "He played too good, I couldn't do much. I have more experience than him and was probably the favorite but

I didn't really play very well, as you can see. I couldn't bring my tennis to the court and he played probably the best game of tennis in his life." Federer cracks the top 10 in the ATP singles rankings the next day by virtue of his results.

2007 – Roger Federer beats Carlos Moya 4-6, 6-4, 6-2 to set up a final-round match-up with Rafael Nadal at the Tennis Masters Series Hamburg. "It's nice to come back from one set down," Federer says. "I came out of it but I am still missing too much. You have to believe that you can come back." Nadal wins his 81st straight match on a clay court with a hard-fought 2-6, 6-3, 7-5 decision over Lleyton Hewitt. "I feel good, it's always a special, interesting match," Nadal says of playing Federer, whom he had beaten all five times they have played on clay, including the final of the Monte Carlo Open earlier in the year. "I have no pressure; win or lose I will go to Paris with the best of confidence." Federer says that beating Nadal, to end his four-tournament streak without a title (the longest since he became No. 1), would be the ideal way to head into the French Open. "That would surely boost my energy, my motivation and my confidence for the French Open," he says.

2013 – Roger Federer and Rafael Nadal play for the 30th time and Nadal registers the most lopsided victory in a best-of-three-set match with a 6-1, 6-3 victory in 69 minutes in the Italian final in Rome. Nadal serves for the match at 6-1, 5-1 but is not able to close out the even more one-sided victory. "For that to happen between two players with not that much difference, it has to be because one player plays very well and the other is having more mistakes than usual," says Nadal, who increases his career head-to-head advantage over Federer to 20-10. "That's all." Says Federer simply, "Rafa was just too good today."

May 20

2007 – Roger Federer ends Rafael Nadal's 81-match winning streak on clay, defeating the Spaniard 2-6, 6-2, 6-0 in the final of the Hamburg Masters in Germany. "It was an incredible performance from my side," says the world No. 1. "I had a great day, it's nice to be playing well again. It's my first title on clay in a couple of years." Says Nadal, who had not lost to Federer on clay in five previous matches, "If I have to lose against anyone, then he is the man. I am not sad to lose to the best in the world."

2002 – Roger Federer enters the top 10 of the ATP Rankings for the first time at No. 9, following his tournament victory at the Tennis Masters Series event in Hamburg, Germany.

May 21

In 2012, tennis historian Steve Flink released his book "The Greatest Tennis Matches of All Time" during the French Open and named the Roger Federer vs. Rafael Nadal 2008 Wimbledon singles final, won by Nadal 6-4, 6-4, 6-7 (4), 6-7(9, 9-7, as the greatest match of all time. Flink rated the match ahead of the No. 2 ranked match, the 1980 Wimbledon men's singles final between Bjorn Borg and John McEnroe won by Borg 1-6, 7-5,

*6-3, 6-7 (16-18), 8-6, and the No. 3 ranked match, the 1926
Cannes final in France when Suzanne Lenglen defeated Helen
Wills 6-3, 8-6.*

*Roger Federer is, without question, one of the greatest shotmakers
in the history of tennis. Mary Carillo, when broadcasting tennis
matches for ESPN, hosted a feature on many occasions called
"The Federer Fun House" that featured highlights of some of
Federer's spectacular shots. At the 2010 Australian Open,
Federer was asked if he is genuinely surprised by some of the
shots he is able to conjure up. "Well, I mean, quite often," Federer
said. "Even though I know I can play really good shots and come
up with great backhands, forehands, serves and volleys, and
stuff, when you can really produce them in the most important
stages of a match it's so rewarding and such a good feeling that
all the hard work you put in in the off-season is so like -- it's
just a beautiful feeling. Then if you can start to hit a dropshot or
dig in the corner and get the ball back that you think you would
never get, but it's a match situation and the adrenaline is there
and you just got that extra speed and you get the ball back and
end up winning the point, it does still obviously surprise me
even today."*

May 22

2000 – Roger Federer begins the week ranked No. 54 in
singles and No. 55 in doubles – the closest Federer ever
comes to having a higher doubles ranking than a singles
ranking. He achieves a career-high doubles ranking of No.
24 on June 9, 2003 when he also ranks No. 5 in the world
in singles.

2006 – Roger Federer is chosen as the "Sportsman of the Year" for the second straight time in the Laureus World Sports Awards.

2013 – Roger Federer, the recently named brand ambassador for Moet & Chandon champagne, heats up a mini-tennis court at the Park Hyatt Hotel in Paris with Moet & Chandon's Tiny Tennis 'Game, Set & Moet Challenge,' refereeing the matches and even taking to the court himself to hit some balls. "It's more than just an honor to be Moët & Chandon's brand ambassador, it's an invitation to be part of a very glamorous tradition," says Federer. "Moët & Chandon has always been the champagne of international trendsetters and I'm proud to be part of a brand that is as dedicated to the pursuit of excellence as I have been throughout my career."

"He simply does not have any more weaknesses left in him. It is such a pleasure to see him play. To me, Roger Federer is the right model for anyone aspiring to be a tennis player. It is such a pleasure to just watch him play. His shot-making has got better and I doubt there is any shot he cannot make in any part of the court...All records will tumble when it comes to Roger. He is such a complete player that I do not see anyone getting better than him for a long time from now."
—*Bjorn Borg on Roger Federer to Gulf News in the Middle East in 2007*

May 23

2005 – Top-seeded Roger Federer opens his 2005 French Open campaign with a 6-1, 6-4, 6-0 victory over Dudi Sela, a qualifier from Israel. Federer confesses after the match that he scouted his opponent only a half an hour before the match. "I warmed up next to him on the same court, that's it," says Federer. "I warmed up with my friend and he warmed up with his friend. I hadn't heard anything about him, so I think you can relax a little bit because he's not supposed to break through in this tournament. If you play tough, you know you should get through. Once I win the first set 6-1, I'm not usually going to lose a match."

2013 – With a message that reads "A little (blue) bird told me that the place to be is @twitter, so here I am!" Roger Federer posts his first message on his @RogerFederer account on Twitter. Federer gains 100,000 followers in five hours after his first tweet. The first four Twitter accounts that he follows are the four major championships that he has won.

"The Chatrier court is really, really big, and I just haven't had enough play on it," said Roger Federer after his 2004 third-round loss to Gustavo Kuerten at Roland Garros. "For me, it's not the surface, it's rather maybe the court."

May 24

2010 – Roger Federer opens up his defense of his French Open crown defeating No. 71-ranked Peter Luczak of Australia 6-4, 6-1, 6-2. Federer commits only 11 unforced errors and loses only 14 of 64 points on his serve and faces only one break point in the match. "It's always important coming back as defending champion trying to get off to a good start," says Federer. "It was like a perfect match to get off the French Open campaign, really." Writes Howard Fendrich of the Associated Press of Federer first stepping onto the Roland Garros clay as the tournament's defending champion, "The French-speaking voice booming through loudspeakers at Court Philippe Chatrier in Paris recited Roger Federer's bona fides during pre-match introductions, detailing his six titles at Wimbledon, five at the U.S. Open, four at the Australian Open and then, reaching a crescendo, concluded this way: "One at Roland Garros, here, last year!" Federer smiled. Fans roared, many rising to applaud."

2013 – In his pre-French Open press conference, Roger Federer is asked only asked about his chief rival Rafael Nadal in the first three questions posed to him from media. The third question posed to Federer concerns the difficulties in returning to the tour after injury as Nadal has in reaching the final of all eight tournaments he has played since being off tour for more than six months. Snaps Federer as an answer to the question, "I don't know. I have never been out for seven months."

2013 – Roger Federer participates in an AMA ("Ask Me Anything") Q&A session on the social news site Reddit under prior to the French Open. When asked whether he will bring out the "Darth Federer" all-black outfit that he wore at the U.S. Open, Federer responds, "I really loved that outfit. Under the lights in NYC. All black. That was awesome. No plans yet to bring it back yet., but we'll see." Federer lists the following as his toughest matches ever, "Hewitt in Davis Cup 03, Del Potro in Olympics 2012, Roddick Wimbledon 09, Nalbandian 05 World Tour Finals, final, Rafa Wimbledon 2008. One of the great matches I've been a part of." When asked if he could play doubles with one player living or dead, who would it be and why, Federer responds, "My three choices would be John McEnroe, Stefan Edberg and Rod Laver. From a historical perspective it would be really fun to play doubles with them as they are all legends."

May 25

1999 – Ranked No. 111 in the world, 17-year-old Roger Federer plays in his first main draw match at a major tournament at the French Open, losing to two-time reigning U.S. Open champion Patrick Rafter of Australia 5-7, 6-3, 6-0, 6-2. Writes Rene Stauffer in the book *Roger Federer: Quest for Perfection*, "He (Roger) jumped out to win the first set against the world's No. 3-ranked player who then was at the peak of his career. However, the sun came out and the conditions became warmer and faster. The clay courts dried out and balls moved much faster through the court. The Australian's attacking serve-and-volley style seemed to run on automatic and he won in four sets. 'The young man from Switzerland could be one of the people who will shape the next ten years,' the French sports newspaper *L'Equipe* wrote during the tournament. Rafter shared the same opinion. "The boy impressed me very much," he said. "If he works hard and has a good attitude, he could become an excellent player.""

2005 – World No. 1 Roger Federer makes headlines at the French Open, not with his easy 6-3, 7-6 (0), 6-2 win over Spain's Nicolas Almagro, but in his post-match press conference where he says that had said he told Jim Curley of the U.S. Tennis Association that he is against the U.S. Open's plans to implement an instant replay system. "I'm absolutely against it," Federer says. "I'm against the challenge system. I'm for the way it is right now; don't change that....I am concerned about the amount of money that will be blown on this for just a few points. It's money that I think we can use for other, different things. I am against the whole idea of replay."

2009 – Roger Federer has little trouble with Alberto Martin in the opening round of the French Open, defeating the Spaniard 6-4, 6-3, 6-2.

May 26

2003 – An expected contender to win the French Open seeded No. 5 and holding an ATP-best 38-8 record, Roger Federer crashes out in the first round at Roland Garros, falling 7-6 (6), 6-2, 7-6 (3) to No. 88-ranked Luis Horna, a player from Peru playing at the French Open for the first time. "I don't know how long I'll need to get over this defeat," Federer says following the match. "A day, a week, a year—or my entire career." Writes Rene Stauffer in the book "The loss undeniably confirmed Federer's reputation as a Grand Slam loser. He showed that he was a player who could not pull out a match even though he was not playing his best tennis—a characteristic that most champion tennis players exhibited, most notably in the present by Lleyton Hewitt, who could win a match on guts and determination alone. Since his victory over Sampras at Wimbledon in 2001, Federer was 0-4 in matches at the French Open and Wimbledon—the last three matches without even winning a set. His last five Grand Slam tournaments ended in defeat at the hands of much lower-ranked players."

2008 – Roger Federer defeats Sam Querrey 6-4, 6-4, 6-3 in the first round at Roland Garros. Federer loses his serve once to the American early in the first set, but counters with five service breaks of his own. "Once I got settled I played a little bit more better," Federer says. "I was able to create myself a few opportunities against his serve, which was sort of good. Hopefully, I can play a bit better the next match."

2010 – Forced off the court by two rain delays, Roger Federer posts a 7-6 (4), 6-2, 6-4 victory over Alejandro Falla in the second round of the French Open. During the rain delays, Federer is told by his Davis Cup captain Severin Luthi to be more aggressive and to use more drops shots, which Federer credits to helping to achieve victory. "Those were good things he told me," says Federer. "Those little details make a crucial difference."

2013 – Starting his French Open campaign by playing on the controversial first Sunday, Roger Federer defeats Spanish qualifier Pablo Carreno-Busta 6-2, 6-2, 6-3. "I told them if they wanted me to play Sunday, whatever, I'm fine with it," says Federer, seeded No. 2, of French Open officials and the Sunday start. "They took that opportunity right away." Federer loses only seven points on his first serve in the match against the No. 164-ranked player, playing in a Grand Slam tournament for the first time in his career. Says Carreno-Busta of first learning he would face Federer in his major tournament debut, "My first thought was 'What bad luck!' I wanted to win and move ahead in the tournament and improve my ranking, and playing against someone like Federer is going to make that difficult. But as I thought about it more ... I tried to appreciate it."

May 27

2004 – Roger Federer staves off two set points in the third set and defeats Nicolas Kiefer 6-3, 6-4, 7-6 (6) to advance into a marquee third round match-up with former world No. 1 Gustavo Kuerten at the French Open. "It's a great match for the tournament and for us too," Federer says of playing Kuerten. "We haven't played much because of injury or playing sometimes on different surfaces. ... So if I can get through him I think that is for me a huge step."

2005 – Roger Federer saves two set-points in a first-set tiebreaker then holds on to defeat No. 25 Fernando Gonzalez of Chile 7-6 (9), 7-5, 6-2 in the third-round of the French Open. After the match, when asked by reporters who he fears most in the tournament, Federer answers, "No one. I'm No. 1. I've beaten everyone. Why should I fear anyone? I respect everyone, that's for sure."

May 28

2002 – Seen as a dark horse favorite to win his maiden Grand Slam tournament title, No. 8 seed Roger Federer is upset by No. 45-ranked Hicham Arazi of Morocco 6-3, 6-2, 6-4 in the opening round of the French Open. Federer, fresh off entering the top 10 for the first time by virtue of his victory in Hamburg, commits 58 unforced errors in the 95-minute match on Court No. 2 at Roland Garros. Federer cites the heavy, wet conditions to contributing to his loss. "They were not suited for my game, obviously," he says. "I've never experienced anything like it, raining consistently for over 21/2 sets. If it rains really [hard], we can stop. But it was just raining enough, so we could keep playing. That was a little bit unlucky."

2006 – In the first ever Sunday start at the French Open, Roger Federer is on the day's schedule, despite not requesting it, and is not pleased. Federer does beat Argentine lucky loser Diego Hartfield 7-5, 7-6 (2), 6-2, in two hours 35 minutes, but vents his displeasure with the scheduling in his post-match press conference. "I only knew one day ahead who I was going to play, and I never heard of his name or never seen him before," Federer says of Hartfield, who replaced Federer's original opponent, Arnaud Clement of France, who pulls out of the tournament the day before due to injury. "I'm happy I didn't lose, because otherwise I'd be very angry right now.... I requested not to play Sunday, so I wasn't happy to play today. But I'm through." Federer then jokes, "I can go home to Switzerland, come back in four days and be ready for Wednesday."

2012 – Roger Federer equals Jimmy Connors' record of 233 Grand Slam match victories defeating Germany's Tobias Kamke 6-2, 7-5, 6-3 in the opening round of the French Open. "Weird with all the press I do, I didn't even know that," Federer says to ESPN's Brad Gilbert when presented with his record-tying stat on live television. Says Federer in his post-match press conference, "I get a great deal of pleasure playing here. When I play well, the numbers come with me. It's great to have played and won here so often. I hope it continues."

2009 – Roger Federer endures a tense second-round match at Roland Garros, escaping the near upset bid of Jose Acasuso of Argentina by a 7-6 (10-8), 5-7, 7-6 (7-2), 6-2 margin. The 45th-ranked Acasuso holds four set points in the first set and, after winning the second, holds another set point in the third set. "Mentally, I've always been very strong, but I'm not being put in a position like this very often, you know," Federer says. "Coming through such a match is always a great feeling. Like I said, I'm not part of such close matches that often." Says Acasuso, "I thought, I could have won this match."

2010 – Top-ranked Roger Federer reaches the fourth round of the French Open beating German qualifier Julian Reister 6-4, 6-0, 6-4. "I feel fine," Federer says. "I haven't faced the top guys yet but the players I have faced are dangerous, they all have their own skills on this surface. The guy today has played five matches here (three qualifiers and two main draw), so I couldn't underestimate him."

May 29

2004 – In a hallmark match in the career of Roger Federer, the world No. 1 and reigning Wimbledon and Australian Open champion is upset in the third round of the French Open by three-time champion Gustavo Kuerten 6-4, 6-4, 6-4. The loss, however, marks the beginning of an unprecedented level of consistency for Federer at Grand Slam tournaments as he reaches at least the semifinals of his next 23 major championships and reaches at least the quarterfinals in his next 36 major championships. Writes Liz Clarke of the *Washington Post* of the upset, "No player had been in better form entering the tournament than Federer, the world's No. 1 player, whose unease on clay appeared to have been remedied. But against Kuerten, a master of the capricious, clay-court surface, Federer lost both his footing and confidence." Says Federer of his play in the loss, "I think my game today had a lot to do with his game. Obviously, usually I can control these kind of matches, but today I couldn't. That's a credit to him."

2005 – Roger Federer has little trouble with an injured Carlos Moya in the fourth round of the French Open, beating the tournament's 1998 champion 6-1, 6-4, 6-3. Moya enters the match with a shoulder injury that prevents him from playing at his best. "He had no faith in his tennis, and was obviously disappointed to have to play like he did," says Federer. "I was surprised he even managed to finish the match, which proves he's a real champion. But I'm glad that I was able to save some energy."

2007 – I don't think he hits the hardest ball," says Michael Russell of Roger Federer after a rain-interrupted 6-4, 6-2, 6-4 first-round French Open loss to the Swiss, "and I don't think he hits the heaviest ball, but there's so much spin on it, you never really feel like you can get him off balance."

2008 – Roger Federer doesn't lose his serve, but drops the first set in beating Albert Montanes of Spain 6-7 (7-5), 6-1, 6-0, 6-4 in the second round of the French Open. "It was tough going down a set, but reaction was good and bounced back strong," Federer tells reporters after the match. "Played really well after that."

2013 – Roger Federer has little resistance with qualifier Somdev Devvarman of India, needing 82 minutes to advance into the third round with a 6-2, 6-1, 6-1 victory. Says the No. 188-ranked Devvarman of playing Federer, "I felt like I was playing wheelchair tennis and he was just playing on a PlayStation."

May 30

2012 – Roger Federer wins his 234th match at a major tournament – moving him past Jimmy Connors as the all-time leader in that category – defeating Romania's Adrian Ungur 6-3, 6-2, 6-7, 6-3 in the second round of the French Open. "That's a big one, because that was longevity," Federer says. "Jimmy is obviously one of the greats of all time and was around for 20 years."

2007 – In the cloud-filled, rainy, early evening, Roger Federer dispatches a stubborn Thierry Ascione of France 6-1, 6-2, 7-6 (10-8) in the second round of the French Open, blowing two match points while serving for the match at 5-4 in the third set and three more in the third-set tiebreaker.

2009 – Playing what Chuck Culpepper of the *Los Angeles Times* describes as "some of the most picturesque tennis imaginable" Roger Federer defeats No. 35-ranked Paul-Henri Mathieu 4-6, 6-1, 6-4, 6-4 in the third round of the French Open.

2010 – Roger Federer beats Olympic doubles partner Stan Wawrinka, 6-3, 7-6 (5), 6-2 in the fourth round of the French Open to set up a Roland Garros final rematch from the previous year against No. 5-seeded Robin Soderling. When asked how he feels about the match-up with Soderling, a man who he has beaten all 12 times they have met, Federer says, "Obviously, that's a good record to have, but because of the improvements he's made, he's an opponent not to underestimate."

2013 – Federer visits the Eiffel Tower in Paris for the first time during an off day from the French Open. Federer sends the seventh tweet of his short life on Twitter with the following message "I really enjoyed going on top of the Eiffel Tower for the first time in my life today."

May 31

2005 – Roger Federer and Rafael Nadal each advance into a highly-anticipated semifinal at the French Open as the No. 1 seeded Federer reaches his first semifinal at Roland Garros without the loss of a set, straight-setting Victor Hanescu 6-2, 7-6 (3), 6-3, while Nadal beats David Ferrer 7-5, 6-2, 6-0. "Well, everybody's been looking forward a little bit to this one – both of us, first time in the semifinals of a French Open," Federer says of their first career meeting a major tournament, also to be played on Nadal's 19th birthday. "So it's going to be really interesting to see. For me, it's a big moment. It's one of those chances to maybe walk away with the title here."

2006 – In a match where the off-court time due to rain delays extends longer than the actual match time, Roger Federer needs 86 minutes to register a 6-1, 6-4, 6-3 win over Alejandro Falla of Colombia in the second round of the French Open. The match is delayed on two occasions by rain for more than an hour and a half combined. "It's not easy to come on and off" the court, Federer says. "You always hope your game is still there and it hasn't left you."

2008 – Roger Federer wins his fifth straight match against Mario Ancic since his first-round loss to the Croatian in the first round of Wimbledon in 2002 with a 6-3, 6-4, 6-2 dismissal in the third round of the French Open. Curiously, the match is contested between two high-profile victims in the sport of glandular fever, Ancic missing six months of the 2007 season with the disease and Federer suffering at the start of the season. "I'm happy with the way I'm playing," Federer says following the win over the No. 46-ranked Ancic. "I haven't lost much energy in the first week and I'm happy to get through and to give myself an opportunity. I'm happy to be in the fourth round and to be the favorite."

2013 – Roger Federer hits 37 winners and wins his 57th career match win at Roland Garros with a 6-3, 6-4, 7-5 third-round win over Julien Benneteau of France. "I'm happy because I have not used much of my energy so far," says Federer, who advances to the round of 16 without the loss of a set. "Mentally, I'm OK. I'm quite confident. I can feel it, which is what you need to be if you want to go deep and have good results here at Roland Garros."

JUNE

June 1

2009 – Roger Federer strikes perhaps the most important single stroke of his career, connecting on an inside-out forehand cross court winner that lands on the line for a winner down two-sets-to-love, 3-4, break point against Tommy Haas in the fourth round of the French Open. The winner prevents Haas from serving for a straight-set upset and marks the turning point in the match as Federer rallies for a 6-7 (4), 5-7, 6-4, 6-0, 6-2 win, capturing 15 of the last 17 games of the match. "I knew I was going to look back on that shot," Federer says of fortuitous forehand. "That saved me on the day, you know." With Robin Soderling's upset the previous day of four-time champion Rafael Nadal, Federer's conqueror the last four years at Roland Garros, Federer's advancement into the quarterfinals continues his more realistic dream of winning his first French Open championship and win a career Grand Slam. Says Haas, "(Novak) Djokovic is out, Nadal is out, maybe Roger was feeling it a little bit knowing this is maybe a great opportunity for him to win and he puts a little extra pressure on him." Writes Chuck Culpepper in the *Los*

Angeles Times of the famous Federer forehand, "It made a gorgeous thwack in the sun. It went screaming across the court and above the net and toward the sideline without a hint of fear. It landed obediently maybe two inches shy of doom. The inside-out forehand Roger Federer struck at midday Monday at Roland Garros already drips with relevance. Already it has rescued the alluring new narrative of the 2009 French Open, the question of whether Federer will capitalize on the shocking removal of his great nemesis Rafael Nadal and win the only Grand Slam china he lacks." Concludes Haas of the Federer shot, "You just got to tip your hat and say, 'That's why he's Roger Federer.'"

2010 – Roger Federer's streak of 23 consecutive semifinal appearances at major tournaments is snapped dramatically in the quarterfinals of the French Open as Robin Soderling avenges his final-round loss at Roland Garros from the previous year with a 3-6, 6-3, 7-5, 6-4 victory in heavy, damp conditions in Paris. The loss was Federer's first to Soderling in 12 previous matches against the Swede. "I didn't think I played a bad match," says Federer of the upset loss to the No. 5 seed Soderling that featured a 75-minute rain delay in the third set. "He came up with some great tennis. It's much easier to digest this way." The loss, combined with Rafael Nadal's eventually winning the championship, also bumps Federer out of the No. 1 ranking, preventing the Swiss from equaling and breaking the all-time weeks-ranked-No. 1-record of 286 weeks set by Pete Sampras. "You take defeat as it comes," Federer says. "You don't think of the consequences. I guess that I am most disappointed that I can't defend my title here. I really felt like my tennis was good enough to come here and do it again, but that was not the case today." Quips Federer of the end of his consecutive major semifinal streak, "It was a great run. Now I've got the quarterfinal streak going, I guess."

2007 – Roger Federer beats Potito Starace of Italy 6-2, 6-3, 6-0 to reach the fourth round of the French Open. "I didn't make any mistakes," Federer says simply after the victory.

June 2

2013 – Roger Federer secures his 900th career ATP singles match victory of his career, rallying from two-sets-to-one down to defeat Frenchman Gilles Simon 6-1, 4-6, 2-6, 6-2, 6-3 in the fourth round of the French Open. The win advances Federer into the quarterfinals of a major tournament for a record-extending 36th consecutive time and also gives Federer his 58th career win at Roland Garros, surpassing the all-time singles match win record among men set by Guillermo Vilas and Nicola Pietrangeli. After leading 3-2 in the second set, Federer falls on the red clay and seems to hurt his wrist and goes on to lose 10 of the next 13 games. He then rallies to win seven straight games to take the fourth set and lead 3-0 in the fifth before closing out the match six games later.

2000 – Reaching the round of 16 of a major tournament for the first time in his career, Roger Federer defeats fellow Swiss Michel Kratochvil 7-6 (5), 6-4, 2-6, 6-7 (4), 8-6 in the third round of the French Open.

2006 – Roger Federer fights off dusk, and a late rally from reigning Olympic champion Nicolas Massu of Chile, to advance into the third round of the French Open by a 6-1, 6-2, 6-7 (4), 7-5 margin. The win sets up a round of 16 match with Tomas Berdych, who beat Federer at the Olympic Games in Athens, Greece, that was eventually won by Massu.

2008 – "He's always very calm," says Frenchman Julien Benneteau of Roger Federer after losing in his second career meeting with the Swiss maestro 6-4, 7-5, 7-5 in the fourth round of the French Open.

June 3

2005 – Rafael Nadal celebrates his 19th birthday and defeats Roger Federer 6-3, 4-6, 6-4, 6-3 in the semifinals of the French Open, the first meeting between the two in a Grand Slam tournament. Says the French Open rookie Nadal, "Federer, for me, is the best player wherever. Not only No. 1 for tennis, but the No. 1 for the person, and for sportsmanship." The two rivals will face each other in the French Open final for the next three years – and again in the 2011 final – Nadal winning each time. "Simple version for me is, um, started bad and finished bad, basically," says Federer of the semifinal loss to Nadal. "Was good in the middle and that was not good enough." Says Nadal, "It's incredible to beat Federer. Winning a semifinal is already incredible and beating Federer is even more amazing. I said to him, 'I'm sorry for you.' He said, 'No, no, you played very well.' He said, 'Good luck for the final. Good luck for the future.'" Writes Lisa Dillman of the *Los Angeles Times*, "Federer's usually trustworthy shot seemed almost to vanish from his arsenal. Somehow, it was fitting that the match ended when a Federer forehand floated long about 9:15 in the Paris evening."

2011 – Roger Federer ends the 43-match win streak of Novak Djokovic in the semifinals of the French Open with a 7-6 (5), 6-3, 3-6, 7-6 (5) victory. Djokovic enters the match undefeated on the year and not having lost a match since Federer beat him on November 27 of the previous year in the semifinals of the ATP World Tour Finals in London. "I wasn't here to spoil the party," says the No. 3-seeded Federer. "Almost feels, somewhat, like I've won the tournament, which is not the case. Silverware is still out there to be won, and I'm looking forward to the match with Rafa." Says Djokovic of the loss, "A loss cannot feel good, that's for sure, but, look, I know what to do. I handle myself better off the court, on the court. I'll just accept it as another loss." Two days later, Federer loses in the final at Roland Garros, falling to Rafael Nadal 7-5, 7-6 (3), 5-7, 6-1.

2007 – Roger Federer extends his Grand Slam streak of sets won to 35, equaling the record set by John McEnroe in 1984, with a 7-6 (3), 6-4, 6-4 win over No. 13 seed Mikhail Youzhny of Russia in the round of 16 of the French Open. Federer's Grand Slam set streak began by winning the last two sets against Andy Roddick in the 2006 U.S. Open final and included a 21-0 record in sets in winning the Australian Open in January and a 12-0 sets won record through four rounds of the French Open. Youzhny becomes only the fifth player since the U.S. Open to extend Federer to a tiebreaker. "He should have beat me here," Federer says. "I got lucky."

2012 – Roger Federer rallies for a 5-7, 7-5, 6-2, 6-4 fourth round French Open win over the boyish-looking David Goffin, a 21-year-old lucky loser from Belgium ranked No. 109 in the world who idolized Federer growing up. "I won't hide the fact that I had photos of Roger everywhere on the walls of my bedroom," says Goffin. "I came out of the qualifiers and I played my best tennis in my first three matches. Then playing Roger was the cherry on the cake. It was like a dream for me playing him here." Says Federer of the win that advances him into the quarterfinals, "I'm not used to playing against an opponent who loves me or loves the way I play. But I was aware that it had to happen someday, because it happened to me when I played against [Pete] Sampras or Andre Agassi."

2009 – In a rematch of a tense semifinal from the year before, Roger Federer again defeats Gael Monfils of France 7-6 (6), 6-2, 6-4 in the quarterfinals of the French Open, calling the match "my most consistent match of the tournament so far."

June 4

2000 – Alex Corretja ends the run of 18-year-old Roger Federer, defeating the young Swiss upstart 7-5, 7-6 (7), 6-2 in the fourth round of the French Open. The round of 16 finish marks the first time Federer had gone that far in a Grand Slam tournament. "Corretja played a great match but Roger was still able to hang in there for two hours," says Federer's coach Peter Lundgren to Rene Stauffer in the book *Roger Federer: Quest for Perfection.* "This experience will give him strength and self-confidence."

2006 – Roger Federer has little trouble with an erratic Tomas Berdych, beating the Czech 6-3, 6-2, 6-3 in the fourth round of the French Open.

2008 – Despite losing three of his first four service games, Roger Federer rallies to reach the semifinals of a major tournament for the 16th straight time with a 2-6, 6-2, 6-3, 6-4 win over Fernando Gonzalez of Chile at Roland Garros. "I was really under pressure in the first set," Federer says. "I felt uncomfortable. I was missing a lot of shots, and he defended well. After that it was a good match." After losing his serve three times in the 25-minute first set, Federer does not lose serve the rest of the match, winning 36 of his final 40 service points, including the last 17 in a row.

2013 – Roger Federer loses before the semifinals at a major event for only the fifth time in nine years as No. 6 seeded Jo-Wilfried Tsonga, spurred by a loud home French crowd, defeats Federer 7-5, 6-3, 6-3 in the quarterfinals of the French Open. "I'm pretty sad about the match and the way I played," says Federer. "Jo-Willy played great today. He was better than me in all areas today. He returned better than I did, served better than I did. I struggled to find my rhythm." Federer, seeded No. 2, leads 4-2 in the first set, but starts to misfire on overheads, easy volleys and loses his serve six times in the match.

June 5

2001 – Roger Federer advances to the quarterfinals of a Grand Slam event for the first time in his career defeating Wayne Arthurs of Australia 3-6, 6-3, 6-4, 6-2 in the round of 16 at the French Open.

2007 – Roger Federer sets a record for most consecutive sets won by a man in Grand Slam tournament play winning the first set from Tommy Robredo in the French Open quarterfinals for his 36th straight set won. Federer, however, has his streak snapped in the second set, but he rallies to advance into the semifinals with a 7-5, 1-6, 6-1, 6-2 win over the No. 9 seeded Robredo. "Well, not looking for excuses, but it was windy," Federer says of the second set. "I didn't play well in that set, that's for sure. But he played solid." Federer's streak of 36 straight sets won breaks the record set by John McEnroe in 1984.

2009 – Roger Federer eludes the upset bid of No. 5-seed Juan Martin del Potro, edging the Argentine 3-6, 7-6 (7-2), 2-6, 6-1, 6-4 to advance into a French Open final against Robin Soderling and not against Rafael Nadal for the first time. The win puts Federer in a favored status to win his first French Open championship to become only the sixth man to complete a career Grand Slam and tie Pete Sampras for the most major singles titles won with 14 men's singles titles. "There's still one more step," says Federer. The semifinal win for Federer ties him with Ivan Lendl for most Grand Slam tournament finals reached in a career with 19 and also marks the 15th time in the last 16 major tournaments where he has reached the final. Of facing in the final Soderling, a first-time major finalist and man who he owns a 9-0 career record against, rather than Nadal, whom he has lost to at Roland Garros the last four years, Federer says, "Obviously, it's nice to see someone else for a change."

2011 – Playing in their fifth career French Open final, Rafael Nadal remains undefeated at Roland Garros against Roger Federer winning his sixth French title with a 7-5, 7-6 (3), 5-7, 6-1 victory in three hours and 40 minutes. "I was able to play my best when I needed my best," says the No. 1 ranked Nadal, winning his sixth French title. "For that reason, today I am here with the trophy." The final marked the eighth time that Federer and Nadal play in a major singles final, the most ever between two men. Says Federer, "It was just important to get to another Grand Slam final, keep on playing well. That's obviously the huge priority right now, to win Wimbledon in a few weeks' time." Writes Henry Chu of the *Los Angeles Times*, "It was the matchup everyone craved but few predicted would happen, a record eighth time the same two men have faced off on the last day of a Grand Slam event. After failing to make it to the four previous major finals -- a terrible drought by his lofty standards -- Federer had been all but written off by commentators convinced of his rapid decline."

2012 – Roger Federer comes back from two-sets-to-love down to defeat Juan Martin del Potro 3-6, 6-7 (4), 6-2, 6-0, 6-3 to advance into the semifinals of the French Open. The Argentine, who upset Federer in the 2009 U.S. Open final, appears to be hampered by a left knee problem that affects his movement in the last three sets of the match. "He called the trainer, but he didn't take a timeout, so I didn't know what they were talking about, if he got painkillers, or what happened," says Federer. "So I was just trying to focus on me, really, because I was in trouble. He wasn't. Maybe his knee was (a problem). I don't know. But doesn't matter how bad that knee is. Maybe he can just sit on it and just say, `OK, here, take the two next sets ... and then I'll come back in the fifth set and I will destroy you.'"

June 6

2006 – Roger Federer straight-sets the persistently-attacking Mario Ancic of Croatia 6-4, 6-3, 6-4 to advance into the semifinals of the French Open. Ancic, however, is treated on the court for a sore shoulder in the second set and for dizziness in the third set. Federer, in his post-match press conference, is asked to project to the potential of playing defending champion Rafael Nadal in the final, and answers, "I'd like to be thinking of Nadal already, but it's not possible."

2008 – Roger Federer talks confidently of facing Rafael Nadal for the fourth straight year and for the third straight final at Roland Garros after his 6-2, 5-7, 6-3, 7-5 semifinal win over Gael Monfils. "I feel I have the right tactics, I have the right game, and I have the fitness to beat him," says Federer in his post-match press conference. "I believe very strongly that this is my year." Chuck Culpepper of the *Los Angeles Times* calls Federer's comments "delusional" writing "Only in this parallel universe, the Kingdom of

Rafael Nadal where opponents quickly turn into yard mulch, could the inarguably great Roger Federer wind up sounding delusional." Continues Federer, "I think maybe three years ago when I played him the first time in the semifinal here, I just, I guess I came in and I thought I could blow him off the court," speaking of his first meeting with Nadal in the 2005 Roland Garros semifinals. "I didn't expect myself to win necessarily, but I really felt like I had the game, you know, by just playing my style of game, I could win. I was very close. I was up a break in the fourth to push it to the fifth set, you know."

June 7

2009 – Roger Federer finally completes a career Grand Slam defeating Robin Soderling 6-1, 7-6 (1), 6-4 in the final of the French Open in Paris. The title is Federer's 14th major singles title, equaling the record of Pete Sampras. Writes Rene Stauffer in the book *Roger Federer: Quest for Perfection*, "Even before he won the last point he had tears in his eyes. He finally won the title that many thought he never would, and only a few weeks after a drastic low and a phase where most people already wrote him off. Federer became the sixth man after Fred Perry, Don Budge, Roy Emerson, Rod Laver and Andre Agassi to accomplish the career Grand Slam, to complete the quartet of major titles within the scope of a career." This might just be the greatest victory of my career. I'm so proud," Federer says after receiving the Coupe des Mousquetaires from Andre Agassi, who also clinched the Career Grand Slam at the French Open 10 years earlier. "It really wasn't easy to deal with my emotions during the match." Writes Mark Hodgkinson of the *Daily Telegraph*, "Federer's defeat of Robin Soderling gave him a first French Open title, made him only the sixth man to achieve the career grand slam, put him level with Pete Sampras on a record 14 majors, and surely brought confirmation that he is the greatest tennis player of all time."

2005 – Roger Federer comes within two points of losing a grass court match since the first round of Wimbledon in 2002, beating Robin Soderling 6-7(5), 7-6 (6), 6-4 in two hours, 20 minutes in the second round of the Gerry Weber Open in Halle, Germany. The win extends Federer's grass court win streak to 25.

June 8

2008 – Roger Federer is drilled by Rafael Nadal 6-1, 6-3, 6-0 to lose his third consecutive French Open final to his biggest rival and again be denied the lone Grand Slam tournament trophy that is missing from his trophy case. Described by Chris Clarey of the *New York Times* as a final "that only rarely resembled anything other than one-way traffic," Nadal hands Federer the worst loss of their rivalry and the most one-sided decision in a French men's final since 1977 when Guillermo Vilas beats Brian Gottfried 6-0, 6-3, 6-0.

2004 – World No. 1 Roger Federer extends his grass-court winning streak to 13 with a 6-3, 6-2 victory over Thomas Johansson in the Gerry Weber Open at Halle, Germany.

2007 – After defeating No. 4 seed Nikolay Davydenko 7-5, 7-6 (5), 7-6 (7) to advance into the final of the French Open, Roger Federer is asked if he would rather face Novak Djokovic or two-time defending champion Rafael Nadal who are set to play the second semifinal. "I mean, I probably prefer Djokovic, to be honest," says Federer. "Never lost against the guy, and the guy has never played in a Grand Slam final. So that would be stupid to say the other guy." Nadal ends up beating Djokovic 7-5, 6-4, 6-2. Federer, one match away from winning his fourth straight major title, faces Nadal the next day, the man whose 81-match win streak on clay he ends in the final of Hamburg just before the French final. Says Djokovic of Nadal, "If you win on clay against him, you've got to do more, you've got to push him more, push him over the limits. You've got to play really great tennis, and it has got to be your day."

2012 – Novak Djokovic avenges his loss to Roger Federer from Roland Garros in 2011 by handing the Swiss a 6-4, 7-5, 6-3 loss a year later also in the French Open semifinals. "I thought I was playing very aggressive early on but it was always going to be hard serving well in the wind and when Novak picks up some good returns my first serve is always going to be difficult," Federer says. "I was actually feeling well in the second set so that one hurts the most to lose. In the third I wasn't able to put a good game together and with a two sets lead it's not the same match anymore and Novak goes for broke."

2010 – Roger Federer needs 63 minutes to register a 6-4, 6-4 win over Jarkko Nieminen of Finland in the first round of the Gerry Weber Open in Halle, Germany.

June 9

2006 – Roger Federer escapes from a 6-3, 3-0 deficit and is given a pass into the French Open final when David Nalbandian is forced to default with a strained abdominal muscle, trailing 3-6, 6-4, 5-2. "I couldn't explain why I had such a bad start," Federer says. "All of a sudden, he pulled away and I couldn't keep the ball in play. That's definitely got something to do with the long history I've had with him." Entering the match, the No. 3-ranked Nalbandian was one of the few active players with a winning record against Federer, winning six of their 11 previous meetings. "In the beginning of today, I feel 100 percent, I feel perfect," Nalbandian says. "And then in the middle of the second set, I feel it again much worse than [against quarterfinal opponent Nikolay] Davydenko. So, that was tough." Says Federer of Nalbandian quitting the match, "It doesn't usually happen that someone actually starts playing a match and then gives up halfway through. It's a bit unfortunate to win a match like this in a semifinal. But I think I worked to put myself in that position."

2004 – Roger Federer needs only 68 minutes to defeat Russia's Mikhail Youzhny 6-2, 6-1 in the second round of the Gerry Weber Open in Halle, Germany, improving his grass-court record to 14-0 over the past two years.

2005 – Roger Federer, the two-time defending champion, has little trouble with Germany's Florian Mayer, registering a 6-2, 6-4 win to ease into the quarterfinals of the Gerry Weber Open at Halle, Germany.

2003 – Roger Federer holds his highest career ATP doubles ranking of No. 24 at the same time that he holds at No. 5 ranking in singles.

June 10

2007 – Roger Federer loses the French Open final to Rafael Nadal for a second straight year, falling 6-3, 4-6, 6-3, 6-4 and again is denied the chance to win the one Grand Slam tournament title missing from his trophy case. "Spin it any way you want—I'm disappointed to have lost. I couldn't care less how I played the last 10 months or the last 10 years. At the end of the day, I wanted to win that match," says Federer. "I couldn't do it. It's a shame. But life goes on." Federer is also denied the opportunity of winning four consecutive major titles, a feat that has not happened in men's tennis since Rod Laver won four straight in winning his second Grand Slam in 1969. Federer says he will win the event one day. "Eventually, if I get it, the sweeter it's going to taste," he says.

2005 – Two-time defending champion Roger Federer extends his grass-court winning streak to 27 matches beating Germany's Philipp Kohlschreiber 6-3, 6-4 in the quarterfinals of the Gerry Weber Open in Halle, Germany.

2010 – Top-seeded Roger Federer needs only 52 minutes to move into the quarterfinals of the Gerry Weber Open in Halle, Germany, beating Alejandro Falla of Colombia, 6-1, 6-2. The two famously meet again on grass 11 days later in the first round of Wimbledon and Federer drops the first two sets before narrowly winning in five sets.

2013 – Roger Federer pairs with Tommy Haas in doubles at the Gerry Weber Open in Halle, Germany, but the duo is beaten in the opening round by Jurgen Melzer and Phillip Petzschner 7-6, 6-4.

June 11

2006 – Roger Federer fails in his quest to win a fourth consecutive Grand Slam title, losing to Rafael Nadal 1-6, 6-1, 6-4, 7-6 (4) in the final of the French Open. Federer, appearing in the French final for the first time in his career, nearly joins Don Budge and Rod Laver as the only men to hold all four Grand Slam titles at the same time. The loss also marks Federer's first defeat in eight career Grand Slam finals. Says Federer of his lost opportunity to win four straight majors, "Obviously, it's a pity, but it goes on, right?" Writes Rene Stauffer in the book *Roger Federer: Quest for Perfection*, "The final was one of the most highly-anticipated matches in memory. Black market prices for the final reached four digit figures in euros. The media outdid itself with previews and headlines—"Prince against the Pirate" ran the headlines of the British *Independent on Sunday*. Former French heavyweight boxing champion Jean-Claude Bouttier said the final reminded him of one of the greatest fights in boxing history. "A stylist is meeting a puncher at this match," he said. "Nadal is Marvin Hagler. Federer is Sugar Ray Leonard." The match began fantastically for Federer. Carried by a wave of sympathy from the spectators accorded the No. 1-seeded "underdog," he won the first set 6-1 on the hot afternoon with temperatures hovering near 90 degrees Fahrenheit. The turning point in the match, however, came quickly and brutally. At 0-1 in the second set and after leading 40-0 on his serve, Federer missed an easy volley at the net to lose his serve and go down an early break in the second set. His tremendous momentum was lost. Months later, Federer said that this moment "broke his neck."'

2005 – Top-ranked and two-time defending champion Roger Federer beats Tommy Haas 6-4, 7-6 (9) in 99 minutes to reach the final of the Gerry Weber Open title in Halle, Germany.

2004 – Top-ranked Roger Federer moves into the semifinals of the Gerry Weber Open in Halle, Germany with a 6-3, 7-5 win over No. 37-ranked Arnaud Clement of France. "I wasn't feeling so good like the last few times but maybe that's got something to do with him because he really came in a lot and never gave me the rhythm," Federer tells reporters after the match. "So I'm happy to have won in straight sets. It was just a really solid performance which it needed to be against such a player."

2008 – Playing in the first match since he won only four games against Rafael Nadal in the final of Roland Garros three days earlier, Roger Federer, with only 90 minutes of pre-event grass court practice, beats Michael Berrer of Germany 6-4, 6-2 in the first round of the pre-Wimbledon tune-up event in Halle, Germany. Federer loses only one point on his serve in the first set of the 61-minute match, his 21st straight win in Halle and his 55th consecutive match win on grass. "My reaction was good, my movement was good, I'm very happy with my first-round performance," Federer says. "This wasn't necessarily expected, the preparation on grass was very short." Federer tells reporters that he loves the unpredictability of grass court play. "Sometimes it can be frustrating on grass, because you don't have a chance when someone is serving good," Federer says. "But I like that, waiting for my chance -- maybe that's why I'm so successful on grass."

2010 – Roger Federer defeats Germany's No. 1 Philipp Kohlschreiber 7-5, 6-3 to advance into the semifinals of the Gerry Weber Open in Halle, Germany. Federer wins five games in a row from 5-5 in the first set before holding on to win his 28th straight match at the German grass court event where he has won the title in 2003, 2004, 2005, 2006 and 2008. He did not play in 2007 or 2009. "Ten strong minutes led to today's success," Federer says of the match win. "It was a bit of a bumpy start, but then I found my rhythm."

2013 – Playing his first singles match since losing to Jo-Wilfried Tsonga in the quarterfinals of the French Open, Roger Federer defeats German wildcard Cedrik-Marcel Stebbe 6-3, 6-3 in 67 minutes to advance into the quarterfinals of the Gerry Weber Open in Halle, Germany.

June 12

2004 – Roger Federer advances to the final of the Gerry Weber Open in Halle, Germany, defeating Jiri Novak 6-3, 6-4. The match is the ninth and final meeting between Federer and Novak, with Federer leading the career series 5-4 with his victory the Czech in Halle. Novak was the first player Federer faced in a Wimbledon match in 1999, winning 6-3, 3-6, 4-6, 6-3, 6-4.

2005 – Roger Federer wins his third straight title at the Gerry Weber Open in Halle, Germany defeating Marat Safin 6-4, 6-7 (6), 6-4 to also avenge his loss to the Russian in the Australian Open semifinals earlier in the year. The win is also marks Federer's 29th career singles title and his 29th consecutive match win on a grass court. "I feel great. My 29th title and my 29th win on grass, that fits perfectly," Federer says. Safin, by comparison, final-round appearance is his first on grass. "It was difficult, tougher than I thought against Marat on grass," Federer says. "But I feel great. It's exactly how I want to feel heading into Wimbledon."

2008 – "Awkward" is how Roger Federer describes his 7-5, 6-3 second round win over No. 342-ranked Jan Vacek of the Czech Republic at the Gerry Weber Open in Halle, Germany. "It was difficult," Federer says. "When it happens — you can't play your game and it isn't working — then it's a surprise. It was an awkward sort of match." The win over Vacek, who had won only one match on the ATP Tour entering the match, extends his grass-court win streak to 56 straight matches, including 22 in Halle.

2010 – Five-time tournament champion Roger Federer wins his 29th consecutive match at the Gerry Weber Open in Halle, Germany – and reaches his first tournament final of 2010 – defeating German Philipp Petzschner 7-6 (3), 6-4 in the semifinals.

June 13

2004 – German fans openly root against Roger Federer after he wins a 6-0 first set in 22 minutes against Mardy Fish in the final of the Gerry Weber Open in Halle, Germany. "Go, Mardy, Go" yell the fans who are entertained with a more competitive second set as Federer needs only 57 minutes in all to win his 16th ATP singles title by beating Fish 6-0, 6-3 to successfully defend his Halle title. The previous year on grass, Fish is the only player to win a set off Federer during his run to his first Wimbledon title, sneaking in third set of his 6-4, 6-1, 4-6, 6-1 third-round loss to the Swiss. "The way I played this week is fantastic – it's unbelievable," says Federer, who extended his grass-court win streak to 17 matches. Says Fish of Federer, "He's unusual because he returns so well. Most players who serve well don't do both. He doesn't have any weaknesses. I just tried to go out and make him beat me with his backhand -- and he did it convincingly."

2002 – Roger Federer advances into the quarterfinals of the Gerry Weber Open in Halle, Germany defeating home favorite David Prinosil 6-3, 6-4 in 66 minutes, benefitting from 11 double faults from his German opponent. Prinosil is not able to mirror the success on the day of his countryman Nicolas Kiefer who defeats seven-time champion Pete Sampras 6-4, 6-3.

2010 – Lleyton Hewitt ends a 15-match losing streak to Roger Federer, defeating the world No. 2 3-6, 7-6 (4), 6-4 in the final of the Gerry Weber Open in Halle, Germany. The loss marks only the second time in seven years that Federer loses a grass-court match, the other being to Rafael Nadal in the epic 2008 Wimbledon final. "I was unfortunate not to come through today, but the loss here does not worry me in any way," says Federer. "I thought it was a good tournament for me." Federer had won his previous 29 matches in Halle before losing to Hewitt. Says Hewitt of finally beating Federer and breaking his streak in Halle, "It doesn't matter how big a favorite you are. He still only has two arms and two legs."

1999 – Roger Federer, 17, loses to American doubles specialist Don Johnson 6-3, 6-2 in the final round of qualifying for the ATP event in Nottingham, England.

2008 – Roger Federer beats Marcos Baghdatis 6-4, 6-4 in the quarterfinals of the Gerry Weber Open in Halle, Germany.

June 14

2013 – Roger Federer registers the second 6-0, 6-0 white-wash of his professional career, delivering a "double-bagel" decision to No. 156-ranked Mischa Zverev of Germany in 39 minutes in the quarterfinals of the Gerry Weber Open in Halle, Germany. "It's not something which is easy to do.

You never go into a match aiming for that score," the No. 3-ranked Federer says following the match. "I was very surprised that it happened today, especially on grass. I think it is disappointing for a serve and volley player to go down like this. It shows also how easy it is to hit passing shots or returns today. I just had a pretty easy time picking up his serve, and I must have made a ton of returns." Says Zverev of the loss, "I'd rather lose 6-0, 6-0 to Roger in a quarterfinal (than to a qualifier in the second round). At least there is something to talk about later." Federer's also wins 6-0, 6-0 over Gaston Gaudio of Argentina in round-robin play at the Tennis Masters Cup in Shanghai in 2005.

2002 – Second-seeded Roger Federer beats Mikhail Youzhny 6-3, 6-4 to advance to the semifinals of the Gerry Weber Open in Halle, Germany.

2003 – Roger Federer reaches the first career grass-court tournament final of his career in Halle, Germany defeating Russian Mikhail Youzhny 4-6, 7-6 (4), 6-2 in the semifinals of the Gerry Weber Open. The win over Youzhny is Federer's tour-leading 42nd of the year.

2006 – Playing three days after losing the French Open final to Rafael Nadal, Roger Federer corrects his course and wins his 37th straight match on a grass court, defeating Indian doubles specialist Rohan Bopanna, ranked No. 267 in singles, 7-6 (4), 6-2 in the first round of the Gerry Weber Open in Halle, Germany.

2008 – Roger Federer wins his 58th straight match on a grass court with a 6-1, 6-4 win over Nicolas Kiefer of

Germany in the semifinals of the Gerry Weber Open in Halle, Germany. Says Federer of the 65 minute victory, "Overall, I played a really good game."

June 15

2001 – Patrick Rafter saves a match point and beats a 19-year-old Roger Federer 4-6, 7-6 (6), 7-6 (4) in the quarterfinals of the Gerry Weber Open in Halle, Germany. The match is the final meeting between Rafter and Federer, Rafter having the rare distinction of never losing a match to Federer, winning all three matches the two played on the ATP Tour.

2002 – Nicolas Kiefer follows up his round of 16 win over Pete Sampras and beats Roger Federer 4-6, 6-4, 6-4 in the semifinals of the grass-court Gerry Weber Open in Halle, Germany. Kiefer is not able to capitalize on beating the past and future grass-court – and all-time greats – in the same tournament and loses to Yevgeny Kafelnikov in the final 2-6, 6-4, 6-4.

2006 – Roger Federer hits 41 unforced errors but is still able to win his 38th consecutive match on grass, edging Richard Gasquet, 7-6 (7), 6-7 (7), 6-4, to advance to the quarterfinals of the Gerry Weber Open at Halle, Germany.

2008 – Roger Federer wins his 10th career title on grass – matching the number won by Pete Sampras in his career – defeating Philipp Kohlschreiber 6-3, 6-4 to win the Gerry Weber Open final in Halle, Germany for a fifth time. Federer wins the tournament without losing his serve, equaling a feat he achieved in Doha, Qatar in 2005, and increases his match-win streak on grass to 59. "That was very special -- and I'm very proud to keep my streak going" says Federer of his efforts.

2013 – Roger Federer advances into the final of Gerry Weber Open in Halle, Germany for an eighth time in his career, avenging his loss to Tommy Haas in the previous year's final. Federer's 3-6, 6-3, 6-4 semifinal win over Haas puts Federer into his second final of the year. "I felt good out there and as I had predicted it was a tough match," Federer says in a courtside interview. "I have not won a title this year, twice I have lost here in the final in the past years. It will not be easy but I am really looking forward to it."

June 16

2006 – "A roller coaster" ride is what Roger Federer calls surviving four match points in beating Olivier Rochus 6-7 (2), 7-6 (9), 7-6 (5) in the quarterfinals of the Gerry Weber Open in Halle, Germany. The win is Federer's 39th straight on grass, two shy of Bjorn Borg's record of 41 straight. Rochus, who holds a 4-2 lead in the final set, also holds three match points in the second set tiebreaker after wasting a chance when leading 6-5 in the final set. Federer wins the match on his sixth match point. "It was a rollercoaster ride and a crazy match from start to finish," says Federer. "Olivier could have won the match on at least two occasions. It's getting more and more likely that I will lose one of my next matches."

2000 – Michael Chang, the 1989 French Open champion whose baseline game never translated well on grass tennis courts, beats 18-year-old Roger Federer, the future five-time Wimbledon champion, 7-5, 6-2 in the quarterfinals of the Gerry Weber Open in Halle, Germany.

June 17

2012 – "If someone had said before that I was going to beat Roger Federer, probably the best player of all time, I would have thought they were mad," says Tommy Haas after the 34-year-old German, ranked No. 87, defeats the 16-time major winner 7-6 (5), 6-4 to win the Gerry Weber Open in Halle, Germany. Haas enters the match having lost his previous nine meetings with Federer over a 10-year period. "This has been one of the best weeks of my career but I reckon I won't really appreciate what's happened until this evening," says Haas.

2006 – Roger Federer beats Tommy Haas 6-4, 6-7 (4), 6-3 in the semifinals of the Gerry Weber Open in Halle, Germany. to win his 40th straight match on a grass court, just one shy of equaling the record set by Bjorn Borg.

2002 – Richard Krajicek, the Wimbledon champion from 1996, returns to competitive tennis for the first time in 20 months due to an elbow injury, but loses to 20-year-old Roger Federer 6-2, 7-5 in the first round of the Ordina Open at Den Bosch, the Netherlands. Following his victory, Federer actually participates in a global media conference call hosted by the ATP to further promote him being one of the rising stars in tennis, and part of their "New Balls Please" marketing program.

June 18

2006 – Roger Federer ties Bjorn Borg's record of 41 consecutive grass-court victories with a 6-0, 6-7 (4), 6-2 victory against Tomas Berdych in the final of the Gerry Weber Open in Halle, Germany. It is the fourth consecutive year he wins the tournament. Says Federer, "Winning this tournament gives me enormous satisfaction. Apart from the Grand Slams, it has been one of the hardest weeks ever." Borg won his 41 straight grass-court matches – all at Wimbledon – from 1976 to 1981.

June 19

2002 – Roger Federer advances to the third round of the Ordina Open at Den Bosch, Netherlands, when his countryman Ivo Heuberger retires with an injury after losing the first set 6-4.

2013 – Roger Federer "tweets" his first mention of Wimbledon, the tournament he is most associated with, by writing "Are you guys as excited as me for @Wimbledon to start?" and attaching a photo of him on the grounds of the All England Club.

June 20

2005 –Roger Federer plays the traditional men's defending champion role at Wimbledon for a second-straight year, opening up play on Centre Court by defeating Paul-Henri Mathieu of France 6-4, 6-2, 6-4. Federer hits four aces in the opening game of the match and is never threatened. "Very important first step," is how Federer labels the one-sided victory that features 18 aces and 33 winners. Writes Liz Clarke in the *Washington Post*, "Federer opened his match cautiously, hugging the baseline until sure of his footing and rhythm, then he ratcheted up his aggressiveness."

June 21

2010 – Defending champion Roger Federer escapes from being the victim of one of the greatest upsets in tennis history as he comes back from a two-sets-to-love deficit to defeat Alejandro Falla of Colombia 5-7, 4-6, 6-4, 7-6(1), 6-0 in the first round of Wimbledon. Falla serves for the match at 5-4 in the fourth set against the six-time Wimbledon champion and is only three points from victory, but Federer is able to magically grind is way to the victory. "Maybe some think I should have never put myself in that position, but he played well," says Federer of the left-handed Falla, ranked No. 59. "He's unconventional. He doesn't look like much, but he plays very solid. Falla had not even won a set from Federer in four previous matches. Writes Diane Pucin in the *Los Angeles Times*, "Playing the traditional defending champion's Centre Court opener, he was often left flat-footed on the baseline, curiously out of place after groundstrokes, definitely in trouble after he lost the first set, then the second, and fell behind in the third and fourth." Says Falla, simply, "I had a big chance to win this match."

2004 – Roger Federer steps on the pristine grass court at Centre Court at Wimbledon as the defending men's champion for the first time and defeats British wild-card entry Alex Bogdanovic 6-3, 6-3, 6-0. Writes Diane Pucin of the *Los Angeles Times*, "He had the honor of inaugurating play on the legendary court when the grass was fresh and slippery, the pristine lines still bright white and when everything seemed possible to everyone."

2002 – Roger Federer, seeded No. 2 behind Lleyton Hewitt, is upset by Sjeng Schalken 3-6, 7-5, 6-3 in the quarterfinals of the Ordina Open in Den Bosch, Netherlands.

June 22

2005 – Roger Federer hits 10 aces and advances into the third round of Wimbledon with a 6-4, 6-4, 6-1 win over Czech Ivo Minar.

1999 – Roger Federer makes his main draw debut at Wimbledon and loses in the first round to Jiri Novak of the Czech Republic 6-3, 2-6, 4-6, 6-3, 6-4. Writes Rene Stauffer of the occasion in his book *Roger Federer: Quest for Perfection,* "It was only Federer's second appearance in the main draw of a Grand Slam tournament, but he once again showed that he could dominate a match over long stretches. It appeared he was on his way to a victory—leading Novak two sets to one—when his concentration began to fade and he became mired down in the first five-set match of his career. Federer's inexperience showed as he was unable to capitalize on eight break points in the deciding set—and lost."

2009 – With defending champion Rafael Nadal sidelined with a knee injury, five-time champion Roger Federer is accorded the honor of opening play on Centre Court at Wimbledon, fit for the first time with a retractable roof, for the 2009 Championships and defeats Yen-Hsun Lu of Taiwan 7-5, 6-3, 6-2. It marks the sixth straight year that Federer plays the first match on Centre Court, the traditional role of the defending champion. Writes Liz Clarke in the *Washington Post*, "Roger Federer thought Centre Court looked smashing, what with its new retractable roof at the ready, all white fabric and steel trusses. The fans at Wimbledon thought Federer looked smashing, too, what with his new collar-up, military-style jacket and formfitting tuxedo vest, all white with gold trim."

June 23

2008 – Leading Dominik Hrbaty 6-3, 6-2, 5-2 in the first round of Wimbledon, top-seed Roger Federer gets a surprise on the last changeover of the match as he finds his 30-year-old Slovakian opponent sitting next to him. "I looked and there he was," Federer says of his good friend and former practice partner. "He asked if he could sit next to me. I said, 'Sure. There's no problem. There's an extra seat.' We go way back. We used to play doubles together. Used to practice a lot together...He said it might be his last Wimbledon," Federer says later, "so it was almost a little bit emotional. So it was quite nice he did that." Writes Chuck Culpepper in the *Los Angeles Times,* "Federer credited Hrbaty with helping teach Federer how to practice, and said Hrbaty once told him that if Federer could ever beat Hrbaty in practice, he surely could become No. 1 in the world. Both those things happened, and Hrbaty said he made the gesture to venerate the friendship, and as they sat there, Hrbaty said it had been an honor to play his friend, and Federer said, "Well, same for me here." In turn, Wimbledon had another addition to its vivid history of sidelights, and Hrbaty had the chance of being remembered as far more than the usual first-round Federer mulch."

2010 – Just two days after surviving a two-sets-to-love deficit in his first round match with Alejandro Falla, defending champion Roger Federer again struggles in his second-round match, needing a fourth-set tie-breaker to defeat little-known Serbian qualifier Ilija Bozoljac 6-3, 6-7 (4), 6-4, 7-6 (5). "I think the first two matches have been tough," Federer says. "I mean, this is hard. I'm excited that I'm still in the tournament. I'm looking forward to my third round, regardless of how I got there."

2001 – Lleyton Hewitt advances to the men's final of the Wimbledon grass-court tune-up event in S'Hertogenbosch, Netherlands defeating Roger Federer 6-4, 6-2.

June 24

2004 – Playing what he called "maybe the most easy match I can remember," Roger Federer crushes Alejandro Falla 6-1, 6-2, 6-0 in only 54 minutes in the second round of Wimbledon. "I had to play well today to beat him because he wasn't a player who was just going to give it to me," says Federer after the match. "I had to fight hard, especially in the first set." The two players famously play six years later at Wimbledon in the first round where Federer escapes from a two-sets-to-love deficit to win in five sets.

2009 – Roger Federer beats Guillermo Garcia-Lopez of Spain 6-2, 6-2, 6-4 to advance in the third round of Wimbledon. The win marks Federer's 35th career straights-sets win at the All England Club.

2013 – Roger Federer opens up Centre Court at Wimbledon for a record eighth time and only needs one hour, eight minutes to defeat Victor Hanescu of Romania 6-3, 6-2, 6-0. Federer, who wins his seventh Wimbledon singles title the year before over Andy Murray, is also given the distinction of opening the tournament in 2009 when defending champion Rafael Nadal is unable to compete in the event, and is given the traditional first start time. Pete Sampras, also a seven-time Wimbledon champion, opens up Centre Court one less time than Federer. The win for Federer over Hanescu gives him his 41st straight first-round Grand Slam tournament win in a row. "I always pack my bags for five sets," Federer says, speaking before arch-nemesis Rafael Nadal makes his premature exit. "In the first round we have seen the surprise losses happen too often. I was always going to give credit to Victor."

June 25

2002 – Tagged as a pre-tournament dark horse favorite to win Wimbledon just one year removed from his stunning round of 16 upset of seven-time champion Pete Sampras, No. 7 seed Roger Federer is bounced in the opening round of Wimbledon by 18-year-old Croatian qualifier Mario Ancic 6-3, 7-6 (2), 6-3. Says the No. 154-ranked Ancic, "I came first time to play Centre, Wimbledon, they put me on Centre Court for my first time. I qualified, nothing to lose, I was just confidence. I knew I could play. I believe in myself and just go out there and try to do my best. Just I didn't care who did I play. Doesn't matter...I knew him (Federer) from TV. I knew already how is he playing. I don't know that he knew how I was playing, but that was my advantage. And yeah, I didn't have any tactics, just I was enjoying." Following the loss, Federer goes on to win his next 40 matches at Wimbledon – including five straight titles – before losing in the 2008 final to Rafael Nadal of Spain.

2001 – In his third appearance in the main draw at Wimbledon, Federer finally wins his first match in the gentlemen's singles competition, defeating Christophe Rochus of Belgium 6-2, 6-3, 6-2 in the first round. Rochus is the brother of Federer's junior doubles partner Olivier, with whom he won his junior Wimbledon boy's doubles title in 1998.

2005 – "I feel a bit relieved," says Roger Federer after escaping 6-2, 6-7 (5), 6-1, 7-5 against former world No. 4 Nicolas Kiefer in the third round of Wimbledon. "The end of the match was definitely intense. I feel happy to have gotten through, because I knew there was danger with Kiefer."

2007 – Roger Federer opens up play on an open, roofless Centre Court at Wimbledon with a 6-3, 6-2, 6-4 win over Teimuraz Gabashvili of Russia. Centre Court, still one year away from having its retractable roof installed, is described by Chuck Culpepper of the *Los Angeles Times* as "open like a cereal bowl and shorn of intimacy." Federer, for a second-straight year, walks onto Centre Court wearing a cream-colored jacket and old-school cream-colored long pants. Writes Culpepper of the unusual atmosphere and occasion, "With all the strangeness, at least the defending men's champion did walk out first per tradition Monday after a rain delay that's also per tradition, and at least that champion did remain Federer, proof this must be Wimbledon."

2008 – Robin Soderling of Sweden takes a consolation of being the first player to break Roger Federer's serve in his last seven matches on grass, but is straight-setted 6-3, 6-4, 7-6 (7-3) in the second round of Wimbledon. Federer appears irked in the post-match press conference when media suggest his road through the Wimbledon draw is made easier by the second-round upset loss of Novak Djokovic, the Australian Open champion, by Marat Safin. The fact "that Novak lost doesn't make my day any better," Federer says. "I'm through to the third round, so that's really what I'm focusing on. But it's true, [Djokovic's loss] is a big upset."

2010 – After surviving a first-round two-sets-to-love comeback win against Alejandro Falla and a tough four-set second round win over Ilija Bozoljac, Roger displays the form he – and the tennis world – is accustomed to from him at Wimbledon, cruising past Arnaud Clement 6-2, 6-4, 6-2 in the third round. Federer saves the only break point he faced, hits 29 winners, makes only 12 unforced errors in the Centre Court tussle. and left Centre Court to a rousing standing ovation. "I get standing ovations 99 percent of the time -- doesn't matter if the performance was great or not so great," Federer says to the media when asked about the standing ovation he receives as he walks off the court. "I think they're happy to see me, and they love tennis. . . . But of course, when I end up winning, and they give me a reception like this, it feels good at the heart."

June 26

2013 – One of the craziest days in the 127-year history of Wimbledon – where seven former No. 1 ranked players are defeated – is capped with Roger Federer's stunning 6-7 (5), 7-6 (5), 7-5, 7-6 (5) second-round upset loss by the hands of No. 116-ranked Sergiy Stakhovsky of Ukraine on Centre Court. The loss ends one of the greatest streaks in professional sports – Federer's run of 36 major tournaments where he reaches at least the quarterfinals that starts at Wimbledon in 2004. The loss is also the seven-time Wimbledon champion's earliest at the All England Club since his first-round loss to Mario Ancic in 2002. It is also his earliest exit at a major since losing to Luis Horna in the first round of the French Open in 2003. It also marks the earliest exit for a defending Wimbledon champion since Lleyton Hewitt loses in the first round to Ivo Karlovic at Wimbledon in 2003, the year Federer first wins at the All England Club. The shocking loss comes just two days after his fellow tennis legend No. 5 seed Rafael Nadal, with whom he is hyped as his potential quarterfinal opponent, loses in the opening round to No. 135-ranked Steve Darcis of Belgium. A solemn but accepting Federer meets with the press following the loss and says, "It's always a disappointing losing a match, particularly here...It was a tough loss today...I just have to get over this one...I am very disappointed that I could find a way... It's very frustrating and disappointing. I am going to accept it and move on and look forward to the next challenge." What makes the upset even more remarkable is that Stakhovsky enters the match with an 0-20 career record against top 10 players – and Roger Federer, the seven-time Wimbledon champion playing on Centre Court at Wimbledon is not your average top 10 player. Stakhovsky calls the victory "magic" to the BBC shortly after the match, saying breathlessly "I am still in disbelief" over his historic victory. When asked how he felt about his streak of 36 straight major quarterfinal showings ending, Federer smirks and says "I'll be OK" before adding "It's a great number. I wish it wasn't going to end here today."

2009 – Media and observers decry "Roger Federer actually lost a set" as Federer hiccups in a third-set tie-breaker but defeats Philipp Kohlschreiber of Germany 6-3, 6-2, 6-7

(3), 6-1 in the third round of Wimbledon. The win gives Federer a 43-1 record (plus a walkover) – losing only 11 sets en route – at the All England Club since 2003. Federer actually leads 4-2 in the third set and appears ready to close out a straight-set win but loses his way, allowing the match to be extended an additional set. "It has been a good first week," Federer says of his first three match victories. "Pretty convincing. I thought this was my best match of the tournament, even though I dropped a set. I'm excited about the second week. It's down to business in the second week. This is where it gets really interesting."

2006 – The only thing that can delay Roger Federer from achieving his record-breaking 42nd straight grass-court victory is Mother Nature. Federer is forced to sleep on a 6-3, 1-2 lead over Richard Gasquet in the first round of Wimbledon as their Centre Court match is postponed due to rain.

June 27

2012 – Prince Charles attends Wimbledon for the first time since 1970 and watches Roger Federer defeat Fabio Fognini 6-1, 6-3, 6-2 in the second round. Prior to and after the match, Federer and Fognini bow to the Prince and his wife Camilla, the Duchess of Cornwall, sitting in the Royal Box on Centre Court. "They do brief you beforehand," Federer tells reporters following the match. "I guess you don't do anything stupid. You behave. Obviously we were asked to bow, which is obviously no problem to do. We're thrilled for the tennis family that they came to watch

Wimbledon today." Federer also meets with the royals following his victory. "They were very nice, very sweet and thought I played great," Federer says, "which was very nice to get some compliments after the match, which was unnecessary, but of course I do appreciate it."

2005 – Roger Federer defeats Spain's Juan Carlos Ferrero 6-3, 6-4, 7-6 (8-6) to register his 33rd straight match win on grass courts to reach the quarterfinals of Wimbledon. "My goal for this year is to be No. 1 in the world and to win Wimbledon," says Federer to reporters after the match. "I'm right in it now but I have to prove it – to myself especially."

2006 – Roger Federer completes his record 42nd consecutive win on grass, closing out a 6-3, 6-2, 6-2 demolition of the 20-year-old Frenchman Richard Gasquet in the first round of Wimbledon. The win moves Federer passed Bjorn Borg, who wins 41 straight matches from 1976 to 1981. "To come through today, that was my only wish and not to break the streak really," says Federer of the 72-minute match played over two days due to rain. In humble fashion, Federer gives more credit to Borg's streak since all of his matches were won at Wimbledon, while his streak also includes wins at the pre-Wimbledon grass court event in Halle, Germany. "Halle is not Wimbledon," Federer says. "Wimbledon stays Wimbledon after all. The five Wimbledons and sixth final is something beyond almost possibilities for any player. So obviously Borg stays a hero."

2003 – Mardy Fish stretches Roger Federer to four sets in the third round of Wimbledon, losing by a 6-3, 6-1, 4-6, 6-4 margin. The set victory for Fish proves to be an interesting footnote for the tournament as it becomes the only set that Federer ends up losing en route to his first singles title at the All England Club.

2004 – For only the third time in 127 years, play is scheduled on the middle Sunday at Wimbledon and Roger Federer defeats Thomas Johansson of Sweden 6-3, 6-4, 6-3 in one hour, 38 minutes in the third round. Rain causes for two complete days of play to be totally washed out and for four others to endure rain delays in the first week, necessitating play on the middle Sunday, traditionally a day of rest. Diane Pucin of the *Los Angeles Times* writes that through the first three rounds of Wimbledon, "Federer has not lost a set, has not lost his serve, and has barely spent enough time on the court to have a good meal with a glass of wine and dessert. He gives his opponents no room to breathe, then greets them with a hug." Says Johannson of Federer, "Against Roger, for me there are no openings. I believe right now that he is on a separate level from others."

2008 – Roger Federer wins his 62nd consecutive grass-court match beating Marc Gicquel 6-3, 6-3, 6-1 in the third round of Wimbledon.

2001 – Roger Federer wins his second career match at Wimbledon, defeating Xavier Malisse of Belgium 6-3, 7-5, 3-6, 4-6, 6-3. Writes Rene Stauffer in his book *"Roger Federer: Quest for Perfection,"* "In the second round, Federer escaped defeat in an unusual five-set win over another Belgian Xavier Malisse. After blowing a two-sets-to-love lead, Federer trailed by a service break in the fifth set before Malisse received a point penalty for insulting a line-judge and faltered, giving Federer the 6-3, 7-5, 3-6, 4-6, 6-3 victory, despite Malisse winning more points and registering more service breaks than the man from Basel."

June 28

2004 – Roger Federer survives the serving bombs from 6-foot-10 Ivo Karlovic, defeating the 25-year-old from Croatia 6-3, 7-6 (3), 7-6 (5) in the fourth round of Wimbledon. The win for the 22-year-old Federer marks his 21st consecutive grass-court match win as he holds serve for 89 consecutive games at Wimbledon since the previous year's quarterfinals.

2006 – In only one hour, 25 minutes, Roger Federer breezes past 31-year-old British favorite Tim Henman 6-4, 6-0, 6-2 in the second round of Wimbledon. Writes Diane Pucin of the *Los Angeles Times*, "Despite the fans doing the wave and stomping their feet to urge on Henman, the four-time Wimbledon semifinalist couldn't muster up even a little challenge to Federer, who has now won 43 straight grass court matches. So dominating was Federer that the second question asked of Henman after the loss was whether he would ever return to Wimbledon. "I don't know," Henman says. "Definitely a few more years."

2007 – Roger Federer plays future rival Juan Martin del Potro of Argentina for the first time in his career and beats the 18-year-old 6-2, 7-5, 6-1 in the second round of Wimbledon to claim his 50th consecutive victory on grass.

2010 – Roger Federer beats former junior doubles partner Jurgen Melzer 6-3, 6-2, 6-3 in their first pro meeting in the fourth round of Wimbledon. The match is so routine that the highlight of Federer's post-match press conference is Federer's thoughts on instant replay usage in tennis versus soccer. "We have it even though we don't need it," Federer, an opponent of the Hawk-Eye system in tennis, says. He adds that soccer "should have it and they don't. I do struggle with soccer because there's so many mistakes from umpires."

June 29

2011 – Roger Federer lets a two-sets-to-love lead slip away for the first time in a major tournament when he falters against Jo-Wilfried Tsonga 3-6, 6-7(3), 6-4, 6-4, 6-4 in the quarterfinals of Wimbledon. Entering the match, Federer holds a 178-0 record when he wins the first two sets of a major singles match. "I think my game was plenty good enough this year to win the tournament, but unfortunately there's only one who can win it, and the rest go home empty-handed," Federer says. "That's what happened to me today, but Jo played an amazing match."

2001 – Roger Federer, age 19 and seeded No. 15, defeats Sweden's Jonas Bjorkman 7-6 (4), 6-3, 7-6 (2) to set up a fourth-round match at Wimbledon against seven-time champion Pete Sampras. Federer falls several times during his victory on the slippery grass, causing a painful groin injury that requires pain-killers to dull the pain.

2007 – Roger Federer dispatches of Marat Safin 6-1, 6-4, 7-6 (7-4) in one hour, 39 minutes in the third round of Wimbledon. "I don't see anybody who can hurt him," says Safin after the Centre Court loss, the 51st straight grass court match victory for Federer. "No-one has enough weapons to beat him on grass." Says Federer, "I knew the danger against Marat. I don't know if I played phenomenal. I just played the right way. I kept the ball in play, served well when I had to and neutralized him from the baseline. I expected him to serve well in one of the three sets and he did in the third but by then it was too late and obviously I played a great tie-break."

2012 – Roger Federer comes back from two sets down to defeat Julien Benneteau 4-6, 6-7 (3), 6-2, 7-6 (6), 6-1 in the third round of Wimbledon. "Oh my God, it was brutal," says Federer of the anxiety of his near defeat. "When you're down two sets to love you have to stay calm, but it's hard because people are freaking out." The match comes a day after the tournament is rocked by No. 100-ranked Lukas Rosol upsets two-time champion Rafael Nadal also in the second round. "I did start to play better and better as the match went on," says Federer. "I had to push deep and extremely hard, and I'm very happy with the way things sort of happened at the end."

2005 – Roger Federer defeats Fernando Gonzalez of Chile, 7-5, 6-2, 7-6 (2) in the quarterfinals of Wimbledon to set up a semifinal-match with Lleyton Hewitt, who is controversially seeded No. 3 behind Andy Roddick, despite being ranked No. 2 and having won Wimbledon in 2002. "I would definitely like it to have been the final, obviously," Hewitt says of the semifinal matchup with Federer. "It's a strange situation. I don't know how many times it would have happened that the top two ranked players would be playing in the semifinal in a Slam." Says Federer of playing Hewitt, "He's beaten me enough to believe in his chance. He knows. He hasn't been playing any tournaments. We don't know how hard he worked, how much he's changed his game and what he's got. And on grass I think anything can happen against him. He knows how to win the title here."

2009 – "I feel perfect" says Roger Federer after defeating Robin Soderling 6-4, 7-6 (7-5), 7-6 (7-5) in the fourth round of Wimbledon, in a re-match of the French Open final from three weeks earlier. Federer describes the match – that features only one service break – as "pretty much of a serving contest" "I thought Robin served great," says Federer who serves 23 aces in the contest. "Thank God he served a double fault in the tie-break otherwise it could have gone to four sets. I'm happy to be through four matches already, I gave myself a chance back in the quarters and I'm looking forward to my next match."

June 30

2004 – Lleyton Hewitt becomes the first man since Sjeng Schalken at the 2003 Wimbledon to break the Roger Federer serve at the All England Club, but double-faults on match point in his 6-1, 6-7 (1), 6-0, 6-4 loss to the Swiss in the Wimbledon quarterfinals. The win is Federer's 22nd consecutive on grass courts. Hewitt winning the second-set tiebreaker marks the first set lost for Federer at the tournament. "I predicted before the match it's going to be difficult," Federer says. "It's going to be a hard battle where I really have to run a lot."

2006 – Roger Federer has his serve broken for the first time in the tournament but still straight-sets Nicolas Mahut 6-3, 7-6 (2), 6-4 to move into the fourth round of Wimbledon.

2010 – Tomas Berdych ensures that for the first time since 2002, Roger Federer will not compete in the semifinals or final at Wimbledon as the 24-year-old Czech, seeded No. 12, beats the top-seeded and six-time champion Federer 6-4, 3-6, 6-1, 6-4 in the quarterfinals. "I couldn't play the way I wanted to play. I am struggling with a little bit of a back and a leg issue," says Federer in his post-match press conference that draws up controversy among the media and some observers that he is reaching for excuses for the loss. "That just doesn't quite allow me to play the way I would like to play. It's frustrating, to say the least." Counters Berdych when told how Federer explained the loss to the press, "I don't know if he was just looking for excuses," Berdych says. "I mean, [injuries] happen to all of us." The loss guarantees that Federer will drop to No. 3 in the rankings after Wimbledon, his lowest ranking since 2003.

2008 – Roger Federer win his 63rd consecutive match on grass, defeating Lleyton Hewitt 7-6 (7), 6-2, 6-4 in the fourth round of Wimbledon, marking his 12th consecutive win over the Australian former world No. 1. Writes Paul Newman in *The Independent* of Hewitt, "There is no grittier competitor who hates losing more than the 27-year-old Australian, but by the end of this one hour 49-minute contest he was offering as much threat to Federer as a koala bear with a hangover."

2003 – Stricken with back pain that nearly ends his Wimbledon dreams, Roger Federer overcomes the pain and an early 0-3 first-set deficit and defeats Feliciano Lopez 7-6 (5), 6-4, 6-4 in the fourth round of Wimbledon. Federer, stricken with back pain, is forced to call a trainer to the court in the first set, where he feels like his chances to win the tournament hung in the balance. "I just couldn't move anymore so I had to call the trainer and hope for a wonder," Federer tells reporters after the match. "It was very tough for me. I don't know. I still now can't explain what happened. I don't know how I won today. As the match went on, it got a little better because the body gets warmer and you get into it and you try to forget it. I didn't think that I would sit here today as the winner after this shock I had. I have to try and take this lucky, lucky match today and get rid of this and then be ready for the quarters. It's a great opportunity I have now and I shall try to use it."

JULY

July 1

2005 – Calm, cool and collected, Roger Federer defeats Lleyton Hewitt 6-3, 6-4, 7-6 (4) in two hours, eight minutes to advance into his third-straight Wimbledon final. Federer, so dominant on the grass courts having won his last 35 matches on the surface and having not dropped a set en route to the final, receives an added advantage for the final when the second semifinal match between Andy Roddick and Thomas Johansson is suspended due to rain with Roddick leading 6-5 in the first set. Writes Liz Clarke from the *Washington Post* of Federer. "There is simply something magical about the way he coasts around the court in pursuit of the ball and, once in the ideal position for swatting it, wields his racket like Merlin wields a wand."

2007 – Roger Federer advances into the quarterfinals of Wimbledon in the easiest of manners, receiving a walkover victory over No. 13 seed Tommy Haas, who cannot play due to an abdominal injury.

2009 – Blackjack for Roger Federer as he advances into his 21st consecutive major semifinal with a relatively easy 6-3, 7-5, 7-6 (7-3) win over hard-serving Ivo Karlovic of Croatia. "Twenty-one in a row. It's amazing," says Federer following the victory. "It means the world to me. It's been quite a streak and I am happy it is still alive." Karlovic is able to do something that no player had done so far in the tournament and that is break the Federer serve, which he manages to do twice, once each in the first and second set of the serving contest. "Rallies were at a premium but Federer made it look easy, dispatching opportunities whenever they presented themselves," writes Owen Gibson in *The Guardian* of the match. "I don't know what else I can do," says Karlovic of playing Federer. "He's maybe the best player ever but on grass he's, you know, the best by far."

July 2

2001 – Nineteen-year-old Roger Federer of Switzerland registers a stunning 7-6(7), 5-7, 6-4, 6-7(2), 7-5 Centre Court upset of seven-time Wimbledon champion Pete Sampras in the round of 16 at Wimbledon, ending the 31-match winning streak at the All England Club for Sampras as well as his quest for a record-tying fifth straight title. Federer calls the match "the biggest win of my life" adding, "This match will give me as much confidence as I can get." Federer, playing on Centre Court for the first time in his career, says that winning the first set after fighting off a set point against him was a key to the match. "I had the feeling that I really can beat him," he says. "I had that feeling all the way. That's probably why I won." Says Sampras of Federer, "I lost to a really, really good player. He played great. He came up with some really good stuff at huge times."

2004 – Playing what Diane Pucin from the *Los Angeles Times* calls "flawless grass-court tennis despite the on-and-off nature of the day," Roger Federer nearly reaches the Wimbledon final for a second-straight year, but his semifinal match against France's Sebastien Grosjean is postponed due to rain with Federer leading 6-2, 6-3, 4-3. Federer and Grosjean go on and off the court three times, the longest stretch off the court being four hours and 43 minutes in one of the rainiest Wimbledon's in history that features two entire days washed out and play on the middle Sunday of the tournament for only the third time in history.

2008 – Roger Federer dominates Mario Ancic 6-1, 7-5, 6-4 in the quarterfinals of Wimbledon. When asked to compare the quality of play in his first-set destruction of Ancic, Federer responds, "Well, one match that comes to mind is probably the Hewitt final at the U.S. Open when I beat him 0-6-0. That was just right from the start until the very end." Federer's win features zero break-point chances for Ancic and marks his 64th straight victory on a grass court and moves him into the semifinals of a major tournament for a 17th straight time. "Sure, I mean, I'll have a chance to win this tournament for the next five or 10 years, you know," Federer says. "Doesn't matter how I play from here. You know, I think my game's made for grass."

July 3

2005 – Roger Federer wins Wimbledon for a third straight year defeating Andy Roddick, 6-2, 7-6(2), 6-4 in the championship match. Says Roddick in an entertaining post-match press conference, "I feel like I played decent, the statistics are decent and I got straight-setted. But I am not going to sit around and sulk and cry. I did everything I could. I tried playing different ways. I tried going to his forehand and coming in. He passed me. I tried to go to his backhand and coming in. He passed me. Tried staying back, he figured out a way to pass me, even though I was at the baseline. Hope he gets bored or something." Says Roddick of his personal feelings for Federer, "I have loads of respect for him as a person. I told him, I've told him before, 'I'd love to hate you, but you're really nice'."

2004 – It takes Roger Federer only 29 minutes to finish off a rain-delayed Saturday victory over No. 10-seeded Sebastien Grosjean, 6-2, 6-3, 7-6 (6), to advance into the Wimbledon final for a second consecutive year. Grosjean is able to break the Federer serve, one of only two times it happens at that point in the tournament, and leads 4-0 in the third-set tiebreaker, before Federer finishes with a flurry. "Last year's grass season was just incredible," Federer explains after the match of his success the last two years at Wimbledons. "I thought, 'Well, I've got so many points to defend [on grass], I hope I can just at least play well at Wimbledon.' I started. Now I've hardly lost a serve, hardly lost a set. For me, it's very difficult to explain why and how it comes."

2006 – After registering a 6-3, 6-3, 6-4 win over No. 14 seed Tomas Berdych of the Czech Republic for his 45th straight match win on grass, Roger Federer expresses his disappointment that no American advances into the Wimbledon quarterfinals for the first time since 2006. "We know that it can happen at the French Open, but now, seeing that it is happening in Wimbledon is obviously a bit of a surprise," Federer says to the assembled press after his victory. "It's disappointing because I like seeing the Americans going far. They've had a great history. I hope it's going to be better for them at the U.S. Open."

2009 – Roger Federer becomes the first man to reach seven consecutive Wimbledon finals in the history of a tournament that began in 1877 with a 7-6(3), 7-5, 6-3 semifinal win over Tommy Haas. "I'm very happy with my performance and it's unbelievable to back into another Wimbledon final," Federer says. "I've had a lot of pressure over all the years, so this is just another great match, great opportunity for me to get into the history books." Federer's position in the Wimbledon final gives him an opportunity to break ahead of Pete Sampras and win his record 15th major singles title. "It's not the only reason why I'm playing tennis because mostly because I love it and I enjoy playing tennis, but sure going for something that big this coming Sunday, it's quite extraordinary," Federer says. Of Sampras potentially attending the Sunday final against Andy Roddick, Federer says, "He might come around, he might not. It's his choice. I'd love to see him because he's a good friend of mine. Very honored of course that I share the record of 14 with him."

2003 – Roger Federer becomes the first Swiss man to reach the Wimbledon semifinals when he wins the last five games of the match and beats No. 8-seeded Dutchman Sjeng Schalken 6-3, 6-4, 6-4 in a rain-delayed quarterfinal. "I am just very, very happy," Federer says after the match. "I have waited a long time for this, and to be in the semifinals is just a great day for me. I definitely didn't play super today because of all the talk of my injury and of his injury, but in fact I had no problems today. I felt fine." Federer joins Marc Rosset was the only Swiss men to reach the semifinals of a major tournament, Rosset reaching the semifinals of the French Open in 1996.

July 4

2004 – Roger Federer wins Wimbledon for a second consecutive time defeating first-time finalist Andy Roddick 4-6, 7-5, 7-6 (3), 6-4. "Somehow I feel even more joy this year because I had so much pressure going into this tournament," says Federer following the final. "Now to see my name on the board twice in a row, I get more joy out of this." Roddick jumps on Federer early, blasting 145 mph first serves and 130 mph second serves before Federer steadies himself and gradually takes control of the match. "Andy was playing really well," Federer says. "He was hitting off both sides, backhand and forehand, very hard and deep into the baseline. All I could do was block the ball back. I couldn't even slice. That is a credit to him."

2001 – Tim Henman gives his home fans on Centre Court at Wimbledon plenty to cheer about as the Englishman beats Roger Federer 7-5, 7-6 (6), 2-6, 7-6 (6) in a tense, three hour, 12 minute quarterfinal played just two days after Federer's upset win over Pete Sampras. "It doesn't get any bigger than this," Henman says referring to giving hope to the manifestation of an Englishman's winning Wimbledon for the first time since Fred Perry in 1936. Writes Rene Stauffer in his book *Roger Federer: Quest for Perfection*, "In contrast to the match with Sampras, the balls did not bounce Federer's way against Henman. He did not play poorly, but his concentration suffered in the crucial moments and he failed to capitalize on key opportunities in two tie-breaks."

2003 – Roger Federer advances to a major final for the first time as he defeats Andy Roddick 7-6 (6), 6-3, 6-3 in the semifinals of Wimbledon. Roddick, seeded No. 5, holds a set point on his serve against the No. 4 seeded Federer at 6-5 in the breaker, but nets a simple forehand and two points later, loses the first set. Federer then rolls to win the second and third sets with a dizzying display of shotmaking. "It's incredible right now," Federer tells the BBC following his victory. "It is my favorite tournament so it is a dream. This was just outstanding. I hope I can keep this up for the final. I'm not thinking about the final at the moment – I'm just celebrating this victory. I'm very happy to have the opportunity to win a Grand Slam." Writes Lisa Dillman of the *Los Angeles Times*, "Roddick could only shake his head and smile when Federer came up with mind-boggling shots, wielding his racket like a magician."

2008 – "It was a perfect match for me" says Roger Federer after defeating Marat Safin 6-3, 7-6 (3), 6-4 to advance into the Wimbledon men's singles final for a sixth straight year. In advancing to face Rafael Nadal in the final for a third straight year, Federer wins his 18th straight set of the tournament, firing 14 aces and does not have his serve broken in the match, his 65th straight victory on a grass court. Writes Liz Clarke of the *Washington Post*, "His gold-trimmed Nike shoes didn't have a grass stain on them, and his tennis whites were spotless enough to wear to perform surgery." Says Federer, "It was quite easy if you look at the score."

July 5

1998 – A 16-year-old Roger Federer defeats Irakli Labaze of the Republic of Georgia 6-4, 6-4 to win the Wimbledon junior singles title, becoming the first player from Switzerland to win such title since Heinz Günthardt in 1976. "I felt satisfied but not overjoyed," says Federer to Rene Stauffer in his book *Roger Federer: Quest for Perfection*, Says Peter Carter, Federer's coach also to Stauffer, "Roger played with the concentration of a professional."

2009 – Roger Federer breaks the all-time record for most major men's singles titles winning his 15th major title with a dramatic 5-7, 7-6 (6), 7-6 (5), 3-16, 16-14 win over Andy Roddick in the Wimbledon final. The match lasts four hours and 16 minutes, including a 95-minute fifth set, lasting 77 games – marking the longest major final in games in history. The tournament win, Federer's sixth at Wimbledon, moves him past Pete Sampras, who flies to Britain to watch the final, along with other tennis legends Bjorn Borg and Rod Laver. "I am happy that I was able the break the Grand Slam record. Wimbledon is the tournament that always meant the most to me," says Federer. Roddick, who loses to Federer in the 2004 and 2005 Wimbledon finals, nearly goes up two-sets-to-love in the match, leading by a set and 5-1 in the second-set tie-breaker and holds four set points in the tie-breaker, losing a critical one at 6-5 with a botched backhand volley into an open court. Writes Bud Collins in *The Bud Collins History of Tennis*, "The Yank might have won had he not bungled a set point volley in the tricky breeze that would have given him a two-set lead. Roger lifted himself from 1-5 in that tie-breaker, cancelling four set points, the Roddick-haunting one at 6-5, the misplayed volley. Never has such brutal serving illuminated a major final. They fireballed each other, scorching the court – Federer with 50 aces (a personal high), Roddick with 27 – while they crafted the lengthiest of major finals. Their 77 games topped the 71 consumed by Gerald Patterson in overcoming Jack Hawkes to seize the Australian trophy 82 years before. It was also a Wimbledon record, surpassing Nadal and Federer's 62 games, merely 12 months previously." Writes Rene Stauffer in the book *Roger Federer: Quest for Perfection*, "His triumph was complete. He reached his dreams. He set new standards in his sport and his career was closer to perfection than ever before. While debating if he is the best player on earth, he provided overwhelming proof and most people gave him the nod as the greatest ever."

2006 – In a match interrupted twice due to rain, Roger Federer beats Mario Ancic 6-4, 6-4, 6-4 in the quarterfinals of Wimbledon. Federer is not shy with reporters after the match explaining the high level of play he had attained. "I've been serving excellent," he says. "I've been returning good and, especially, my passing shots have been incredible." Writes Diane Pucin of the *Los Angeles Times*, "Federer finishes off his victory with an ace and a wink at his coach, Tony Roche. Ancic, who is the last man to beat Federer here -- four years ago, applauded his opponent once during a game, after Federer's lob had touched the baseline just out of Ancic's reach. And he applauded Federer at the end. The Centre Court fans didn't immediately leave when Federer was gone. They stood in awe and talked to each other about what they had just witnessed."

2007 – Roger Federer play his first match in five days at Wimbledon and defeats Juan Carlos Ferrero 7-6 (2), 3-6, 6-1, 6-3 in the quarterfinals. Federer last plays on Friday, June 29 against Marat Safin, then has the weekend off due to Wimbledon not conducting play on the middle Sunday, then benefits from Tommy Haas withdrawing from their fourth round match on Monday with an abdominal injury. "Yeah, I went to the city once or twice," Federer tells reporters of what he did on his extended time not playing matches. "Went to the hairdresser. Watched movies. Played cards." Writes Chuck Culpepper in the *Los Angeles Times* of Federer's reemergence on the Wimbledon courts, "The audience quit chitchatting and applauded. As in the gauzy memories of last month, Federer redefined dapper in his cream-colored jacket and matching warmup trousers. He set down his bags. He removed the jacket and sat down briefly. The clock showed 3:02 p.m., a mere 138 hours 38 minutes since he walked out on Friday night, June 29."

July 6

2008 – In what is widely described as one of the greatest tennis matches – if not *the* greatest tennis match – ever played, Rafael Nadal defeats Roger Federer in a Wimbledon final for the ages. Nadal wins his first men's singles title at the All-England Club and stops the run of five-straight Wimbledon titles of Federer in a gripping 6-4, 6-4, 6-7 (5), 6-7 (8), 9-7 final in the longest singles final in Wimbledon history at four hours, 48 minutes. Nadal, the four-time French Open champion, becomes the first man to win the French title and Wimbledon in the same year since Bjorn Borg in 1980 and prevents Federer from winning his sixth straight Wimbledon men's singles title, an unprecedented feat in the modern era of tennis and only achieved by Willie Renshaw from 1881 to 1887 when reigning champions only had to play the final defend their championship. In addition to holding a two-sets-to-love lead, Nadal holds two match points in the fourth-set tie-breaker – at 6-5 and 8-7 – the latter being snatched away with a brilliant backhand passing shot from the reigning champion. Federer himself is two points from victory in the fifth set leading 5-4. Three rain delays highlight the match, including a dramatic pause at 2-2, deuce, in the final set. The loss snaps Federer's 40-match win streak at the All-England Club and his 65-match grass court winning streak. Praise for the match comes from all observers of the game, including John McEnroe, the three-time Wimbledon champion and TV commentator who labels the encounter, "The greatest match I've ever seen." Jon Wertheim of *Sports Illustrated* describes the match as "a spell-binging men's final that will stand as the benchmark against which all future tennis matches will be measured."

2003 – Roger Federer wins a major tournament for the first time defeating Mark Philippoussis 7-6 (5), 6-2, 7-6 (3) in the final of Wimbledon. The 21-year-old Federer becomes the first Swiss man in 117 editions of The Championships to win the title. Federer hits 21 aces and 50 winners against only nine unforced errors in the one hour, 56-minute final. "It's an absolute dream for me coming true," says Federer after the victory.

2012 – Roger Federer beats world No. 1 and defending champion Novak Djokovic 6-3, 3-6, 6-4, 6-3 to reach a modern-record eighth Wimbledon final. "I have one more match to go. I'm aware of that," says the 30-year-old Federer. "Still, it's always nice beating someone like Novak, who has done so well here last year, the last couple years." The win places Federer in his 24th major singles final, also a men's record, against Britain's Andy Murray, a semifinal winner earlier against Jo-Wilfried Tsonga. Writes Greg Garber on ESPN.com "Roger Federer reached back to his vintage years and took down the best player in the world."

July 7

2006 – Roger Federer plays flawless tennis and allows Jonas Bjorkman only four games in a 6-2, 6-0, 6-2 win in just 77-minutes in the Wimbledon semifinals. The lopsided affair is the most one-sided men's semifinal at Wimbledon since 1922 and moves Federer into his fifth-straight major final, a record in the Open era of tennis. Says the 34-year-old unseeded Bjorkman, "I just felt it was, in a way, nice to be around and see how someone can play the nearest to perfection you can play tennis." The win sets up a final-round match up with Rafael Nadal for the first time at Wimbledon and gives Federer his 47th consecutive grass court match victory.

2007 – Roger Federer reaches his ninth consecutive major final beating Richard Gasquet 7-5, 6-3, 6-4 in a Saturday semifinal at a rain-affected Wimbledon. "It has become sort of a routine, but I'm still so excited to be back in the final," says Federer, who advances to face Rafael Nadal for the second straight year. Says Federer of his upcoming match with Nadal, "On clay I always feel like he is in the driver's seat, whereas on grass, I feel like I'm in the driver's seat."

1998 – Ranked No. 702, sixteen-year-old Roger Federer plays his first ATP Tour match losing to lucky-loser, No. 88-ranked Lucas Arnold of Argentina 6-4, 6-4 in the first round of the Swiss Open in Gstaad. Federer is given a last-minute wild-card entry into the event after he wins the Wimbledon junior singles title and he rushes from the All-England Club to Gstaad, skipping the traditional

Wimbledon champion's dinner. Federer is due to play Tommy Haas in the first round, but the German pulls out of the match due to stomach trouble just minutes before he is set to play. Writes Rene Stauffer in his book *Roger Federer: Quest for Perfection*, "There was no doubt that the tournament was a few sizes too big for him. His purpose, however, was just to gather some experience and be presented, on this grander sporting stage, to a larger portion of the Swiss public."

July 8

2007 – With Bjorn Borg watching from the Royal Box, Roger Federer wins his fifth-straight Wimbledon men's singles title – equaling the mark set by Borg from 1976-1980 – with a dramatic 7-6 (7), 4-6, 7-6 (3), 2-6, 6-2 win over Rafael Nadal. Writes Elizabeth Clarke of the *Washington Post*, "With his idol looking on and his fiercest rival across the net, Roger Federer put an end to a five-set battle of artistry and stamina in Sunday's Wimbledon championship with a thunderous overhead slam. Then he dropped to his knees, fell on his back and wept. The pressure Federer had shouldered with such grace this Wimbledon fortnight erupted in the form of tears the moment his winning shot delivered his fifth consecutive Wimbledon championship, equaling the mark set from 1976 to '80 by the masterful Bjorn Borg, who watched with approval from the Royal Box." Says Federer, "I'm just happy with such a great run, especially at Wimbledon, the most important tournament of my life. I'm loving every moment of it."

2012 – Roger Federer wins his seventh Wimbledon title – and his 17th major singles title – with a 4-6, 7-5, 6-3, 6-4 win over Andy Murray. The win vaults the 30-year-old Federer back to the No. 1 ranking and prevents Murray from becoming the first British man since Fred Perry in 1936 to win at the All England Club. The seventh Wimbledon singles title for Federer ties the men's record shared by William Renshaw, a Brit who played in the 19th century, and American Pete Sampras. "I mean there was so much on the line, so I didn't try to think of the world No. 1 ranking or the 7th or the 17th," Federer says. "So I think that's going to actually, for a change, take much longer to sort of understand, what I was able to achieve today. Yeah, it was crazy how it all happened under the circumstances. Yeah, I played terrific." The final is started outdoors but after two hours and two minutes of play, with the score 1-1 in the third set, rain causes for the retractable roof to be closed after a delay of 40 minutes and the match is resumed indoors, the first Wimbledon final to be played indoors. Writes Christopher Clarey in the *New York Times* of the final, "This was also Federer's 17th Grand Slam singles title, padding his lead in the career men's standings. But this victory, though not the most significant or emotional of his career, was particularly reaffirming because it was his first major title in more than two years at an age when tennis superstars are usually past their primes."

2003 – Just two days removed from winning on first major title on the grass of Wimbledon, Roger Federer steps foot on the clay of Gstaad, Switzerland and beats qualifier Marc Lopez 6-3, 6-7 (4-7), 6-3 in the first round of the Swiss Open. "I have to thank the crowd for its support today. I really needed it," Federer says following the match. "In view of the state I'm in, I'm not sure what I can expect here. I'll just have to go match by match and hope for the best."

2013 – Following his second-round loss to Sergiy Stakhovsky at Wimbledon, Roger Federer drops to No. 5 in the ATP World Tour rankings, his lowest ranking since 2003.

2011 – After almost a two-year absence, Roger Federer returns to the Swiss Davis Cup team, and for the first time, he plays in the zonal competition. In the Europe/Africa Zone I quarterfinal against Portugal in Bern, Federer defeats No. 93-ranked Rui Machado 5-7, 6-3, 6-4, 6-2 for his 38th Davis Cup win in his 49th match (singles and doubles). Federer last plays for Switzerland in a play-off tie against Italy in 2009, where he wins both his rubbers in a 3-2 win that keeps the Swiss in the World Group.

July 9

2004 – Roger Federer wins two matches – playing six tough sets – in one day in a rain-troubled Swiss Open in Gstaad. In the morning, he defeats Ivo Karlovic of Croatia 6-7 (5), 6-3, 7-6 (4) and then defeats Radek Stepanek 6-1, 5-7, 6-4 to reach the semifinals of the post-Wimbledon clay-court event.

2006 – Roger Federer ends a five-match losing streak to Rafael Nadal defeating his Spanish rival 6-0, 7-6 (5), 6-7 (2),

6-3 to win his fourth consecutive Wimbledon title, joining Björn Borg and Pete Sampras as the only men to win four straight men's singles titles at the All England Club. Says Federer of winning his eighth career major singles title, "I'm very well aware how important this match was for me. If I lose, it's a hard blow for me. It's important for me to win a final against him for a change and beat him for a change. Wimbledon I knew was going to be the place for me to do it the easiest way and it turned out to be tough."

2011 – Roger Federer teams with Stanislas Wawrinka to defeat Federico Gil and Leonardo Tavares 6-3, 6-4, 6-4 to clinch victory for Switzerland in Davis Cup over Portugal in Bern.

July 10

2001 – "Saying I just had too many things against me today," Roger Federer is defeated in the first round of the Swiss Open in Gstaad, losing decisively to Croatia's Ivan Ljubicic 6-2, 6-1. Federer's loss comes only a week after dramatically beating Pete Sampras in the round of 16 of Wimbledon.

2004 – Roger Federer, overcoming rain delays and fatigue, edges Potito Starace 6-3, 3-6, 6-3 in one hour and 30 minutes to advance to final of the Swiss Open in Gstaad. Federer wins two matches the day before due to rain delays throughout the week. His match with Starace is interrupted for 30 minutes overall by rain.

July 11

2004 – Putting an exclamation point on a week that followed his second Wimbledon title, Roger Federer wins his first pro singles title on Swiss soil at the clay court Swiss Open in Gstaad defeating Igor Andreev of Russia 6-2, 6-3, 5-7, 6-3 in the final. Writes Rene Stauffer in his book *Roger Federer: Quest for Perfection*, "Federer was the first Swiss champion at Gstaad since Heinz Gunthardt in 1980 and attendance at the Swiss Open during his performance was record-breaking. His relief was as great as his weariness." "I always believed that I could win in Switzerland," says Federer after finally winning a title on Swiss soil, after losing the 2003 Gstaad tournament final and in finals in his hometown tournament in Basel in 2000 and 2001.

2003 – Roger Federer advances into the semifinals of the Swiss Open in Gstaad when David Sanchez of Spain withdraws due to a foot injury.

July 12

2003 – Roger Federer beats Gaston Gaudio 6-1, 7-6 (6) to reach the final of the Swiss Open in Gstaad, Switzerland for the first time. Federer leads 6-4 in the second-set tiebreaker, but loses his chance to close out the match on a controversial circumstance. A shot hit by Gaudio is hit wide, but is not seen or called by the line judge due to Federer blocking the view. The chair umpire then refuses to check the mark on the court. Federer then calls to the court the tournament referee, who agrees with the chair umpire. Federer then loses the next point to make the score 6-6 in the tie-breaker, before winning the next two points to close out the match.

"Well, I think when I look at Roger, I mean, I'm a fan. I'm a fan of how he plays, what he's about... he's a class guy on and off the court. He's fun to watch. Just his athletic ability, what he's able to do on the run. I think he can and will break every tennis record out there."

—Pete Sampras, 2006

July 13

2003 – Roger Federer has his 15-match winning streak halted in a 5-7, 6-3, 6-3, 1-6, 6-3 loss to Czech Jiri Novak in the final of the Swiss Open at Gstaad. Federer enters the event in his home country after his break-through victory at Wimbledon where he beats Mark Philippoussis in the final to become the first Swiss man to win a Grand Slam title. Federer falls short in his attempt to win his first title on home soil after having reached the final twice in his hometown indoor tournament in Basel in 2000 and 2001, losing both times.

"I am amazed, not only by the beauty of Roger's game, but also the consistency of his tournament wins. Even more amazing is the fact that he seems to love what he is doing and he handles the pressure so well. Roger is a great champion and ambassador for our sport."

—John McEnroe on Roger Federer in 2007

July 14

2013 – Roger Federer arrives in Hamburg, Germany to compete in the Bet-at-Home Championships, the first time Federer has played in the northern German city since 2008. Federer posts a photo on his Facebook page of him hitting a serve in practice with the caption "I'm really happy to be back in Hamburg. Just finished my practice and now going to have a relaxing evening!" Federer decides to play in two summer clay-court events – in Hamburg and at the Swiss Open in Gstaad – after losing in the second round at Wimbledon to Sergiy Stakhovsky. "At Wimbledon, it was strange to go out so early and I didn't know what to do," says Federer. "But I had a clear plan 48 hours later to play at Hamburg and Gstaad."

July 15

1996 – Roger Federer plays his first ITF world junior tournament in Davos, Switzerland at the age of 14 and defeats Lakas Rhomberg of Austria 6-1, 6-0 in the first round.

2013 – Roger Federer conducts a pre-tournament press conference before competing in the Bet-at-Home Championships in Hamburg, Germany, saying that the tournament that he won four times when it was a "Masters Series" event holds a special place in his heart. "I first entered into the Top 10 [of the ATP Rankings] at Hamburg in 2002," Federer tells the assembled press. "That is something that can never be taken away from

Hamburg or me. It was one of my dreams. I have always enjoyed coming back here, winning here. I have had milestone victories here and also times when I have learnt a lot." Federer also tells the media that he did not watch the Wimbledon final between Andy Murray and Novak Djokovic, but did pass along a congratulations text message to Murray, the man whom he beat to win the Wimbledon title 12 months earlier. "I didn't see anything but I did send him a message," Federer says. "I was happy for him. I think he's been very consistent for a long time. Last year, was a huge year for him winning the [London] Olympics, making the Wimbledon final and winning the U.S. Open. I thought after missing Paris to come back and win Wimbledon it was amazing."

July 16

1999 – Seventeen-year-old Roger Federer is thrust into the role as the leader of the Swiss Davis Cup team as its No. 1 player as its top-ranked player Marc Rosset is not able to compete due to illness against Belgium in the Davis Cup quarterfinal in Brussels. After Federer's teammate Lorenzo Manta loses the opening match to Xavier Malisse, Federer, ranked No. 109, loses to No. 146-ranked Christophe Van Garsse 7-6 (4), 3-6, 1-6, 7-5, 6-1 to put the Swiss in an 0-2 hole. Van Garsse suffers from cramps in the fourth set, but Federer is not able to close out the victory in four sets and himself suffers from cramps.

2013 – Roger Federer and Tommy Haas visit the Inner Alster Lake (Binnenalster) in the middle of the city of

Hamburg on a promotional photo opportunity to promote the Bet-at-Home German Tennis Championships.

July 17

2013 – Roger Federer plays his first ATP World Tour match with a new Wilson racquet with a 98-square inch face and struggles past Daniel Brands 3-6, 6-3, 6-2 in his opening match at the Bet-at-Home German Tennis Championships. After dropping to No. 5 in the ATP rankings following a shock second-round upset loss at Wimbledon, Federer makes the switch to the larger racquet after winning 17 major singles titles with a 90-square inch racquet. "I'm pleased how it's playing," Federer says of the racquet after his win over Brands. "I kind of knew it from practice, so it wasn't like just jumping into the water, but I'm very happy that under match conditions I was feeling comfortable with it. I'm satisfied." Federer plays tentative from the start in his first career meeting with Brands, losing the first set, but doesn't lose a point on his first serve in the second set (17 for 17) to square the match. Federer's confidence grows in the third set and he streaks to victory. "After I lost at Wimbledon, I thought this is a good time to go and test the racquets, to take a bit of time off and then add some tournaments and see was there enough time to change or not," Federer says. "I'm happy I did the change and now we'll see how it goes. So far, so good." Federer says his extended time off from his loss at Wimbledon and the start of the summer hard-court season in the United States provided an ideal time to try out new models of racquets. "I've been very close on numerous occasions to change racquets in a bigger way," he says. "But then very often, time was the issue. Maybe also just the records of Grand Slams – I was always keeping on playing quarters and semis – so then it was also a bit more difficult to change it because of the time. This time around, all of a sudden I just had the extra 10 days, two weeks I was looking for, and I really was very serious about it. Wilson flew to Switzerland and we went through the whole process and I was very happy how things went over there."

July 18

1999 – In a battle of talented teenagers, Roger Federer, 17, loses to Xavier Malisse, 18, 4-6, 6-3, 7-5, 7-6 (5) as Belgium clinches victory over Federer's Switzerland in the Davis Cup quarterfinals in Belgium. The match between the No. 109-ranked Federer and the No. 111-ranked Malisse is played in hot and humid conditions and both players suffer from cramps in the three hour, 30 minute match. Writes Rene Stauffer in the book *Roger Federer: Quest for Perfection*, "At the time, Federer was an inconsistent player with the fascinating repertoire of strokes. He still had trouble concentrating and often couldn't find his way to winning matches, despite his technical superiority. This was especially the case in matches that exceeded three sets, where stamina, patience and tactical maturity—not brilliance—were required." The match is the first meeting between Federer and Malisse and Federer wins all the other matches between the two (ten in total) in the following thirteen years before Malisse's retirement in 2013.

2013 – Saying "I'm just still looking for the timing and the rhythm here," Roger Federer plays his second match with his new 98-square inch racquet frame and advances into the quarterfinals of the Bet-at-Home German Tennis Championships in Hamburg with a 6-4, 6-3 win over Czech qualifier Jan Hajek. "The longer I stay in the tournament, the more confident I am that I'm going to play better and better as the tournament goes on," says Federer of adjusting to his new racquet frame. "I guess it's to a degree some more getting used to, just to see how it reacts on every single shot. Clearly it reacts better to some shots. But it's important not to think of it the whole time, not to talk about it all the time, but more just sort of go with it, fight for every point, have the right mindset, be optimistic about playing here now and wanting to achieve a good result and that's what I'm doing." Against Hajek, the No. 5-rakned Federer wins only three of 13 break points and needs six match points to close out the No. 140-ranked player.

July 19

2013 – Roger Federer causes a stir by losing a set for the first time in four meetings against Florian Mayer of Germany – and sporting a black sweater vest in the second set – in his 7-6 (4), 3-6, 7-5 victory in the quarterfinals of Bet-at-Home German Tennis Championships in Hamburg. "It was extremely difficult," says Federer of the evening match. "I started really well. I thought we were both hitting the ball well in the first set and not giving each other that many chances. It went down to the wire. I'm happy I played a good tie-break. I should have been up early with a break in the second set; he got me there. It was a bit of a rollercoaster till the very end of the match. Just had to tough it out." Federer sporting the black sweater vest causes an uproar on the social network Twitter as many fans watching the match on television and on-line express their stylish approval of clothing addendum. "The conditions were cold and heavy, the clay was heavy," says Federer of the conditions. "So, it was different than we had expected at the beginning of the day when we thought we would play at 5:15pm. I have to say that I really enjoyed the match. It was a tough match and Florian fought hard."

July 20

2013 – Qualifier Federico Delbonis of Argentina, ranked No. 114 in the world, stuns No. 5-ranked Roger Federer 7-6 (7) 7-6 (4) in the semifinals of the Bet-at-Home German Tennis Championships in Hamburg. "He was better than me," says Federer, who takes a wildcard entry into the tournament to help him adjust to a new racquet with eight more square inches on the racquet face. "I don't think it had much to do with the racquet. Both sets could have gone either way. It's clearly a pity I couldn't win either of the sets because I was starting to feel better towards the end of the match. Unfortunately I couldn't push him further and create more chances. I tried everything I could at this tournament. It's been a difficult week." Entering the match, Delbonis had won as many career matches on the ATP Tour as Federer had won major singles titles (17) "I feel like I'm dreaming," says Delbonis. "My key was to enjoy the match and enjoy playing this kind of player, because he's the best of all time."

July 21

2000 – Roger Federer, 18, beats Vladimir Voltchkov 4-6, 7-5, 7-6 (1), 5-7, 6-2 to give Switzerland a 2-0 lead over Belarus in the Davis Cup Qualifying Round in St. Gallen, Switzerland.

"Some hit the ball more mightily off the forehand side, and others were flashier, but Federer's forehand is the best I have ever seen. His capacity to station himself inside the baseline and shorten the court for his opponent has surpassed all others. Once he is inside the court, he can go either way—inside-in or inside-out—and hit winners at will. In top form, he clips more lines with his majestic forehand than anyone and yet he makes very few mistakes for someone so adventuresome."
– Steve Flink on ranking Roger Federer's forehand No. 1 all time in his book "The Greatest Tennis Matches of All Time."

July 22

2000 – Pairing with Lorenzo Manta, Roger Federer clinches victory for Switzerland over Belarus in the Davis Cup Qualifying Round with a 2-6, 7-6(5), 7-5, 7-6(4) victory over Max Mirnyi and Vladimir Voltchkov in St. Gallen, Switzerland.

2013 – "It's good to be back, but it's been a long time," says Roger Federer in his pre-tournament press conference upon returning for the first time in nine years to the Swiss Open in Gstaad, the site of his ATP debut in 1998. "I can't believe it's been nine years. It's been 15 years since my first time here, so time flies on tour. Every day in Switzerland is special – especially playing in this country, I love it. I'm really excited to be starting here in a few days." After his stunning second-round loss at Wimbledon, Federer adds Hamburg and Gstaad to his summer schedule to work out the kinks in his game as well as trying out a larger-faced racquet. His appearance in Hamburg ends with a shocking semifinal loss to No. 114-ranked Federico Delbonis of Argentina. "I feel okay," the 31-year-old Swiss says. "It's been a tricky season, to say the least. Clearly I've been asking myself questions of how can I get out of, I wouldn't call it a slump because I did win Halle in between, and I know that the game's just around the corner. It's just important that I take the right decisions, how to move forward from here and then how I bounce back, because usually when things don't go so well I find a way, and that's what I'm looking for right now." Federer, however, says he hopes the Swiss crowd will be able to lift him to new successes. "I feel like I play home almost everywhere I go; I have so much support all around the world, but there's nothing like playing in front of your own," says Federer. "There's no doubt about it that it's extra special – more friends and family can come support you and see you. Also once the match is over you go hang out with them more often, so it's really comfortable as an environment. It's nice, it's home, it's the cows, it's the Alps, it's everything you know about Switzerland and more, especially here in Gstaad. It's a very unique event and I'm happy to be part of it again this year."

2005 – Roger Federer announces that he is pulling out of the Roger's Cup in Montreal, Canada due to a nagging foot injury.

July 23

2009 – Roger Federer and his wife Mirka become parents to twin girls, Myla Rose and Charlene Riva. "I have some exciting news to share with you," Federer says on his web site and Facebook page. "Late last night, in Switzerland, Mirka and I became proud parents of twin girls....This is the best day of our lives."

2008 – Playing in his first match since his July 6 Wimbledon final loss to Rafael Nadal, Roger Federer falls to Gilles Simon 2-6, 7-5, 6-4 in his opening match at the Rogers Cup in Toronto. "The problem was my game today," says Federer.

2013 – Roger Federer is presented with a gift of a cow named Desiree during a ceremony celebrating the Swiss star's return to the Swiss Open in Gstaad for the first time in nine years. Ten years earlier at Gstaad, the tournament presents him with another cow, named Juliette, on the same court to celebrate Federer's first Wimbledon title. "She won't be in my trophy room, that's for sure," says Federer of Desiree. "But we'll find a good solution, she needs a nice place and enough to eat."

July 24

2013 – Roger Federer announces that for the first time in 11 years, he will begin his Australian tennis season by playing in a pre-Australian Open ATP event on Australian soil at the Brisbane International. "I've always hoped that I could come there (to Brisbane), so I am happy we are all able to make it work," Federer says. "I'm not just coming there for the Australian Open, especially when I commit so early in advance, it's also to win in Brisbane." Says Brisbane Tournament Director Cameron Pearson, "Roger Federer is a global superstar and arguably the most accomplished tennis player in history. His attendance at this event will be a legacy for future generations." Federer once visits the Queensland area of Australia with his family on vacation when he 14 years old and since then, has had a high affinity for the Australian people. "I have been to Queensland some time ago now ... when I was 14 years old, and I travelled through Queensland with my family ... it was our last vacation before I entered the National Tennis Centre when I came back to Switzerland," Federer says. "We visited Rainbow Beach; we spent a few nights in Brisbane, and then went up to Cairns. We also went to the Great Barrier Reef ... we had a good time and ever since I've loved Australia. I've also had Australian coaches as many know, and always enjoyed coming back to Australia."

July 25

2013 – The summer of woe for Roger Federer continues as the seven-time Wimbledon champion loses his opening round match at the Swiss Open in Gstaad to No. 55-ranked Daniel Brands of Germany 6-3, 6-4 in only 66 minutes. The loss to Brands comes on the heels of Federer's second-round loss to No. 116-ranked Sergiy Stakhovsky in the second round of Wimbledon and a semifinal loss in Hamburg to No. 114-ranked Federico Delbonis. Federer admits after the match that he only decided to take the court just before the start of the match due to back problems. "I only decided after today's warm-up whether I would play or not," Federer says. "I'm happy that I was able to play because I've had problems for some time now, already in Hamburg. But it didn't get worse during today's match. I'm positive and I felt that it was getting better during the last few days." Federer, playing his second tournament with an experimental racquet with a bigger 98-square-inch hitting area, says he was troubled by the strong serving performance from Brands, who connects on 11 aces, as well as his powerful forehand. "I wasn't consistent enough in the end," says Federer, who could not convert any of his five break-point opportunities. "He was serving well and I couldn't do enough with my return."

2003 – Roger Federer, just weeks after winning his first major title at Wimbledon, announces his withdrawal from the Legg Mason Classic in Washington due to a back injury. Federer reflects on his Wimbledon victory to Rene Stauffer in his book *Roger Federer: Quest for Perfection*, "A Wimbledon victory changes your entire career, your entire life, your inner world. People look at you much differently. I would always want to win my first Grand Slam title at Wimbledon. That's where it all began. The all-white clothing, the grass—it's simply a classic."

July 26

2010 – Roger Federer announces on his RogerFederer.com website that he has started to work with Paul Annacone as his new coach on a trial basis. Annacone, the former top 20 ranked pro, previously worked with Pete Sampras and Tim Henman and was most recently the head of men's tennis for Britain's Lawn Tennis Association. Writes Federer on his website, "I've been looking to add someone to my team and I've decided to spend some days with Paul Annacone. As Paul winds down his responsibilities working for the Lawn Tennis Association [where he's currently the men's head coach], we will explore our relationship through this test period. Paul will work alongside my existing team and I am excited to learn from his experiences." The trial basis turns into a more permanent role and Annacone helps Federer win a 17th major singles title at Wimbledon in 2012.

July 27

2012 – After carrying the Swiss flag in the Opening Ceremonies at the last two Olympic Games, Roger Federer defers the honor to his gold-medal winning Olympic doubles partner Stanislas Wawrinka for the

Opening Ceremonies at the London Games. "I felt it was important to give someone else a chance," Federer says. "I told Switzerland they should choose someone else and they then chose my partner Stan, and I think it's a great honor for him because I couldn't have won Olympic gold without him and everybody knows that. That's why I think they chose the right guy. I thought about it for a long time, what I should do with it when they offered it to me. First, I obviously hoped they would offer it to me and only later when I did accept it, I thought it was better for me to give it to someone else actually."

"I've never enjoyed watching someone playing tennis as much as Federer. I'm just in awe. Pete Sampras was wonderful but he relied so much on his serve, whereas Roger has it all, he's just so graceful, elegant and fluid—a symphony in tennis whites. Roger can produce tennis shots that should be declared illegal."

—Tracy Austin, 2004

July 28

2004 – Roger Federer finishes off a 6-3, 7-5 win over Hicham Arazi to advance to the second round of the Tennis Masters Series Canada tournament in Toronto. Federer had won the first set the previous night before play is suspended because of rain.

2012 – Three weeks after winning his seventh Wimbledon title, Roger Federer again steps onto Centre Court at Wimbledon, but is surrounded by unfamiliar purple banners in his first-round match at the Olympic Games.

Sporting a red shirt, not allowed during play at Wimbledon due to its "all-white" clothing policy, Federer struggles in his London Olympic opener with Colombia's Alejandro Falla, edging out a 6-3, 5-7, 6-3 victory. Federer leads Falla 5-3 in the second set and holds three match points, but suffers through a stretch of unforced errors, bad footing on the slippery grass and some excellent play from his opponent to lose the second set. "I've struggled against him in the past at times," Federer says following the match, referencing his two-set-to-love comeback against Falla in the first round of Wimbledon in 2008 on the very same court. "I was able to mix it up and played well for the first set and a half then, all of a sudden, I missed the match points. Things got difficult and he played a great match to come back, so I'm relieved."

July 29

2002 – Unseeded Guillermo Canas of Argentina upsets world No. 10 Roger Federer 7-6 (10), 7-5 in the first round of the Tennis Masters Series Canada in Toronto. It is the first meeting between Federer and Canas, who enjoys considerable success in his career against Federer, winning three of six career meetings.

2004 – Roger Federer plays two singles matches in a day at the rain-affected Tennis Masters Series – Canada in Toronto, advancing into the tournament's quarterfinals by defeating Robin Soderling 7-5, 6-1 and then eliminating Max Mirnyi 7-6 (3), 7-6 (4). The two wins extend Federer's unbeaten streak to 20 matches since his loss to Gustavo

Kuerten in the third round at the French Open. "If someone had told me after the French I wouldn't lose a match until now I would've told them this was almost impossible," Federer says. "I'm happy with the way I'm playing. I'm winning my matches in straight sets, I couldn't ask for more."

2008 – Robby Ginepri serves for a straight-sets upset of Roger Federer in Federer's opening match, but falters, loses a second-set tie-breaker, injures his stomach and loses 6-7 (2), 7-6 (5), 6-0 at the Cincinnati Masters. Says Ginepri of the loss, "I was feeling a little under par at the end of the first set and just could never kind of rebound back from it. Just kind of got caught up in the match, the situation. My body was kind of freezing up, tightening up a little bit. Could never really fully relax out there. It was tough running around and having trouble breathing out there."

July 30

2012 – Following his 6-2, 6-2 victory over Julien Benneteau in the second round of the London Olympic Games at Wimbledon, Roger Federer says that winning an Olympic gold medal in singles would be a "dream come true" drawing on inspiration from fellow Swiss Marc Rosset who wins Olympic singles gold in 1992. "That was huge news in Switzerland," says Federer. "I definitely felt like I was inspired by that on an Olympic level. Then I just remember following all the great Olympians for many years. I also hoped one day I could take part in the

Olympics. So when I got the call in 2000 to be part of the Sydney Olympics 12 years ago, I got there, I stayed in the village. I was there for over two weeks. I had the best time following sports, being there with the athletes, playing so well. I almost overachieved in that tournament. Ever since it's been something very important in my life. I'm happy to be back here healthy and having a chance to do great."

2004 – Roger Federer increases his match win streak to 21 by beating Fabrice Santoro 7-5, 6-4 to reach the Tennis Masters Series Canada semifinals in Toronto. Says Federer of winning streak, "Obviously, I start to wonder how many is that all together. I thought about it last night and said 'I am not here to just keep that streak going. I am here to actually concentrate on each and every match and hopefully try to win the tournament. And if the streak continues, that's fine."

July 31

2004 – Roger Federer wins his 22nd straight match defeating Thomas Johansson 4-6, 6-3, 6-2 in the semifinals of the Tennis Masters Series – Canada in Toronto. "It was a good match, I had to fight hard," Federer says. "I was missing my rhythm at the start and there was a bit of wind. But in the end I got it right, I'm glad. I've won 22 now, I'd like to keep that streak going."

2008 – Ivo Karlovic puts Roger Federer's No. 1 ranking in serious jeopardy after beating the Swiss 7-6 (6), 4-6, 7-6 (5) in the third round of the Cincinnati Masters. Federer, the world No. 1 for 235 consecutive weeks, loses the Wimbledon final to Rafael Nadal earlier in the month and fails to reach the third round in Toronto the previous week. "This year was hard, I guess, with the start of the year. But nevertheless, I still think it's been a good year," Federer says after the loss, citing his early season diagnosis of mono. "I just hope I can show it now at the Olympics and the U.S. Open. I'm looking forward for the next two tournaments. Those are really the ones that can make this season from a good one to a great one again."

AUGUST

August 1

2004 – On Switzerland's national holiday and on the second anniversary of the death of his childhood coach Peter Carter, Roger Federer defeats Andy Roddick 7-5, 6-3 in the final of the Canadian Open in Toronto. Federer becomes the first player since Björn Borg in 1979 to win three consecutive tournaments on three different surfaces—grass, clay and hard courts. Says Federer, "I hope to be able to have coffee with Borg sometime and have a talk about these series." Federer avenges his semifinal loss to Roddick from the previous year at the event, played in Montreal. "Andy, I'm sorry you didn't win another final," Federer says in the post-match presentation. "But in the future I'm sure we'll play many, many more great matches, and you'll get your fair share of them." Quips Roddick, who lost to Federer in the Wimbledon final a month earlier. "I'd like to congratulate Roger. You're certainly becoming very annoying."

2012 – After defeating Denis Istomin of Uzbekistan 7-5, 6-3 in the third round of singles, Roger Federer and Stan

Wawrinka are defeated in their second-round doubles match at the London Olympic Games by the Israeli pair of Andy Ram and Jonathan Erlich 1-6, 7-6 (5), 6-3. "It was really on our racquet," says Federer of not being able to advance in the defense of the Olympic gold he won with Wawrinka in men's doubles at the 2008 Beijing Games. "It was a pity we couldn't create a few more maybe opportunities throughout the second set, but obviously they found a bit of a way to get back into the match. Then in the tiebreak, there's always going to be a shot here or there. That was the same thing in the third set. Just didn't fall our way."

2002 – Peter Carter, Roger Federer's childhood coach since the age of 8, dies tragically in a car accident while on vacation in South Africa.

"Roger is a complete player. What he has—and it's not luck—is the ability to change his game slightly as to what his opponent's doing to him...He's not known as a great aggressive player, but he's so good on the defense and so good at the return of serve that he's forcing the other player, mentally, to get a little bit of scaredness. 'I've got to serve a little better or Roger's going to knock it by me. ... I've got to make a better approach shot or he's going to pass me.' He's getting errors because of the threat of his skills. That's why he's the champ."
—Tennis legend Jack Kramer, born August 1, 1921, on Roger Federer to the Associated Press in 2004.

August 2

2012 – Two swings of the racquet is the razor thin difference between Roger Federer and John Isner in the quarterfinals of the London Olympic Games on Centre Court at Wimbledon. Federer, the world No. 1, tops the American No. 1, 6-4, 7-6(5) – with Federer benefiting from a net-cord winner that dribbles over onto Isner's side of the net off a return of serve on match point. "You just feel bad really, but relief because it's finally over," says Federer of the net-cord winner. "I felt I hit the return actually well. I hit it perfect. I don't remember if I thought it was going to go over or actually straight in the net, but I had a good contact. I played well throughout, so maybe I just got really lucky today. I don't know how fortunate I am." The only service break of the entire match comes at 4-4 in the first set when Isner misses a sitter forehand on break point, allowing Federer to serve out the first set 6-4.

2013 – After three consecutive tournament losses against low-ranked opponents, Roger Federer announces his withdrawal from Rogers Cup in Montreal. He does not officially cite a reason but it is later learned to be back trouble. "I am disappointed not to be playing in Montreal next week," Federer says in a statement released by the tournament. "It is a great tournament with amazing fans. I look forward to competing there in the future." Federer loses to No. 116th-ranked Sergiy Stakhovsky in the second round of Wimbledon, then loses in the semifinals of Hamburg to No. 114th-ranked Federico Delbonis, and then follows with a loss to No. 55th-ranked Daniel Brands in Federer's opening match on clay at Gstaad, Switzerland.

2004 – The day after beating Andy Roddick in the finals of Toronto – and a month after beating Roddick in the Wimbledon final – Roger Federer is asked by the media in his pre-event press conference in Cincinnati if he and Roddick have started to develop a bit of a rivalry. "In a way, a little bit, especially now that we've played each other twice in finals in – what is it in three or four tournaments we've played," says Federer. "Now that we face each other, it's always in the finals because he's No. 2, I'm No. 1. So it's good for tennis, I think, that the best players play each other more often than in the past. Because in the past, you know, there were a lot of surprises all the time. And for people who didn't follow tennis that much, it was very, I think, tough to understand how come the top guys are not winning all the time. Now that me and Andy, we've been dominating a little bit, I think it's good for tennis."

August 3

2012 – In what many described as the greatest Olympic tennis match ever played, Roger Federer defeats Juan Martin del Potro 3-6, 7-6 (5),19-17 in four hours, 26 minutes in an epic Olympic men's semifinal on Centre Court at Wimbledon. The win places Federer into the gold medal match and guarantees his first-ever Olympic medal in singles, and Switzerland's first medal of the 2012 Games. Federer, who won Olympic gold in doubles in 2008 in Beijing and lost the bronze medal match in 2000 in Sydney, is empathetic to the man who beat him in the 2009 U.S. Open final. "Juan Martín did so well to hang in there," Federer says. "I don't think I have ever played as long a set in a best of three-set match. It was very physical at the end and so mental. I feel horrible for Juan Martín, but he can be very proud." The Federer-del Potro match is the longest best-of-three set men's singles match on record, besting the four hour, three minute match between Novak Djokovic and Rafael Nadal in the semifinal in Madrid in 2009 and the previous longest Olympic best-of-three-set men's singles match, Jo-Wilfried Tsonga defeating Milos Raonic 6-3, 3-6, 25-23 in three hours, 58 minutes in the 2012 second round just days prior. Says del Potro, "To lose this way hurts a lot. It's very hard to talk about it right now. Everyone has their time. The U.S. Open was my time, not today."

2004 – Roger Federer's 23-match winning streak ends in a shocking first-round upset loss to Dominik Hrbaty 1-6, 7-6 (7), 6-4 in his opening round match at the Tennis Masters Cincinnati. Federer, the world No. 1, had not lost in the first round of an event since the French Open in 2003. "I had a great run," says Federer after the loss, his first since falling to Gustavo Kuerten in the French Open third round in May. "The streak's ended now. I'm going to take a few days off."

2011 – Five days before his 30th birthday, Roger Federer speaks to the media in a conference call to promote the U.S. Open Series tournaments in Cincinnati and Canada and discusses his upcoming milestone birthday. "Birthdays happen," he says. "They're part of life. I'm happy I'm getting older. I'd rather be 30 than 20, to be honest. To me it's a nice time. Like I said in the preparation, nothing changes. Do you listen to your body more? Yes, you do. Are you more wise? Yes, you are. Are you more experienced? Yes. Do you have a thousand matches in your body? Yes, you do. You just go with what you have. The important thing is I work hard, I'm professional, I enjoy my time on tour, and I have that going for me. I'm very happy about that."

August 4

At the 2010 Australian Open, Roger Federer was asked if he has ever been intimidated by a player going into a match. "I'm never intimidated," Federer said. "Not that that's good or bad. I'm just saying that sometimes you're nervous before a match and you don't know why that is."

On the eve of the retirement ceremony for Pete Sampras at the 2003 U.S. Open, Roger Federer was asked about the career and retirement of Sampras. "Well, first of all, I would like to say I'm lucky I played him one time," Federer said. "You know, that was always something I've always looked forward to, that I would get that chance. Better for me, it was Centre Court in Wimbledon, plus I beat him in an unbelievable five-set match. But now, you know, it's not a big shock for all of us because he hasn't been playing for over a year. But still, you know, it's a pity, you know, that he's leaving. But, he's older and it's his decision. And if he's happy this way, we all respect that."

In Rome in 2002, Roger Federer was asked about the most important goal in his career, after being reminded that previously he had stated that his goal was to the top athlete in Switzerland. "My goals, my aim is higher," Federer said. "I wish and hope that I can win a Grand Slam or be No. 1 in the world. But this is all still far away, and hopefully one day I can reach it, though.

August 5

2012 – Four weeks after losing a heart-breaking Wimbledon singles final to Roger Federer, Andy Murray of Britain turns the tables on the greatest tennis player of all time on the very same court in dramatic fashion, easily defeating the seven-time Wimbledon singles champion from Switzerland 6-2, 6-1, 6-4 to win the Olympic gold medal. Winless in four major singles finals, including his 2012 Wimbledon loss and three previous major singles finals to Federer, Murray finally breaks through and wins on one of the grandest stages in all of sport. Murray, ranked No. 4 in the world, is energized throughout the one hour, 56-minute match against the No. 1 ranked Federer, lifted by the strength of his serving game and his blistering returns of serve. While the raucously pro-Murray crowd lifts the spirits and adrenaline of Murray, the 30-year-old Federer appears sluggish at times and disconsolate as the one-sided match wears on. Federer is only two days removed from his four hour, 26-minute 3-6, 7-6 (5),19-17 victory over Juan Martin del Potro in the semifinals. If there was a turning point in the match, it was the third game of the second set when Federer is not able to connect on any of his six break point opportunities that could have placed him back in the match. Instead, the 25-year-old Murray consolidates his service break to take a 3-0 lead, then breaks Federer again to take 4-0 lead and the rout is

THE DAYS OF ROGER FEDERER

on. Murray actually sweeps nine straight games during the stretch from 2-2 in the first set until 5-0 in the second set, breaking Federer's serve an incredible four straight times. "I think this is as good as I could do during these championships; Andy was much better than I was today in many aspects of the game," Federer says. "For me, it's been a great month. I won Wimbledon, became world No. 1 again, and I got silver. Don't feel too bad for me."

2003 – Roger Federer struggles but wins the last four games of his 6-4, 3-6, 7-5 first round win over Gaston Gaudio at the Tennis Masters Series Canada tournament in Montreal.

August 6

At the 2008 Australian Open, Roger Federer was asked what his relationship is with the sport of tennis, for good and for bad, and how his attitude towards the game has accounted for his longevity in the sport and on top of the game. "I mean, for me probably it's a bit different because I'm at the very top and I'm facing sort of different pressure," he said. "It's maybe not such a grind day in and day out. It's more the pressure I'm facing. But honestly, I still also want it to be what I wanted it to be in the first place: love for the game. I always said this is what I always wanted to do and when it came along and it became all crazy with media and sponsors and stuff, I didn't really think part of it. I told myself, You got to enjoy the ride. It's part of it now. Don't let that scare you away. Honestly, I've enjoyed it starting with local media back in the day when I was a junior, and going all the way, I've enjoyed the changes. I'm happy it didn't take away the pleasure of playing, because that's what it comes down to for me in the end. I like practice, but in the end I love the matches out on the tennis court in front of the supporters, which is nice."

At the 2010 Australian Open, Roger Federer was asked about being such a good frontrunner when he wins the first set and what kind of mindset change he has after winning the first set in a match. "It's just maybe more comfortable being in the lead," he said. "You don't ask yourself any questions of, 'Do I need to change anything around?' because what you've been doing has been working, so you keep that up and you can go for a bit more maybe. I think that's what top guys do really well overall. If you look at it, I obviously have done it so many times I know exactly what I need to do. Also, when I'm down, I just try and react and stay with it."

August 7

2003 – Third-seeded reigning Wimbledon champion Roger Federer beats No. 16 seed Tommy Robredo 6-4, 6-3 to advance to the quarterfinals of the Tennis Masters Series Montreal.

2006 – Meeting with the press before competing in the Rogers Cup in Toronto, Roger Federer, fresh off a three-week vacation in Dubai, discusses the responsibility of being the No. 1 player in the world. "I kind of really started to find out about that once I turned No. 1 in the world," Federer says. "That was for me a very special moment at the Australian Open in '04. I felt it right after.

I was being asked many more questions about different things not related to tennis, then a lot of things also about tennis. They really cared all of a sudden what I had to say. I only maybe realized in what a position I was later on, you know, a few months after that. I think it's very important for the No. 1 player in the world, you know, to represent the sport as good as he can."

August 8

1981 – In the morning hours at the canton hospital in Basel, Switzerland, Roger Federer is born. "He was named Roger because it could also be pronounced easily in English," writes Rene Stauffer in his book *Roger Federer: Quest for Perfection*. "Roger's parents, even in the first hours of his life felt that one day it could be beneficial for their son to have a name that was easy to pronounce in English."

2003 – Roger Federer celebrates his 22nd birthday by setting up a semifinal match with Andy Roddick at the Tennis Masters Montreal with a 6-2, 7-6 (3) victory over Max Mirnyi.

2007 – The Montreal crowd serenade Roger Federer with a Quebecois version of "Happy Birthday" and the Rogers Cup tournament staff present him with a birthday cake on court after the world No. 1 celebrates his 26th birthday with a 7-6 (2), 7-6 (3) victory over Ivo Karlovic in his opening round match. "I had no chance on his serve. I couldn't read it at all," Federer says of the 6-foot-10 Karlovic. "There was no way to prepare for a match like this, as he takes control away from you with his serve. I was pleased with how I played, especially in the tiebreakers."

2006 – On his 25th birthday, Roger Federer beats Paul-Henri Mathieu 6-3, 6-4 in the first round of Toronto. "I do enjoy birthdays. Yeah, I do like to be the center of attention once in a while," the world No. 1 says in his post-match press conference. "I get that already enough through tennis. But then on birthdays, it's even kind of more unique, you know. I had a nice day today with Mirka. She gave me flowers. It's nice. She knows I like that."

2008 – Roger Federer is bestowed one of the great honors of his career as he carries the Swiss flag in the Opening Ceremony of the Olympic Games in Beijing, China on his 27th birthday. Federer also carries the flag in the Opening Ceremonies at the 2004 Olympics in Athens, Greece and turns down the honor in 2012, asking the Swiss Olympic Committee to share the honor with another athlete, which ends up being his gold-medal winning doubles partner Stan Wawrinka.

August 9

2003 – Andy Roddick avenges his semifinal defeat to Roger Federer at Wimbledon by beating the world No. 3 6-4, 3-6, 7-6 (3) in the semifinals of the Canada Masters in Montreal. The win marks Roddick's first career win over Federer, having lost the previous four meetings. "It definitely wasn't looking good out there, but to win a match where I was down and fought back and clawed and scrapped feels good," Roddick says after the win. The loss costs Federer a chance to overtake Andre Agassi as the world's No. 1 player. "It's a pity," Federer says. "I've never been No. 1, but I've never been No. 2, either, and now I'm No. 2. So let's take the positive side of the story."

2006 – Roger Federer wins his 50th straight match in North America beating Sebastien Grosjean 6-3, 6-3 in the second round of the Rogers Cup at Toronto. Following the match, Federer is asked by media about what records in tennis he would most like to break. "I mean, I guess the one with the most Grand Slams," says Federer, a winner of six major singles titles at the time. "If you could choose, that is probably the one you would want to beat because that's where you probably are measured up at the end of your career. Of course, it would be nice to be the longest No. 1 in the world or the most titles. I think one of those three is definitely very special."

2007 – In a match that takes all of 45 minutes, Roger Federer rolls into the quarterfinals of the Rogers Cup in Montreal with a 6-1, 6-1 win over Italy's Fabio Fognini. Federer tells the media after the match that easy matches like this can have mental challenges. "Mentally it was difficult because fans want to see more," Federer says. "At the end of the first, and the beginning of the second, of course, they start cheering for your opponent and you feel like if the guy's going to get one chance, he's going to take it. That is the kind of pressure they put on you. It's not easy but I think I handled it well today. I've gotten used to it over the years, but every time it happens again, it's a tough situation to be in, because you're playing so well, and normally would think everybody wants you to win it so quickly, but that's not how it works. They want to see more. And this is where they start cheering for your opponent, so it's okay."

2010 – Roger Federer holds a pre-tournament press conference at the Rogers Cup championships in Toronto and speaks of playing his first tournament since Wimbledon, his first tournament since turning 29, his first tournament with Paul Annacone as his coach and of being ranked No. 3 in the world for the first time since November of 2003. "Being ranked No. 3 in the world is something I haven't been in a very long time," Federer says. "So it gives me motivation and a drive to come forward again." Writes Greg Bishop in the *New York Times*, "All great athletes, even Federer, get older. Federer himself acknowledges he is no longer the player who captured 11 of 16 Grand Slam championships from 2004 to 2007. He knows, as well as anyone, that the last player 29 or older to win at a Grand Slam was Andre Agassi, at 32, at the 2003 Australian Open. Federer has not won a singles title since the Australian Open. And after 23 straight appearances in Grand Slam semifinals, he fell in -- gasp -- the quarterfinals at the French Open and Wimbledon. For most players, those results in one calendar year of Grand Slam tournaments -- a title and two quarterfinal appearances -- would constitute progress. But Federer is not most players, never has been."

August 10

2006 – Dmitry Tursunov puts in a scare to Roger Federer but the world No. 1 rallies for a 6-3, 5-7, 6-0 victory over the Russian in the third round of the Rogers Cup in Toronto. Says Federer of the match, "I was happy the way I scrambled. It's just here and there I don't feel like my balance is quite right."

2007 – Defending champion and top-seeded Roger Federer beats Lleyton Hewitt 6-3, 6-4 to register his 10th straight victory over his long-time rival in the quarterfinals of the Rogers Cup in Montreal. Federer breaks the Hewitt serve once in the first set and twice in the second set. "I think it was a tough match," Federer says. "Maybe the score and everything, it looked like I was pretty much in control. If you look at the first set, it took 45 minutes. We had our chances, both of us, on both serves. It went my way in the end because I served well in the important moments. I think the second set, once he broke back, I knew this was going to be now one of those tough matches against Lleyton again. Thank God I played a good game to break him. In the end really I served well. I was just more consistent from the baseline. My forehand was great today."

2010 – Playing in his first match since losing in the quarterfinals of Wimbledon to Tomas Berdych, Roger Federer beats Juan Ignacio Chela 7-6 (9-7), 6-3 in his opening match at the Rogers Cup in Toronto. "I thought it was a good match, overall," Federer says. "It's always nice to come back after six weeks and get the win. I think that's what counts the most tonight. It's normal that you're a bit rusty after six weeks."

2011 – Playing his first match after turning 30 years old, Roger Federer defeats 21-year-old Vasek Pospisil of Canada 7-5, 6-3 in his opening round match at the Rogers Cup in Montreal. "It felt good. I'm still able to move," quips Federer when asked by media how his first match as a 30-year-old felt. "The match was tough because I was playing against a player I don't know so well. It was my first match outdoors on hard courts. It was a bit tough. I believe I didn't play so well, wasn't aggressive enough. But also I must say he didn't give me the opportunity to do that. He was playing well. So I'm happy I came out of it and I will have a second chance tomorrow."

2013 – Saying his motivation is still "sky high," Roger Federer discusses the most disappointing season in a decade with reporters prior to the start of the Western & Southern Open in Cincinnati. "The motivator is the passion, clearly," Federer says. "If passion doesn't overweigh the rest, the end is extremely near. Because as nice as the travel is, and playing matches, and practicing, and all these things, I think if the passion's not there, it just becomes so much harder. Coming into Cincinnati, Federer suffers a shocking second-round loss at Wimbledon to No. 116-ranked Sergiy Stakhovsky, ending his streak of 36 straight appearances in Grand Slam tournament quarterfinals. He experimented with using a larger-framed tennis racquet at events in Hamburg, Germany and Gstaad, Switzerland, suffering upset losses to Federico Delbonis and Daniel Brands, respectively, but also suffered from back problems that impeded his play. "I was ready to get over the Wimbledon loss as quick as I could - which I did. Took a short break, and then started practicing extremely hard, and things were great. Tested rackets, and was ready to go to Hamburg and Gstaad and play tournaments I really enjoy playing. But I couldn't enjoy them in the end, then, because I just had too many problems with my back, and my body."

August 11

2006 – Roger Federer edges a junior rival Xavier Malisse, defeating the No. 41-ranked Belgian 7-6 (7-4), 6-7 (5-7), 6-3 in the quarterfinals of Toronto. Federer says he only felt threatened when facing a break point at 5-5 in the first set. "I think this is really when I thought, Okay, this could be a tough match now, all of a sudden after being up a break and anything," Federer says. "I ended up winning the tiebreaker. Really after that I was never really in doubt too much." When told that Malisse confesses in his post-match press conference that he was working to muster the belief to beat him, Federer says feelings like this give him a significant advantage, as it did after he wins the first set. "That's why for me there's no reason to panic," says Federer. "We're back to zero. He's got to win another, I don't know, 40 points or so to win the set. That's a long way, especially against me. I'm very well-aware of that. I try to take that for me positive, even though I might not also feel that great and the momentum has shifted at that point. I know Xavier since a long time. I used to play him in juniors under-16s. He used to toy with me back then.

He beat me on the first occasion on the ATP Tour, as well in Davis Cup. After that I came back and beat him every time. We always had close matches. I think once you're about the same age, I think the opponent always believes in his chance. On top of that, we haven't played I think for three or four years and these have been my dominant years. I knew he was going to believe in his chance tonight and I think he did. This was a close match."

2007 – Roger Federer registers a 7-6 (6), 6-2 victory over Radek Stepanek in the semifinals of the Rogers Cup in Montreal to set up a final-round meeting with up-and-coming Serb Novak Djokovic, who beats Rafael Nadal in the other semifinal. "Novak's absolutely a tough player at this moment," says Federer. "He's got a good serve and return, and he always makes you work hard."

2008 – It's a busy day for Roger Federer at the Beijing Olympic Games as he defeats Dmitry Tursunov 6-4, 6-2 in the opening round of men's singles, then receives congratulations from one of the spectators, U.S. basketball star LeBron James, then pairs with Swiss teammate Stan Wawrinka and beats Simone Bolelli and Andreas Seppi of Italy 7-5, 6-1. In his post-match press conference, Federer talks about the importance and the uniqueness of Olympic tennis, "It's such a nice change to the regular tour we play in, first of all. But then also, being part of the biggest sort of sports event in the world. Now that tennis is finally accepted by the Olympic Committee, it's something I wish to sort of move it forward in a way. I guess when I speak to some players now, who didn't used to play the Olympics back in maybe '96, 2000, you name it, I know that some of them have regrets that they didn't play it, seeing how big the Olympics has become in tennis and how important tennis has become to the Olympics really. I hope that with my presence, and also, let's say, Rafa's presence, you know, Roddick's presence, Hewitt's presence in the past years, I think that's only gonna make it more important for the future generation, as well. So I think that's one of the reasons I play. But then also having the chance to represent my country is the second one. Third, just sort of living the dream, as well, being part of the Olympic Village, the Olympic spirit. Just being here is something that is quite unique, especially after spending an incredible couple of weeks in Sydney, which for me will always stay in my memories as one of the greatest sports experiences I ever had. It was, for me, clear that I would never want to miss an Olympic Games ever again if I would have the chance to compete in them."

2009 – Playing his first match since he won his record 15th major singles title at Wimbledon – and his first match as a father – Roger Federer registers a 7-6 (3), 6-4 win over Canada's Frederic Niemeyer at the Rogers Cup in Montreal. Niemeyer, age 33 and ranked No. 487th, puts up a strong resistance against the world No. 1. Says Federer, "After five or six weeks of not playing matches, just practice matches, you're a little slow on the returns."

2011 – Jo-Wilfried Tsonga duplicates his upset win over Roger Federer in the quarterfinals of Wimbledon – and in Montreal from two years earlier – in defeating the world No. 3 7-6 (7-3) 4-6, 6-1 in the round of 16 of the Rogers Cup in Montreal. When asked how Tsonga was able to hurt him the most, Federer responds, "Well, he's confident right now and he played an excellent third set. The first two sets were tighter. I should maybe have won the first one. I had some opportunities. In the second I was able to hold my serve. I might have won, but he was able to finish off the match very well."

August 12

2003 – Wimbledon champion and world No. 2 Roger Federer saves seven match points in barely surviving a 4-6, 6-3, 7-6 (10) first-round match in Cincinnati against No. 114-ranked qualifier Scott Draper of Australia. Federer fends off two match points in the 12th game of the third set against Draper and then falls behind 6-2 in the tie breaker. Federer clinches the match on his fourth match point, which he secures when Draper double faults at 10-10 in the final-set tie-breaker. "Well, what can you do, you know?" says Federer of what he was thinking being down so many match points. "It's a pity, fighting so hard and then being down 6-2. So you hope that he's not gonna close out the match and just hope you're gonna get another chance but normally it should be over, you know, so..."

2006 – Roger Federer registers a 6-1, 5-7, 6-3 victory over Fernando Gonzalez of Chile to reach the final of the Rogers Cup in Toronto. The win marks his 53rd consecutive win in North America since 2004. Federer wins his first set in 20 minutes, winning the first five games of the match, and endures a third successive three-set match. "It started excellent," says Federer of his form. "I was a bit worried going into the match really because, you know, you have these feelings before matches where you feel good or you feel average. I felt kind of average going into the match."

2007 – In his fifth career meeting with Roger Federer, Novak Djokovic registers his first win over his future Swiss rival in a 7-6 (2), 2-6, 7-6 (2) upset over the world No. 1 in the final of the Rogers Cup in Montreal. With wins over No. 3 Andy Roddick and No. 2 Rafael Nadal, Djokovic becomes the first player to beat the world's top three in the same tournament since Boris Becker in Stockholm in 1994. "It's a dream come true to win such a strong tournament as this and to win against probably the best player ever in the sport," says Djokovic.

2010 – In a wild, straight-set match at the Rogers Cup in Toronto, Roger Federer withstands the serve-and-volleying, drop-shotting and trick-shot antics of Michael Llodra in his 7-6 (2), 6-3 victory that moves him into the tournament's quarterfinals. Llodra, who starts the match with a 4-1 lead, even attempts an under-handed serve at one stage, Federer telling reporters after the match that it is the first time it has happened to him in his career. "It was a different kind of tennis today," says Federer of his first ATP Tour level meeting with the left-handed 30-year-old Frenchman. "But it was fun playing against Michael today. I thought he played well." At the conclusion of the match, Llodra asks Roger for his pink Nike shirt as a memento of the match. Says Llodra of the shirt-exchange, "Roger is a legend. It's a good present for my kids."

2008 – Competing against Rafa – No. 447-ranked Rafael Arevalo of El Salvador and not main rival Rafa Nadal – Roger Federer advances into the third round of the Olympic Games in Beijing with a 6-2, 6-4 victory. Says Federer of the match, "Obviously, for me a very interesting match in such an tournament in my life to be playing a player with a very low ranking in a very big pressure situation for me. I have nothing to win, only to lose. It wasn't easy today. But I think Rafael, he did well. I think he played like a clay courter to me. He kept the ball in play, played it with a lot of spins. Really, I felt like he believed in his chance, which I think was key in terms of mental approach in a match like tonight, where he could easily go into this match and hope, 'Okay, I hope I play a good match, a few games, and I'm happy,' but I think he wanted more."

August 13

2003 – "I will beat him if I know," snaps Roger Federer on being asked what is it about the game of David Nalbandian that he struggles with after losing to his Argentinean rival for a fourth time in four pro meetings, 7-6 (4), 7-6 (5) decision in the second round of Cincinnati. "You look at the statistics," he says to reporters of his one-sided rivalry with Nalbandian. "I haven't beaten him in the seniors. I've beaten him in junior one time. He's tough for me, so..." Federer scoffs at the idea that the opportunity to capture the No. 1 ranking with a strong performance in Cincinnati contributed to the loss. "I was too much occupied with the matchup," he says. "I knew it's gonna be tough. We've always had actually tough matches; he came through every time – 6-4 in the fifth at the Australian Open, I was up a set then a break in Basel and I lost in three. Then now here 6 and 6. We've always had tough matches, but he came through. And I was not thinking about the No. 1 spot because for those who were here in the first press conference, you know, the road is too long to the semifinals."

2006 – Roger Federer wins his 40th career title defeating Richard Gasquet of France 2-6, 6-3, 6-2 in the final of the Canadian Open in Toronto. Say Federer of his slow start against the Frenchman, "'I just always believe that I can turn any match around. That's what happened today. I know that once I turn it around, once I would take the lead then it would be very difficult for my opponent. That's what I always tell myself. Maybe it's an illusion sometimes, but it definitely works." The title is Federer's second in Canada and the win over Gasquet is his 54th straight in North America as he improves his record to 62-4 on the year, all of this losses coming against Rafael Nadal.

2008 – Roger Federer avenges his upset loss to Tomas Berdych from the second round of the Athens Olympic Games by beating his Czech rival 6-3, 7-6(4) in the third round of the Beijing Games. Since their famous meeting in 2004, Federer only allows Berdych only one set in six matches, but Federer admits beating the Czech at the Olympics is extra special. "We've played a lot since then," Federer says of their Athens Olympic meeting, "but it was nice to get him back here." Berdych warns of Federer's future form, despite his inevitable drop to the No. 2 ranking in the next week. "He can't win all the time. It is not humanly possible," Berdych says. "I think now, the pressure is off, so watch out."

2009 – For the first time since the ATP was founded in 1973, the top eight ranked men all reach the quarterfinals of an event, clinched when Roger Federer beats his Olympic doubles partner Stan Wawrinka 6-3, 7-6 (5) in the round of 16 at the Rogers Cup in Montreal. "It's actually a little bit easier here because the top eight had a bye, but at the same time it's not just the top eight seeds it's the top eight ranked players in the world," Federer tells reporters of the history-making occasion after his win. "It's definitely a special occasion. It just shows the top guys now are really consistent and they're showing up at the big events. It's nice it finally happened."

2010 – Roger Federer comes back from 2-5 down in the third set to beat Tomas Berdych 6-3, 5-7, 7-6 (5) in the quarterfinals of the Rogers Cup in Toronto, avenging his quarterfinal loss to the Czech at Wimbledon. "It was a tough match to go through," says Federer. "I started off great, was doing all the right things. I had some opportunities to defend in the beginning of the second, where he had a couple of break-points early on in two of the service games, and then I had really big chances of my own. I was struggling to see the ball in the night – that was tricky going from day to night. He also had one service game where he, all of a sudden, served two double faults and I had the same thing. I just couldn't take advantage of it and he could. The third set was lucky. I tried and he got into a good momentum. He started to play better, loosened up a bit and got in a lead, but I just tried to hang with him. Those are the kind of matches I lost earlier on this season, so I'm happy this one went my way." Writes Steve Simmons of the *Toronto Sun*, "It was something to see, something unforgettable. Maybe not a match for the ages but a match for the Canadian ages."

2013 – After struggling through two tournaments experimenting with a racquet with a 98 square-inch face, Roger Federer returns to his 90-square-inch frame in his first summer hard-court tournament of the summer and beats Germany's Phillip Kohlschreiber 6-3, 7-6 (7) in his opening match at the Western & Southern Financial Masters in Cincinnati. Federer, who was struggling with a sore back that prevented him from playing the previous week in Montreal, ends a two-match losing streak with the victory. "It was important to play a clean match," Federer, the defending champion, tells reporters after the match. "I had a few tough weeks, months behind me, I was happy to play a clean match. I told myself I was not going to come back until I felt no pain in my back. Eventually I started to work out very hard. It is a tournament I have always played in lead up to the U.S. Open, I like it here. I love the calmness of this place." The win extends Federer's career record against Kohlschreiber to 7-0.

August 14

2008 – World No. 1 Roger Federer of Switzerland is upset in the quarterfinals of the 2008 Olympic in Beijing, losing to American James Blake 6-4, 7-6 (2). The loss continues to leave Federer, an owner of 12 major singles titles, without any Olympic hardware having finished fourth in 2000 and losing in the second round in 2000. "Big disappointment, obviously," Federer says. "It was one of the goals of the season to do well here. The quarterfinals is not going to do it." Blake enters the match having lost all eight previous matches with Federer, but benefits from 56 unforced errors from the Swiss and a first serve percentage that at one point in the second set falls to 46 percent. "Roger had an off-day," Blake says. "We're all human. Although at times, it seems like he has been inhuman. It doesn't by any means mean I'm better than him because I beat him one out of 10 times."

2009 – Jo-Wilfried Tsonga stuns world No. 1 Roger Federer 7-6 (5), 1-6, 7-6 (3) in the quarterfinals of the Rogers Cup in Montreal, Tsonga's first victory over Federer in their second career meeting. Federer leads 5-1 in the third set, but allows Tsonga to make the improbable comeback. "Well, it happens in tennis," says Federer of blowing the 5-1 lead. "It's never over until it's over. It showed today. I thought it was a very up-and-down match, obviously. I think I should have won the first and he completely lost his game for an hour there, through the second, the third. It was unfortunate I couldn't serve it out."

2010 – Roger Federer dramatically beats Novak Djokovic 6-1, 3-6, 7-5 in the semifinals of the Rogers Cup in Toronto. "Well, look, I thought he was pretty tired at the end -- and he's the younger guy," jokes Federer after the victory. "So that's a good sign."

2002 – Roger Federer attends the funeral service for his childhood coach Peter Carter in Basel, Switzerland. Carter is killed in a car accident while on vacation in South Africa. Federer withdraws from the Legg Mason Tennis Classic in Washington, D.C. to attend the service. "This is the first time a close friend of mine has died," Federer says the day after Carter's death on August 1. "He helped me a lot with my career when I was younger. We traveled together and spent a lot of time together."

August 15

2005 – Returning to tennis after a five-week post-Wimbledon break, due also to a sore foot, Roger Federer fends off an intense James Blake 7-6 (3), 7-5 in his opening round match at the Cincinnati Masters. Blake leads by a break 3-0 in the second set, but Federer remains steady to break back and close out the match in straight sets. "I just told myself focus on that serve, you know, don't give him any easy points, which I thought I gave him," says Federer to the media of what he thought when down 3-0 in the second set. "Maybe just had a concentration lack maybe for just a couple of points, and then he had another few good points. I just hoped I could hang in there in the second and give myself a chance. He definitely didn't play a great game where I broke back. But I just needed also same -- like he broke me, I just needed to play one or two good shots and that was enough. Once I was back in the second set, I had a good feeling that I could close it out in two."

2007 – In a match described by the Associated Press as being "devoid of surprises," top-ranked Roger Federer beats qualifier Julien Benneteau of France 6-3, 6-3 at the Western & Southern Financial Group Masters in Cincinnati. The match is the first career meeting between the two players. Following the match, Federer is asked in his post-match press conference if he thinks at all about being only three major singles titles away from equaling the record of Pete Sampras of 14 major singles titles. Says Federer, "I think about it when I'm playing the Slams, not when I'm playing Cincinnati. But it is great to be so close. So close yet so far in a way, because Slams are not easy to get. But I've done a very nice job the last few years picking of as many Slams as possible and giving myself a chance over and over again. So it's one of the big goals for me in my career to not only equal it but break it as well."

2010 – In a final delayed four times due to rain, Andy Murray beats Roger Federer 7-5, 7-5 to defend his Rogers Cup title in Toronto and increase his head-to-head advantage over Federer to 7-5. Federer fails to win his first singles title since he beat Murray in the Australian Open final in January, while Murray wins his first title of the year. Federer, while praising Murray's effort and accomplishment, also reminds observers that the Scotsman has still to win on the grandest stage saying, "it's obviously nice, but it still doesn't give you a Grand Slam title."

2013 – Trailing 6-1, 3-1, Roger Federer comes back to win a confidence-building third-round match against Tommy Haas 1-6, 7-5, 6-3 at the Western & Southern Financial Masters in Cincinnati. "I think I had too many of those small hiccups that kept on adding up, because overall I wasn't playing terrible. I was just missing by a margin or putting myself in a tough spot," says Federer. "Then on top of that, Tommy took advantage of it, played well when he had to... I was just hanging on, and I'm happy I did because it paid off. At the end, I'm very happy I was able to turn a match around like this. Those are the matches I knew just kind of what I need right now," kind of what I need right now. "Every minute more in a match court is a good thing right now. It gives me a lot of opportunity in the next match to do better." Federer wins 92 percent of points on his first serve in the final set. "Federer himself looked like a man hopelessly lost and out of touch with all that has made him great," describes Peter Bodo on Tennis. com of Federer's form for the first hour of the match.

2006 – Roger Federer hands No. 45-ranked Paradorn Srichaphan of Thailand his 15th first-round loss at a tournament for the year, winning his 55th consecutive match on North American hardcourts with a 7-5, 6-4 win in the first round of Cincinnati. Federer trails by a service break in both sets, but is able to close out the victory in 84 minutes. "I was very worried today, obviously," Federer tells reporters after the match. "The court was quick. He was playing very, very well, and I had a bad feeling when I was down in that first set. I thought this match could be over in a hurry, you know, the other way."

2008 – Roger Federer clinches his first ever Olympic medal, albeit in doubles, as he and Stan Wawrinka upset the top-seeded team of Bob and Mike Bryan of the United States 7-6 (6), 6-4 in the semifinals of Olympic men's doubles in

Beijing. Says Federer to reporters when asked how it feels to be guaranteed of his first Olympic medal, "I think at the moment really the emotions winning the semifinals, sort of being excited being in the finals. Obviously the medal is an issue right now. You're like, you know, we've sort of made it, but you want more, right, if already you've got the opportunity. Yeah, so just very excited. I think we played fantastic tennis. Yeah, we deserve to be in the finals."

2012 – In exactly one hour, Roger Federer defeats No. 58-ranked Alex Bogomolov 6-3, 6-2 in his opening match at the Western & Southern Financial Masters in Cincinnati, his first match since losing the Olympic gold medal match to Andy Murray in London. "It was a quick match, a good one for me," says Federer. "I served well. I was able to play some good points on the offensive, and overall I'm very pleased. Obviously the turnaround from grass to hard court might not be an easy one this year. The ball definitely bounces so much higher here and plays much faster than Wimbledon, so it just takes some getting used to. I'm happy I was able to find a way."

August 16

2008 – Roger Federer and Stan Wawrinka win the gold medal in men's doubles for Switzerland at the Beijing Olympics defeating Simon Aspelin and Thomas Johansson of Sweden 6-3, 6-4, 6-7 (4), 6-3. Writes Rene Stauffer in the book *Roger Federer: Quest for Perfection* of Federer's first Olympic medal, "After the 6-3, 6-4, 6-7 (4), 6-3 victory, the two Swiss embraced each other as Olympic champions.

They celebrated doing their unique "fire dance" where Federer warmed his hands by his partner who lay on his back and pretended to be a campfire, to symbolize how hot he was." Says Federer of the gold medal, "To process Olympic gold is almost harder for me than a Grand Slam title. It was an unbelievable moment. Every time I see Stan we both can barely believe it." Federer falls one win shy of an Olympic medal at the 2000 Games in Sydney, losing to Arnaud DiPasquale of France in the bronze medal playoff and is upset early in singles and doubles at the 2004 Games in Athens, Greece. In Beijing, Federer loses in the quarterfinals of the singles event to James Blake, but prevails in the doubles competition with Wawrinka. "It is like a fantastic dream comes true, I feel really happy to win the gold medal. It is great, I enjoy that," Federer says following the final. "I have tried for several times (to get a medal), and I came really close to the medal in Sydney where I finished fourth. Since then I can't stop thinking that If I am the best player in the world, I should do the same in the Olympics, and then finally I made it, it is really special also because it is for Switzerland, you know, our country cannot get so many medals at one Olympics, maybe one or two, but this time I got a gold medal, it is for my country, I really feel different, as it is for my country, it is different from the Grand Sam where I did it for just myself."

2006 – Roger Federer's 55-match winning streak in North America comes to an end in a 7-5, 6-4 loss to Andy Murray of Britain in the second round of Cincinnati. "The streaks? I don't care about those now that they're over," says Federer, who had not lost in straight sets in his last 194 matches. "It's going to be a relief for everybody and now we can move on." Says Murray, "I know Federer didn't play his best match, but how many guys beat him when he's playing badly anyway?" Federer's last loss on the continent also comes at Cincinnati when he loses to Dominik Hrbaty in the first round on Aug. 3, 2004. The straight-set loss was his first in 194 matches and also ends his streak of reaching at least the final in his last 17 tournaments, one shy of equaling Ivan Lendl's Open era record of 18 straight in 1981-82.

2013 – In perhaps the most curious end to a Roger Federer – Rafael Nadal match, Nadal's match-winning forehand winner down-the-line, that appears to land on the line, is actually shown via Hawk-eye instant replay to land a millimeter wide. Federer, however, does not challenge the call and walks to the net and shakes Nadal's hand as the 5-7, 6-4, 6-3 loser in the quarterfinals of the Western & Southern Financial Masters in Cincinnati. When he is told that the shot was indeed wide in his post-match press conference, Federer snips, "At this point, it doesn't matter. I am sitting here." The loss extends Nadal's lead over Federer in their career head-to-head to 21-10 and, more importantly, gives him a 7-6 lead in the career head-to-head on hard courts. "I'm happy with my progress along the way," Federer says, entering the tournament with a two-match losing streak. "Could have won tonight; should have won tonight. Who knows? But at the end, I think Rafa's confidence and the way he's playing at the moment got him through." The loss also guarantees that Federer, the defending champion, will drop to No. 7 in the next ATP rankings, his lowest ranking since October 28, 2002.

2004 – World No. 1 Roger Federer beats up-and-coming Russian player Nikolay Davydenko 6-3, 5-7, 6-1 in the opening round of the 2004 Olympic Games in Athens, Greece. "It's actually the best I've beaten Davydenko," says Federer in his post-match press conference. "After two times I've played him, I beat him, 7-5 in the third. This is a hell of an improvement. I'm happy about it."

2007 – Marcos Baghdatis blows four set points when serving for the first set at 6-5 against Roger Federer – two on double faults – and loses to the world No. 1 7-6 (5), 7-5 in the third round of Cincinnati. "It was a struggle out there," Federer tells reporters. "It was tough to keep the ball in play and they were really quick conditions. I am just really happy I got through."

2010 – A video is posted on YouTube of what looks like behind-the-scenes activity at a Roger Federer commercial shoot for Gillette where Federer seemingly knocks a bottle off the head of a guy with his serve, the style of another Swiss hero William Tell. The video becomes an instant viral hit, quickly viewed by millions of fans. Federer later is coy on whether the video is actually real or not. "Well, there's a lot of debate at the moment" he says later. "You know how it is with magicians. They don't tell how their tricks work, you know."

2011 – Playing in top form described as "a wondrous sight" by Kevin Mitchell in *The Guardian*, Roger Federer defeats a No. 19-ranked and rehabilitating Juan Martin del Potro 6-3, 7-5 in his opening round match at the Western & Southern Financial Masters in Cincinnati. "I expected a tough match with Juan Martin for obvious reasons, and it went better than I thought," says the No. 3-ranked Federer of Del Potro, returning to the ATP Tour after sitting out almost a year rehabilitating from wrist surgery. Says Del Potro of Federer's play, "Roger played like No. 1 in the world tonight."

2012 – Dropping just 13 points on serve and not facing a break point, Roger Federer beats Bernie Tomic 6-2, 6-4 in 62 minutes to reach the quarterfinals of the Western & Southern Financial Masters in Cincinnati.

August 17

2004 – In a self-described "terrible day," Federer's Olympic dreams come to an end in a matter of hours as he is eliminated from both the singles and doubles competitions at the Athens Olympics. In singles, Federer is dismissed in the second round by upstart Czech Tomas Berdych 4-6, 7-5, 7-5, then, with partner Yves Allegro, he loses to Mahesh Bhupathi and Leander Paes of India 6-2, 7-6 (7). "What can I say? It's a terrible day for me, losing singles and doubles," Federer says. "Obviously, I was aiming for a better result than this, but that's what I got. So I have to live with it."

1999 – Bjorn Phau of Germany claims a victory over a 19-year-old Roger Federer in the first round of Washington, D.C., by a 6-2, 6-3 margin. Federer reflects on the loss to Phau eight years later after he beats the German in straight sets in the opening round of the Australian Open. "I had a real drought of six months where I was really struggling to win matches. That's when I lost to Bjorn," says Federer. "That match was really hot I remember in Washington. I could hardly walk anymore after five games. So I had that problem, but then also I had no confidence. If you have no confidence against a player who's steady from the baseline, you're always going to lose. That's where I was just not good enough yet. I went through a patch where I had many losses."

2005 – Losing his serve four times, Roger Federer is still able to hold on and defeat Nicolas Kiefer 4-6, 6-4, 6-4 in the second round of the Cincinnati Masters at Mason, Ohio. "There's a reason he's No. 1 -- he makes the important points," says Kiefer of Federer, playing in his first tournament since winning his third straight Wimbledon the previous month. Federer blames his spotty play on his long break from play that hurts his confidence. "The way you read the game, I have the feeling that's missing most," he says. "Then doubt suddenly creeps to your mind."

2007 – Roger Federer survives a furious stretch of brilliant play from Nicolas Almagro, defeating the Spaniard 6-3, 3-6, 6-2 in the quarterfinals of the Western & Southern Financial Masters in Cincinnati. Writes the Associated Press, "The 21-year-old Almagro had the crowd behind him during the second set, when he matched Federer shot for shot, moved him around the court and won the only break point of the set." Says Federer, "I had one really bad game and it cost me the set. It happens. I'm happy that it doesn't happen every match."

2012 – World No. 1 Roger Federer beats No. 10 seed Mardy Fish 6-3, 7-6(4) to set up a semifinal clash with Olympic doubles partner Stan Wawrinka at the Western & Southern Financial Masters in Cincinnati. Federer wins 88 percent of his first serve points and does not face a break point en route to beating Fish for the eighth time in nine meetings. "It was a great atmosphere," says Federer. "I think it was sellout crowd. That always makes it exciting. Playing an American here in America, it's always special. It was pretty straightforward. Whoever was going to be more aggressive, serve more consistent, and then play maybe a tiny bit better from the baseline was probably going to win. I'm happy I was that guy tonight."

August 18

2005 – Roger Federer beats Olivier Rochus, the man with whom he won the 1998 Wimbledon junior boys' doubles title with, 6-3, 6-4 to reach the quarterfinals of the Cincinnati Masters. "He was just too good," Rochus says. "If you are going to beat him, you have to beat him in the first round. He gets better the more matches he plays."

2007 – Roger Federer comes back from a break down in the third set and beats Lleyton Hewitt 6-3, 6-7 (7), 7-6 (1) in the semifinals of the Western & Southern Financial Group Masters in Cincinnati. Federer comes back from 2-3 down in the third set to beat Hewitt for the 11th straight time. "I think it was the best match I've played this week, no doubt," Federer says. "I think he played well, too. In the end I've got to be happy I came through. It's nice to win a third-set tiebreak." Federer holds a match point at 6-5 in the second-set tiebreaker after winning four straight points from 2-5 down, but Hewitt then wins three points in a row to force the final set. Says Federer of Hewitt, "He's like a cat, with seven lives. How many do they have? Nine, yeah, thought so, seven would have been easy."

2008 – Roger Federer's record 237 consecutive-week reign as the No. 1 ranked player in the world ends as Rafael Nadal assumes the top ranking on the ATP computer. Federer regains the No. 1 ranking again from Nadal 46 weeks later on July 6, 2009.

2012 – Roger Federer is guaranteed to go into the U.S. Open with the No. 1 ATP Ranking – and likely the No. 1 seed – when he wins his ninth straight match against countryman Stan Wawrinka – a 7-6(4), 6-3 decision in the semifinals of the Western & Southern Open in Cincinnati. "The goal has already been achieved by getting back there," says Federer of the No. 1 ranking. "I have to look at the long term, and I would like to stay around for as long as I can. For that reason I have to pace myself at times, but I'm happy I'm playing so well again right off the bat again here in the States."

2010 – After only 28 minutes and seven games of play, Roger Federer wins his opening round match in Cincinnati when Denis Istomin of Uzbekistan retires with an ankle injury with Federer leading 5-2 in the first set.

2011 – Roger Federer needs only 55 minutes to beat James Blake 6-4, 6-1 to reach the quarterfinals of the Western &

Southern Financial Masters in Cincinnati. "Against James it's always a fast-paced match from start to finish," says Federer. "You hope you get on a roll and he doesn't. I was able to counter his attacking style. I was able to play clean on my service games. In the second set he didn't play so well, and the scoreline shows that."

August 19

2012 –Roger Federer posts a 6-0, 7-6 (7) win over world No. 2 Novak Djokovic to give him a record-breaking fifth title at the Western & Southern Financial Masters in Cincinnati and a record-tying 21st "Masters 1000" level ATP tournament title, tying Rafael Nadal for the most all time. The win was also Federer's 76th career singles title, one shy of John McEnroe's third-place tally of 77 singles titles. Only Jimmy Connors (109 titles) and Ivan Lendl (94 titles) have won more men's singles titles than McEnroe and Federer in a career. Djokovic has his serve broken by Federer in the opening game of the match, and then two more times en route to losing the set 6-0 in just 20 minutes. "I was hoping for a good start — but not like that," Federer says. "I'll take it." Federer wins the title without having his serve broken, the first man to win a title of this level to make that distinction, and only faced three break points the entire week but none against Djokovic. "It's been another amazing week for me, and I'm having a magical summer," Federer says during the trophy ceremony. "So it's obviously very nice. And I'm excited about New York now. But I'll first savor this one for a bit."

2007 – Roger Federer wins his 50th career singles title defeating James Blake 6-1, 6-4 in the final of the Western & Southern Financial Group Masters in Cincinnati. Says Federer, "I was mentally much more relaxed today than I was in the first round. I was playing really worried in the first round this week…That was totally different today. I felt I was going to win every point, and that's just huge change of the maybe mental ability, I don't know. But I've had many tournaments I've won happening this way. I didn't feel great in the first round and towards the end of the tournament I played the best tennis of my life, and that was similar today."

2005 – After beating Jose Acasuso 6-4, 6-3 to advance into the semifinals of the Cincinnati Masters, Roger Federer is asked by media to explain to explain his "squash shot" forehand shot that is seen more and more in his repertoire of shots, including one on set point in his match against the Argentine. "Usually I have the feeling if you can play a squash shot, you can play a normal shot, too," Federer says. "It's the first reflex you sometimes get. I don't know where it comes from, you know, the reflex, but I don't like to use it, to be honest, because it really says that you're in an awful position. It's tough to come back from there. Because forehand slice is not really my favorite shot to play, but as long as I don't miss it and sometimes win a few crucial rallies like I did on set point, I think that's great."

2008 – Rafael Nadal is announced as the No. 1 seed at the U.S. Open, marking the first time since January 2004 that a man other than Roger Federer is given the top spot at a Grand Slam tournament.

2009 – Roger Federer faces only one break point and beats world No. 51 Jose Acasuso 6-3, 7-5 in his opening round at the Western & Southern Financial Masters in Cincinnati. Federer connects on 70 percent of his first serves and cracks 14 aces. The match is the fifth and final meeting between the two players, Federer winning on all occasions. Federer is asked in his post-match press conference to discuss the differences between the world No. 1 and No. 51. "I guess we have the advantage, the ones at the top, that we have always a very high standard of play, no matter who we play" Federer says. "Maybe in practice we push it a little bit harder, I don't know. But it's really marginal. People might think guys ranked outside of the top 50 for us it's not a challenge. But I almost lost to Acasuso in Paris, which today probably nobody even remembers anymore. But I was down 5-1 in the third, and looked like I was out of it almost, you know, at one set all. That's why you cannot underestimate any opponents."

2010 – Roger Federer reaches the quarterfinals of the Western & Southern Financial Masters when Germany's Philipp Kohlschreiber withdraws because of a painful right shoulder. Federer's opening round match is decided by an injury as Denis Istomin retires against Federer trailing 2-5 with a foot injury. Federer spends a total of 28 minutes on court in advancing into the quarterfinals.

2011 – Failing to earn a single break-point, Roger Federer is dismissed by a hot Tomas Berdych 6-2, 7-6 (3) in the quarterfinals of the Western & Southern Financial Masters in Cincinnati. The loss is the first for Federer in Cincinnati since 2008. "I definitely didn't feel like I was getting a great read on his serve today, and that definitely cost me a bit of maybe giving myself more opportunities and just getting into the rallies more on his service games, which then maybe would have allowed me to try out a few things and so forth," says Federer. "I thought he served well. He played a good match. Unfortunately I didn't play a very good tiebreaker, and yeah, he was better than me today."

2013 – Roger Federer receives the No. 7 seeding for the U.S. Open, his lowest seed at a major tournament since the 2002 U.S. Open, when he is seeded No. 13.

August 20

2005 – Playing on windy day, with air temperatures in the mid 90s, Roger Federer rallies to beat Robby Ginepri 4-6, 7-5, 6-4 in the semifinals of the Cincinnati Masters. When asked to sum up a final-round match-up with the winner of the Andy Roddick – Lleyton Hewitt semifinal (that is won by Roddick), both of whom he has dominated of late, Federer says, "I'm not overconfident, I'm very confident. I just know what I have to do. I know my game's in place now. Once I win a certain amount of matches, my level of play, I know what I can do, what I can't do. And so I play the percentages I think extremely well in finals, and on big points usually I'm -- well, I've been unbeatable, you know, so that's always what I'm looking for."

2009 – Roger Federer wins his ninth match in nine meetings with David Ferrer, but drops only his second set against the Spaniard in his 3-6, 6-3, 6-4 win in blustery conditions in the third round of the Western & Southern Financial Group Masters. Federer is asked by media after the win on how he keeps his composure in tight matches. "It's something you kind of develop, I guess, over the years," he says. "You have a certain attitude out there and certain approach. Mine you know many years ago was that I tried to stay calm and not give too much away to my opponent and try to hang in there. And even when it's tough sometimes, accept it and try to turn it around. There's never a guarantee, obviously. Today I didn't think I was going to because I thought David was playing a great match. That's why the satisfaction is maybe greater now."

2010 – Playing his first full match of the tournament, Roger Federer defeats Nikolay Davydenko 6-4, 7-5 to reach the quarterfinals of Cincinnati. Federer enters the match having only played seven games in his previous two matches, advancing on a retirement and a walkover. Says Federer, "I was really hoping to kind of get a decent match in today, play solid, and come through and then feel really like I am really in the tournament, because before it didn't really kind of feel that way. So there's a bit of a sense of relief from my side."

2013 – Roger Federer attends the 270th anniversary party for Moet & Chandon, one of his sponsors, at Chelsea Piers in New York City and toasts to the champagne brand that was founded in 1743.

August 21

2002 – Seeded No. 2, playing one week before the start of the U.S. Open, Roger Federer loses his opening match at the TD Waterhouse Cup in Commack, N.Y, falling to Nicolas Massu of Chile 6-7 (5), 6-1, 6-3.

2005 – Roger Federer wins for a 22nd straight time in a tournament final defeating Andy Roddick 6-3, 7-5 to win the Cincinnati Masters championship – his ninth title of the year. The win is Federer's sixth in a row against Roddick and improves his career record against the American to 10-1. "Today I got the feeling occasionally that this is great tennis again," Federer says. The win increases Federer match record for the season to 64-3 match and to 138-9 for the last two years. It also marks his 28th consecutive victory on a hard court and increases his overall winning streak to 18.

2009 – Roger Federer extends his winning streak over Lleyton Hewitt to 13 matches with a 6-3, 6-4 victory in the quarterfinals of the Western & Southern Financial Masters in Cincinnati. Federer connects on 89 percent of his first serves and never faces break point. Says Federer of his run of success over Hewitt, "it is a great run. Well, obviously I'm surprised myself, because he's a top-quality player. He's beaten me so many times in the past that I didn't expect myself to all of a sudden go on such a great run against him. But I guess with the power I have in my shots and when I grew stronger, that maybe made a quite a significant difference in our games. And as I was going up, maybe he was coming down just a touch, especially the last few years. But it seems like he's hanging in there. I never really think going into a match with Lleyton that it's for sure that I will win. That would be foolish."

2010 – Roger Federer has little difficulty in beating Marcos Baghdatis 6-4, 6-3 in 70 minutes to advance into the final of the Cincinnati Masters to face Mardy Fish, a 4-6, 7-6 (3), 6-1 winner over good friend Andy Roddick. "I didn't get broken today, so that was a first in this Northern American tour for me," Federer says in his post-match press conference. "I thought I played a good match. I was able to mix up my serve well and always kept him off balance. So it kind of worked for me."

August 22

2009 – Never facing deuce on his serve, Roger Federer ends a four-match losing streak to Andy Murray, beating the Scotsman 6-2, 7-6 (8) in the semifinals of Cincinnati, benefitting from a Murray double-fault on match point. "I was just happy that I managed to keep it close in the second set, because I returned poorly and served poorly," says Murray. "Against Roger, if you do both of those things, it's going to be very difficult."

2010 – Ending a seven-month title drought, Roger Federer beats Mardy Fish 6-7 (5), 7-6 (1), 6-4 to win the Cincinnati Masters for the fourth time and for his 63rd career pro singles title, equaling the number of singles titles Bjorn Borg wins in his career. The title is the first for Federer since he won his 16th major singles title at the Australian

Open the previous January. "I've been playing well the last couple weeks, and today was just another proof that I'm playing really well," Federer says.

2008 – Don King, the legendary boxing promoter, appears with Roger Federer and Rafael Nadal for a promotional event for Nike in advance of the U.S. Open in New York City. "You had the 'Thrilla in Manila.' You had the 'Rumble in the Jungle.' Now, the 'Grapple in the Apple,'" says King at the event. Writes Christian Red in the *New York Daily News*, "But this is no second coming of Ali-Frazier in the Philippines. No rematch between Ali and Foreman in Zaire. The only punches likely to be thrown are a right or left uppercut after winning a point." Says Federer, "I'm happy we don't have contact sports, especially with Rafa's biceps."

August 23

2009 – Playing a month after his twin girls were born, Roger Federer wins his first title as a father beating Novak Djokovic 6-1, 7-5 in the finals of Cincinnati. "That's the special part, especially winning for the first time as a dad," Federer says. "It gets me going emotionally a little bit, because I know it's been a wonderful summer." Federer breaks Djokovic's serve in the match's second game, a 13-minute game that features 22 points.

2013 – On the 40th anniversary of the debut of the ATP rankings, Roger Federer and 18 other ATP world No. 1 ranked players marks the occasion at the Waldorf Astoria in New York City. Federer is joined by the first ATP world No. 1 Ilie Nastase as well successors John Newcombe, Jimmy Connors, Bjorn Borg, John McEnroe, Ivan Lendl, Mats Wilander, Stefan Edberg, Jim Courier, Marcelo Rios, Carlos Moya, Yevgeny Kafelnikov, Gustavo Kuerten, Lleyton Hewitt, Juan Carlos Ferrero, Andy Roddick, Rafael Nadal and Novak Djokovic. The elite group of players take part in question and answer sessions, share their experiences of reaching the elusive ranking and pose for a group photo. Federer, who holds the No. 1 ranking for a record 302 weeks, speaks about sharing the stage with the players who inspired him, particularly Edberg. "It was very important for me to have someone to look up to. Stefan was one of them, so it's nice to see you here tonight and all the others players," he says. "We've put such huge effort in the game, and that's a platform we can enjoy today. So it's unbelievable. Thanks for being an inspiration Stefan, all of you here today."

2008 – In his pre-event U.S. Open press conference, fresh off winning the Olympic gold medal at the Beijing Olympics with Stan Wawrinka, Federer is asked about the satisfaction of winning doubles gold after losing out on singles gold with a quarterfinal loss to James Blake. "Some people ask me that, you know, if sort of if it made up for losing the singles, but it's completely irrelevant because it's two completely different things," says Federer. "I had hopes to make gold in singles and maybe in doubles, and once I lost the singles I right away played doubles. So there was no time really to be disappointed about it, even though that was the big goal of the season for me, as well. Like winning Wimbledon and then winning the Olympic gold. So I still got my Olympic gold, but in doubles. Honestly the celebration was much more intense. It was very different to winning alone on a tennis court. You might have heard that. So for me it was very special winning with my teammate."

August 24

2003 – In his pre-U.S. Open press conference, Roger Federer is asked if he feels any different coming into this U.S. Open after having finally broken through and winning a major title at Wimbledon. "Yeah, totally different," Federer responds. "I feel much more relaxed. The pressure I've felt over the last few Grand Slams hasn't been so much fun. So I'm very happy to have come over that stage. Now it's about proving more that Wimbledon title, not about just prove that I can win one. It's totally different. I feel much more relaxed inside."

2013 – Roger Federer conducts his pre-U.S. Open press conference and shares his thoughts at being ranked and seeded No. 7 – his lowest standing in a decade. "I think the rankings, they fluctuate a lot, especially if you don't play so well," Federer says. "If you play great you move up or go down rather quickly. No. 7 I don't think is a huge drop from No. 4, but people are going to say what they like. Important is that I concentrate on my game and, that the passion is there, that I work the right way, that I'm prepared, and then that I feel like I can win a tournament. Then the ranking actually itself is secondary. But I have looked at the rankings my whole life. I used to be incredibly excited on Monday seeing how many spots my ranking went up or down. Usually it was more excited that it was going up. The older you get the less you pay a bit of attention about it."

In a U.S. Tennis Association hosted conference call from August 3, 2011, Roger Federer discussed his feelings about the U.S. Open. "(I get) just a great feeling coming back to New York, honestly," Federer said. "I liked it from day one. It was one of those tournaments I right away fell in love with. Just the buzz and energy over there. Sure, it was a bit overwhelming at first. I kind of always liked to play there. Difficult with the wind, humidity, the city behind it, the whole deal. Having to deal with that was quite interesting. Every time the U.S. Open rolls around, I'm very, very excited."

August 25

2007 – In a benign pre-event U.S. Open press conference, Roger Federer is asked by the media of his feelings on night matches at the U.S. Open. "I do like the night sessions. I prefer them over the day sessions, to be honest," he says. "Even though the schedule is tough, you know, because you finish late, then it's hard to get back into the rhythm. But, still, I do prefer to play at night because it's more special, electrifying. The crowds come out in big numbers. Yeah, somehow you always have the feeling you're playing better at night than during the day." Federer enjoys the night matches so much at the U.S. Open that he goes 23-0 in night-session matches at Flushing Meadows from 2000 until 2012, when he loses in the quarterfinals to Tomas Berdych.

2008 – Roger Federer joins fellow U.S. Open men's and women's singles champions for a special on-court ceremony at the U.S. Open to celebrate the 40th anniversary of the Open Era of professional tennis. Federer, John McEnroe and Billie Jean King are the only three former champions to receive a standing ovation when introduced to the Arthur Ashe Stadium crowd. Federer discusses the reception he receives following his first-round victory the following night. "You never know what kind of a reception you're going to get, especially like last night being next to so many other legends and champions and people that inspired me as a player, as a person, and then also people who were so influential in the game," he says. "And then to walk out and almost get a bigger roar than them, it's almost a little bit uneasy. At the same time it's very nice, and I appreciate it very much, especially not being an American."

2010 – Roger Federer participates in the Nike "Lights On Lights Out Primetime Knockout" event in New York City prior to the U.S. Open and discusses how he gets involved with his match outfits before big tournaments. "We try to be involved, I like to talk colors and cuts," Federer says as reported by Priya Rao of the *Wall Street Journal*. "I ask [Vogue editor Anna Wintour] what she thinks. She gives a second opinion. A very strong second opinion. I asked her about the pink color I was wearing last week and she was like, 'Are you sure about that, Roger?'" The event also features Serena Williams, Maria Sharapova,

John McEnroe, New York Giants football star Justin Tuck, model Bar Refaeli and others.

2005 – Prior to the U.S. Open in New York, Roger Federer participates in the launch of the *Men's Vogue* brand and meets admirer Anna Wintour, the editor of *Vogue* magazine. Two days later, in his pre-U.S. Open press conference, Federer discusses the launch and his fashion style. "My style, I like quite elegant more and more," he says. "I'm very much into shopping the last especially two years. Got to meet Anna Wintour, and of course you get inspired when you meet people like this. I like to dress up."

2012 – In his pre-tournament U.S. Open press conference, Roger Federer tells reporters of what he drew from losing in the semifinals of the tournament a year ago, after holding a two-sets-to-love lead on Novak Djokovic and blowing two match points, and his return to the world No. 1 ranking. "I think it's not only last year's match that made me get back to world No. 1," Federer says. "There's been a lot of sacrifices done before this match here. Remember, I also had a tough loss at Wimbledon (to Jo-Wilfried Tsonga). That also shook things up a little bit. And then when it happened a second time around after being up two sets to love, I took a bit of a break after going to Sydney for Davis Cup the following week after here. I took some time to assess the situation and how should I move forward. And then of course it was great to start off with a win in Basel last year in my hometown. Then the rest we know. So it's been a great last 12 months. I was able to stay injury-free. I mean, I always did believe that if things turned for the better for me I was always going to be very near to world No. 1. I wasn't far off, but I couldn't plan on Novak going on a 40-match winning streak or Rafa going for almost four Grand Slams in a row, as well. Other guys also have their part to play in it. It's not only up to purely myself. That's where you have to be patient sometimes and just keep working hard and believing that what you're doing is the right thing as well."

August 26

2002 – Saying "I don't see much positive out of this match really" No. 13-seeded Roger Federer snaps a four-match losing streak beating No. 157-ranked Jiri Vanek 6-1, 6-3, 4-6, 7-5 in the first round of the U.S. Open. "The only thing that really helps right now is to win a few matches because lately I haven't been winning at all," Federer says. "Kind of missing the matches. Always a lot of practice in between. You just get bored with practicing the whole time because you want to go out there and play matches and compete. That's missing a little bit right now. It would just be nice to get a few more matches here. I'd be more happy." Federer enters the U.S. Open losing in the first round of Canada to Guillermo Canas, Cincinnati to Ivan Ljubicic and in Long Island to Nicolas Massu, after losing in the second round of Gstaad to Radek Stepanek and in the opening round, before that, to Mario Ancic at Wimbledon.

2008 – "Never saw my opponent before. Never saw him play, obviously, 'cause I never saw him" says Roger

Federer after his 6-3, 6-0, 6-3 first-round victory over No. 118-ranked Maximo Gonzalez of Argentina at the U.S. Open. Gonzalez enters the match having never played an ATP-Tour level hard court match or any main draw match at a Grand Slam tournament. "It's unbelievable for me," says Gonzalez after the match of playing Federer. "It was like a dream. I was so happy... I played so good, he played unbelievable, I think, all the time. For me he's No. 1 always."

2007 – Roger Federer sits at the No. 1 ranking for a 187th consecutive week, setting the record for weeks spent consecutively in the top ranking, besting Steffi Graf's mark. Earlier in the year, Federer beats Jimmy Connors's men's record of 160 weeks in a row. "It was not something new," says Federer of the record.

2006 – In his pre-event U.S. Open press conference, two-time defending champion Roger Federer tells reporters that it's actually less pressure coming into a tournament as a two-time defending champion than as a defending champion. "I think it's easier to come back the third time, you know, when you come around and try to defend a title," Federer says. "When you come around the second time, you're defending that title for the first time and you feel a lot of pressure, everybody's talking about you. By now I've gotten used to how to defend big tournaments, and I don't look at it as a big pressure, I just try to prove to myself again that I can do it all over again."

August 27

2013 – Roger Federer equals a remarkable record of consistency in men's tennis, playing in his 56th consecutive Grand Slam tournament, tying the record set by Wayne Ferreira from 1991 to 2004, with his 6-3, 6-2, 7-5 victory over Grega Zemlja of Slovenia in the first round of the U.S. Open. In his post-match press conference, Federer is asked if his passion for tennis is as high as it has ever been. "Yeah, I think so," Federer says. "Clearly when you win everything, it's fun. That doesn't necessarily mean you love the game more. You just like winning, being on the front page, lifting trophies, doing comfortable press conferences. It's nice. But that doesn't mean you really actually love it, love it. That maybe shines through maybe more in times when you don't play that well. For me, I knew it, winning or losing, practice court or match court, that I love it. So I've been around for too long. Clearly when I had my two girls, I also wasn't sure right off the bat how it was going to be after that. Was I going to be able to play the same schedule? Was my love for the game as big? Were we going to be able to cope with the whole thing, having twins or not? Managed it totally fine. They were at the court today. I'm so happy to see them before and after the match. I'm in a good spot right now. I want to enjoy it as long as it lasts."

2012 – Seeded No. 1 at the U.S. Open for a sixth time, Roger Federer begins the U.S. Open with a 6-3, 6-2, 6-4 win over American Donald Young, a player who the week before at the Winston-Salem Open ended a 17-match ATP losing streak. "First round at the U.S. Open can always bring a lot of pressure with it," says Federer. "It was very windy out there and extremely humid. I'm just happy I was able to weather the conditions and a dangerous opponent."

2005 – UNICEF, the world's leading children's organization, presents Roger Federer with a plaque as a token of its appreciation for the efforts of the ATP and pro tennis to rapidly raise funds to support UNICEF's relief efforts in south Asia immediately after the tsunami struck the region. Federer accepts the framed photograph at the U.S. Open's Arthur Ashe Kids' Day on behalf of all players. "I'm very honored to accept this from a great organization like UNICEF," says Federer. Says Charles J. Lyons, President of the U.S. Fund for UNICEF, says, "The ATP, its players, employees and fans have raised significant funds and awareness to support our mission. As soon as the ATP and the players heard about the disaster, they wanted to help in any way they could. This partnership will continue to go a long way in helping children around the world lead happier, healthier lives and develop to their full potential." Federer is the lead organizer of the tsunami fundraising exhibition in March at the Pacific Life Open in Indian Wells -- called ATP All-Star Rally for Relief -- and secures the participation of nearly every Top 10 player in the world, including Andy Roddick, Andre Agassi, Lleyton Hewitt, Marat Safin and several leading Sony Ericsson WTA Tour players. Federer also donates money and memorabilia for fund-raising auctions. His on-going charitable work in South Africa on behalf of the Roger Federer Foundation is featured on the stadium's big screen. "We all did individual things, but I wanted to get all of us together to do something as a group," Federer says. "It was great fun, but more importantly it raised more needed funds for the tsunami victims."

2003 – Beginning play on the first Wednesday of the U.S. Open, Roger Federer, the reigning Wimbledon champion, plays his first Grand Slam tournament match as a major champion defeating Jose Acasuso of Argentina 5-7, 6-3, 6-3, 2-0, retire. Acasuso retires from the match with a back injury, but Federer says in his post-match press conference that he felt firmly enough in control of the match at that point. "I was already winning when he got injured and I felt in control so I wasn't too worried," says Federer. "I felt really good during the match from a physical point of view. I was a little impatient early on but I bounced back and I was serving pretty good." Federer says walking onto the Grand Slam stage for the first time as a major champion gave him a shot of confidence. "Once you walk on the court, doesn't change much, maybe a little bit more confidence," he says. "You have the No. 2 seed next to your name. Doesn't really matter in the end. I'm not looking at this whole thing very different than I used to."

2007 – Roger Federer has little trouble with Scoville Jenkins in the first round of the U.S. Open, defeating the American wild-card entrant 6-3, 6-2, 6-4. "It was a good match, tough match," he says. "Didn't allow my opponent many chances on my serve."

2005 – Entering the U.S. Open as the defending champion for the first time, Roger Federer, in his pre-tournament press conference, tells the media of the pressure that constantly feels as the world No. 1. "Well, pressure's there, you know, especially going into Grand Slams where you have a win from last year," Federer says. "I've experienced it on a couple of occasions. It's not the easiest thing to do, so you really want to, you know, not take any chances in your preparation and really focus on what's been working in the past and try to do that again without being too crazy. For me, it's been working. Since I'm No. 1, I've been playing with less pressure, I have the feeling. But obviously sometimes it comes back."

2011 – Conducting his pre-U.S. Open press conference as Hurricane Irene approaches New York, Federer discusses how the coming storm will affect his pre-tournament training sessions. "I kind of usually always take a break anyway shortly before the tournament. So, you know, I'm not anxious now having to hit tomorrow," Federer says. "I won't be playing tomorrow. It's not an issue. I'm not even going to try to. It wasn't on the plan anyway to do so, but sure it's somewhat scary because we don't know how hard it's gonna hit us. I've got family. We're in New York City, you know, it's not just a regular city. It's quite something with all the buildings. So it's unusual, but we'll follow the news closely and we'll try to stay as safe as we can so we get through it."

August 28

2001 – Roger Federer, playing only his second match since his spectacular Wimbledon performance where he upsets seven-time champion Pete Sampras, beats Lars Burgsmuller of Germany 6-4, 6-4, 6-4 in the first round of the U.S. Open. After losing to Ivan Ljubicic in the first round of the post-Wimbledon Swiss Open in Gstaad, Federer sits out the entire rest of the summer recuperating from a groin injury.

2004 – Seeded No. 1 at the U.S. Open for the first time, Roger Federer conducts a pre-event press conference at Flushing Meadows and discusses his chances to step up and move deep into a U.S. Open draw after three fourth-round finishes. "I feel like I've played good here, but not great," Federer says. "I never played bad. Three times fourth round, it's not bad, but now I think it's time for me to step it up because I've played so well in the last few Grand Slams. I know the surface. I have no problems with New York or – how do you say – the crowd or the busy, big life. It's a nice change for me. I really hope I can play better this year."

2010 – In his pre-tournament press conference at the U.S. Open, Roger Federer is asked how it feels to enter the tournament not as the defending champion for the first time in five years. "I look back at the last six years I guess of being incredibly successful. Now, being defending champion or not doesn't change a whole lot," Federer says. "Okay, maybe I don't have as many points to defend, but I don't have sleepless nights over that kind of stuff anymore. That was back in the day when I was trying to make a move in the rankings. I was thinking, What do I have next week to defend? I don't play that game anymore. It's about performing well and trying to win the U.S. Open again. Maybe there is an extra incentive for me to try to win it again after being two points away last year.

It was a disappointing loss for me. I felt like that was one of the finals I should have never lost. At the end, Del Potro played great and deserved the victory. It was a tough one to swallow. But, yeah, I've had a bit of an up and down season so far. I've won the Australian Open, so I have a chance to win a second one this season. There's still a lot to play for. That's why I'm excited to be back in New York and feeling great."

August 29

2003 – Roger Federer advances into a third-round match with American James Blake at the U.S. Open by defeating Jean-Rene Lisnard, 6-1, 6-2, 6-0. "I expect a good match, a fair match especially, because he's a nice guy," says Federer of playing Blake. "We've never played. It's going to be a first time. It's nice to play a crowd favorite also. It's going to be a good crowd. I think it's going to be a good match. Looking forward to it." Federer says his concentration and focus early in each set is key to decisive victory over Lisnard. "You always got to concentrate in the beginning of the sets," says Federer. "This is when it went well for me. I made sure I had a lot of first serves in, you know, so I didn't have to go for my second serve, because that's what he wanted. I kind of like his game – already did in Gstaad. I didn't expect to beat him again so easy."

2002 – Roger Federer, seeded No. 13, is devastatingly efficient in dismissing Michael Chang 6-3, 6-1, 6-3 in the second round of the U.S. Open. "Against Michael, you always get into the rally because his second serve is not very good, so you can kind of put it into play quite easy," Federer says. "For me, obviously it's quite convenient because either I can chip and charge sometimes on big points or I can just play deep and then get into the point. From the baseline with him I feel like he can't really hit a winner against me, I can always run them down. I don't put too much pressure on myself to hit the winner right away. I know even if he attacks me, it's not so, so dangerous maybe like somebody else. But, yeah, I'm happy the way it went today."

2007 – Debuting an all-black tennis outfit that earns him the nick-name "Darth Federer," Roger Federer beats Paul Capdeville of Chile 6-1, 6-4, 6-4 in a second-round night match at the U.S. Open. Says Federer to reporters of his new outfit, "I thought it was a cool mix with kind of the tuxedo kind of look, all black. Why not? Especially at night. During the day you could never wear a black shirt anyway because it would be too hot. I kind of like to do sophisticated statements. Also at Wimbledon with the jacket, I kind of took a chance. I thought I was going to look like an idiot. But kind of people liked it. I thought actually it was a great idea. So I backed it up this year with an entire outfit, and here in New York with a black one. So it's good stuff." Federer's win sets up a third-round match up against up-and-coming American John Isner, a wild-card entry into the tournament. After Isner beats qualifier Rick De Voest of South Africa in his second-round match, he jokes in his on-court interview of playing Federer, "I don't know much about the guy. I've heard he's good."

2008 – Saying "I was never really in danger, so it was actually pretty good for me," No. 2 seed Roger Federer advances into the third round of the U.S. Open beating No. 137th-ranked Thiago Alves of Brazil 6-3, 7-5, 6-4. "I knew the longer the match would go the more tired we would get, so it was a good match for me" says Federer of the match against the qualifier in which he approached the net 42 times (winning 24 of the points).

2011- Roger Federer registers his 224th career Grand Slam singles win, tying him with Andre Agassi for second-place all-time, defeating Santiago Giraldo of Colombia 6-4, 6-3, 6-2 in the first round of the U.S. Open. Federer trails only Jimmy Connors who won 233 Grand Slam tournament matches. Says Federer of his opening night performance, "It's always one of those moments you train for, to get on the first night of the U.S. Open. You try to put on a good show and I was able to play a good match today, so I'm pleased. It could have been swifter maybe but I'm happy."

2013 – Hitting 37 winners against 25 unforced errors, Roger Federer, seeded No. 7, advances into the third round of the U.S. Open beating Carlos Berlocq of Argentina 6-3, 6-2, 6-1. Says Federer of his victory, "It's one of those matches I expect myself to win if possible in straight sets, and, you know, gain confidence in the process. All those things happened, so, yeah, I'm pleased about it."

August 30

2001 – "I had no idea who he was," says Roger Federer of American Robby Ginepri, ranked No. 327, after his 6-2, 7-5, 6-1 second-round win at the U.S. Open. "I just had to find out a little bit more how he plays." Federer also tells reporters in his post-match press conference that his injured groin, that keeps him out of all but one tournament leading into the U.S. Open following his monumental upset of Pete Sampras at Wimbledon, is greatly improved. "I would say 95%. I'm still not 100%, for sure," Federer says of his groin. "Still when I'm pushing really hard, I feel a little bit. I think as long as I don't slip, really have a terrible movement, it shouldn't be a problem."

2004 – Roger Federer's true quest for perfection is shown at his disgust with himself for not serving out a straight-set win over Albert Costa in the first round of the U.S. Open. Federer has his serve broken while trying to close out Costa, leading 7-5, 6-2, 5-2, before serving out the match on his second opportunity two games later. "I definitely wish it was different at the end," Federer says. "Obviously to win, but to close it out like I usually do, just serve it out. I guess it seems like I was too dominant for a while. There was not enough rallies suddenly, and that worked against me because the game I lost, I was against the wind. Actually to get the 5-2 lead, I think if I get that lead, I'm not going to give it away. But I got broken, and then when I served for the match, I just had a terrible service game. I went for too much. That's how quickly it goes."

2005 – A trio of breadsticks is what Roger Federer offers Czech Ivo Minar in a 6-1, 6-1, 6-1 dismantling in the first round of the U.S. Open in 61 minutes.

2006 – Roger Federer beats Yeu- Tzuoo Wang of Chinese Taipei 6-4, 6-1, 6-0 in the first round of the U.S. Open. "I thought I was always in control," Federer says of his easy victory. "I thought I played pretty well. Not too many mistakes. I played aggressive, and it worked out. So it was a good match, all in all." Federer fires seven aces and faces only one break point in the 99-minute match. Says Federer, "The hard work as all paid off, and now I'm always in the position where I'm the big, big favorite for every tournament I play. That has been tough sometimes for other players."

2010 – One year after hitting perhaps the signature shot of his career – a tweener winner against Novak Djokovic in the semifinals of the U.S. Open – Roger Federer thrills crowds at the U.S. Open yet again with the same shot in the first round against Brian Dabul of Argentina. Federer hits the shot with Dabul serving down 6-1, 5-3, ad-in, but rates the one he hit in the second-to-last point against Djokovic as more important, due to the round and circumstances. "Maybe in terms of difficulty, maybe this one was harder, because I had the feeling I had to run a longer distance, and I was farther back somehow," Federer says of the shot after his 6-1, 6-4, 6-2 victory. "I had to really give the last big push at the end. I didn't have time to set it up. So I felt like this one was incredible again. I turned around and couldn't believe the shot landed in the corner." Writes Diane Pucin of the *Los Angeles Times* of the shot against

Dabul, "It came from deep in the back of the court, when Federer was almost running into the wall; it was born partly of desperation but also partly of confidence, a forehand hit between his legs, across the court and skipping across the sideline, a winner past helpless Brian Dabul of Argentina. The night session crowd at Arthur Ashe Stadium roared and Federer offered a little bow and a sheepish smile."

2012 – Roger Federer advances into the third round of the U.S. Open with a 6-2, 6-3, 6-2 win over Bjorn Phau of Germany. In his post-match press conference, Federer is reminded of Phau's victory over him 13 years earlier in Washington, D.C. and Federer reflects back on their early careers. "It is quite fascinating actually how careers go, sometimes how juniors really don't matter, even though I probably was a better junior than he was. I wasn't as tough as a competitor back in the day. I remember going to a future in Greece, spending some time with him there. I think we were both waiting for lucky losers at one point. He got in and I didn't because he was ahead of me in the rankings. Here we are on center court at the U.S. Open. It's quite amazing. I'm glad we both got the opportunity to experience something like we did tonight. Of course, I never believed in that moment that I was going to become such a great player. I remember walking off practice courts and telling my partner in practice, I'm sorry, I don't enjoy it right now, I have to stop because I'll just ruin your practice instead of toughening it out and making a good practice for him, at least. I was so weak back then. It was just different times, look. I'm happy I turned the corner at the right times, learned from my mistakes. Now I can enjoy it so much more. I was able to make it on the big stage. That I did react in time, I am very relieved that that happened in my career."

August 31

2003 – Connecting on only three of 23 break point opportunities, Roger Federer beats American James Blake 6-3, 7-6 (4), 6-3 in the third round at the U.S. Open in a Sunday night match. Federer has 20 of his break point opportunities in the second set, converting on only one. Blake saves eight break points in one game alone. Writes Lisa Dillman of the *Los Angeles Times*, "The break points kept coming and coming, almost as if they were on a conveyer belt. Blake would knock one away and another would pop up, almost like in the famous episode of "I Love Lucy." Blake was ordinary at deuce, extraordinary at ad out." Says Federer of missing all of his break points, "It happens."

2008 – A convincing 6-3, 6-3, 6-2 win over No. 30 Radek Stepanek in the third round of the U.S. Open helps restore Roger Federer's invincibility factor, in the views of the tennis media in his post-match press conference. "That's the advantage I have," the No. 2-ranked Federer says of restoring the aura that he has around him, after losing earlier in the year at Wimbledon, and the French and Australian Opens. "If I were to win a big tournament, again, one of the Slams, right away I have the invincibility factor again, which is great for me." On whether his easy win over Stepanek will send a message of the rest of the U.S. Open field, Federer says, "It's good for me to not waste any energy. I'm playing well and moving on in the draw. At the end of the day, what counts is winning the tournament. And anyway, you forget who you beat, how you won. You forget all the unforced errors you made, and all anybody's going to talk about is the finals. That's how I look at things. I don't try to impress anybody in the early rounds. If it happens, that's great. I don't really care that much." Writes Marc Carig in the *Washington Post* after Federer's victory, "After winning match point, Federer briefly extended his index finger toward the sky, just a second before the song "Still the One" blared over the loudspeakers for the third time in the last week."

2009 – Playing a self-described "tricky match" against "a guy whose got absolutely nothing to lose" world No. 1 Roger Federer has his serve broken twice against NCAA singles champion Devin Britton from the University of Mississippi in a 6-1, 6-3, 7-5 first-round victory at the U.S. Open.

2002 – Roger Federer beats Xavier Malisse 4-6, 6-3, 6-4, 6-4 to reach the round of 16 of the U.S. Open. After entering the tournament with a four-match losing streak and losing five of his last six matches, the No. 13-seeded Federer says he finally feels like his game is coming around after also beating Jean-Rene Lisnard in the first round and Michael Chang in the second round at Flushing Meadows. "Even though I lost the first set, I was just staying positive out there, trying to come back strong the second set," says Federer. "That worked really well. I felt mentally I was very good already against Chang. Compared to the first-round match, I was still very, very negative, very down on myself, very disappointed quickly. So now in the last two matches, I really felt like this is how I can play, should play, and I am playing. That was a nice feeling today."

2013 – Roger Federer needs only 81 minutes to register a 6-3, 6-0, 6-2 victory over world No. 63 Adrian Mannarino in a third-round night match at the U.S. Open. Says Federer of playing night matches at the U.S. Open and how it affects his preparation, "I have played I think 20 plus matches under the lights here and other tournaments as well around the world for years, so for me there is not a special preparation I need to do. Very often during on the tour I play later in the day, usually, you know, 6:00, 7:00, 8:00, 9:00 p.m. It's something I'm used to. But in this stadium with this crowd it's always very particular, clearly, because it is the biggest stadium in the world, it is New York City, and you don't ever know how many times more you're going to play on this court. You always want to enjoy it."

SEPTEMBER

September 1

2001 – Roger Federer advances into a fourth-round match-up with Andre Agassi after beating No. 24-ranked Sjeng Schalken in the U.S. Open third round 6-4, 7-5, 7-6(3). "Well, seeing a draw the beginning of the week, I was hoping to play him in the fourth round" Federer says of his pending match with the No. 2 seed. "But you don't really think about that yet, because you've got too many matches to come. So now that it's a fact, I'm looking forward to it. Most likely we gonna play on center court, so it's nice to play here."

2004 – World No. 1 and reigning Australian Open and Wimbledon champion Roger Federer drops a rare set in a second-round match at a major championship, to a qualifier none-the-less. The qualifier is, however, future top 20 player Marcos Baghdatis of Cyprus, who would also win a set from Federer 18 months later in the final of the Australian Open. On this day in the second round of the U.S. Open, Federer wins by a 6-2, 6-7 (4-7), 6-3, 6-1 margin.

2006 – Roger Federer evens his career head-to-head with Tim Henman at 6-6 with a 6-3, 6-4, 7-5 win in the second round of the U.S. Open. Henman is an early nemesis for Federer, winning the first round meetings and six of the first seven. The match is played at 11 a.m. on Arthur Ashe Stadium, a rare starting time for the defending men's singles champion and the No. 1 seed. After the match, Federer is asked if he prefers the raucous night session atmosphere over the quiet morning atmosphere on Ashe Stadium. "Yeah, I mean, of course, because there (at night) you have the more electrifying atmosphere," Federer says to reporters. "The focus is more on this one night session match than all around the grounds and everything. I got to keep on winning to get my night session here, I think. That's fine. Maybe it's going to be an advantage to have played early because of the rain coming in. I mean, I've played some night sessions here, so I don't mind getting out early for a change. I haven't played for a while at 11:00. But I think it's good for Europe, too. Two Europeans playing each other, it's good for the time change. I hope they showed a lot of it in Europe."

2007 – Roger Federer is momentarily shell-shocked by the booming serves of 6-foot, 10-inch 22-year-old American upstart John Isner but steadies the boat after dropping the first set and advances to the fourth round of the U.S. Open with a 6-7 (4), 6-2, 6-4, 6-2 victory. Says Federer of his thoughts after losing the first set, "I'm thinking, this could be a really difficult match from now on. I knew it from the start, but now I have proof. I was worried, you know, but I was staying calm. I knew for him to serve five sets this way was almost impossible." Says Isner of playing

Federer, "By far that was the most fun I've had playing a tennis match; it was amazing. Especially after winning the first set. The feeling of beating Roger Federer in a set, sitting down, it was crazy."

2011 – Roger Federer wins his 225th career match at a Grand Slam tournament – breaking out of a second-place tie with Andre Agassi – with a 6-3, 6-2, 6-2 win over Dudi Sela of Israel in the second round of the U.S. Open.

2012 – Winning 26 of 27 points at the net, Roger Federer advances into the quarterfinals of the U.S. Open with a 6-3, 6-4, 6-4 win over Fernando Verdasco.

September 2

2002 – Playing on a non-show court for the last time at the U.S. Open, Roger Federer, seeded No. 13, loses on Court 7 at the USTA National Tennis Center to No. 34-ranked Max Mirnyi 6-3, 7-6 (5), 6-4 in the round of 16.

2005 – In a highly-entertaining second-round match featuring fantastic ball-striking, Roger Federer advances into the third round of the U.S. Open with a thrilling 7-5, 7-5, 7-6 (2) victory over the crafty double-fisted groundstroker Fabrice Santoro of France, ranked No. 76. "I had a blast out there today because rarely the crowd really gets into a match like this," Federer says. "I knew it from the start, this could be a very interesting match, the way he plays, the way I play. This is a night session at the U.S. Open, I knew it could be a great one."

2008 – In a three-hour, 32-minute five-set, fourth-round match, featuring 60 unforced errors and plenty of media-described "guttural yells," Roger Federer advances into the quarterfinals of the U.S. Open with a 6-7 (5), 7-6 (5), 6-3, 3-6, 6-3 decision over Russia's Igor Andreev. Federer credits the rowdy Arthur Ashe Stadium crowd for his rare on-court animations – "that feeling of going crazy" – as the four-time defending champion staves off the upset bid. Chuck Culpepper of the *Los Angeles Times* describes the Federer-Andreev affair as "a long, stirring slog of a match" that "had Federer as a sort of mini-Connors impersonating a jackhammer and vibrating his body in a double fist pump after a pivotal break of service in a fifth set." Says Federer to the media of his five-set effort, "I was really happy because in five sets you go through different stages of feelings, of playing well, playing bad. And in the fifth set you try not to make that many errors, and hopefully, you know, you'll get off on a good start. That's exactly what happened. I was just really pleased with my fighting spirit."

2009 – Punctuated by his eighth ace of the match, five-time defending champion and top-seeded Roger Federer beats 28-year-old Simon Greul of Germany 6-3, 7-5, 7-5 in the second round of the U.S. Open.

2010 – Labeling his first two rounds at the U.S. Open as a "perfect start," Roger Federer beats Andreas Beck of Germany 6-3, 6-4, 6-3 in the second round of the U.S. Open. "I played Monday, had two days off. I had another easy one physically today and here I am in the third round feeling like I'm completely in the tournament. I got a sense for how the court speed is again. I got the sense of the crowd and the wind now as well. I played one night, one day. I have all the answers after two matches. Obviously they weren't the most difficult matches. I didn't have to save multiple break points or whatever. Even though I got broken today, I feel really good. Tougher matches will only be coming up now, I guess. I underestimate nobody."

2013 – For the first time since 2003, Roger Federer loses before the quarterfinals of the U.S. Open, losing for the first time in a sanctioned-match in his career to Tommy Robredo by a 7-6 (3), 6-3, 6-4 in the fourth round. "I kind of self-destructed, which is very disappointing," says the 32-year-old Federer, who won all 10 previous matches with Robredo. "It was a frustrating performance." The No. 7-seed Federer hits 43 unforced errors and converts on only two of 16 break points. Federer's loss prevents a blockbuster quarterfinal match-up with Rafael Nadal, which would have been his first career meeting with his rival from Spain in Flushing Meadows. The Federer-Robredo match is played on Louis Armstrong Stadium, the No. 2 court at the U.S. Open, after being moved from Ashe Stadium due to rain delays.

September 3

2001 – Andre Agassi, 31, cruises over twenty-year-old Roger Federer 6-1, 6-2, 6-4 in the fourth round of the U.S. Open. Agassi dominates from the start, jumping on Federer 5-0 in the first set. "He started off playing very well," says Federer. "I didn't actually have the feeling I was playing terrible in the beginning. I was always just one shot behind. Just missed a little bit early. But he put a lot of pressure on me. I didn't serve as well as I did the first few matches. My serve didn't help me at all today. That's why it was very tough for me." Says the No. 2-seeded Agassi of his victory, that set up a quarterfinal match against Pete Sampras, "It was like I was in third gear, then switched into fifth gear. Today I absolutely stepped it up in every department. You need it to happen that way sometimes." Agassi, however, says he has great respect for Federer, especially after his Wimbledon upset of Pete Sampras. "I had a lot of respect for his game going out there," Agassi says. "I had a lot of respect for how I felt he could still have turned it around late in that third set."

2006 – Saying "Not losing a set the first three rounds is always awesome," Roger Federer wins his third consecutive straight-set match at the U.S. Open defeating Vince Spadea 6-3, 6-3, 6-0 in the third round of the U.S. Open, in a match played on Louis Armstrong Stadium. "I think it was a great atmosphere out on Armstrong," Federer says. "I've had some great matches out there, you know, playing against Ferrero years ago, like six years ago. Other ones, too. The crowd's much closer to you. There's less space behind you. They're much more into it. So it's good for a change again to play on that court."

2000 – Roger Federer is beaten by No. 12 seed Juan Carlos Ferrero 7-5, 7-6 (6), 1-6, 7-6 (6) in the third round of the U.S. Open.

2007 – "That's awesome. Come on. What have I done?" is Roger Federer's response when media present him with the fact that he wins an incredible 35 straight points on his serve in his 3-6, 6-4, 6-1, 6-4 fourth-round night victory over Feliciano Lopez at the U.S. Open. Federer trails 0-40 in the first game of the third set before reeling off his streak that ends in the final game of the match. "I was feeling great on the serve, my God," says Federer. "I was serving well and playing aggressive, and things really turned around for me. Yeah, it was an awesome match. I really enjoyed it because he did play very well. Right off the bat was hitting his best shot, and that was tough for me. I was relieved when I got that second set, no doubt."

2003 – David Nalbandian continues his mastery over Roger Federer, scoring his fifth victory in five career pro meetings against the Swiss – a 3-6, 7-6 (7), 6-4, 6-3 win on Arthur Ashe Stadium in the fourth round of the U.S. Open. "I never felt I had a great day playing against him," says the No. 2-seeded Federer, who hits 62 unforced errors in the match. "I'm still trying to figure out how to beat him." The first set is delayed twice by rain – for 45 minutes with Federer leading 3-2 in the first set and for another hour after the players return to the court playing only one point on resumption of play. After Federer secures the first set 6-3, he goes down 0-5 in the second set, but, remarkably, wins five games in a row to tie the score at 5-5. After Nalbandian is able to win the second-set tiebreaker, he cruises in the third and fourth sets and upsets the Wimbledon champion. "In the second set I thought I could hang in there," Federer says. "I thought I could get back, but in the end I didn't win. It's a pity."

2011 – Roger Federer escapes a tough test from No. 27-seeded Marin Cilic, defeating the Croatian 6-3, 4-6, 6-4, 6-2 in the third round of the U.S. Open. "I thought it was a tough match," Federer says. "Coming in I knew it was gonna be tricky, and I'm happy that I was able to counter his pace and his good play. It was a tricky match, especially at one set all. In the third set sort of in the beginning I thought that was a key moment because he had momentum on his side. I was not returning and serving exactly the way I wanted, but I was able to turn it around and finished strong in the set. Then in the fourth things were a bit easier. Tough match from start to finish, really, because also the first set could have gone differently. I know that."

September 4

2004 – Top-seeded Roger Federer beats No. 31 Fabrice Santoro 6-0, 6-4, 7-6 (7) to advance to the fourth round of the U.S. Open. "It's just about keeping your focus," Federer says of advancing through the draw. "You take it one match at a time, and pretty soon you're in the final stages of the tournament. After winning three matches, you start to feel comfortable. You start to think about winning."

2005 – Roger Federer beats close friend Olivier Rochus of Belgium 6-3, 7-6 (6), 6-2 to reach the fourth round of the U.S. Open and, in his post-match press conference is asked where he gets the beauty and grace in his game that he is so admired for. "Technique-wise, I think I've always gotten many compliments because everything looks very easy, smooth," Federer says. "On top of that, I think I've really improved my physical shape, so my movement is even better, quicker, smoother. All those things make it now look, you know, basically perfect for some. So I think that's why I get all the compliments. You don't see many guys playing one-handed backhand. That definitely helps, too. I think the one-handed backhand always looks nicer in a way than the double-handed. Obviously, I get commitments because I'm No. 1 in the world. If Olivier would be No. 1 in the world, everybody would be saying how nice he plays. That's just how it is."

2008 – Claiming his 32nd consecutive match victory at the U.S. Open, Roger Federer advances into the semifinals with a 7-6 (7-5), 6-4, 7-6 (7-5) victory over No. 130th-ranked qualifier Gilles Muller of Luxembourg. Federer holds 11 break points but converts only one, in the second set. "It was tough today, especially to break against the wind. It was almost impossible," says Federer. "He's a big guy. He gets great angles and he's got a lot of, you know, safety in his serve, especially the first serve. He does have great variety. So I always knew it was going to be hard to break against that, and it makes it frustrating in itself." Says Mueller of Federer following the match, "I think players have too much respect for him. I mean, he's a nice person outside of the court, and he's a good player, so everybody has a lot of respect for him. But on the court, nobody should have respect for him."

2010 – Enduring blustery conditions, Roger Federer advances into the fourth round of the U.S. Open without the loss of a set, straight-setting Paul-Henri Mathieu 6-4,

6-3, 6-3 in one hour and 39 minutes to improve his career record against the Frenchman to 5-0. "The wind was very strong," says Federer. "I think you could tell Mathieu was really struggling after being down in the score. His serve, his returns, everything kind of falls into pieces. That's what the wind can do to you. I kind of felt comfortable, because you can also use it to your advantage and play really great tennis. You have to be careful with it. After four games or so, I knew what I could do and what I couldn't do."

September 5

2012 – For the first time since 2003, Roger Federer is eliminated at the U.S. Open before the semifinals as the world No. 1 is defeated by Tomas Berdych 7-6 (1), 6-4, 3-6, 6-3 in the quarterfinals. "I really expected myself to play better tonight, especially at night, I have had such a great record," Federer says of the loss, his first in 23 Arthur Ashe night session matches at the U.S. Open, "I felt good. It's such an amazing summer I had. I really thought I was going to come out and play a solid match. I didn't do that tonight. Obviously there is a bit of a letdown now."

2007 – It is not until the third set when Roger Federer gets to break point on Andy Roddick in their quarterfinal match at the U.S. Open, but Federer is still able to tame the American 7-6 (5), 7-6 (4), 6-2 marking his 10th consecutive win over his rival. "There was nothing I could do on his serve for two and a half sets. I didn't see a breakpoint," says Federer. "I definitely played well on my service games. I think I was really consistent. I'm happy he couldn't convert his one breakpoint he had. I played great in the tiebreak. Obviously he had more pressure in the second tiebreaker than in the first one. And once he's down two sets to love in two tiebreaks, that's a hard thing to go against. Obviously against me, as well. I thought it was a very high-standard match. I was very pleased with my performance. I thought actually Andy also played very well." Says Roddick, "I'm not walking off with any questions in my head this time. I'm not walking with my head down. I played my [butt] off out there tonight. I played the right way."

2009 – For a 14th consecutive time, Roger Federer beats Lleyton Hewitt, dispatching the former world No. 1 4-6, 6-3, 7-5, 6-4 in the third round of the U.S. Open. "Maybe, you know, I have too much variation for him" says Federer, when asked by media to explain his run of success over Hewitt. "I guess it's really the details because this match was close. It could have gone either way."

September 6

2004 – Roger Federer advances into the quarterfinals of the U.S. Open for the first time in his career – and without striking a ball – as No. 16 seed Andrei Pavel withdraws from his fourth-round match with Federer with a back injury.

2005 – Losing a set for only the second time in his last 11 Grand Slam matches, Roger Federer advances into the quarterfinals of the U.S. Open with a 6-4, 6-7 (3), 6-3, 6-4 win over Nicolas Kiefer. Ironically, Kiefer also is the only player to win a set from Federer during his run to his third Wimbledon final earlier in the summer. "At the beginning of the year, people were shocked when I lost a set," Federer says. "Not so much now. I wish could win three. But I'm happy as long as I win. I lost a set, but four sets is easier on your body. In the fourth set, I felt I was in control again. I didn't feel like that early. Momentum was all on his side."

2006 – Not losing a point in the first three games of the match, Roger Federer beats Marc Gicquel 6-3, 7-6, 6-3 in the fourth round of the U.S. Open. Playing on Louis Armstrong Court for a second straight match, Federer needs only an hour and 46 minutes to advance.

2008 – With Tropical Storm Hanna heading towards New York, Roger Federer is able to beat the weather, and Novak Djokovic, and advance into his fifth straight U.S. Open final with a 6-3, 5-7, 7-5, 6-2 victory, in a reprise of the previous year's U.S. Open final. Federer is fortunate to finish his match on Arthur Ashe Stadium, where the other men's semifinal match between Rafael Nadal and Andy Murray is started on Louis Armstrong Stadium and not completed, Murray holding a two-sets-to-one lead before the rains cancel play for the day. "I'm happy I got my match through," Federer says in his courtside interview. Of his form in his win, Federer tells reporters in his post-match press conference, "I had moments out there where I really felt, 'This is how I normally play on hard court.' You know, half volleys, passing shots, good serving, putting the pressure on, playing with the wind, using it to my advantage. I definitely had moments during today where

I thought, 'This is how I would like to play every time.' So it was a very nice feeling to get that that feeling back."

2010 – Advancing into his 26th consecutive Grand Slam quarterfinal, Roger Federer straight-sets No. 13 seed Jurgen Melzer of Austria 6-3, 7-6 (4), 6-3, winning his 12th straight set of the tournament. Federer tells reporters that despite not being the defending champion and being the No. 2 seed, he still feels the glare of the tournament spotlight. "I always feel the spotlight's on me regardless of what my ranking is and how I'm playing. I've still got to attend press conferences and all that stuff, so nothing changes from that side," Federer says. "It's hard to read because I get recognized more than ever. Crowds are fantastic, you know, regardless of what my ranking is."

2011 – Roger Federer and Juan Monaco finish their fourth-round match at the U.S. Open at 1:14 am, Federer giving up only three games in 6-1, 6-2, 6-0 rout of his No. 36-ranked opponent. Federer hits 42 winners and hits 14 aces – including four in one game – to win the match in 82 minutes. "Other sports start at 8 in the morning, like golf. It's crazy how our schedules change all the time," says Federer. "As tennis players, it makes it extremely difficult to be on your 'A' game every single day."

September 7

2006 – Saying "The score says it all. The match could have gone either way," Roger Federer edges James Blake 7-6 (7), 6-0, 6-7 (9), 6-4 in a high-energy night match in the U.S.

Open quarterfinals. "It was tough," Federer says. "It was a match of extremely high quality. It takes a lot for two people hitting the ball so hard. I was happy with my game. I didn't make many unforced errors. I pretty much could rely on my serve except for a couple of match points here and there. With so much back and forth, it turned out to be a real thriller."

2009 – Roger Federer cruises against No. 14 seed Tommy Robredo after winning a hard-fought first set, advancing into the U.S. Open quarterfinals with a 7-5, 6-2, 6-2 victory. When asked what made the first set so difficult, Federer responds, "I tried to figure him out a little bit the way he played me. I thought he really played my backhand a lot. I expected him to open it up sometimes towards my forehand, but he didn't. I was a little bit unsure for a while there, how I should play him. He was doing a good job of keeping me off-balance and being intense from the baseline. So it was a key to get the break and not having to maybe go through the tiebreak. I was even down breakpoints, so it was kind of tough. Once I got the lead, I could also hit a bit more freely. That didn't allow him to play his game anymore. I got on top of him and played good tennis."

September 8

2005 – After admitting that he was up until 1:30 am the previous night watching the Andre Agassi and James Blake match, Roger Federer joins Agassi in the U.S. Open semifinals but in a one-sided manner, beating David

Nalbandian 6-2, 6-4, 6-1 in only one hour, 40 minutes. Says Federer of his surprisingly one-sided match against Nalbandian, the man who beats him in the their first five pro matches, "I was expecting a five-set match. I'm surprised this was over so quickly.... I was a little tense going into this match because I knew of his record against me. I was particularly happy I played well." Says Nalbandian of the loss, "Today, he played better than other days. When he plays like this, he's really tough to beat. That's why he's No. 1 in the world. That's why he's lost only three matches this year."

2007 – Nikolay Davydenko is able to break Roger Federer's serve three times in a row, but is still not even able to secure a set against the world No. 1, falling 7-5, 6-1, 7-5 in the semifinals of the U.S. Open. The win puts Federer into a 10th straight major final. "I'm always very well-prepared for the majors," Federer tells the media of his consistency in major tournaments. "I know what it takes. I don't have any hiccups early on in the slams, don't have any, let's say, stupid five-setters, matches I could have won in three or four sets, I end up maybe scraping through in five or maybe even losing those matches. So I stayed away from those moments. In the end, when the second week comes around, I play my best. The points get tougher, like here. I played basically really good against Davydenko and against Roddick too." Writes Bill Dwyre of the *Los Angeles Times* of Federer, "The superlatives emanating from TV and print media will be both excessive and warranted."

2008 – Seeded in the unusual position of No. 2, Roger Federer wins his fifth-straight U.S. Open men's singles title – and his 13th major singles title – defeating Andy Murray 6-2, 7-5, 6-2 in a rain-delayed Monday final. The title also marks Federer's 13th major singles title, one shy of Pete Sampras's record 14 men's singles Slams. "One thing's for sure. I'm not going to stop at thirteen," Federer says after the final. "I really feel tennis is in a great place right now. We have incredible athletes." The victory prevents Federer from finishing the year without a major singles title for the first time since 2002.

2004 – Roger Federer and Andre Agassi battle in a marquee Wednesday night U.S. Open quarterfinal and, shortly after Federer takes a two-sets-to-one lead after winning the third set 7-5, the match is delayed by rain and later postponed with Agassi serving at deuce in the first game of the fourth set.

2010 – Roger Federer advances into his seventh straight U.S. Open final, exacting revenge on Robin Soderling, the man who ended his record run of 23 straight Grand Slam semifinal appearances earlier in the year in the French Open quarterfinals. Federer, however, says that his 6-4, 6-4, 7-5 victory is not motivated on revenge for his loss to the Swede in Paris. "I just feel happy that I played a good match under tough circumstances against a player who's really hard to beat these days, especially on the hard courts," says Federer. "For me, this is obviously a big victory. It's always nice beating fellow top 10 players and moving on in tournaments and giving yourself chances, and that's what I've been able to do. I don't need revenge to fuel my motivation. It really doesn't, because I love playing in the stadium in front of people like this. I love tennis, and that's enough motivation for me to really get it going on a night like this."

2011 – After blowing a two-set lead against Jo-Wilfried Tsonga in the quarterfinals of Wimbledon, and losing to the Frenchman at the Rogers Cup in Canada, Roger Federer beats the No. 11-ranked player 6-4, 6-3, 6-3 to advance into the semifinals of the U.S. Open. Federer and Tsonga play five games under the lights at Arthur Ashe Stadium before play is delayed for over an hour due to rain. After closing out the straight-set victory, Federer is asked by the media if Tsonga's comeback victory from Wimbledon entered his mind when up two sets to love. Says Federer, "A little bit, yeah. Why not, right? Little flashbacks, you know, forehand goes by, serve I can't reach. But I felt like -- I was returning way better this time around, or his serve wasn't going through the court as much as at Wimbledon, and I just felt I was in control from the baseline, from on my serve, on my return. I just felt like I had my teeth in the match. Sure, it could have changed. I felt the same way at Wimbledon, but obviously at Wimbledon the margins are a bit smaller, I feel. Today I felt I took the right decisions out of the matches we had in Wimbledon, and especially in Montreal where I was very unhappy with my game. I think the Montreal match was actually key for me winning this match today."

September 9

2007 – Saving a combined total of seven set points, Roger Federer wins his 12th major singles title – and his fourth straight U.S. Open men's singles title – defeating Novak Djokovic 7-6 (4), 7-6 (2), 6-4 in the final. Federer trails by a service break in each set and Djokovic holds five set points in the first set and two in the second, but is unable to put away the world No. 1. Jokes Djokovic following the match, "My next book is going to be called, 'Seven Set Points." Says Federer "I think straight sets was a bit brutal for Novak, to be honest. He deserved better than that. He's had a fantastic run, not only this tournament but the entire year. I told him at the net 'keep it up.' We're going to have many more battles I think." Says the 26-year-old Federer of possibly breaking Pete Sampras' record of 14 major titles, "I think about it a lot now. To come so close at my age is fantastic, and I hope to break it."

2004 – Resuming their U.S. Open quarterfinal match postponed the previous night due to rain, Roger Federer and Andre Agassi battle through very windy conditions before Federer wins in five sets 6-3, 2-6, 7-5, 3-6, 6-3. Federer leads by two-sets-to-one before rain delays the conclusion of their match. "Today it felt like you were playing out on a field, where there is no wind breakers," says Federer. "So this has been one of the toughest experiences I've had with the wind in a match situation, especially in such a big one. So I'm happy to have coped well with that."

2006 – Roger Federer becomes the first man since Rod Laver in 1961 and 1962 to reach six straight major singles finals when he beats Nikolay Davydenko 6-1, 7-5, 6-4 in the semifinals of the U.S. Open. "You don't think of making history or something at that moment itself," says Federer, the two-time defending Open champion. "Once you get there, you think of each and every point. You don't think, 'This could be my third U.S. Open.' You just hope to win this U.S. Open. After that, it kind of sinks in when you lift the trophy like, 'I've been in this situation before. It's great that I have the opportunity to lift it again.'" Of playing American Andy Roddick in the final in front of a pro-American crowd, Federer says, "They make you get the better out of you, really. Against Americans here, it's automatic that you'll have the crowd support the American. I've seen how it was with [James] Blake and with [Andre] Agassi over the years. I don't think there will be any difference when I play Roddick in the final."

2009 – In a match that first appears to be a routine romp turns into a dog-fight as Roger Federer fends off the late surging Robin Soderling 6-0, 6-3, 6-7 (6-8), 7-6 (8-6) to advance into the semifinals of the U.S. Open, his 22nd consecutive Grand Slam semifinals appearance. Federer wins the first two sets in just 59 minutes and is just two points from a straight-sets victory in the third set, before Soderling wins the third-set tiebreaker to extend the match. Soderling actually holds a set point at 6-5 in the fourth-set tiebreaker to extend the match to a fifth set, but Federer holds on, winning the last three points of the match. "It was so close towards the end. It's a great relief to come through, because Robin started playing better and better as the match went on," Federer says after the match. "I knew he'd be tough, but the beginning was way too easy. He found his way into the match." The win gives Federer a 12-0 record against Soderling, including his win over him in the French Open final earlier in the year.

September 10

2006 – With golfing great Tiger Woods sitting in his box, Roger Federer wins the U.S. Open for a third consecutive year, defeating Andy Roddick 6-2, 4-6, 7-5, 6-1 in the final. "I can relate to what he's going through ... with the success I've had over the years now," Federer says of Woods. "I follow him a lot. I'm always happy when he wins...More and more often, over the last year or so, I've been kind of compared to Tiger. I asked him how it (is) for him (and) it's funny because many things (are) similar. He knew exactly how I kind of felt out on the court. That's something I haven't felt before, a guy who knows how it feels to be invincible at times, when you just have the feeling there's nothing going wrong any more. In the fourth set, for instance, it's I guess (like) him in the final round. He knows exactly how it feels."

2011 – Roger Federer suffers one of the most disappointing losses of his career, letting a two-sets-to-love and two match points fall away in a 6-7(7), 4-6, 6-3, 6-2, 7-5 loss to Novak Djokovic in the semifinals of the U.S. Open. The loss marks the second straight year that Federer lets two match points slip away against Djokovic in a U.S. Open semifinal. Federer breaks Djokovic's serve to take a 5-3 lead in the fifth set and comes to double match point at 40-15. Djokovic, almost in resignation, slaps a cross-court forehand return winner to save the first match, then saves the second, breaks Federer's serve and wins the next three games to seal the incredible comeback victory. "It's awkward having to explain this loss because I feel like I should be doing the other press conference. But it's what it is," says Federer. "It's the obvious, really. He came back; he played well. I didn't play so well at the very end. Sure, it's disappointing, but I have only myself to blame."

2005 – Roger Federer beats Lleyton Hewitt for a ninth straight time, posting a 6-3, 7-6 (0), 4-6, 6-3 victory over his Australian rival to advance into a final-round match at the U.S. Open against Andre Agassi. Federer fights off five set points in the second set before he plays a perfect tie-breaker to take a commanding two-sets-to-love lead and holds on for the four-set victory. When asked to discuss saving the five set points Federer responds "That's how it goes." When asked to elaborate, he says "I don't know. That was luck, I think" and then says, "Not pure luck, but there was a lot of luck involved, I think. Because five set points normally don't come out. I was in some rough situations there, and obviously I was serving all right, but in the end I think he should have deserved that set. But tennis can be tough sometimes."

2001 – Mirka Vavrinec, the future Mrs. Roger Federer, reaches her career high singles ranking on the WTA computer at No. 76.

September 11

2005 – Andre Agassi calls Roger Federer to best player he has ever faced in losing to Federer 6-3, 2-6, 7-6 (1), 6-1 in the final of the U.S. Open. "Pete (Sampras) was great, no question," Agassi says. "But there was a place to get to with Pete. It could be on your terms. There's no such

place with Roger. I think he's the best I've played against."
Says Federer of Agassi's comments, "It's fantastic to be
compared to all the players he's played throughout his
career. We're talking about the best – some are the best in
the world of all time. And it's still going and I still have
chances to improve." The title is Federer's sixth major
tournament victory and second in Flushing Meadows.

2004 – Roger Federer thrashes nemesis Tim Henman 6-3,
6-4, 6-4 in the semifinals of the U.S. Open, needing only
one hour, 46 minutes to reach his third major final of the
year, after winning the Australian Open and Wimbledon
earlier in the year. Entering the match, Henman holds
a 6-2 head-to-head record against the world No. 1, but
does not contend much in his first U.S. Open semifinal
showing. Federer advances to face Lleyton Hewitt in
the final, as Hewitt advances earlier in the day defeating
Joachim Johansson. "There is a lot on the line for me,"
Federer says of playing Hewitt in the final, following his
win over Henman. "My finals record, which is very good.
Then obviously it's another Grand Slam. For me to move
to four would be fantastic, and third of the year. I hope I
can cope with all of those things, plus there's a very tough
opponent."

2010 – Roger Federer lets two match points slide away
and loses 5-7, 6-1, 5-7, 6-2, 7-5 to Novak Djokovic in the
semifinals of the U.S. Open. A win for Federer would have
placed him in seventh straight U.S. Open final where he
would have faced his main rival Rafael Nadal. Djokovic
saves his two match points while serving at 4-5, 15-40 in
the fifth set – the first one with a swinging volley winner

and the second with a forehand winner. Federer is then broken at 5-5 and Djokovic fights off a break point in the next game, before closing out the match. "I closed my eyes and hit," Djokovic says with a grin in his post-match press conference. "If it goes in, OK. If it goes out, it's just another loss to Roger Federer at the U.S. Open." Federer had beaten Djokovic the previous three years at the U.S. Open – in the 2007 final and the semifinals in 2008 and 2009. Writes Bill Dwyre of the *Los Angeles Times*, "The unexpected, but not unthinkable, had happened. Federer had lost just his second match in seven years at the U.S. Open, and had done so in a flurry of racket-frame miss-hits and shanks. There was little wind." Says Federer of the match, "It's a tough loss ... but it's only going to fuel me with more motivation to practice hard and get back to Grand Slam finals."

2001 – Roger Federer, like most people, have strong memories of where they were on September 11, 2001 during the terrorist attacks to the United States that destroyed the World Trade Center in New York City. As published in the *Sydney Morning Herald*, Federer relayed his thoughts on that terrible day: "I was at the National Tennis Centre in Biel, Switzerland and working out in the gym. I heard something was going on. I don't know if I got a message on my phone or someone ran down and told me and I started to tell all my friends to turn on the TV and see this incredible news. I couldn't believe what was happening, you know. I guess I didn't quite understand it almost until I came back to America the next time, or when I came to New York the next time. It was almost surreal that something like this was possible that someone would want to do that, so that was very heavy. For us, it left a big impact because as tennis players we don't really have the choice not to travel, right? We are a part of the travelling circus with planes and so forth. We didn't really like to see it, I think all of us. I think you're never quite safe. Doesn't matter what you do. I guess what you try to do in life is try to be as safe as you can be without living in a golden cage, either. You have to go out there and live life, right?"

September 12

2004 – A 23-year-old Roger Federer wins the U.S. Open for the first time, overwhelming Lleyton Hewitt 6-0, 7-6(3), 6-0 in one hour, 51 minutes in the men's singles final. The U.S. Open title adds to his Australian and Wimbledon titles also won in 2004 making Federer the first player since Mats Wilander in 1988 to win three Grand Slam tournament titles in the same year. Federer is also the first man to win his first four Grand Slam singles finals. "I think in the circumstances, against Hewitt, first U.S. Open final for me, I couldn't have hoped for more really," says Federer. "I got the start I wanted, I was dreaming of. In the end, to win it in straight sets is just fantastic. Because actually, honestly, going into this final today, I had kind of a strange feeling because of all the talk, nobody has ever won four in a row, their first (four) Grand Slam finals. So I started wondering, you know, so... Now that I did it, it's great."

September 13

2009 – Roger Federer executes perhaps the signature shot of his career, slamming a "tweener" passing shot winner past Novak Djokovic in his second-to-last point of his 7-6 (3), 7-5, 7-5 semifinal victory at the U.S. Open. Federer calls it "the greatest shot I ever hit in my life" saying, "I was in a difficult position. I had nothing to lose. We (practice that) a lot actually but it never works." Says Djokovic, "On those shots, you just say, 'Well done, too good.' What can you do?" Writes Diane Pucin of the *Los Angeles Times* of the famous shot, "On the next-to-last point of the match, Federer hit what he called the best shot of his life. Djokovic was serving and seemingly in control of the point, standing at the net and watching for his just-hit lob to land out of Federer's reach. Except Federer materialized at the baseline just when the lob landed. With his back to the net, Federer swung the racket between his legs -- and hit a clean winner past Djokovic. The crowd roared, and Federer's forehand return winner that followed on match point was anticlimactic."

1998 – Roger Federer is defeated in the boys' singles final of the U.S. Open, falling to future pro rival David Nalbandian of Argentina 6-3, 7-5. Federer conducts his first official U.S. Open press conference after the match, but is asked only five questions. When asked to talk about the match, Federer responds simply, "I didn't play my best tennis. He played well. He's a tough player." When asked why he didn't play his best, Federer says, "My return was not as good as the returns during the whole tournament. I was negative a little bit during the whole match, I couldn't find my game." Despite the loss, Federer says he is pleased with his runner-up showing. "I'm actually happy with the tournament," he says. "I would have liked to win it, of course, but I'm happy for him."

September 14

2009 – Roger Federer falters in his attempt to win a sixth straight men's singles title at the U.S. Open – and equaling the six straight U.S. titles won by Bill Tilden from 1920-25 – losing to No. 6 seed Juan Martin del Potro of Argentina 3-6, 7-6 (7-5), 4-6, 7-6 (7-4), 6-2, in four hours, six minutes. Federer had won 40 consecutive matches at Flushing Meadows and 33 of his previous 34 Grand Slam matches. Federer is two points from a two-sets-to-love lead, serving at 5-4, 30-0, but is not able to close out the 20-year-old Argentine, who squares the match by winning the second-set tie-breaker. Del Potro breaks Federer's serve in the second game of the fifth set and holds on and closes out the upset victory. "I thought it was a tough match from the start," Federer says. "I think even the first set was pretty close. I got off to a pretty good start, and had things under control as well in the second set. I think that one cost me the match eventually. But I had many chances before that to make the difference. So it was tough luck today, but I you thought Juan Martin played great. I thought he hung in there and gave himself chances, and in the end was the better man."

2012 – Roger Federer overcomes wet and windy conditions on a temporary outdoor clay court in Amsterdam to beat

No. 159-ranked Thiemo De Bakker 6-3, 6-4, 6-4 to give Switzerland the 1-0 lead over the Netherlands in the Davis Cup Qualifying Round. "On the serve it can play tricks on you," Federer says of the gusty wind. "The ball, after you tossed it, it was moving away from you and you had to adjust the whole time. So to find a way to move the serve was pretty difficult."

September 15

2012 – Aiming to close out a 3-0 advantage over the Netherlands in the Davis Cup Qualifying Round, Roger Federer and Stan Wawrinka are upset by Robin Haase and Jean-Julien Rojer 6-4, 6-2, 5-7, 6-3 in Amsterdam. The loss is the third in a row for Federer and Wawrinka in Davis Cup play, having lost earlier in the year to Mike Bryan and Mardy Fish of the United States and to Lleyton Hewitt and Chris Guccione of Australia in 2011.

In a U.S. Tennis Association hosted conference call in 2011, Roger Federer was asked which of his five straight U.S. Open singles titles stands out the others. "Well, I guess the first one always kind of stands out just because of it being the first one," said Federer. "The finals were so incredible for me against Hewitt that I kind of look back on that one in a big way. I think actually the year I defended I think it was against Andre Agassi in the finals, I had to play him there. I thought he might retire if he won the U.S. Open. There was a huge buzz before the match. I was the new world No. 1 who was almost unbeatable. He played a great match, got really close in the match, was able to come through. For me those two stand out a lot. All the other ones are very important to me, too. If I had to pick two, I would pick those two maybe. I'm not sure."

September 16

2012 – Roger Federer wins by a 6-1, 6-4, 6-4 margin against No. 50-ranked Robin Haase to clinch Switzerland's victory over the Netherlands in the Davis Cup Qualifying Round in Amsterdam. "The first set actually on the score looks the easiest but could have been one of the tougher ones," Federer says. "The result doesn't always show how tough it was. But I was in control most of the time." The match lasts two hours, 38 minutes.

2011 – Roger Federer beats long-time rival Lleyton Hewitt 5-7, 7-6 (5), 6-2, 6-3 on grass at the Royal Sydney Golf Club to even the Davis Cup Playoff tie between Switzerland and Australia at 1-1. Federer, who trails by a set and 3-1 in the second, hits 22 aces in the match and 87 winners, against 62 errors. The match comes eight years after one of Federer's most difficult defeats, losing to Hewitt at Rod Laver Arena in five sets – after leading two sets to love – in the Davis Cup semifinals in 2003. "I'm not that kind of guy that I need to get him back to sleep at night," says Federer of any feelings of revenge against Hewitt from their 2003 Davis Cup encounter.

September 17

2011 – Roger Federer and Stan Wawrinka lose to Lleyton Hewitt and Chris Guccione 2-6, 6-4, 6-2, 7-6 (5) as Australia takes a 2-1 lead over Switzerland in the Davis Cup Playoff Round 6-2, 4-6, 2-6, 6-7(5) on grass at the Royal Sydney Golf Club.

2009 – Roger Federer is fined $1,500 for profanity while arguing with the chair umpire during the final of the U.S. Open. Courtside microphones pick up Federer's in a profanity-laced argument with chair umpire Jake Garner over the length of time elapsed before his opponent Juan Martin del Potro challenges a line-call with the Hawk-Eye instant replay system.

September 18

2011 – Roger Federer beats Bernard Tomic 6-2, 7-5, 3-6, 6-3 to even up the Australia vs. Switzerland Davis Cup World Group Playoff series at 2-2 at the Royal Sydney Golf Club. "It was tough conditions today, but I really had a pleasure coming down here and playing; we'll see how it all works out in the fifth rubber," says Federer. "I think we were both able to play well. Bernie, I think he did a good job as well, making it difficult for me today so also credit to him for a good weekend." The following day, Federer's teammate Stan Wawrinka outlasts Lleyton Hewitt to give Switzerland the 3-2 victory.

2009 – Roger Federer registers a 6-3, 6-4, 6-1 win over Simone Bolelli to give Switzerland a 2-0 lead against Italy in the Davis Cup Playoff Round on the red clay courts at the Valletta Cambiaso Club in Genoa. Stan Wawrinka opens the series with a 6-4, 6-1, 6-2 win over Andreas Seppi. "From the Swiss side we're very happy with today's start," says Federer. "It was surprisingly comfortable matches today for Stan and myself. We expected much tougher. We knew these were key matches, and that we were able to get both gives us a great opportunity on the weekend."

September 19

2003 – In a repeat of the 2003 Wimbledon final, Roger Federer once again defeats Mark Philippoussis in straight sets 6-3 6-4 7-6(3) as Switzerland ties Australia 1-1 after day one of the Davis Cup semifinal at Rod Laver Arena in Melbourne. The Australian leads 5-3 in the third set, but is unable to close out the set. "I feel fine. I would also feel fine playing four or five sets," says Federer. "It's just basically three matches and if you can't handle three matches, I think something's wrong as a 22-year-old."

2008 – Roger Federer shows some rare frustration requesting a change of line judges before going on to beat Belgium's Kristof Vliegen 7-6(1) 6-4 6-2 to give Switzerland a 2-0 lead in a Davis Cup World Group playoff in Lausanne. Upset by a baseline call that led to him lose serve and trail 2-0 in the second set, Federer walks to his chair and calls for match referee Norbert Peick to change the line judges. "It was an annoying call for me and I just asked him to change them, that's all I did," Federer says. "Who knows, maybe I overreacted, but I was so irritated by the call because for me it was such an obvious call."

September 20

2008 – Reigning Olympic gold medal-winning doubles champions Roger Federer and Stan Wawrinka save a set point on serve in the second set tie-breaker and go on to defeat Xavier Malisse and Olivier Rochus 4-6, 7-6(6), 6-3, 6-3 for an unbeatable 3-0 lead over Belgium in the Davis Cup Playoff Round in Lausanne, Switzerland.

2009 – Roger Federer clinches victory for Switzerland over Italy in the Davis Cup Playoff Round beating Potito Starace 6-3, 6-0, 6-4 in Genoa, Italy. Federer endures a two-hour rain delay before completing the victory. "I have to go on holiday badly," Federer says following the victory. "I have a problem with my leg, I have a problem with my arm – everything is hurting. And I've got to do some baby-sitting. I've been spending a lot of time on the tennis court the last few weeks." It is Federer's first Davis Cup series since he becomes a father to his twin girls.

2003 – Roger Federer and Marc Rosset are defeated by Wayne Arthurs and Todd Woodbridge 4-6, 7-6 (5), 5-7, 6-4, 6-4 as Australia takes a 2-1 lead over Switzerland in the Davis Cup semifinals in Melbourne.

2000 – Roger Federer plays his first Olympic singles match defeating David Prinosil of Germany 6-2, 6-2 in Sydney.

2002 – Roger Federer squares Switzerland even with Morocco at 1-1 on the opening day of the Davis Cup Playoff Round in Casablanca with a 6-3, 6-2, 6-1 win over Hicham Arazi.

September 21

2003 – Leading two sets to love and 5-3 in the third set, Roger Federer suffers one of his most disappointing losses of his career, falling to Lleyton Hewitt 5-7, 2-6, 7-6, (7-4), 7-5, 6-1 as Australia clinches a spot in the Davis Cup final. Federer serves to even the series at 2-2 at 5-4 in the third set and is two points from victory at 30-30, but Hewitt stages an incredible comeback to win in three hours, 31 minutes. "This beats the hell out of winning Wimbledon or the U.S. Open," Hewitt says after the victory. Prior to the crucial third set, Federer had won 31 consecutive sets in Davis Cup singles play. "I still believe it was one of my toughest losses I've ever had as a player," Federer says eight years later of the loss.

2007 – On a fast carpet surface in Prague, Roger Federer loses a set, breaking a streak of 23 straight sets won in Davis Cup play, and survives against Czech Radek Stepanek by a 6-3, 6-2, 6-7(4), 7-6(5) margin. Federer wastes a match point serving at 5-4 in the third set, but races to a 4-2 lead in the fourth-set tie-breaker and converts his seventh match point when Stepanek nets a backhand return. "I made it more difficult for myself," says Federer, putting the Swiss team up 1-0. "I played very well in the first three sets. It's a pity I couldn't serve it out."

2002 – Roger Federer and George Bastl defeat Karim Alami and Younes El Aynaoui 6-4, 6-1, 6-4 to give Switzerland a 2-1 lead over Morocco in the Davis Cup Playoff Round in Casablanca.

September 22

1997 – Less than two months after turning 16 years old, Roger Federer debuts on the ATP computer with a world ranking of No. 803. Nearly six and half years later, the man from Basel, Switzerland moves into the No. 1 ranking on the computer, and keep the top spot for more consecutive weeks than any player in the history of the sport.

2000 – Roger Federer defeats Karol Kucera of Slovakia 6-4, 7-6 (5) in the second round of the Sydney Olympic Games. Kucera was a first-round upset winner over No. 7 seed Tim Henman of Great Britain, a player who was an early nemesis for Federer who beat the future Swiss No. 1 in six of their first seven matches, but at the time, only one time to date entering the 2000 Olympics.

2002 – Roger Federer defeats Younes El Aynaoui 6-2, 6-2, 6-1 to win his third point for Switzerland and almost single-handedly accounting for his team's Davis Cup victory over Morocco in the Davis Cup Playoff Round in Casablanca. Federer beats Hicham Arazi by the exact same scoreline in Friday's opening singles.

2007 – Roger Federer and Yves Allegro fall to Tomas Berdych and Radek Stepanek 3-6, 5-7, 7-6 (7), 6-4, 6-4 in three hours, 15 minutes as the Czech Republic takes a 2-1 lead over Switzerland in the Davis Cup Playoff Round in Prague. Federer and Allegro hold a match point at 6-5 in the third-set tiebreaker but are unable to convert. It marks the second time that Federer blows a two-sets-to-love lead in a doubles match, the previous time being at Wimbledon in 2000 when he and Andrew Kratzmann of Australia lose in the quarterfinals to Paul Haarhuis and Sandon Stolle 6-7 (5), 5-7, 7-6 (2), 6-2, 6-3.

2006 – Roger Federer gives Switzerland a 1-0 lead over Serbia in the Davis Cup Playoff Round as he defeats No. 92-ranked Janko Tipsarevic 6-3, 6-2, 6-2. Federer drops his serve once during this straightforward victory in one hour and 27 minutes on an indoor hard court in Geneva.

September 23

2007 – Roger Federer saves a set point in the first set and five set points in the second set and beats Tomas Berdych 7-6 (5), 7-6 (10), 6-3 to draw Switzerland even with the Czech Republic at 2-2 in the Davis Cup Playoff Round in Prague. "This match reminded me a lot of the U.S. Open final against [Novak] Djokovic when I was down and came back too," says Federer. "It was close, he had his chances but he missed them." However, Radek Stepanek beats Stanislas Wawrinka 7-6 (3), 6-3, 7-6 (4) to give the Czech Republic the 3-2 victory in the decisive fifth match.

2006 – Roger Federer and Yves Allegro notch a 7-6, 6-4, 6-4 win over Ilija Bozoljac and Nenad Zimonjic to give

Switzerland a 2-1 lead over Serbia in the Davis Cup Playoff Round in Geneva.

2005 – Roger Federer returns to the Swiss Davis Cup team after a 17-month absence and crushes world No. 262 Alan Mackin of Great Britain 6-0, 6-0, 6-2 in 75 minutes on an indoor clay-court in Geneva. "It would have been a disaster if I'd lost," Federer says. "I don't remember the last time I played such a low-ranked player and it wasn't that difficult today." Federer skips the first round in 2005 – Switzerland losing 3-2 to the Netherlands – conceding that his singles career is the biggest priority in his career. He goes on to skip Switzerland's Davis Cup world group first round ties also from 2006 to 2010.

September 24

2004 – Top-ranked Roger Federer reaches the second round of the Thailand Open in Bangkok defeating Nicolas Thomann of France 6-4, 7-6 (7-4).

2000 – Roger Federer advances to the quarterfinals of the Olympic Games in Sydney defeating Mikael Tillstrom of Sweden 6-1, 6-2. Rather than facing world No. 1 and freshly-minted U.S. Open champion Marat Safin of Russia in the quarterfinals, Federer is drawn to face Karim Alami of Morocco after Safin loses in the opening round to Fabrice of Santoro of France.

2005 – Roger Federer faces Andy Murray on the doubles court as Federer and Yves Allegro post a 7-5, 2-6, 7-6(1), 6-2 win over Murray and Greg Rusedski to give Switzerland the insurmountable 3-0 lead over Great Britain in the Davis Cup Playoff Round in Geneva. "I'm not going to rush any decision," Federer says of his involvement in the 2006 Swiss Davis Cup team. "I really would like to play – especially as [next time] it will be about more than just trying to stay in the World Group." Federer, however, does not play in a Davis Cup World Group match for Switzerland until 2012.

2006 – In his second career meeting with Novak Djokovic, Roger Federer beats his 19-year-old future rival 6-3, 6-2, 6-3 to clinch Switzerland's Davis Cup Playoff Round series in Geneva. The one-sided encounter for Federer marks the most lopsided scoreline between the two players in a best-of- five-set match. Afterward, Federer criticizes the No. 21-ranked Djokovic for simulating injury. "You know I don't trust his injuries, no it's not funny, I mean I'm serious, and I think that he's a joke when he comes down to these injuries," Federer says. "The rules are there to be used but not abused and that's what he's been doing many times. That's why I wasn't happy to see him doing that and then running around like a rabbit again. Yeah it was a good handshake for me. I was happy to beat him."

September 25

2000 – Roger Federer eliminates Karim Alami of Morocco 7-6 (2), 6-1 in the quarterfinals of the Olympic Games in Sydney, Australia. It is the only career meeting between the two players.

In his all-consuming tennis encyclopedia "The Bud Collins History of Tennis," Hall of Fame journalist Bud Collins wrote of Roger Federer, "Performing in a smooth, seemingly effortless, style, a right-hander using one-handed backhand, he occupies his status as the best in men's tennis with rare grace and competitive verve, always in the right place to deliver the right shot from his peerless all-court arsenal of angles, spins, volleys, pinpoint serves. Is there a weakness, a flaw? Doubtful."

September 26

2000 – Roger Federer loses to Tommy Haas 6-3, 6-2 in the semifinals of the Olympic Games. Federer, at age 19, is looking to position himself as the youngest Olympic gold medalist in modern tennis, but is tentative against his German rival who, with a ranking of No. 48, is actually ranked 12 spaces below Federer.

September 27

2000 – Unheralded Arnaud DiPasquale of France, ranked No. 62 in world, defeats 19-year-old Roger Federer 7-6 (5), 6-7 (7), 6-3 to win the bronze medal playoff at the 2000 Olympic Games in Sydney. Federer holds a 3-0 lead in the first-set tie-breaker, but loses seven of the next nine points. He also leads by a break 2-1 in the final set, DiPasquale beginning to suffer from cramps, but Federer is unable to close out the victory. "Considering how the match was going, I should never have lost," Federer says after the loss. "I really wanted to be standing on the podium. Now I have nothing to take home except my pride."

September 28

2005 – Defending champion Roger Federer advances to the second round of the Thailand Open in Bangkok, defeating Marcos Daniel, 7-6 (3), 6-4.

"I'm a fan of his game, his temperament, the way he handles himself on and off the court. I do picture myself how I would play him. Now that I'm sitting on my couch watching, I just kind of marvel at the things he's able to do. He's a great mover, does great things off both sides of the court, can come in when he has to, and has a pretty big first serve. He has the whole package. There's really nothing he can't do. I just love it. He just makes it look easy. He's smooth, a great athlete." —Pete Sampras on Roger Federer in 2007

September 29

2005 – Roger Federer extends his winning streak to a career-high 28 matches by defeating Denis Gremelmayr 6-3, 6-2 to reach the quarterfinals of the Thailand Open in Bangkok.

September 30

1998–Seventeen-year-old Roger Federer defeats Guillaume Raoux of France 6-2, 6-2 in the first round in Toulouse for his first ATP singles match victory. Rene Stauffer, in his book *Roger Federer: Quest for Perfection,* summarizes Federer's achievement, "Yet, before the chase for the year-end No. 1 junior ranking reached its decisive phase, the unexpected happened. Federer achieved his first great breakthrough on the ATP Tour. With a ranking of No. 878, he traveled to Toulouse, France at the end of September and, to his own surprise, advanced through the qualifying rounds to progress into the main draw of the tournament. In only his second ATP tournament, the 17-year-old registered an upset victory over No. 45-ranked Guillaume Raoux of France—his first ATP match victory—allowing the Frenchman just four games. In the next round, Federer proved this win was not a fluke by defeating former Australian Davis Cup star Richard Fromberg 6-1, 7-6 (5). In the quarterfinals—his sixth match of the tournament including matches in the qualifying rounds—Federer lost to Jan Siemerink 7-6 (5), 6-2, with a throbbing thigh injury hampering him during the match. The Dutchman was ranked No. 20 and went on to win the tournament two days later, but Federer was also handsomely rewarded. He received a prize money check for $10,800 and passed 482 players in the world rankings in one tournament—moving to No. 396."

2004 – Roger Federer advances to the quarterfinals of the Thailand Open in Bangkok defeating fellow Swiss Ivo Heuberger 6-1, 6-3.

2005 – Roger Federer cruises into the semifinals of the Thailand Open in Bangkok with a 6-4, 6-3 win over Gilles Muller.

OCTOBER

October 1

2004 – World No. 1 Roger Federer defeats Sweden's Robin Soderling, ranked No. 50, 7-6 (3), 6-4 to reach the semifinals of the Thailand Open in Bangkok. The Swede is two points away from taking the first set serving at 5-4, but is not able to convert. The match is the second career meeting between to the future rivals, Federer winning their first meeting earlier in the year in the second round of Toronto. Federer fires 14 aces in the 82-minute match.

2005 – Defending champion Roger Federer defeats No. 42-ranked Jarkko Nieminen of Finland 6-3, 6-4 in 59 minutes in the semifinals of the Thailand Open in Bangkok. The win is the 30th straight for Federer, the longest winning streak on the ATP Tour since Thomas Muster won 35 on the trot in 1995.

October 2

1998 – Ranked No. 878 in the world, seventeen-year-old Roger Federer is defeated by No. 20th-ranked Jan Siemerink of the Netherlands 7-6 (5), 6-2 in the quarterfinals of the Toulouse Open in France. It's Federer's first ATP tournament in which he wins his first main-tour-level matches. Prior to the match, Federer, the reigning junior Wimbledon champion, had won both his qualifying rounds and his first two main draw matches in straight sets.

2001 – Ranked No. 12 and seeded No. 3, Roger Federer is upset in the opening round of the Kremlin Cup in Moscow, losing to No. 39-ranked Nicolas Kiefer of Germany 6-3, 1-6, 7-6 (4).

2004 – Top-ranked Roger Federer posts a three-set victory over hometown hero Paradorn Srichaphan of Thailand to set up a No. 1 vs. No. 2 final final at the Thailand Open in Bangkok against Andy Roddick. Federer defeats the No. 20-ranked Srichaphan 7-5, 2-6, 6-3 in 115 minues, hitting seven aces.

2005 – Roger Federer plays Andy Murray for the first time in his career, beating his future rival 6-3, 7-5 in the final of the Thailand Open in Bangkok. The match is the first ATP tournament final for the No. 109-ranked Murray. The win increases Federer's winning streak in ATP finals to 24. "It was intimidating playing someone like Roger" says the beaten finalist.

October 3

2004 – Roger Federer defeats Andy Roddick 6-4, 6-0 in just 58 minutes in the final of the Thailand Open in Bangkok for his 10th title of the year. Federer is the fifth player to win 10 titles in one season in the past 20 years, joining John McEnroe (13 titles in 1984), Thomas Muster (12 in 1995), Ivan Lendl (11 in 1985, and 10 in 1989), and Pete Sampras (10 in 1994). The win is also Federer's 12th straight in a tournament final and he joins Bjorn Borg and John McEnroe as the only players to achieve that feat in the past 25 years. "I hurt my elbow yesterday against Marat Safin, but I don't think that made a difference," explains Roddick. "I was playing with half a deck of cards and I have a bad record against Roger with a full deck of cards, so it was a little disappointing."

October 4

2006 – Roger Federer plays his first match in Japan at the AIG Japan Open in Tokyo and registers a 7-6 (2), 7-6 (3) win over No. 276-ranked Viktor Troicki of Serbia, playing in his first career ATP tournament. "It was a really tough match," says Federer. "I didn't know his game. I've never seen him play and it always takes time to figure a player out."

October 5

2006 – Injuring his leg while having a nightmare in his hotel room, Roger Federer is still able to defeat defending champion Wesley Moodie of South Africa 6-2, 6-1 to reach the quarterfinals of the Japan Open in Tokyo. Federer tells his blog on the ATP website that he hits the corner of his bed and had to be restrained by his girlfriend Mirka Vavrinec. "I must have had a nightmare. I jumped out of bed and stood up screaming in a state of shock," Federer writes. "I did not know where I was, and I ran back and hit the corner of the bed, which is solid wood and sharp. Luckily Mirka was there. She grabbed me and told me to relax." Federer needs only 52 minutes to beat the No. 73-ranked Moodie, but only hits two aces.

2013 – Roger Federer conducts a whirlwind of pre-tournament activities in advance of the Shanghai Masters. He makes a surprise appearance at the tournament's draw ceremony, joining fellow tennis legend Rod Laver. He also takes part in a kids clinic at the event's Qizhong Stadium and helps debut the court at the tournament's opening ceremony.

October 6

1998 – Playing for only the third time in the main draw of an ATP Tour level tournament, Roger Federer is given a tennis lesson by all-time great Andre Agassi, who defeats the hometown boy 6-3, 6-2 in the first round of the Swiss Indoors in Basel. Agassi, ranked No. 8, needs only 55 minutes to dispose of the 17-year-old Federer, ranked No. 396. Agassi breaks in Federer's opening service game in each set. "He proved his talent and his instinct for the game a few times," Agassi says of Federer. "But for me it was an ideal first round where I didn't have to do all that much and where I could get accustomed to the new conditions."

2006 – In a self-described image-saving match that would have been the worst loss ever by a world No. 1-ranked player, Roger Federer defeats local wild card Takao Suzuki, ranked No. 1,078 and playing his first tournament in almost 12 months, by a 4-6, 7-5, 7-6 (3) margin in the quarterfinals of the Japan Open in Tokyo. "It was a difficult match and I was afraid I might lose it," Federer says after the match. "I could see the headlines, 'Federer loses to a guy outside the top 1,000.' I'm glad I won, it saved my image. He mixed up his serves well and hit all the corners. I got a bit of luck here and there in the third set which helped."

October 7

2006 – Top-ranked Roger Federer cruises to a 6-3, 6-4 win in one-hour over No. 72-ranked Benjamin Becker of Germany to advance to his first Japan Open final in Tokyo. "It was pretty straight forward," says Federer to reporters after the match.

2013 – Playing only his second doubles match of the year, Roger Federer pairs with Chinese No. 1 player Ze Zhang and beats Kevin Anderson and Dmitry Tursunov 6-2, 6-1 in the first round of the Shanghai Masters. "It's been a pleasure playing with him today and I'm looking forward to the next match of course," Federer says of his partner, ranked No. 271 in the world, following the match.

2012 – In China to compete in the Shanghai Masters, Roger Federer is surprised and disappointed at the level of attention that is given to a death threat he receives, posted online via one of his fans' websites. "I'm a bit disappointed that it became a lot more public and came out in the press," Federer says to media in Shanghai. "It was very small on a website, nothing very clear and concrete – people debating. To make that kind of big news is a bit surprising for me." While saying "I've felt very safe here. The authorities have been wonderful" Federer tells reporters that he first learned of the threat around 10 days earlier. "The government has been very supportive and I've felt great since I've been here. Obviously it's been a different type of preparation and it's a little bit of a distraction – there's no doubt about it. You have to be aware of what's happening around about you but that is the case anywhere today with my fame and all that stuff. But it's been fine. I'm happy I'm here and I feel I'll have a good preparation to start."

October 8

2006 – Roger Federer wins his 42nd career title – but his first in Japan – defeating former nemesis Tim Henman 6-3, 6-3 in the final of the Japan Open in Tokyo in the Swiss maestro's maiden trip to Japan. The win is Federer's sixth straight over Henman to take the lead in their head-to-head series 7-6. The final-round showing is the 28th and last final-round appearance for Henman, who wins 11 of the 28 championship matches during his ATP career. Says Henman of his match with Federer, "I'm not the first guy to lose in a final to Roger and I won't be the last. I would have loved to have won today but he was simply too good."

1999 – Roger Federer and Tim Henman play against each other for the first time, squaring off in the quarterfinals of the Swiss Open in Basel with Henman, the defending champion ranked No. 6, defeating Federer, ranked No. 106, 6-3, 7-5. Henman becomes an early nemesis for Federer in his career, winning their first four meetings and six of their first seven meetings. Federer, however, wins the career head-to-head with the British great 7-6, winning the last six matches before Henman's retirement in 2007.

2013 – Roger Federer hosts an entertaining "#AskRF" question and answer session on Twitter while competing in the Shanghai Masters in China. In response to a fan's question on if he has taught his twin daughters tennis, Federer tweets back "I have but they don't listen to me! #BadCoach" When asked if he watches any TV shows and what are his favorites, he responds "I loved watching LOST, Prison Break, Entourage and Heroes. And then I had kids. #cyaTV" When a fan suggests that he is drinking whiskey during his question and answer session, Federer responds, "I don't drink and tweet #responsibleRF"

October 9

2013 – Playing in his first singles match since his fourth-round loss to Tommy Robredo at the U.S. Open, 32-year-old Roger Federer defeats Andreas Seppi 6-4, 6-3 in his opening-round match at the Shanghai Masters. "It was a big maybe shall I say 20 minutes going up a set and a break, really started to feel comfortable" Federer says after the win. "Even though it remained tough, Seppi did a good job of hanging around. That's the kind of first round match you want in this particular situation I'm in right now."

American tennis historian and journalist Steve Flink rated the Roger Federer serve No. 5 all time in his book "The Greatest Tennis Matches of All Time" "Because he dazzled so many learned observers across the years with his propensity to hit virtually any shot in the book at any given moment, we tend to overlook Federer's incomparably smooth and purposeful first serve," wrote Flink. "At his best, Federer's serve is the most precise in the game."

October 10

2000 – Ranked No. 31, nineteen-year-old Roger Federer defeats world No. 4 Magnus Norman of Sweden 4-6, 7-6 (4), 6-4 at the first round at the CA Trophy tournament in Vienna. Federer leads 4-1 in the first before losing five straight games, while in the second set, Norman serves for the match at 5-4 before faltering. Each player win 114 points in the match, which marks their only career meeting.

2002 – Roger Federer, ranked No. 13, defeats Tommy Robredo, ranked No. 36, 6-2, 6-7 (5), 6-4 in the second round of the CA Trophy in Vienna, Austria. Federer squanders a match point in the second set, but rallies to defeat the Spaniard in 116 minutes, striking only four aces.

2012 – Playing in the shadow of a death threat from a Chinese blogger, Roger Federer wins his opening match at the Shanghai Masters in China, defeating Taiwanese qualifier Yen-Hsun Lu 6-3, 7-5. "I felt fine" Federer says. "There was maybe one quick thought. I saw one of the bodyguards outside of the court. I thought, still around, obviously. I have bodyguards every time I play a match on a center court, which is normal."

2013 – Gael Monfils says he "feels a bit sorry" for Roger Federer in beating the struggling 32-year-old seven-time Wimbledon champion 6-4, 6-7 (5), 6-3 in the round of 16 of the Shanghai Masters. "It's a good win for me. I feel a bit sorry for him because I know he's running for London, but it's tennis," says Monfils and his efforts to qualify for the ATP year-end championships in London. Federer trails 3-5 in the second set and 3-5 in the second-set tie-breaker, winning the last four points of the second set, before faltering in the third. Federer also falls in doubles play following his singles loss, losing in a super tie-breaker with Chinese partner Ze Zhang 6-1, 1-6 (10-8) to Wimbledon finalists Ivan Dodig and Marcelo Melo.

October 11

2010 – Roger Federer conducts his pre-tournament press conference in advance of the Shanghai Rolex Masters and compares present day China and his career with 2002, the first year he played in Shanghai during the 2002 ATP year-end championships. "A lot has changed since 2002," says Federer to the media. "I maybe had, I don't know, four titles. Now I have 63 I think. I'm not even sure. So it's been an amazing run for me, the last eight years, with a lot of success, incredible streaks, a lot of fun, becoming somewhat of a national hero back home in Switzerland, which is a hard thing to do. Being here in 2002 obviously has been very different to being here, let's say, two years ago. When you come back now, every time you play, you're one of the big favorites. In 2002, I was just happy to be part of the tournament. Only later did I realize the power and the potential I had, and especially this country had to embrace tennis and to see what they really wanted to achieve here in this part of the world, especially here in Shanghai where people seem so excited about this sport. There are flags everywhere from the airport when you arrive till here, to the Qizhong Stadium. The excitement they have to come here, it's a lot of fun for the players. Have an incredibly strong fan base it seems here in China. That's why I loved playing at the Olympics in Beijing and finally I'm back here again after missing last year. So I feel like I'm very connected to China."

2012 – Roger Federer guarantees himself the No. 1 ranking for the 300th week of his career by defeating Davis Cup teammate and Olympic doubles partner Stan Wawrinka

4-6, 7-6 (4), 6-0 in the third round of the Shanghai Masters in China. "I'm happy I've been able to reach 300 weeks," says Federer after the win. "It's an amazing number and record for me. That's a big thing I've been able to achieve."

2003 – Losing just one point on his serve in the first set, defending champion Roger Federer defeats Max Mirnyi 6-2, 7-6 (2) to advance to the final of the CA Trophy in Vienna for the second consecutive year. Federer takes revenge on the No. 28-ranked Mirnyi for a semifinal defeat to "the Beast" in the Rotterdam semifinal eight months earlier.

October 12

2003 – Roger Federer wins his 10th career ATP singles title and successfully defends a title for the first time in his career when he defeats Carlos Moya of Spain 6-3, 6-3, 6-3 to win the CA Trophy in Vienna, Austria. Says Federer of successfully defending a title for the first time, "I'm over the moon about that."

2013 – Roger Federer announces on his website that he and his coach of more than three years Paul Annacone have parted ways. Writes Federer on his website, "After a terrific 3 ½ years working together, Paul and I have decided to move on to the next chapter in our professional lives. When we started together we had a vision of a 3 year plan to win another Grand Slam title and get back to the number #1 ranking. Along with many other goals and great memories, these 2 main goals were achieved. After numerous conversations culminating at the end of our most recent training block, we felt like this was the best time and path for both of us. Paul remains a dear friend, and we both look forward to continuing our friendship. I want to thank Paul for his help and the value he has added to me and my team." Federer's 2013 season sees his ranking drop from No. 2 to No. 7 and he does not reach a major final for the first time since 2002.

2005 – Roger Federer announces on his website that he has injured a ligament in his right foot during practice, forcing him to miss at least two weeks of tournaments, including his hometown event in Basel, Switzerland.

October 13

2002 – Roger Federer wins an emotional final at the CA Trophy in Vienna against Jiri Novak 6-4, 6-1, 3-6, 6-4 to win his first tournament since the death of his childhood coach Peter Carter. Federer dedicates the title to his former coach, who dies in a car accident in South Africa the previous summer. "I dedicate this title to him," Federer says with glistening eyes at the award ceremony.

2000 – Richard Krajicek fails to convert on any of his seven break point chances against Roger Federer and loses to the future Wimbledon champion in the quarterfinals of the CA Trophy in Vienna by a 6-4, 6-3 margin. Krajicek, ranked No. 20, fails to convert on three of his break point chances in the ninth game of the first set against the No. 31-ranked Federer, who then reels off five consecutive games.

2010 – Roger Federer, playing his first match since the U.S. Open, hits another of his trademark between-the-legs shots in his 6-3, 6-4 victory over John Isner at the Shanghai Masters. The signature shot comes in the second set when Federer chases down a lob and hits the ball back between his legs, causing Isner to hit his volley into the net. "The reaction was amazing, as it usually is after a shot between the legs," Federer tells reporters of the shot after the match. "But it's something that happens so rare, you know. Usually happens maybe once a tournament and then you have to play the score. Depends on the opponent you play against. Could have done anything different. But I'm hitting that shot so well now, it's almost the most consistent shot in tennis these days. I've attempted it like four times in the last few years, every time I made it and won the point off it. I played it great again. The ovation from the fans was absolutely amazing again."

2012 – Highlighted by two rain delays and a stretch where Roger Federer hits three double faults in a row, Andy Murray increases his head-to-head advantage over Federer to 10-8 with a 6-4, 6-4 win in the semifinals of Shanghai Masters. Federer loses his serve in the fifth game of the first set when he hits three straight double-faults from 0-15 down. When asked if he had ever hit three straight double-faults in a match before, Federer responds, "It has happened, and today again. It happens, unfortunately." The match is delayed briefly at 1-1 in the second set and again by 30 minutes with Murray serving for the match at 5-4. The players leave the court for about 30 minutes while the eight-petal magnolia-shaped roof is closed to continue the match. When play resumes, Murray needs only five points to close out the victory. Says Murray of the victory, "I was able to be very aggressive on his second serve. He, maybe, slowed down his first serve a little bit so I was able to take a few more chances on his first serve."

October 14

2000 – Roger Federer loses to Tim Henman 2-6, 7-6 (4), 6-3 in the semifinals of the CA Trophy tennis championships in Vienna. The match-up is the second of 13 career meetings between Federer and Henman, the Brit winning six of the first seven meetings. In the second set, Federer has many chances to advance to the final, but is not able to convert. The event is Federer's 40th main-level tournament and his first career ATP defeat despite holding a match point.

2010 – Roger Federer defeats No. 58-ranked Andreas Seppi 6-3, 6-4 in 74 minutes in the third round of the Shanghai Master in China. It is the second consecutive win of Federer by the same scoreline (the day before he defeats John Isner 6-3, 6-4). "The points were tough we were both feeling it there for a while, but I was happy to come back. It was a good match in the end," says Federer.

October 15

2010 – Roger Federer routs No. 5-ranked Robin Soderling 6-1, 6-1 in only 54 minutes in the Shanghai Masters quarterfinals. "It's a great match for me," says Federer.

"Surprising that it all went so fast. [It was] somewhat close in the beginning to get the 4-1 lead. I guess that was the hard work."

2003 – Roger Federer beats Alex Corretja, ranked No. 127 in the world, 6-4, 6-3 in his opening round match at the Madrid Masters in Spain and discusses his elusive pursuit of the No. 1 ranking which fell out of his grasp. "I'm happy to be in contention, to have a chance to become No. 1," Federer says. "Obviously, it's a pity I missed my chance in Montreal and Cincinnati and the U.S. Open. But for me it's just important now to play a good, solid indoor season. Last year was good, but I want to do even better this year. You know, it was a perfect start (to win in) Vienna. This tournament and Paris are very important for me. Basel obviously, too, but not points-wise. Then obviously the Masters Cup. I'm going to try to come as close as I can to win all of them."

2013 – Roger Federer makes chocolate creations with Swiss school children at a special event for his sponsor Lindt chocolate at the chocolatier's headquarters in Kilchberg, Switzerland, near Zurich. The event is supported by the Roger Federer Foundation, in partnership with Winter Aid Switzerland. "As a father of two little children, I experience on a day-to-day basis how important it is to support them in all possible ways," says Federer in a statement. "That is why I take particular personal interest in getting involved with underprivileged children here in Switzerland, too. It was great fun spending an exciting day at the Lindt Chocolateria together with the kids we support through the program of Winter Aid."

October 16

2001 – Defending champion and No. 36-ranked Wayne Ferreira administers a near lethal blow to Roger Federer's chances of qualifying for the year-end championships, defeating the No. 11-ranked Federer 7-6 (1), 3-6, 6-2 in the second round of the Masters Series event in Stuttgart, Germany. "Well, I mean, from now on I probably can stop talking about Sydney," Federer tells reporters after the loss and his more distant chances of playing at the year-end championships in Australia "If I'm playing that bad or I can't even go past the first round, why should I talk about Sydney? I'm just not playing well enough to be there anyway. So I'm just going to try to play as well as I can the next two tournaments and we'll see what happens." The loss is Federer's second in the first round in his last three tournaments. After reaching the final at his hometown event in Basel, Switzerland, Federer's season ends with a first round loss to Jiri Novak at the Paris Masters.

2002 – Roger Federer beats Marcelo Rios 6-4, 6-2 in his opening round match at the Madrid Masters in Spain. Says Federer of victory, "I have to say it was very difficult today because I only had one and a half hours of play on the outside courts, then a half hour this morning on the center court to get ready for the first match. I really didn't know what to expect because the balls are different, the center court is different, everything is different. I had to get used to it first. That took me a few games. I was very nervous before the game because I didn't know how good Marcelo was playing, how good I was going to play. Right now I'm very happy that I won, first of all. Doesn't matter the result. 6-4, 6-2 is also good for my condition."

2007 – Playing in his first match on tour in more than five weeks, Roger Federer defeats Robby Ginepri 7-6 (2), 6-4 in the second round of the Madrid Masters in Spain. "I took a rest so I could be 100 percent here and now I'm fresh and eager to play here again," says Federer, who extends to his winning streak against Americans to 39 straight matches, spanning four years.

2008 – "It's very nice to have records. Sure, money is important in life but it's not everything," says Roger Federer on becoming the ATP Tour's career leader in prize money after his 6-4, 6-1 win over Jo-Wilfried Tsonga that puts him in the Madrid Masters quarterfinals. The win guarantees that Federer will overtake the $43.3 million won by Pete Sampras following the tournament. The match is also the first meeting between Federer and Tsonga, a highly anticipated match since Tsonga defeated Rafael Nadal in the Australian Open semifinal ten months earlier. "I tried to put him under pressure there, the conditions allow you to do that," Federer says. "At this stage you're looking for the knockout punch, like in boxing."

2003 – Roger Federer beats Mardy Fish 6-3, 7-6 (4) to reach the quaterfinals of the Madrid Masters.

2010 – Roger Federer defeats Novak Djokovic 7-5, 6-4 in the semifinals of the Shanghai Masters, avenging his loss to the Serb in the semifinals of the U.S. Open and guaranteeing that he will regain the No. 2 ranking that he loses to Djokovic after his loss in New York."I think the first set could have gone either way," Federer says following the win. "It was really an open battle. I got the better of him at the end of the first set. I think for 10 minutes he was a bit out of it and I was able to take advantage of that."

October 17

2003 – Roger Federer needs two hours and 16 minutes to defeat Feliciano Lopez 4-6, 7-6 (3), 6-4 in the quarterfinals of the Masters Series event in Madrid. The Wimbledon champion is on the verge of being eliminated when trailing 0-40 on his serve at 4-4 in the second set. "Well, if I could choose, I'd always choose an easy match, obviously," says Federer after the match. "I just hung in there. I could have lost in straight sets 6-4, 6-4. I was down Love-40 in the second. I really battled hard tonight. I gave everything I had."

2002 – Roger Federer defeats Nicolas Lapentti 6-3, 6-4 to reach the quarterfinals of the Madrid Masters in Spain.

1999 – Playing in the semifinals of an ATP event for the first time in his career, Roger Federer loses to No. 7-ranked Greg Rusedski 6-3, 6-4 in the semifinals of the CA Trophy tennis championships in Vienna. En route to the semifinals, Federer beats Vince Spadea, Jiri Novak and Karol Kucera. Says Rusedski of beating the 18-year-old Federer, "I really didn't have to do anything spectacular. I just had to wait for him to make the mistakes."

2006 – Top-ranked Roger Federer wins his first match indoors in almost a year, hitting 28 winners in defeating Nicolas Massu 6-3, 6-2 in his opening match at the Madrid Masters. "I think it's always nice to beat the Olympic champion," says Federer of beating Massu, the 2004 Olympic gold medalist. "That's what I think. I enjoy playing against him."

2008 – Withstanding 11 first-set aces from Juan Martin del Potro, Roger Federer advances to the semifinals of the Madrid Masters with a 6-3, 6-3 win. Federer only allows one second-set ace from his 6-foot, 6-inch opponent – and his out-aced 12 to 3, but credits his slice backhand as the key to his victory. "The slice goes nicely on this court," Federer says after the match. "I felt good using it to counter Juan Martin's height."

2010 – Breaking Roger Federer's serve four times, Andy Murray defeats Federer 6-3, 6-2 to win the Shanghai Masters, his eighth win in 13 meetings with the Swiss. "I love the challenge of playing against him," Murray says of playing Federer. "I don't fear playing him. I don't know if my game matches up well against his or not, but I've played some of my best tennis against Roger."

October 18

2002 – For the second time in three matches, Fabrice "The Magician" Santoro beats Roger Federer, this time 7-5, 6-3 in the quarterfinals of the Madrid Masters. The No. 7-ranked Federer blows a double-set point with the No.

50-ranked Santoro serving at 3-5, 15-40 in the first set. The two players play another eight times in their career, Federer not losing even another set to the double-handed French player.

2003 – In an indoor match between the reigning French Open champion and the reigning Wimbledon champion, world No. 1 Juan Carlos Ferrero beats the Wimbledon winner Roger Federer 6-4, 4-6, 6-4 to reach the Madrid Masters final in Spain. "I wasn't too happy with my game," Federer says after a defeat hurts his chances in his three-way battle with Ferrero and Andy Roddick for the achieving the year-end world No. 1 ranking.

2007 – After surprisingly losing twice earlier in the year to Guillermo Canas, Roger Federer finally gets a win against his Argentine nemesis, defeating the 14th-ranked Canas 6-0, 6-3 to reach the quarterfinals of the Madrid Masters. In March, Canas beats Federer in consecutive tournaments – in Indian Wells and in Key Biscayne. Federer needs only 21 minutes to win the first set and 53 minutes for the match.

2008 – Roger Federer loses his chance to finish as year-end No. 1 for a fifth straight year as he is defeated by Andy Murray 3-6, 6-3, 7-5 in the semifinals of the Madrid Masters. The loss guarantees that Rafael Nadal will end the year at No. 1, becoming the first Spanish player in the Open era to end the year with the No. 1 ranking. Murray breaks the second-ranked Federer in the final set on his seventh break point chance in the 11th game.

October 19

2006 – A strong opponent of the Hawk-Eye replay challenge system, Roger Federer wins his round of 16 match at the Madrid Masters against Robin Soderling by using a challenge that overrules an original call on match point. In the final point of his 7-6 (5), 7-6 (8) victory over the Swede, Federer challenges the linesman's call on Soderling's cross-court forehand winner, which the Hawk-Eye replay reveals to be out. Says Federer of the final replay, "I thought it was really funny, especially waiting like this for the match point. This has never happened before and I thought it was kind of silly."

2007 – Converting on only one of 11 break point chances is all Roger Federer needs to beat Feliciano Lopez 7-6 (4), 6-4 in the quarterfinals of the Madrid Masters."I couldn't break early on," Federer says of the match that also features Lopez hitting 34 unforced errors."I was starting to get a bit concerned."

October 20

2006 – Roger Federer ties the 24-year-old record of Ivan Lendl for consecutive 80-win seasons with a 6-3, 7-6 (4) win over Robby Ginepri that puts him through to the semifinals of the Madrid Masters for the first time since 2003. "It's obviously great to win. It always is a sign of the hard work paying off somewhere. And the best way that it pays off is in wins," says Federer after the historic victory. "So you can imagine, I've walked off the court 80 times as a winner this season, only five times as a loser. That's a great record for me. I'm really proud of those last two years now. I've only lost a small number. The 80 is not more special than 70 or 90, but it's a great number to reach that's for sure."

2007 – Top-ranked Roger Federer wins his 18th straight match and reaches his 10th final in his last 13 events with a 6-4, 6-4 win over Nicolas Kiefer in 84 minutes in the semifinals of the Madrid Masters. Federer breaks Kiefer's serve twice and is near-perfect on first serve points, winning 31 of 34 for the match, including 10 aces.

2008 – Roger Federer loses a rare set in a first-round match as American Bobby Reynolds extends Federer to three sets in the first round of the Swiss Indoors in Basel, Federer winning 6-3, 6-7(6), 6-3.

October 21

2007 – David Nalbandian pulls of a rare "trifecta" in men's tennis defeating No. 1 Roger Federer 1-6, 6-3, 6-3 in the final of the Madrid Masters in Spain, giving the Argentine the distinction of beating the No. 1, No. 2 and No. 3 ranked players in the same tournament. Nalbandian, ranked No. 25, beats No. 2 Rafael Nadal in the quarterfinals and No. 3 Novak Djokovic before dismissing Federer in the final. "I usually play better in the finals, but it had something to do with the way he played today," says Federer, the defending champion. "I guess when you beat Djokovic and Nadal back-to-back, you come into the final here very ready." Nalbandian becomes only the third player in 13 years to perform the sweep of the top three players in the same event – Novak Djokovic turning the trick earlier in the year in Canada – and Boris Becker pulling off the feat in Stockholm in 1994.

2006 – Winning the last eight games of the match, Roger Federer routs David Nalbandian 6-4, 6-0 in the semifinals of the Madrid Masters. Federer's backhand produces four winners on the day, including a superb passing shot that puts him in front 5-4 before he breaks Nalbandian for the second time to take the set. "My second set was phenomenal," Federer says. "I was able to put more pressure on him and at 3-0, you start to think this is his last chance. If he plays another poor game, he won't have a chance and you start to feel it."

2010 – In his 900th match on the ATP Tour, Roger Federer cruises into the Stockholm Open quarterfinals with a 6-1, 6-2 win over Taylor Dent in 51 minutes. "In 1998 I played my first match and now I just played my 900th," says Federer. "It's crazy. I have a great win-loss record and I couldn't have asked for a better career. And it was nice to actually win my 900th match."

2013 – Roger Federer opens up play for the 14th time at his hometown tournament, the Swiss Indoors in Basel, Switzerland, with a 6-4, 6-2 win over No. 62-ranked Adrian Mannarino of France. "I think it was a pretty good performance for a first round," says Federer. "I had some good spells and some that were tougher. I fought through and stayed positive throughout. I kept playing aggressive, the way I would like to play for the week."

October 22

2006 – "I am the best right now, in history we'll never know, unless I break all records, but that's still a long way to go," says Roger Federer after he defeats Fernando Gonzalez of Chile 7-5, 6-1, 6-0 to win the Madrid Masters singles title. The title is his 10th of the 2006 season, giving Federer the distinction of becoming the first player in the Open era to win 10 or more titles in a season for three consecutive seasons. Federer finishes the season with 12 titles – to go with the 11 titles he wins in both 2004 and 2005. Federer does not drop a set in Madrid while winning his 19th straight match and third straight final. "I've really come a long way in the last four years, and I really hope I stay healthy and improve," says Federer.

2010 – Trailing his Olympic doubles partner 6-2, 2-0, Roger Federer recovers to beat Stanislas Wawrinka 2-6, 6-3, 6-2 to reach the Stockholm Open semifinals. "It was looking pretty bad, Stan was playing well and things were going quickly for me," Federer says. "I had no timing and was shanking balls."

October 23

2007 – World No. 1 Roger Federer loses a rare set in a first-round match as he defeats No. 56-ranked Michael Berrer of Germany 6-1, 3-6, 6-3 at his hometown tournament, the Swiss Indoors in Basel. Says Federer, "I'm now having to explain why I lost a set. It's almost laughable. It happens."

2012 – Defending champion Roger Federer opens up his bid for a sixth title at his hometown tournament, the Swiss Indoors in Basel, with a 7-5, 6-3 victory over German Benjamin Becker. "Ever since my first win here, the pressure has actually gone instead of increased, in my opinion," Federer says. "I feel I can come here and just perform, enjoy and try my best. It's pretty simple, actually, the approach. I know if I lose, I lose points, but I've so long gone over this hurdle of having to defend points and this whole rankings system – I know how it works, so it doesn't really consume me. For me it's all about trying to play my best, enjoy the crowd and show them what I got. Coming back here as the World No. 1 is an amazing feeling, so I think more of that than the pressure of having to win or having to defend or having to win again."

2008 – Despite being down two set points in the first set, Roger Federer admits he never feels in danger against Jarkko Nieminen of Finland in his 7-6 (6), 7-6 (1) win in the second round of the Swiss Indoors in Basel. Nieminen, ranked No. 29, holds two set points leading 5-3 in the first set, but is not able to convert and loses the match in one hour, 36 minutes. "I have such a good record against him that I never felt in danger," says Federer who improves his career record against the Finn to 10-0. "We played doubles 10 years ago as juniors and we know each other well."

2010 – Roger Federer moves himself to within one match victory of tying Pete Sampras for career titles after defeating No. 17-ranked Ivan Ljubicic 7-6 (5), 6-2 to reach the final of the Stockholm Open in Sweden. Federer seeks to win a the 64th title of his career, matching Sampras for fourth place in the Open era, trailing only Jimmy Connors (109), Ivan Lendl (94) and John McEnroe (77). "It's been a good a year when it comes to making the finals, but I don't have the best win-loss record this year," says Federer, who holds a 2-4 record in finals in 2010, most recently a loss in the Shanghai final to Andy Murray. "In the past I've had an amazing run. I think I won 24 straight finals at one stage, so this could be the start of the streak again."

2013 – "It's an amazing atmosphere for me to play in," says Roger Federer of playing at his hometown tournament, the Swiss Indoors in Basel, after defeating Denis Istomin 4-6, 6-3, 6-2 in the event's second round. "As a kid I was always thinking about Wimbledon and Basel," Federer says. "For me those were the two great things. It's important to never forget that dream. It's the dream I have been chasing after since I was a kid." Federer overcomes a slow start and fights off four break points in the second game of the final set, before reeling off the last five games of the match. Federer credits the home crowd to helping him avoid the upset loss. "I think the crowd rarely gets the opportunity to see me play three sets, whether good or bad," Federer says. "It was nice seeing the crowd fight for me and try to get me back into the match. It gives you that extra push to try harder."

October 24

2010 – Roger Federer beats Germany's Florian Mayer 6-4, 6-3 to win the Stockholm Open and match Pete Sampras' total of 64 career titles, tying him for No. 4 all time. "It's amazing that I'm there where Pete's ended his career on," Federer says. "You never know when it's your last one. That's why you want to savor every tournament victory." The match victory is also the 50th for Federer on the year giving him the distinction of becoming only the fifth man, and the first since Sampras, to win 50 matches in at least nine straight years in the Open era. "Early on, I think that feeling of wanting to prove yourself to the world and all the doubters is a very strong one, so you're very aggressive in your ways of winning and not enjoying them," Federer says. "Today it's much more of the enjoyment part because I don't need to prove myself to anyone anymore, except to myself." Sweden's Crown Princess Victoria presents the tournament championship trophy to Federer, who is appearing at this tournament for the first time in a decade. "For me, every tournament victory is special," Federer says. "This is one I'll definitely remember, maybe more than other ones." The title is Federer's first tournament title in Sweden and the 18th country in which he has won a title. "It feels great winning any tournament, but especially in a country where I've never been successful before," Federer says.

2012 – Roger Federer edges Thomaz Bellucci 6-3, 6-7 (6), 7-5 to advance into the quarterfinals of the Swiss Indoors in Basel, Switzerland. Federer, a winner in Basel five out of the last six years, advances in just over three hours with eight aces and two breaks of serve. "It was a tough match but a very enjoyable one," Federer says. "I maybe had some luck at the end. I also had a rest while he was playing yesterday after a long trip. But Thomaz played really well. I had to work for this one."

2006 – Winning 12 of the first 15 points of the match – including a service game that features four aces – Roger Federer easily advances to the second round of the Swiss Indoors in Basel beating No. 151-ranked Tomas Zib 6-1, 6-2. Federer loses only six points on serve in the 49-minute match.

2008 – Roger Federer defeats Simone Bolelli 6-2, 6-3 in 67 mnutes to reach the semifinals at the Swiss Indoors in Basel. "I'm very satisfied by how it went," Federer says of the match. "I tried to step up the pressure and so far that's worked well."

October 25

2001 – Not facing a break point, Roger Federer, ranked No. 4, beats Xavier Malisse, ranked No. 39, 6-3, 6-4 in 63 minutes to advance to the quarterfinals of the Swiss Indoors in Basel.

2002 – In their third career meeting, No. 8-ranked Roger Federer beats No. 12-ranked Andy Roddick 7-6 (5), 6-1 to advance to the semifinals of the Swiss Indoors at Basel.

2007 – Roger Federer plays Juan Martin del Potro for the second time in his career and beats the Argentine, ranked No. 49, 6-1, 6-4 to advance to the quarterfinals at the Swiss Indoors in Basel, Switzerland. "I got out of the blocks fast and when he made errors I took advantage.I kept my errors to a minimum" says Federer, who fires 10 aces in the 58-minute match.

2008 – Roger Federer defeats No. 39-ranked Feliciano Lopez 6-3, 6-2 in the semifinals of the Swiss Indoors in Basel, Switzerland, firing an impressive 15 aces in the 61-minute match. "I had a bit of difficulty at the start," Federer acknowledges after the match. "But then I found my rhythm and my serve was working even better than normal so I'm really happy about that."

2013 – Roger Federer plays the player affectionally known as "Baby Fed," Grigor Dimitrov of Bulgaria, for the first time in his career, and defeats the man who plays with a style quite similar to him by a 6-3, 7-6(2) margin in the quarterfinals of the Swiss Indoors in Basel, Switzerland. Federer recovers from a 3-5, 0-40 deficit in the second set to win his 50th career match at his hometown event. It is the fifth different tournament Federer has won 50 or more matches, also achieving the feat at the Australian Open, the French Open, Wimbledon and the U.S. Open.

October 26

2001 – In the first of 24 career meetings, Roger Federer beats Andy Roddick 3-6, 6-3, 7-6 (5) in the quarterfinals of the Swiss Indoors in Basel, Switzerland. Federer comes back from a 3-5 deficit in the deciding tie-break and hits one of the most spectacular shots of his career, hitting an overhead passsing shot winner from behind the baseline, near the front row of spectactors, off of Roddick's overhead. Roddick responses to Federer's incredible shot by jokingly throwing his racquet in his direction on the other side of the net in disbelief.

2008 – In their 18th – and second-to-last – career meeting, Roger Federer defeats David Nalbandian 6-3, 6-4 to win the Swiss Indoors in Basel for his 57th career singles title, and his third straight title in his hometown."Things are back into a groove the way I like it," says Federer, increasing his head-to-head advantage over his once nemesis to 10-8, after losing the first five pro meetings against the Argentine. "I'm happy with the way I'm playing. It feels great to win at home. Once you had it you want more of it and you want to do it over and over again."

2002 – In their second meeting as professionals, David Nalbandian, ranked No. 18, defeats No. 8-ranked Roger Federer 6-7 (2), 7-5, 6-3 in the semifinals of the Swiss Indoors in Basel, preventing Federer from advancing into the final of his hometown tournament for a third straight year. Nalbandian leads 5-3 in the first set, before faltering while Federer leads by a service break in the two following sets, before also faltering.

2013 – Roger Federer advances into the final of his hometown tournament, the Swiss Indoors in Basel, for a 10th time, edging 23-year-old Vasek Pospisil 6-3, 6-7 (7),

7-5. The 32-year-old Federer serves for a straight-sets win at 5-3 in the second set, but is broken and loses the second-set tie-breaker. He also loses his serve to trail 1-3 in the final set, but rallies for the victory with some brilliant late form. "It's not easy to play someone you basically worshipped growing up," says the 40th-ranked Pospisil after the loss. "You want to win, but you have a great amount of respect. It's tough to compete if you give too much respect. I was battling with myself a bit."

2012 – Roger Federer breezes into the semifinals of the Swiss Indoors beating No. 46-ranked Benoit Paire of France 6-2, 6-2 in just 55 minutes in his first meeting against the Frenchman.

2007 – Top-ranked Roger Federer cruises into the semifinals of the Swiss Indoors at Basel defeating Nicolas Kiefer 6-3, 6-2.

2006 – Winning the last eight games of the match, Roger Federer advances to the quarterfinals of the Swiss Indoors in Basel with a 6-2, 6-0 win in 53 minutes over Spain's Guillermo Garcia-Lopez.

2004 – Roger Federer pulls out of the Swiss Indoors after injuring his left thigh in a practice session in Basel, Switzerland. It marks the first time in Federer's career as a pro that he does not play the Swiss Indoors, first playing the event in 1998.

October 27

2006 – Playing the second-longest tie-breaker of his career, Roger Federer beat No. 15-ranked David Ferrer 6-3, 7-6 (14) to reach the semifinals of the Swiss Indoors in Basel. Federer's 30-point tie-breaker in the second set is second to his 20-18 tie-breaker against Marat Safin at the Tennis Masters Cup in Houston in 2004, what also is the longest in the history of men's singles tennis on the ATP Tour. Federer saves six set points in the tie-breaker against Ferrer at 5-6, 6-7, 8-9, 9-10, 12-13 and 13-14, three of the points on his return of serve. "I think I was trying to risk a bit more in front of my home crowd today, so I'm just lucky that it paid off in the end," says Federer. "It's been a while since I dropped serve at the start of a match, so it was important that I reacted well."

2007 – In a match that features no service breaks, top-ranked Roger Federer defeats No. 25-ranked Ivo Karlovic 7-6 (6), 7-6 (5) to move into the final of the Swiss Indoors tournament in his hometown of Basel. Federer saves a set point at 4-5 in the first set in the 98-minute match. Federer is out-aced by Karlovic 16-10.

2001 – Firing 10 aces, Roger Federer, ranked No. 13, beats Julien Boutter of France, ranked No. 64, 7-6 (3), 6-4 to reach the final of his hometown tournament, the Swiss Indoors in Basel, for the second straight year. Earlier in the year, Federer beats Boutter in the Milan final for his first ATP tournament victory.

2012 – Roger Federer advances into the final of the Swiss Indoors for the ninth time in his career, defeating Paul-Henri Mathieu 7-5, 6-4. Federer, chasing his sixth title in seven years at his hometown event, fires 10 aces and does not allowed the No. 101st-ranked Mathieu a break-point chance in the match.

2013 – Playing in the final of his hometown tournament, the Swiss Indoors in Basel, for a 10th time, Roger Federer is beaten by Juan Martin del Potro 7-6 (3), 2-6, 6-4, marking the second straight year he loses to the Argentine in the Basel final. A win for Federer would have qualified him for the season-ending ATP World Tour Finals in London and would have given him his 78th career ATP singles title, moving him into third place all-time ahead of John McEnroe (77 titles) and behind Jimmy Connors (109 titles) and Ivan Lendl (94 titles). "It's always a pleasure playing against you," Del Potro tells Federer during the on-court trophy ceremony. "I know you are the hero here and for me a big inspiration, too."

October 28

2012 – Saying "I didn't play a good tiebreaker in the third and that was the story of the match," Roger Federer is beaten by Juan Martin del Potro in the final of Swiss Indoors in Federer's hometown of Basel by a 6-4, 6-7 (5), 7-6 (3) margin. Del Potro ends a six-match losing streak to Federer, including his four-hour, 26-minute 19-17 in the third-set loss in the semifinals of the Olympic Games. "This time it was for me," says Del Potro, who doesn't drop serve in the match and improves to 3-13 lifetime against Federer with the win, the 13th tournament title of this career. "It was an unbelievable final. You can't wait, you have to go to (get) the victory."

2007 – Roger Federer beats Jarkko Nieminen 6-3, 6-4 to win his hometown tournament, the Swiss Indoor Championships in Basel, for a second consecutive year. The win officially clinches the year-end world No. 1 ranking for Federer for a fourth consecutive year. Federer joins Pete Sampras, Jimmy Connors, John McEnroe and Ivan Lendl as the only men to finish the year ranked No. 1 for at least four years since the rankings began in 1973. Says Federer, "It's nice to win again and go into the next year as No. 1 again." Of playing at his hometown tournament, Federer says, "It's always emotional at the end (of the tournament). I remember being here as a ball boy myself. I know 50 percent of the people working at the tournament."

2006 – Roger Federer rallies in a third-set tiebreaker to reach the Swiss Indoors final in Basel, defeating Paradorn Srichaphan 6-4, 3-6, 7-6 (5) for his 23rd straight victory. Federer is down 3-5 in the deciding tie-breaker, but manages to win the last four points of the match. "I knew from the start it was going to be a difficult match," Federer says. "(Srichaphan) played well, he started to serve better. I found it hard to get into his return games consistently. It was obviously a bit lucky in the end. You need that in a tiebreak in the third set, so I hung in there and am really excited to be through to the final."

2000 – Ranked No. 34, Roger Federer saves a match point and beats No. 9-ranked Lleyton Hewitt of Australia 6-4, 5-7, 7-6 (6) to reach the final of his hometown tournament, the Swiss Indoors in Basel, for the first time in his career. Hewitt actually wins one more point than Federer – 112-to 111 – in the two-hour, 31-minute match.

2001 – For a second straight year, Roger Federer loses in the final of his hometown tournament, the Swiss Indoors in Basel, falling to No. 11-ranked Tim Henman 6-3, 6-4, 6-2 in the best-of-five-set final. Henman breaks the No. 13-ranked Federer's serve twice in the first set, once in the second set and twice in the third set.

October 29

2000 – Roger Federer plays in the final of his hometown tournament, the Swiss Indoor Championships in Basel, for the first time in his career, but falls to No. 6-ranked Thomas Enqvist of Sweden 6-2, 4-6, 7-6 (4), 1-6, 6-1. Federer holds two set points in the third set at 6-5 (40-15) that would have given him a two-sets-to-one lead. "I was really lucky to win the third set," Enqvist says after the two-hour, 54-minute match.

2006 – In his seventh attempt, Roger Federer finally wins his hometown tournament, the Swiss Indoors in Basel, Switzerland, beating Fernando Gonzalez 6-3, 6-2, 7-6 (3) in the final. The tournament win is his fourth straight title and 11th of the year. "It is indeed magnificent," Federer says of winning the event where he once worked as a ball boy and of winning four straight titles on tour. "Different countries, different titles, they all have a different meaning. Winning Basel, my home tournament, it's one of those moments I'll never forget." The final is a rematch of the previous week's Madrid Masters final, also won by Federer in three sets. Federer fires 14 aces against Gonzalez, the defending Basel champion, to win his 24th consecutive match and improves his record to 9-0 against the Chilean and to 87-5 on the year.

2008 – Roger Federer saves two set points in a second-set tiebreaker and beats Robin Soderling 6-4, 7-6 (7) to reach the third round of the Paris Masters. "He was a potentially dangerous opponent, he's been playing well indoors," Federer tells reporters of Soderling, whom Federer would beat in the final of the French Open seven months later. "I knew he was a player on a roll but I did well. I served well, I was just surprised that he did not return better."

2012 – The ATP announces that due to Roger Federer withdrawing from the Paris Masters, Novak Djokovic will finish the season as the world No. 1.

October 30

2013 – With a 6-4, 6-4 win over Kevin Anderson in his opening round match at the Paris Masters, Roger Federer qualifies for the year-end ATP World Tour Finals in London for a 12th time. The No. 6-ranked, 32-year-old Federer, suffering through his worst season on tour in a decade, was in danger of missing out on the prestigious year-end tournament that he has won six times, but a final-round showing at his hometown tournament in Basel, Switzerland helped him qualify as one of the top eight players for the season. "I'm just happy right now to have made it again [to the World Tour Finals]," Federer says. "It's one of the goals I set myself at the beginning of the year. I could feel out there that the way I was taking decisions, the way I was moving, it was very clear-cut. No second guessing. I know why the year was difficult for me. It's not because I can't make a forehand anymore. It's because I had physical injuries, and I still played in spite of the injuries because I'm not going into a corner and waiting for four months. Little by little I lost my confidence in my movements, in my game. But it was not that bad, because I just qualified for London."

2006 – Top-ranked Roger Federer pulls out of the Paris Masters because of fatigue. Federer's withdrawal comes a day after he wins the Swiss Indoors for his 11th title of the year.

2008 – Roger Federer reaches the quarterfinals of the Paris Masters defeating No. 25-ranked Marin Cilic of Croatia 6-3, 6-4 in 71 minutes. The match is the first career meeting between the two players.

October 31

1999 – Roger Federer beats Max Mirnyi 7-6 (4), 6-3 to win his first ever "Challenger" level professional singles title at the Brest Challenger in France. Federer had previously won a "Satellite" level event in Switzerland in 1997.

2002 – Roger Federer, ranked No. 8, beats Tommy Haas, ranked No. 7, 6-2, 7-6 (2) to reach the quarterfinals of the Paris Masters. Haas does not play another ATP Tour match after this one until February of 2004, a span of 15 months, due to a shoulder injury and time spent off the tour to tend to the health of his parents due to a serious motorcycle accident.

2007 – Top-ranked Roger Federer beats No. 24-ranked Ivo Karlovic 6-3, 4-6, 6-3 in the second round of the Paris Masters. The final few games of the second set go so quickly that neither player is sure the set is even complete. "I thought it was 5-3. I didn't think it was over," Federer says after the match. "When I looked up on the scoreboard it was the set, so I asked the umpire if he could just double check...but some games went really fast. Maybe we forget a couple of games here or there." Federer is out-aced 16-6 by Karlovic in the 104-minute match.

2008 – For the first time in his career, Roger Federer is not healthy enough to complete a tournament as he gives his opponent James Blake a victory by walk-over in the quarterfinals of the Paris Masters due to a bad back. "I've had a lot of back pain over all the years of playing tennis... (but) it's just the first time it's acute during a tournament and it makes me pull out," Federer tells the media. "I'll check it out for the next few days."

NOVEMBER

November 1

2013 – Winning 19 of the last 25 points, world No. 6 Roger Federer defeats world No. 5 Juan Martin del Potro 6-3, 4-6, 6-3 to advance to the semifinals of the BNP Paribas Masters in Paris. Federer wins 17 of 20 points at the net in the match to set up a semifinal confrontation with world No. 1 Novak Djokovic. "That's definitely good for my confidence, because those are the kind of wins I need right now," Federer says. "It was clearly a huge victory, giving myself a chance to be in the semis here, and playing Novak is clearly very exciting."

2002 – Thirty-six unforced errors befuddle Roger Federer as he is defeated by world No. 1 Lleyton Hewitt 6-4, 6-4 in the quarterfinals of the Paris Open.

2007 – David Nalbandian beats Roger Federer for the second time in less than two weeks, registering a 6-4, 7-6 (3) win in the third round of the Paris Masters. The result evens the series between the two players at 8-8 and ends

Federer's streak of reaching the final in eight straight tournaments.

2010 – Alexandr Dolgopolov of the Ukraine is forced to retire with an ankle injury against Roger Federer with Federer leading 6-4, 5-2 in the first round of the Swiss Indoors in Basel, Switzerland.

November 2

2013 – In the 30th career meeting between Roger Federer and Novak Djokovic, the world No. 1 Djokovic fights back from being down a set and a break to beat Federer 4-6, 6-3, 6-2 in the semifinals of the Paris Masters. After winning the first set, fighting off three break point chances, Federer breaks Djokovic to take a 1-0 lead in the second set, but is not able to consolidate and Djokovic pulls away to beat Federer for the 14th time in his career.

2009 – Saying "I was eager to come out and play again," Roger Federer returns from a six-week break and beats old friend and rival Olivier Rochus of Belgium 6-3, 6-4 in the opening round of the Swiss Indoors in Basel.

November 3

2010 – Roger Federer eases into the quarterfinals of the Swiss Indoors in Basel, defeating Janko Tipsarevic 6-3, 6-4.

2013 – In his pre-event press conference before competing in his 12th season-ending ATP World Tour Finals, Roger Federer declares his confidence is back after a year that saw him win only one tournament and his ranking drop from No. 2 to No. 7. "I'm happy with my game," Federer tells reporters. "My confidence is back again and that can carry you a really long way, to be honest. So that's good." Federer qualifies for the year-end event in London in the last week of the season, bolstered by a final-round showing in Basel and a semifinal finish in Paris, playing nine matches over 12 days, including five three-setters. Says Federer of his year as a whole, "I know that the year has been a bit more difficult. Most of the time I was just focusing on myself to get things right in my life, with my back and so forth, and now finally that I did I feel like it's coming together at the right time for me. But [this season] has a different feel. It hasn't been as consistent, as good, as solid as it has been in previous years. So I'm maybe still a little bit — I don't want to say insecure — but unsure about how high is my level of play even though it has been good these last three weeks."

"Yes, I really hit with him when he was 15, during a tournament in Basel, and I knew then he would be good, but not this good. If he stays healthy, it will actually be a miracle if he doesn't win more Grand Slams than Pete [Sampras]. The way he picks his shots is unbelievable. He is fast, he has a great volley, a great serve, great backhand, great everything. If I was his coach, what can I tell him? He is a magician with a racquet. Even when he is playing badly, which is rarely, he can still do things with his racquet nobody else can do."
—Goran Ivanisevic to The Independent, 2004

November 4

2012 – Despite Novak Djokovic being assured as the No. 1 year-end ranking, Roger Federer is asked by media in his pre-ATP World Tour Finals press conference if the winner of the event in London will be considered by fans as the real year-end No. 1 with Andy Murray winning the Olympics and the U.S. Open, Federer winning Wimbledon, Djokovic winning the Australian Open and Rafael Nadal, who is injured and not competing in London, winning the French Open. "I mean, the real No.1, we know who that is. It's going to be Novak. I don't think there should be any debate around that," says Federer. "I think No. 1, you don't get there by chance. The rankings is something that shows you how you've played over a 365-day period. Okay, it might all change again in two months at the Australian Open, there's no doubt about that. But right now, it's clear. I don't think whatever happens should take anything away from anybody."

2009 - Roger Federer reaches the quarterfinals of the Swiss Indoors in Basel by beating Andreas Seppi, 6-3, 6-3.

Growing up Roger Federer's favorite player was Boris Becker, followed by Stefan Edberg and Pete Sampras, according to Rene Stauffer in his book "Roger Federer: Quest for Perfection"

November 5

2013 – Just three days after facing each other in the semifinals of the Paris Indoors, Roger Federer and Novak

Djokovic play again in their opening round-robin match at the ATP World Tour Finals in London, Djokovic winning the rematch of the previous year's tournament final 6-4, 6-7(2), 6-2 in two hours, 22 minutes. "I thought I had a chance today," Federer says. "So that's the part where I'm unhappy. I wasn't able to take advantage of it. Because I was actually feeling much better than I was in Paris overall, physically. I think at this point it's very mental, just making sure I don't get too negative on myself because of the loss today. I mean, it was against Novak after all. It's not against some journeyman." With his appearance in the year-end championships, Federer equals Ivan Lendl's mark for most successive appearances at the season-ending championships with 12.

2012 – The ATP announces that Roger Federer is the winner of the ATP World Tour's Stefan Edberg Sportsmanship Award for the eighth time and extends his reign as the ATPWorldTour.com Fans' Favorite to a record 10th straight year. Federer wins the award, named after one of his childhood heroes and voted on by his fellow players, for six straight years from 2004-09 before Rafael Nadal breaks the streak in 2011. The 31-year-old Swiss wins ATPWorldTour.com Fans' Favorite presented by RICOH for a record 10th straight year, receiving 57 per cent of all votes cast.

2010 – Roger Federer beats Radek Stepanek 6-2, 6-3 to advance into a semifinal showdown with Andy Roddick at the Swiss Indoors in Basel.

November 6

2011 – Roger Federer wins his fifth singles title at his hometown event, the Swiss Indoors in Basel, defeating Kei Nishikori 6-1, 6-3 in the first meeting between the two players. The victory gives Federer five titles or more at an event for the fifth time and his 68th career title. "I'm very happy, as I got better as the week went on," Federer says "I definitely saved the best for last at the tournament. I played really well today in the final."

2012 – Claiming a record-breaking 40th career match victory at the ATP World Tour Finals, Roger Federer defeats Janko Tipsarevic 6-3, 6-1 at London's O2 Arena in his opening round-robin match in his 11th appearance at the season-ending championships. The win moves Federer ahead of Ivan Lendl, who won 39 career matches in the season-ending championships. "I'm happy with my performance today," says Federer. "No pain anymore anywhere. I'm happy with my level of play today against Janko, who is obviously a good player."

2009 – Three-time defending champion Roger Federer advances into the semifinals of the Swiss Indoors in his hometown of Basel with a 6-3, 6-2 win against Russian qualifier Evgeny Korolev.

2010 – Playing for the first since their epic Wimbledon final 16 months earlier, Roger Federer and Andy Roddick engage in a semifinal confrontation at the Swiss Indoors in Basel. On this occasion, Federer more easily dispatches of Roddick 6-2, 6-4 in just 69 minutes against their four hour,

16-minute Wimbledon final that ended in Federer winning by a 16-14 score in the fifth set. Federer breaks Roddick's serve twice in each set and fires 13 aces to the American's four to win for the 20th time in 22 career meetings with Roddick.

2013 – Roger Federer receives three year-end awards in an on-court presentation at the ATP World Tour Finals in London. Federer is selected by his peers as the winner of the Stefan Edberg Sportsmanship Award for a ninth time and by fans as the ATPWorldTour.com Fans' Favorite presented for an 11th straight year. Federer is also awarded the Arthur Ashe Humanitarian of the Year for a second time in recognition of his foundation's support of children in Africa and Switzerland.

November 7

2010 – Avenging his crushing loss to Novak Djokovic from the U.S. Open semifinals, Roger Federer defeats his Serbian rival 6-4, 3-6, 6-1 to win the Swiss Indoors in Basel for a fourth time. Federer's win also avenges his loss to Djokovic from the previous year's Basel final that ends his three-year-reign as champion of his hometown tournament. "I've played really well all week long," says Federer, who does not drop a set en route to the final.

2006 – Roger Federer announces that he will not represent Switzerland against Spain in the first round of the 2007 Davis Cup, dispelling any notion that he and Rafael Nadal could play against each other in the international team event.

2009 – Roger Federer defeats childhood friend Marco Chiudinelli, 7-6 (7), 6-3 to advance to the final of the Swiss Indoors in Basel.

2013 – Converting on his sixth match point in a 16-point final game of the match, Roger Federer defeats Richard Gasquet 6-4, 6-3 to even his round-robin record at 1-1 at the ATP World Tour Finals in London. The win is Federer's 43rd in his 12 appearances at the season-ending championships. "Richard does a good job of making you feel uncomfortable at the same time as well, because he uses heights [and] spins really well," says Federer. "He likes extended rallies. I'm trying to force the issue. But I guess those are the kind of matches I need right now – straight sets against a good player."

November 8

2012 – Roger Federer increases his record to 14-0 in his career against David Ferrer with a 6-4, 7-6 (5) win that advances him into the semifinals of the ATP World Tour Finals in London. In 10 years of facing each other, Ferrer has won only three sets against Federer. "I had a lot of chances ... I can't do it," says Ferrer. "Sometimes with these players, if I don't take my chance, I don't win the important points; it's very difficult to win these matches." Says Federer of his feelings towards the ATP World Tour Finals, a tournament he has won a record six times, "This is a very special tournament in many ways. It's always been the tournament I wanted to be part of when I started playing at the beginning of the year, many years now. I had breakthrough results at this event. I learned a lot. I think I really have taken advantage of what this tournament offers, also sort of for my personality, for just how tough you have to be because it's not a gimme that you're entered into this tournament every year. It's really a lot of hard work beforehand, and then you should actually enjoy it, but then comes more hard work. I think that was a good learning process for me. I've loved everywhere I've played over the years at the World Tour Finals. But I think this one is obviously special, because it's in London and the O2 is an amazing venue, and I'm happy it's going to stay here for the next few years."

2009 – Novak Djokovic ends the three-year run for Roger Federer as the tournament champion at his hometown event, the Swiss Indoors in Basel, defeating Federer 6-4, 4-6, 6-2. "It's disappointing to lose at home in the finals, no doubt," Federer says. "I thought I missed plenty of opportunities. I'm not looking for excuses. He played tough and he played well when he had to, and saved a ton of break points that were crucial." Says Djokovic of what it took to beat Federer, "I have to produce something special to win."

November 9

2013 – Playing Juan Martin del Potro for the third time in three weeks, Roger Federer comes back from 0-3 down in the final set to defeat his Argentine rival 4-6, 7-6 (2), 7-5 to qualify for the semifinals of the ATP World Tour Finals in London. Federer finishes second in his round-robin group with a 2-1 record, behind Novak Djokovic, who posts a 3-0 record. Says Federer, "I think it's one of those matches he probably should have closed out, [but I] found a way. I also played actually good tennis coming back into the match." Del Potro beats Federer in the final of the Swiss Indoors in Basel two weeks earlier before Federer wins in the quarterfinals at the Paris Indoors the next week. Federer qualifies for the semifinal round at the season-ending championships for an 11th time in 12 appearances.

2006 – Roger Federer is in the golf gallery following Tiger Woods in the opening round of the HSBC Champions tournament in Shanghai, China. Federer is also in town preparing for the season-ending Tennis Masters Cup.

2010 – Roger Federer beats Richard Gasquet 6-4, 6-4 to reach the third round of the Paris Masters, but spends most of his post-match press conference discussing allegations that Ted Forstmann, the man who owns IMG, the agency that represents him, bet on professional tennis, betting on Federer to win matches after speaking with him. Federer denies that he was aware that Forstmann was betting on his matches. "I would never do such a thing," Federer says. "I reached out and told him (Forstmann). I want to know everything about it, how this came about. And he's been, you know, nice enough obviously to tell me from his side and has been very open in the press already. So that's O.K. He's not my agent. Tony (Godsick) is my guy, but still, it's a firm that does a lot in sports, so it's just something that for me is important to know what is going on from their side, too."

November 10

2003 – Roger Federer beats Andre Agassi for the first time, saving two match points in a 6-7 (3), 6-3, 7-6 (7) decision in the opening round-robin meeting at the Tennis Masters Cup in Houston. Federer, 0-3 in his career against Agassi entering the match, fires 20 aces and hits 63 winners, while overcoming 50 unforced errors. Says Federer of finally beating Agassi in his career, "We haven't actually played too much, you know, against each other. First time was in my home tournament in Basel, which was when I was 17 years old. I couldn't expect to win there. But I came close in the Miami finals and, I wouldn't say finally, but it's just nice to beat such players, you know, one time in your career."

2012 – Having already clinched a position in the semifinal round, Roger Federer loses his final round-robin match at the ATP World Tour Finals in London, falling to Juan Martin del Potro 7-6 (3), 4-6, 6-3. The loss is the first for Federer at the tournament since 2009 and gives him a 2-1 round-robin record. The win clinches a semifinal berth for del Potro, who coupled with his win over Federer in the finals of Basel two weeks earlier, gives him the distinction of being the first player to beat Federer in two straight indoor tournaments since Lleyton Hewitt. "It's a little record, but really tough to do it," Del Potro said. "To beat Federer is not easy, for sure. But I didn't think about the semis or trying to qualify for the next round. Just was thinking about my match, doing the same things like in Basel." Says Federer, "Good effort (from) his side to get me twice in a row now. I hoped I didn't have to lose against him again today."

2008 – Committing 50 unforced errors against 29 winners, Roger Federer is upset by Gilles Simon 4-6, 6-4, 6-3 in the round-robin opener at the season-ending Tennis Masters Cup in Shanghai, China. Despite pulling out of the Paris Masters 10 days earlier with back pain, Federer says it was not a problem. "Definitely today shots maybe I miss, I normally don't miss," Federer says. "I think that's just lack of practice and just uncertainty where my back was today. All this comes together at the end the day, sometimes against top players it's not enough. Now at least I have a match under my belt, especially three sets, and I hope I can play better in the next match." Simon, ranked No. 9, only enters the elite eight-player field when world No. 1 Rafael Nadal withdraws with a knee injury

2013 – In their 32nd career meeting, Roger Federer and Rafael Nadal face off in the semifinals of the ATP World Tour Finals in London, Nadal registering his first win over Federer on an indoor surface with a 7-5, 6-3 victory. The win increases Nadal's career head-to-head advantage over Federer to 22 wins against 10 losses. Thirty-two unforced errors from Federer does in the six-time winner of the year-end championships. "He was playing more consistent. He was playing more solid," says Federer. "He plays the way he always plays. I just couldn't come up with the shots when I needed them, forehand or serve, moving forward."

November 11

2009 – Roger Federer is dismissed in his opening round match at the Paris Masters, falling to Julien Benneteau of France 3-6, 7-6 (4), 6-4, continuing Federer's dismal record in the prestigious indoor event. "He played incredible at the end. Julien went out and got the victory," says Federer, playing in the event for a seventh time and never advancing past the quarterfinals. "I definitely had chances. I missed them. I feel fine physically, and mentally I was fresh to do really well here."

2011 – Roger Federer wins his 800th career victory beating Juan Monaco of Argentina 6-3, 7-5 to reach the semifinals of the Paris Masters. Federer becomes the seventh player in ATP history to reach the 800-win plateau, joining Jimmy Connors (1,242), Ivan Lendl (1,071), Guillermo Vilas (923), John McEnroe (875), Andre Agassi (870) and Stefan Edberg (806). "I knew going in today that this could be something special, something I could remember," Federer says to the media following the match. "So it's just another win, but it's a special one nevertheless, because 800 is definitely a big number."

2012 – Roger Federer advances into the final of the year-end ATP World Tour Finals for an eighth time, beating

Andy Murray 7-6 (7-5) 6-2 in one hour and 33 minutes in the semifinal in London. "It was a special match. It was the third time in London this year for the two of us and the crowd was electric," says Federer, the two-time defending champion, who beat Murray in July's Wimbledon final, but loses in the London Olympic final in August. "I have been around the block a few times and that was something. You can't tire of nights like this. That is why I keep practicing in front of no people, it inspires you to keep working hard." While the event is played in front of Murray's home British crowd, the fans are not necessarily pro-Murray. "Almost all the times when you play Roger anywhere in the world he gets great support everywhere. He deserves that because of everything that he's achieved," says Murray.

November 12

2012 – Appearing in the ATP World Tour Finals for an eighth time, Roger Federer, ranked No. 2, loses to world No. 1 Novak Djokovic 7-6 (6) 7-5 in London in two hours, 14 minutes, despite leading by a service break in both sets. Federer, the six time winner of the tournament and the two-time defending champion, rushes out to an early 3-0 lead, winning 12 of the first 14 points of the match. However, Djokovic comes back to win five of the next six games. In the second set, Federer breaks Djokovic in the opening game and serves to square the match at one set apiece at 5-4, but, incredibly, while leading 40-15, double-set point, he loses four straight points as Djokovic breaks serve to even the set at 5-5. After holding serve the next game, Djokovic silences the raucously pro-Federer

London crowd with a backhand down-the-line passing shot on his first match point to break serve and close out the victory. "There's no wild card, no free gifts, I am very proud to take part in this tournament," says Federer in the runner-up speech.

2007 – For the first time in four years, world No. 1 Roger Federer loses consecutive matches as the Swiss maestro is a shock loser to hard-hitting Fernando Gonzalez of Chile in the opening round-robin match of the year-end Tennis Masters Cup in Shanghai, China. Gonzalez's 4-6, 7-6 (1), 7-5 win comes after Federer loses to David Nalbandian in the semifinals of the BNP Paribas Masters in Paris earlier in the month. The win is Gonzalez's first over Federer in 11 meetings and Federer's first-ever loss in a round-robin match in 15 previous round-robin matches at the event. Says Federer, "It was a tough loss. I thought I played pretty good. I wish I had an excuse…You can't do much when he drills it into the corners. It was ridiculous." Says Gonzalez, who lost to Federer in the final of the Australian Open at the start of the year, "I have really a lot of motivation. After 10 times, it's my turn now. I think the key of the match was my serve and don't be scared to go for my shots. That was really important."

2006 – In a re-match of the previous year's Tennis Masters Cup final, Roger Federer avenges his 2005 tournament loss to David Nalbandian with a 3-6, 6-1, 6-1 win to opening up round-robin play in Shanghai. The win is Federer's eighth in 14 career meetings with Nalbandian, a player he struggled to beat early in his career, losing their first five professional meetings. Federer tells reporters of the process of learning to beat Nalbandian in his post-match press conference. "I guess just losing, winning a lot of matches, just playing against all sorts of different players," Federer says of how the process evolved in learning to beat Nalbandian. "You always have the fast runners, the big servers, the serve-and-volleyers, the aggressive baseliners, the counterpunchers. I think at the beginning of your career all you're really trying to get is a feel for how to play each and every one of them. It's obvious that you like one style of play. But to beat all the different styles, I think that's the hard part."

2003 – Two days after beating Andre Agassi for the first time in his career, Roger Federer finally is able to register a pro victory over David Nalbandian, registering a 6-3, 6-0 win over the Argentine who entered the match with a perfect 6-0 pro record against the Swiss. Says Federer of the long-awaited victory, "I've been always hoping to beat him, you know, in the seniors. I beat him in juniors, so... Today's my first time and I'm happy about it."

2002 – Roger Federer plays his first career match at the ATP year-end championships, beating Juan Carlos Ferrero 6-3, 6-4 in his opening round robin match at the Tennis Masters Cup in Shanghai.

2008 – After Andy Roddick withdraws from the year-end Tennis Masters Cup in Shanghai with an ankle injury sustained in practice, Roger Federer faces substitute player Radek Stepanek, who has to borrow racquets, socks and plays the round-robin match without his contact lenses. Federer wins the match 7-6 (4), 6-4 to even his round-robin record at 1-1 after dropping his first round-robin match to Gilles Simon.

2010 – Roger Federer reaches the semifinals of the Paris Masters for the first time in his career defeating Jurgen Melzer of Austria 6-1, 7-6 (4).

2011 – For the first time in his career Roger Federer advances into the final of the Paris Masters with a 6-4 6-3 victory over Tomas Berdych. Federer, 30, also becomes the first player to reach the final of all nine Masters 1000 tournaments in a career. "I am very happy to have made the final," says Federer, ranked No. 4 in the world. "I am very happy with my level of play at the moment. I had six weeks off (after the U.S. Open), and that has been very good for my mind and my body. I look at the big picture. The ranking system is 365 days. It is all year round. I am not 20 and I can't play seven straight weeks and expect to win in Paris. I was carrying a few injuries, but the rest has been good. I'm very hungry and aggressive (on the court)."

November 13

2005 – Playing for the first time in seven weeks due an injured ankle, Roger Federer opens up play at the Tennis Masters Cup in Shanghai with a 6-3, 2-6, 6-4 victory over David Nalbandian. "I had no expectations whatsoever, to be honest," says Federer of the match. "For me, this is one of the better moments in my career because coming back from the worst injury I've ever had, to come back and win a match at the Masters Cup, it's great for me."

2011 – Playing at the BNP Paribas Paris Masters for a ninth time, Roger Federer finally is able to win the title at Bercy for the first time, defeating Jo-Wilfried Tsonga 6-1, 7-6 (3) in the title match. "Look, I have had many attempts trying to win Paris-Bercy, and for some reason, you know, I wasn't able to win it earlier," says Federer. "But this one obviously feels great, and it's a special victory for sure." Federer's victory makes him the second man — after Andre Agassi — to win the French Open and the Paris indoor tournament in a career.

2010 – Gael Monfils registers his first win over Roger Federer, staving off five-match points in the 12th game of the final set in his 7-6 (7), 6-7 (1), 7-6 (4) win in the semifinals of the BNP Paribas Masters semifinals in Paris. Monfils, who also trails 1-4 in the final set, enters the match having lost his previous five matches against the Swiss. "I'm happy I won against Rog. He's someone I admire a lot. He's a legend of tennis, 'the' legend, and beating him is a beautiful victory," says the No. 12-seeded Monfils of his two hour and 41-minute victory over the No. 2-ranked Federer. "I will remember that for my whole life," declares Monfils. "And also it happened in very special conditions for me, in Paris, so it's only happiness."

November 14

2003 – Needing only 54 minutes, Roger Federer, the Wimbledon champion, defeats Juan Carlos Ferrero, the French Open champion, 6-3, 6-1 to post a perfect 3-0 record at the conclusion of round-robin play at the Tennis Masters Cup in Houston. Federer also beats Andre Agassi and David Nalbandian in round-robin play to advance in the event's semifinal round. "I'm happy the season is over after this," says Federer. "I'm happy to go on holidays. But I still have the weekend ahead of me which is gonna be very important for me. I'm happy I played so well in this Round Robin. There was tough group ahead. To come through so easily – the last two matches, especially – is quite surprising."

2006 – Andy Roddick lets three match points fall by the wayside – and a golden opportunity to beat the near-unbeatable world No. 1 Roger Federer – in a 4-6, 7-6(8), 6-4 loss in round-robin play at the year-end Tennis Masters Cup in Shanghai, China. Says Federer of Roddick, "He served out of a tree. It was incredible. He was serving a lot of aces. Pretty much for two sets I was trying to stay in and I was a bit lucky in the end because the second-set tiebreak, he should have gotten it. He served for it at 6-4 and he was disappointed, I think, but for me it was a hell of a win. I think he played the perfect match for two sets. Maybe he lacked one serve in the end, so it was unfortunate for him. I tried my best. It's always hard to control against Andy when he's serving so big like in the first two sets. I got a bit lucky in the end. In the third set I was pretty much in control from the start. I'm really, really happy to not be under pressure like he is now." Says Roddick, "I put myself in a position to win tonight. With the progress I've made over the last four or five months, I feel like I'm only getting better each time I step out there on the court.

It's tough right now, but it definitely feels like it's on the upswing tonight. I felt I was unlucky not to win this one."

2007 – Roger Federer beats Nikolay Davydenko 6-4, 6-3, to even his round-robin record at 1-1 at the season-ending Tennis Masters Cup in Shanghai, China. The win moves Federer's career record to 11-0 against Davydenko. After his opening round-robin loss to Fernando Gonzalez two days earlier, Federer tells to reporters that it is a bit unusual for him to be playing again two days later at the same tournament after a loss. "It's just a different situation coming back after losing, playing basically the same tournament," Federer says. "I'm used to losing, going on, playing maybe two days later in a first-round match. The only thing here is, you lose and you play another top 10 guy. This was a top four guy. So it doesn't get any easier."

2008 – Roger Federer fails to qualify for the semifinal round at the Tennis Masters Cup in Shanghai as Andy Murray rallies to a 4-6, 7-6 (3), 7-5 win to give Federer a 1-2 round-robin record. Federer says after the match that he is in discomfort and compensates with muscular problems in his lower back but says he did not consider quitting during the match. Says Federer, "I don't quit once I step on court. Guess you got to drill me one in the eye, then maybe. But otherwise I don't quit."

November 15

2002 – Roger Federer defeats Thomas Johansson 6-3, 7-5 to conclude round-robin play at the year-end Masters Cup in

Shanghai. Johansson is an alternate for Andre Agassi, who withdraws from the tournament with a hip injury.

2003 – World No. 3 Roger Federer beats world No. 1 Andy Roddick 7-6 (2), 6-2 in the semifinals of the year-end Masters Cup in Houston, his fifth win in six meetings against the American. The win moves Federer into the championship match against Andre Agassi. "The week is not over so the week has been okay till now," says Federer after the win over the world No. 1. "But, still, tomorrow is the biggest one of all, I guess. So I'm really looking forward. I'm happy with my performance this whole week until now. But it's not over yet. So I still have to play one big match."

2004 – Playing for the first time since tearing a left thigh muscle on October 25, Roger Federer registers a 6-1, 7-6 (4) victory over French Open champion Gaston Gaudio in his opening round-robin match at The Masters Cup in Houston. "With my game, I'm very happy with it," says Federer. "Coming back from basically not six weeks, no tournament, but two weeks not playing at all, that is something I never have except at the end of the season, which is coming up. To come back and beat a player like Gaston today was very satisfying. I thought I played a great first set. Obviously, I missed a lot of opportunities in the second set. But I still thought I played well."

2005 – Despite trouble with his right leg that requires on-court treatment from a trainer, Roger Federer clinches a spot in the semifinals of the Tennis Masters Cup in Shanghai defeating Ivan Ljubicic 6-3, 2-6, 7-6 (4) to win his second round-robin match at the event. Playing in only his second match since suffering an ankle injury prior to the Swiss Indoors, Federer extends his winning streak to 33 matches with the victory. "I'm not really worried about the ankle," says Federer. "It's just more having the stamina of being able to go physically through a tough three-setter. But again, tennis gives you the opportunity, and especially my game, to play on my terms, deciding how long I want the rally to last. So basically it's okay."

November 16

2003 – Roger Federer routs Andre Agassi 6-3, 6-0, 6-4 to win the year-end Tennis Masters Cup for the first time in his career. Playing at the Westside Tennis Club in Houston, Texas, Federer fires 11 aces in the 88-minute match, delayed two-and-a-half hours due to rain. "It was one of the best matches for me this season," says Federer, who wins Wimbledon, his first major title, earlier in the year. "I'm very happy how the whole year went, especially this tournament. I worked hard this year. You always have ups and downs but I feel this season has been complete." The win moves Federer to a year-end ranking of No. 2. "Andy [Roddick] deserves to be No. 1," he says. "I'm very happy with No. 2, and the fact that I won seven titles and won on all four Surfaces - grass, clay, hard and indoor."

2002 – Top-ranked Lleyton Hewitt defeats Roger Federer 7-5, 5-7, 7-5 in the semifinals of the season-ending Masters Cup in Shanghai, clinching the match on his fourth match point. Hewitt breaks Federer's serve in the ninth game of the third set, but fails to serve out the match. Serving at 5-5, Federer hits back-to-back double faults to lose his serve. Hewitt then fights off one break point in the next game before closing out the victory.

2006 – Roger Federer registers a 7-6 (2), 6-4 victory over Ivan Ljubicic in round-robin play at the Tennis Masters Cup in Shanghai. Federer's win gives him a perfect 3-0 record in his flight of the tournament and leaves David Nalbandian, Andy Roddick and Ljubicic tied for second in their group at 1-2, but Nalbandian advances into the semifinals because of sets won. "I'm pretty happy with the way I'm playing," Federer says. "I thought today was getting a bit better. Towards the end I started to read the serves better. Just from the baseline I had the feeling. I was making more returns. My serve was getting reliable on the big points and everything. So that's always a good sign looking forward."

2007 – Roger Federer beats Andy Roddick 6-4, 6-2 in round-robin play at the Tennis Masters Cup in Shanghai, China and qualifies for the semifinals with a 2-1 round-robin record. "Well, it seems like most times we play he's on top of his game, which is a little annoying," Roddick says. "I guess I just have to figure out, you know, what about my game brings out the best in him and try to adjust. You know, you see some of the guys who beat him are quick, (David) Nalbandian types who can run a little bit more. Unfortunately, that's not my strength." Says Federer of the importance of breaking Roddick in his second service game, "With the break I could play a little bit more relaxed.

He's not the fastest from the back of the court. That's why he must serve really well."

November 17

2005 – Suffering a second-set hiccup, Roger Federer wins his 34th consecutive match, defeating Guillermo Coria 6-0, 1-6, 6-2 at the Tennis Masters Cup in Shanghai. "I got off to a bad start," Federer says of the second set. "I figured if I would have kept on top of things, the result would have been very different. But that's how it goes. In the end, I'm happy I didn't use too much energy and came through. That's what counts." The win gives Federer a 3-0 round-robin record at the event and also improves his record to 80-3 for the year.

2007 – In their 14th career meeting, Roger Federer fires 11 aces and dominates Rafael Nadal 6-4, 6-1 in only 59 minutes in the semifinals of the season-ending Tennis Masters Cup in Shanghai. The win is the sixth for Federer against Nadal. "If he is playing very good, I have to play unbelievable," says Nadal. "If not, it's impossible, especially if he's playing with good confidence." Says Federer, who advances to the final to play David Ferrer, "'I'm happy to have proved myself, you know, yet again."

2004 – In a rematch of the U.S. Open final from two months earlier, Roger Federer defeats Lleyton Hewitt 6-3, 6-4 in one hour, 16 minutes to give him a 2-0 round-robin record at the season-ending Tennis Masters Cup in Houston. "I played a good match, obviously not as good as at the U.S. Open," says Federer. "I thought Lleyton played a good match. I always have to play well to beat him. I think we had better matches against each other, but, obviously, very pleased to be through again in straight sets. I always feel like I have room for improvement. I think the best players, up there with the best athletes in the world, they always have the desire to become better. I have the same."

November 18

2007 – Roger Federer wins the year-end Tennis Masters Cup for a fourth time, defeating surprise finalist David Ferrer of Spain 6-2, 6-3, 6-2 in Shanghai, China. The title is Federer's 53rd of his career and his eighth on the season, which for the third time, sees him win three of the four major tournaments (Australian Open, Wimbledon and the U.S. Open.) Says Federer. "It was a nice victory, especially proving it, to myself and the world, that I can do it over and over again. This is the year-end tournament that only the best can make it to…I practiced hard to get (to) this level. So when it all comes together in a final like today against Ferrer – it's fantastic." By winning $1.2 million in Shanghai, Federer becomes the first player to surpass the $10-million mark in a season in prize money.

2004 – Roger Federer defeats Carlos Moya 6-3, 3-6, 6-3 to finish round-robin play with a perfect 3-0 record at the season-ending Tennis Masters Cup in Houston.

2006 – Playing his Spanish rival for the first time in an indoor setting, Roger Federer defeats Rafael Nadal 6-4, 7-5 in a No. 1 vs. No. 2 semifinal showdown at the Tennis Masters Cup in Shanghai, China. The win is the third for Federer in nine career meetings with Nadal. When asked by media if he has finally figured out Nadal's game, Federer says, "Obviously, I do. For me it's nice to win on kind of my surfaces – grass and indoors, you know. I maybe lost the ones I'm supposed to maybe on clay, but I was awfully close there. For me, there's definitely a way, you know, moving forward. I definitely feel like I've learned a few things, you know, and maybe now it's maybe a little more up to him to change his games. I don't know because it was really close game. Depends obviously a lot on the surface, you know, how the points are played. I think it was an excellent match with high quality. I think that's what we always see when we play each other."

November 19

2006 – Roger Federer concludes one of the most dominating seasons in tennis history, defeating James Blake 6-0, 6-3, 6-4 in the final of the Tennis Masters Cup in Shanghai, China. Federer finishes the year with 12 titles in 16 final-round appearances in 17 total tournaments played and wins three major championships (Australian Open, Wimbledon and the U.S. Open) and becomes the first player to exceed $7 million in prize money in a season with a $8.34 million haul during the 2006 campaign. Only two players manage to beat Federer during the year – Rafael Nadal and Andy Murray. Says Blake of the undisputed world

No. 1, "Obviously, we're all chasing Roger. It's no secret. He's playing head and shoulders above the rest of us." Says Federer of his epic year, "To finish it off by winning the Masters Cup, the world championship so to speak, it's the perfect ending to an incredible season. There's not much more I could have done." Federer is one match from winning the Grand Slam – losing in the final of the French Championships to Nadal. He finishes the year with a 92-5 record – winning his last 29 matches.

2005 – World No. 1 Roger Federer blanks Gaston Gaudio of Argentina 6-0, 6-0 in the semifinals of the year-end Tennis Masters Cup in Shanghai, China – the first ever white-wash in the 35-year history of the year-end men's championships and Federer's first-ever double-bagel in professional tennis. "I think it's nice to have, but no more than that," Federer says.

2013 – GQ magazine unveils its most stylish athletes of 2013 and Roger Federer ranks No. 7 on the list, which is topped by Miami Heat basketball player LeBron James. "'Grand Slam' is a title that could just as easily be applied to Federer's off-court style as the tennis ace's graceful moves on clay or grass extend to the red carpet as well," writes GQ. "Federer favours subdued colours and simple menswear mixes, usually anchored by a crisp white shirt, and the timeless kits are what separate him from athlete pack. Even his white Nike-sponsored uniform, with interlocking gold initials, looks more like luxury menswear than any performance piece in play." Federer is tops among tennis players on the list, Andy Murray ranking No. 18 and Tomas Berdych ranking No. 20.

November 20

2005 – David Nalbandian of Argentina stuns Roger Federer 6-7 (4), 6-7 (11), 6-2, 6-1, 7-6 (3) in four hours and 33 minutes to win the year-end Tennis Masters Cup in Shanghai, China. Nalbandian's win snaps Federer's 35-match win streak and ends his streak of 24 straight victories in singles finals. Says Nalbandian to Federer in the post-match ceremony, "After knowing you a long time, don't worry, you'll win a lot more trophies. Let me keep this one." Federer finishes his 2005 season with an 81-4 record.

2004 – World No.1 Roger Federer wins a 38-point tie-break - the longest tiebreak in the history of men's singles tennis - as he defeats Marat Safin 6-3, 7-6 (20-18) in the semifinals of the Tennis Masters Cup in Houston, Texas. The tiebreak equals the mark last set at the 1993 U.S. Open when Goran Ivanisevic and Daniel Nestor also play a 38-point tiebreak in the third set. "The tie-breaker was very special," Federer says. "I've never played a tie-breaker like it. That was really fun, going back and forth, all big points, match points, set points, and the level of play was high too. We were pushing each other to the limits." Federer needs eight match points to break through and win the 26-minute tiebreaker while saving six set points.

2011 – Roger Federer defeats Jo-Wilfried Tsonga 6-2, 2-6, 6-4 in his opening round-robin match at the ATP World Tour Finals in London. Federer wins the first set in only 21 minutes, but is broken in third game and eighth game of the second set as Tsonga ties the match, gaining the momentum. Federer then breaks Tsonga in the final game of the match to clinch the victory. "With me, it was just trying to stay calm, trying to wait for my chance, trying to create chances when he was not serving as well as he did at times," says Federer. "I was going to take those chances and hopefully come through with the victory, which it all came that way, exactly the way I hoped it to be."

2007 – Roger Federer beats Pete Sampras 6-4, 6-3 in an exhibition match in Seoul, South Korea, the first of three scheduled exhibition matches in Asia between the two.

November 21

2004 – Roger Federer wins an Open Era record 13th singles final in a row, defeating Lleyton Hewitt 6-3, 6-2 in the final of the year-end Tennis Masters Cup in Houston, Texas. The tournament victory, his 11th during the calendar year – the most since Thomas Muster wins 12 in 1995 – caps a fantastic season for the Swiss world No. 1, who also wins the Australian Open for the first time, Wimbledon for a second time and the U.S. Open for a first time. He posts a 74-6 match record and goes 18-0 against his fellow top 10 players. Says Federer, "It's just an unbelievable end to a fantastic season for me."

2010 – Roger Federer defeats David Ferrer 6-1, 6-4 in his opening match of the season-ending ATP World Tour Finals at London, his 11th match victory in 11 career matches with Ferrer. "I'm really happy the way I was able to get out of the first match here," Federer says. "Starting off with a feisty top-10 player is never easy."

November 22

2011 – With a 28-4 advantage in winners, Roger Federer dominates Rafael Nadal 6-3, 6-0 in round-robin play at the Barclays ATP World Tour Finals in London. The win is Federer's ninth against Nadal in their 26 meetings. "It was a great match for me basically from start to finish," says Federer. "I was able to do what I was hoping to do: dominate from the baseline, play close to the baseline, serve well, take his time away. [It] hasn't always worked...I always knew I could beat Rafa. The question is sometimes it was hard to do because he has a big say, as well, in how the matches go. The quicker the court, the more I favor myself. Maybe Rafa didn't play his very best tonight. But on an indoor court, it all happens very quickly as we saw at the end. For me it was an exciting match to play." The win moves Federer to a 2-0 record in the round-robin event, qualifying him for the semifinals, and drops Nadal to 1-1.

2007 – Roger Federer and Pete Sampras play the second of their three scheduled Asian tennis exhibition matches as Federer defeats Sampras 7-6 (6), 7-6 (5) in Kuala Lumpur, Malaysia. "He played some unbelievable shots, but then again, he is capable of doing that," says the 26-year-old Federer of the 36-year-old Sampras. "He had an incredible serve which was so difficult to read tonight."

2009 – Roger Federer fights through an erratic forehand and rallies to beat Fernando Verdasco 4-6, 7-5, 6-1 in the round-robin play at the ATP World Tour Finals at London. "I was down a set, and only the second set was I able to sort of get the ball into play, find my range, find my rhythm. I think this is also when I started to feel like I had chances," says Federer. "It was a crucial match for me to get off with a win in the round robin stages because Fernando is a great player and I'm happy I was able to come through."

November 23

2010 – Losing only eight points on his serve, Roger Federer beats Andy Murray 6-4, 6-2 at the ATP World Tour Finals in London to give him a 2-0 round-robin record and his sixth win against Murray in 14 career meetings. "I'm surprised. I really am, that I was able to win my service games that comfortably," says Federer. "I heard I dropped eight points on my serve. That's not to the norm against Andy, who is one of the best return players, if not the best, in the game right now. So I'll take it. That is all I can say"

Hall of Fame tennis journalist Bud Collins, in his book "The Bud Collins History of Tennis," labeled Roger Federer with the nicknames of "The Lord of the Swings" and the "Basel Dazzle."

November 24

2007 – In their third and final Asian exhibition match, Pete Sampras sneaks out a 7-6 (8), 6-4 victory over Roger Federer at the Venetian in Macao, China. Sampras never faces a break point and converts on one of his two break point chances, while saving two set points. Sampras plays down the win, citing Federer's long season and the considerably fast court that more well-suites his booming serve. "Let's not get carried away," he says. Says Federer, "I'm sort of surprised. This guy can play tennis, you know." Earlier in their exhibition series, Federer beats Sampras 6-4, 6-3 in Seoul, South Korea and 7-6 (6), 7-6 (5) in Kuala Lumpur, Malaysia.

2009 – Roger Federer clinches the year-end No. 1 ranking for a fifth time with his 3-6, 6-3, 6-1 win over Andy Murray in his second round-robin match at the ATP World Tour Finals in London. "That was one of my big goals for this season and it's one of the greatest performances I think I've achieved," says Federer of his five years as year-end No. 1. "Seeing also what happened off the court, getting married, having twin girls, reaching all four major finals, you know. Playing so well at the most important moments, it's been the key this year, and staying healthy. Especially after having a rough 2008, coming back this year and being able to dominate and play at the top when the depth in tennis is so, so great at the moment. I think it's a wonderful achievement. Of course, it's official. It's a wonderful feeling."

2011 – In a round-robin match at the ATP World Tour Finals in London of no significance, Roger Federer beats Mardy Fish 6-1, 3-6, 6-3 to conclude round-robin play with a 3-0 record, while Fish finishes 0-3. Federer shrugs off suggestions from the media that his intensity drops due to already winning the round-robin group and qualifying for the event's semifinal round. "I feel I give a hundred percent every time I step on the court," says Federer. "It's a matter of trying to do the exact same thing, knowing I don't really need to win, but maybe because I know that somewhere you just maybe don't play the same way. Who knows?"

November 25

2010 – World No. 2 Roger Federer clinches a semifinal spot in the ATP World Tour Finals defeating Robin Soderling 7-6 (5), 6-3 to win round-robin Group B with a perfect 3-0 record. The win improves Federer's career record over Soderling to 15-1, the lone loss coming earlier in the year in the quarterfinals of the French Open. "He always brings out something different every time he plays me, because he has to try different things," Federer says of Soderling. "I was able to handle it well, which was a very happy feeling for me to have."

"I've probably run out of adjectives to describe him on the court to talk about his excellence. He's just unbelievable."
—James Blake on Roger Federer in 2006

November 26

2011 – Roger Federer advances to the final of the ATP World Tour Finals for a seventh time defeating David Ferrer 7-5, 6-3 in the semifinals at the O2 Arena in London. The win is Federer's 12th in 12 matches against the Spaniard. Says Federer of his perfect record over Ferrer, "It's not so easy as it might look and seem. It's a lot of hard work. I think today, again, was very close. I've maybe had some easier matches against him, but lately they've all been very tough, very physical."

2009 – Roger Federer scrapes out a second-set tie-breaker against Juan Martin del Potro, fending off his not qualifying for the semifinal stage of the tournament, but loses to the Argentine 6-2, 6-7 (5), 6-3 at the conclusion of round-robin play at the ATP World Tour Finals in London. Del Potro and Federer, however, both barely advance into the semifinals by a three-way tie-breaker between the two and Andy Murray. All three players finish round-robin play with two wins and identical 5-4 set records. However, Murray is eliminated after winning the lowest percentage of games. Had Del Potro lost one more game against Federer, Murray would have advanced instead of the Argentine. Federer officially qualifies for the semifinal round when he wins one game in the third set of the match. "Obviously the focus is completely on my own qualification," Federer says. "I knew I wasn't looking very good at whatever, 6-2, 4-All. I also had a tough start to the breaker. I just tried to hang in there. I knew I couldn't lose in two sets because I knew that was going to knock me out. That's why I was very excited having won the second set. For me it's a tough loss, but, sure, I'm happy I'm through. That he got so close with the other two guys, it's quite incredible. I am in a way surprised myself it came down to a couple games."

November 27

2010 - Roger Federer wins his fourth consecutive straight-set match at the ATP World Tour Finals in London, dominating Novak Djokovic 6-1, 6-4 to advance into the final against Rafael Nadal. "It's been a great tournament so far, clearly, having not lost a set and beaten so many good players, close rivals," Federer says. "Today was another great match. Obviously I'm really looking forward to playing against Rafa tomorrow. Who wouldn't? I'm no different."

2011 – Roger Federer becomes the first player to win six titles at the Barclays ATP World Tour Finals defeating Jo-Wilfried Tsonga 6-3, 6-7(6), 6-3 in the final. Federer, 30, also becomes the oldest titlist at the year-end championship and wins his 70th career ATP singles title in his 100th career final. "It feels very special, indeed," says Federer of his title. "I know it's one of my greatest accomplishments."

November 28

2010 – Roger Federer wins his fifth title at the year-end ATP World Tour Finals defeating Rafael Nadal 6-3, 3-6, 6-1 in London. Federer wins an incredible 92 percent of the points played on his first serve and loses only 13 points on serve the entire match. "I was able to stay offensive. Rallies were never that long," says Federer. "That kind of maybe frustrated him."

2009 – Top-ranked Roger Federer is upset in the semifinals of the ATP World Tour Finals in London, losing to Nikolay Davydenko 6-2, 4-6, 7-5, Davydenko's first win over Federer in their 13th career meeting. "It's disappointing, but not to lose against him; just to lose the semis," Federer says. "Coming so far in a tough group, in a tough tournament, I had hopes to get through to the final and maybe win again. I missed the start again, and I guess that's what cost me the match at the end."

November 29

2013 – In an interview posted on the website of his sponsor Credit Suisse, Roger Federer discusses the state of his career and his relatively disappointing 2013 season, highlighted by his second-round upset loss at Wimbledon and winning only one tournament title. "Defeats are part of tennis," Federer says. "What matters is how you react. What is also important for me is that I am honest with myself. I am the sort of person who often questions everything; I did the same when things were going really well for me. That's why I am not affected much by the criticism, which I don't think is justified."

November 30

"To the dismay of many fans, Federer's game is not interactive like that of Jimmy Connors, who fed off the roar of the crowd the way catfish feed off muck. Federer's game, rather, is a thing to behold, like a Grecian urn."

—Liz Clarke of the Washington Post, Wimbledon, 2005

DECEMBER

December 1

"He's probably the most talented person to ever carry a racquet around—the shots that he can come up with, the way he's kind of become a totally complete player. But I think off the court, it's huge. There have been a lot of good champions, but he's just classy. He is never high and mighty in the locker room or anything like that."
—Andy Roddick, in 2005, on Roger Federer

December 2

"You bring up tennis in this day and age and a lot of people roll their eyes, and they're not interested. But listen: if you're not paying attention to this guy, if you appreciate sports, you have to take a moment to appreciate this guy. It's like Tiger Woods. A lot of people are your meat-and-potatoes sports fans: I like football, I like basketball, I like baseball. If you don't appreciate golf, that's fine. You don't have to watch it, and you don't have to pay attention to it, but you have to appreciate the greatness of Tiger Woods. It's the same with tennis. You don't appreciate tennis? I'm not telling you that you have to. But, if you don't give Roger Federer his due, then you're just missing

the boat. Roger Federer is the best player in any sport today, and it's not close. It's not close." —Mike Greenberg of ESPN Radio's Mike & Mike in the Morning in 2006 on Roger Federer.

December 3

2009 – Roger Federer announces his 2009 tournament schedule on his RogerFederer.com website and reveals he will play in just two clay-court tournaments before the French Open, the only Grand Slam event he hasn't won. Federer's schedule reveals that he will play only in Rome and Madrid before the French, as opposed to playing in four pre-French Open clay court tournaments in 2008. The formula ends up working for Federer who wins his first French title in 2009, although Federer adds the Monte Carlo Open to his schedule, entering as a last-minute wild card.

How does Roger Federer live up to his high standards day after day? "You get used to it after a while, having the pressure from the media or the fans, the expectations and everything," Federer said in Toronto in 2006. "But losing is a normal thing, too. You can't just win, tennis especially, because a lot has to do also with the day form. Sometimes you run into another guy who's playing excellent tennis, then it's also important to understand that today you were not better than your opponent. In the last few years, I've been able to eliminate many matches where maybe I would have lost in the past because of mental fatigue, physically tired. That hardly ever happens any more these days because my preparation is so much better, my belief, my understanding for the game has improved so much that now actually I've kind -- for me, I've passed all the tests.

It's just now for me really to enjoy the tour out there, try to win as many matches because that's what makes me most happy."

December 4

2012 – Roger Federer arrives in Brazil where he is scheduled to compete in a series of exhibition matches around South America. "I am happy that I have finally made it to Brazil! Just arrived in Sao Paulo!" Federer writes on his Facebook page of arriving in Brazil for the first time in his life.

"I guess you don't get very often standing ovations after three sets. It means a lot to me. I got a standing ovation when I beat [Pete] Sampras as well. And you kind of look in the crowd and they actually don't realize, but somehow you don't see any seats anymore, everything is just people." – Roger Federer on receiving a standing ovation after beating Andy Roddick in the 2003 Wimbledon semifinal on Centre Court at Wimbledon.

December 5

2012 – Roger Federer announces the launch of his official YouTube channel www.YouTube.com/RogerFederer that will live stream his South American tennis exhibitions.

Dubai in the United Arab Emirates is the preferred training ground for Roger Federer. Why is that? "It never rains, which is a good thing, because I can practice on a hard court," Federer said. "In Switzerland we struggle with outdoor hard courts. You never know when the rain. I can really concentrate on tennis over there. I have no distractions, whereas in Switzerland maybe I still have so many friends, families, I want to do things. I'm maybe not there to really focus on tennis, whereas in Dubai it's totally different. Maybe, as well, you have the beach. If you want to go, have a day off, like an afternoon off, you can even go to the beach, take it easy. It's just a good feeling in Dubai for me to practice."

December 6

2012 – Roger Federer loses to Brazil's Thomaz Bellucci 7-5, 3-6, 6-4 in Sao Paulo, Brazil in the first of his six South American exhibition matches. World No. 33 Bellucci is serenaded with chants and songs in a carnival-like atmosphere during the match. "It's a special feeling to play this guy (Federer) here," Bellucci says after the match. "He is the best of all time and it was a pleasure to share the court with him." Says Federer after the match, "I am very happy to be here. It took me a while to finally come to Brazil. Everybody has been really good to me and I can't thank you all enough for showing your support." In his press conference prior to the match, the 31-year-old Federer tells reporters that he'll cut the number of tournaments he'll play each year and that he hopes to return to Brazil in 2016 for the Olympic Games. "I have to make sure that I take care of my schedule, of my body, of my mind," Federer says. "Hopefully I can still stay on tour for many more years and hopefully play the Olympics here in three and a half years or so, so I have to look far ahead and not just the next six months."

December 7

2013 – Roger Federer hosts a two-hour "#AskRF" session with fans on Twitter and responds to questions about if he'd look like his mustached father when he gets older, Mirka's role on Twitter, the last song he sang, on his dancing skills, his 2014 hairstyle, and his thoughts on the passing of South African leader Mandela.

Roger Federer, at the 2003 Tennis Masters Cup in Houston, discussed American tennis crowds saying, "Americans always scream a lot. Less clapping, more screaming. That's okay. All the crowds should be different. That's the difference."

December 8

2012 – Roger Federer beats Jo-Wilfried Tsonga 7-6 (3) 6-3 in Sao Paulo, Brazil in the second of his six South American exhibition matches.

Many pinpoint Roger Federer's first-round loss to Mario Ancic as one of the worst losses of his career, but years after the loss, Federer said that it taught him a valuable lesson. Said Federer, "What it taught me was not to underestimate any opponent, no matter where they're from, what technique they have, what ranking they have."

December 9

2012 – Taking time off from his Gillette Federer tennis exhibition in Brazil, Roger Federer meets with fellow sporting legend, the Brazilian soccer star Pele. "Today I had the great honour of meeting the legendary Pele," Federer writes on his Facebook page. "He was so nice and his energy is amazing." Federer posts a photo of he and Pele, each holding tennis and soccer shirts that they present to each other as gifts. Writes Pele on his Twitter page, "I love playing tennis and today one of the greats of the game dropped by to say hello. Roger Federer, you are a champion on the court and in life." Later in the day, Federer beats Tommy Haas 6-4, 6-4 in the third of his six South American exhibition matches.

"I noticed right away that this guy was a natural talent," Adolf Kacovsky, a tennis coach of Roger Federer's at his childhood club The Old Boys Tennis Club in Basel, Switzerland, said to Rene Stauffer in his book "Roger Federer: Quest for Perfection." "He was born with a racquet in his hand. We began giving him private lessons that were partly funded by the club. Roger was a quick learner. When you wanted to teach him something new, he was able to pick it up after three or four tries, while others in the group needed weeks."

December 10

After winning the Paris Masters for the first time in 2011, Roger Federer was asked whether he has a list of accomplishments that he would like to achieve in his career and answered in a slightly annoyed demeanor. "Honestly, I do not have a list to tick off stuff," he said. "I just think that's so wrong, and it's not how it's supposed to be. I have had much more success than I ever dreamed of, and then all of a sudden to start, 'O.K., I need to tick off everything possible in the game of tennis so I feel complete at the end of my career' — that's not how I see it."

December 11

"He's a real person. He's not an enigma. Off the court he's not trying to be somebody. If you met him at McDonald's and you didn't know who he was, you would have no idea that he's one of the best athletes in the world." —Andy Roddick on Roger Federer in 2005

"I really consider myself a top five player in the world, which it doesn't mean that I am close to Roger."
                                    —Ivan Ljubicic on Roger Federer in 2006

December 12

2012 – Roger Federer loses to Juan Martin del Potro 3-6, 6-3, 6-4 in the first Copa Claro Nokia exhibition in Buenos Aires, Argentina.

2013 – The *New York Times* runs a story reporting that Roger Federer and his agent Tony Godsick have formed a boutique sports marketing agency called "Team8" and that one of Federer's main rivals, Juan Martin del Potro, is the agency's first client. "We're trying to be a boutique agency that will manage just a small stable of iconic athletes,"

Godsick says in a telephone interview with Chris Clarey of the *New York Times*. "I can sell Roger Federer really well, but nobody sells Roger better than Roger. I always joke with him, 'Look, you've been really successful on the tennis court, but I promise you, you'll be more successful when you're done playing tennis.' "

December 13

2013 – In an interview with Australian media to promote his January 8 charity exhibition event at Rod Laver Arena against Jo-Wilfried Tsonga, Roger Federer insists he is a better player now than when he won the first of his four Australian Opens back in 2004. "I always believe that I have improved over the last 10 years, you know, that I've not gone backwards, and I've been able to win (the Open) 10 years ago, so I always feel as I move forward I am a more complete player, a better player," Federer says. "That's why I will always believe that I can win, as long as my body is holding up and mentally I'm really hungry travelling the world and playing matches, and that is the case right now – I'm very healthy and training extremely hard."

2012 – Roger Federer defeats Juan Martin del Potro in their second exhibition match in as many days, winning 6-4, 7-6 (1) in Buenos Aires, Argentina.

December 14

At a satellite tennis tournament in Kublis, Switzerland in 1998, a 17-year-old Roger Federer was fined for violating the "Best Effort" rule. "He simply stood unmotivated and non-chalantly on the court and double-faulted twice each game," tournament referee Claudio Grether said to Rene Stauffer in the book "Roger Federer: Quest For Perfection" of Federer's first-round loss to fellow Swiss Armando Brunold. Grether imposes a $100 fine against Federer for the lack of effort, which put together with his prize money earnings of $87,meant that Federer leaves the tournament with a $13 deficit. It is the only professional tournament Federer plays where he loses money.

December 15

2012 – Roger Federer ends his South American exhibition tour defeating Jo-Wilfried Tsonga 7-6, 2-6, 6-3 in front of a 14,000 fans in Bogota, Colombia.

"What he's done in tennis, I think, is far greater than what I've done in golf. He's lost what ... five matches in three years? That's pretty good." —Tiger Woods to the Associated Press on Federer after Woods was told of his selection over Federer as AP Athlete of the Year, 2006

"Obviously I feel I can return his serve. That's what I said yesterday in the press conference. I'm not scared of his serve. Because every time I played him, I read it well. I don't want to say it breaks down, but he gets kind of frustrated because I read it....Often when I play him, he praises my game. Somehow, he enjoys watching me play against him. Always once in a match we laugh at each other because something

ridiculous happens." —Roger Federer of Andy Roddick after defeating him in the 2003 Wimbledon semifinals.

December 16

2012 – Roger Federer is named "Swiss Male Athlete of the Year" for a fifth time. Federer also wins the honor in 2003, 2004, 2006 and 2007.

2009 – Roger Federer finishes in third place in the Associated Press athlete of the decade voting behind the winner, Tiger Woods, and six-time Tour de France winner Lance Armstrong. Woods earns 56 votes, followed by Armstrong with 33 and Federer with 25.

2013 – Roger Federer posts on Facebook and Twitter that he just completed a week of training with former world No. 1 Stefan Edberg as he prepares for an assault on the 2014 Australian Open. "Stefan Edberg just finished doing a training week with me and my team. It was great spending time with one of my childhood heroes!" writes Federer.

December 17

2007 – Roger Federer is named world champion for 2007 by the International Tennis Federation for a fourth straight year, joining Pete Sampras as the only men to earn the honor four straight years.

"Federer is adored and respected. When he walks onto a court. The court is his. He is the lord of the manor and, as such, his every movement and stance is uniquely monitored and examined." —Neil Harman from his book "Court Confidential: Inside The World Of Tennis"

December 18

At Wimbledon in 2004, Goran Ivanisevic is asked to compare the serve of Pete Sampras with the serve of Roger Federer. "Some things Roger does better than Pete," Ivanisevic said. "On the court he's like a magician. Pete was destroying. When you played Pete, you couldn't touch his serve. But Federer, the way he plays, he's back, he comes in. When you look at him you think tennis is a very easy sport, but it's not."

"The metaphysical explanation is that Roger Federer is one of those rare, preternatural athletes who appear to be exempt, at least in part, from certain physical laws. Good analogues here include Michael Jordan, who could not only jump inhumanly high but actually hang there a beat or two longer than gravity allows, and Muhammad Ali, who really could "float" across the canvas and land two or three jabs in the clock-time required for one. There are probably a half-dozen other examples since 1960. And Federer is of this type—a type that one could call genius, or mutant, or avatar. He is never hurried or off-balance. The approaching ball hangs, for him, a split-second longer than it ought to. His movements are lithe rather than athletic. Like Ali, Jordan, Maradona, and Gretzky, he seems both less and more substantial than the men he faces. Particularly in the all-white that Wimbledon enjoys getting away with still requiring, he looks like what he may well (I think) be: a creature whose body is both flesh and,

somehow, light." — *David Foster Wallace on Roger Federer in 2006 in the New York Times Magazine*

December 19

2007 – Roger Federer is named by *Tennis* magazine as the men's player of the year for the fifth year in a row.

2013 – Roger Federer, in full training for playing in the pre-Australian Open tournament in Brisbane for the first time in his career, tweets from his "@rogerfederer" Twitter account "Doing some fitness training ahead of @brisbanetennis that starts December 29th. Can't wait to play in #Queensland"

1998 – Roger Federer avenges his loss to David Nalbandian from the final of the U.S. Open junior championships by beating the Argentine 6-4, 6-2 in the semifinals of the Orange Bowl junior championships in Key Biscayne, Florida.

December 20

1998 – Roger Federer ends his career as a junior player by winning the prestigious singles title at the Orange Bowl in Key Biscayne, Fla., defeating Guillermo Coria of Argentina 7-5, 6-3 in the final. Writes Rene Stauffer in the book *Roger Federer: Quest for Perfection*, "Federer won the Orange Bowl and left Miami with a bowl full of oranges—

and bleached-blond hair after a spontaneous $250 hair-styling adventure."

December 21

1998 – Roger Federer becomes the No. 1 ranked junior player in the world for the first time in his career, fresh off his victory at the Orange Bowl championships in Key Biscayne, Fla. Federer, however, does not immediately clinch the year-end No. 1 junior ranking until Federer's main rival for the year-end top spot, Julien Jeanpierre of France, loses in the semifinals of the final event of the year, the Yucatan Cup in Mexico, to an upstart young American player named Andy Roddick.

2010 – Roger Federer beats Rafael Nadal 4-6, 6-3, 6-3 before 10,000 fans in Zurich to open a two-match exhibition series for charity between the world's top ranked tennis players. The exhibition is called "The Match for Africa" and raises $2.6 million. "This money is going to a really good cause for the kids in Africa," Federer says after the match. "I'll look back at it with fond memories." Says Nadal, "This will be the first time the Foundation will introduce an event of this magnitude to so many people... We are friends and we are both very committed to solidarity." Nadal arrives in Zurich at 11 am local time and is personally picked up and driven to his hotel by Federer, who also entertains his rival for lunch and a tour of the city.

2009 – Roger Federer finishes second in the Associated Press Male Athlete of the Year voting behind NASCAR driver Jimmie Johnson.

December 22

2010 – Rafael Nadal beats Roger Federer 7-6 (3), 4-6, 6-1 in Madrid in the second of two exhibition matches staged to raise money for the pair's each respective charitable foundations. The event, named the "Joining Forces For the Benefit Of Children" match, is played at Madrid's Caja Magica and attracts an all-star crowd, including Spain's Queen Sofia. "I say thank you very much to Roger for coming here to Madrid and supporting my foundation today," Nadal says. "Both of us are very happy that we can finally have this event and raise a lot of money for these kids. I know that with what we're going to raise... it's not going to be decisive but it will be a help. It's going to be important to improve this world a little bit."

"Roger Federer is perfect for stately Wimbledon. His shirt is neatly pressed; his shorts are crisp and tidy. His hair is long but always pulled back in a tight ponytail without a stray hanging loose. When he plays, the tennis is noiseless. He moves so lightly across the grass it seems as if the blades aren't being touched. Federer does not seem ruthless. He is a gentle man in his speech and with words." —Diane Pucin, Los Angeles Times, Wimbledon, 2004

December 23

2009 – The Associated Press names Roger Federer's record 15th major singles championship at Wimbledon as the third biggest sports story of the 2009 season behind the baseball steroids revelations, which is the No. 1 story, and Jimmie Johnson's fourth consecutive NASCAR title, which is No. 2.

"Roger is like a good red wine, he's getting better with age. I think his best years are ahead of him. I think his big years will be when he is 26, 27, 28, as that is when he will be both mature and at his physical peak. I think he will become a better player in many respects. Roger hasn't even started to use a lot of his game. It's a challenge for all those trying to stop him. But they are playing against a man who will probably enter tennis history as the best ever. That should be motivation enough."
— Tony Roche on Roger Federer to The Age in 2007

December 24

2003 – The Roger Federer Foundation—with headquarters in Bottmingen, Switzerland— is founded. The foundation's goals are to support needy children and to promote youth sports. At Indian Wells in 2011, Federer is asked about giving back and his foundation, stating, "It's been something that's been a lot of fun for me to do, to have the opportunity, first of all, with my fame and my fortune, to be able to give back to others who need it so much more," he says. "I took the choice of having my own foundations instead of just donating, you know, shirts, racquets, and money to other foundations. I said I'd like to start my own and really focus on a key area, which was South Africa in the beginning. We've expanded towards Africa in terms of all those projects. And some projects I do, support more women, for instance, because, they become moms. They are the ones who take care of the kids and so forth, and it's important to have education, I always felt, because education is something you cannot take away from someone. That's why I always felt like that was really important to me. And my mom, like you said, even my dad, as well, obviously, have been very helpful. They work extremely hard today still for the foundation. It's a lot of fun."

2013 – Roger Federer tweets that his wife Mirka is once again pregnant. Tweets Federer, "Mirka and I are very happy to share the news that Myla & Charlene will be big sisters in 2014! Happy Holidays....."

December 25

2006 – Roger Federer finishes third in the AP male athlete of the year voting behind winner Tiger Woods and runner-up San Diego Chargers running back LaDainian Tomlinson.

"I'd like to be in his shoes for one day to know what it feels like to play that way." —Mats Wilander to the Associated Press, 2004

"[In the modern game], you're a clay court specialist, a grass court specialist or a hard court specialist ... or you're Roger Federer."
— *Jimmy Connors to the BBC, 2006*

December 26

"Most observers easily envision Federer releasing his sweepingly beautiful forehand or his effortless serve, but not enough has been made of his excellent overhead. The Swiss displays his athleticism and astounding coordination whenever he hits an overhead. His preparation is impeccable, his execution sound, his ability to put his smashes anywhere he wants unarguable. Federer's overhead is one of the most underrated shots in the modern world of tennis." — *Steve Flink on rating the Roger Federer overhead No. 4 all time in his book "The Greatest Tennis Matches Of All Time."*

December 27

2013 – Roger Federer announces on his website that he will work with his childhood idol Stefan Edberg as his coach for 10 weeks in 2014. "I am happy to announce that beginning in Melbourne, Stefan Edberg will join Severin Lüthi on my coaching team," says Federer in a statement. "Severin, who has been part of my team for the last seven years, will do most of the weeks and Stefan has agreed to work with us for at least 10 weeks starting at the Australian Open in Melbourne. Stefan was my childhood hero, and I am really looking forward to spending time and learning from him." Says Edberg in a statement, "I'm really excited to be part of Roger's team and I hope together we can bring out his best tennis." Federer and his previous coach Paul Annacone end their formal relationship two months earlier.

2013 – In an article published in his hometown paper in Basel, Switzerland *Basler Zeitung*, Roger Federer says he will play with a larger 98-inch racket head at the start of the 2014 tennis season. Federer previously uses a 90-inch racquet, except during a failed experiment in tournaments in Hamburg and Gstaad the previous summer. "I'm going to play in Australia with a similar model as in my first attempt," Federer says. "Actually, I wanted to switch back after the U.S. Open again, but then I had so much to do with myself and my game, that I kept it on hold. Now, I had more time to make more small changes and together with my supplier company Wilson worked on the fine details of the racket....But now I have the feeling that this is the right time for a change in the racket. I've played through two and a half weeks with the new model and am confident. The racket is very good in the hand. But the truth will come out on the court. We'll see how it affects me in the tournaments in Australia."

December 28

2013 – After a 14 hour flight from Dubai to Brisbane, Roger Federer conducts a 7 am press conference at the Brisbane airport upon arriving in Australia for the Brisbane International. "It's the first time in a year that I could practice three, four weeks in a row without any setbacks... I was able to do more than I thought which is very encouraging," Federer says of his recent training session in Dubai. "I didn't play any exhibitions which allowed me to train extremely hard and for a longer period of time... Every time I had training (in the past) I had setbacks, little aches and pains, especially in the back from time to time... which cost me confidence. These last few months have been important for me, feeling that movement is not an issue any more."

"(Andy) Roddick could only shake his head and smile when Federer came up with mind-boggling shots, wielding his racket like a magician. One of those instances was on set point in the second. "I remember thinking to myself, 'I played a pretty good game to make him serve it out and I lost it at love,'" said Roddick,, who smiled at Federer after the game. "The last shot was just ridiculous. He came full steam ahead, half-volley, but swinging like half, like not in the air, though. I don't know if anybody else can do that shot. It was almost like he was trying to do a trick shot out there." Federer agreed, saying: "It was a ridiculous shot." Afterward, Becker analyzed that point on BBC. "All the shots in the book on one rally," he said. By then, Federer *was rolling, a stretch of momentum that started after he won the tiebreaker.* —Lisa Dillman, Los Angeles Times *on the 2003 Wimbledon semifinal*

December 29

2002 – Roger Federer loses to Lleyton Hewitt 6-4, 0-6, 6-4 and then, pairing with his future wife Mirka Vavrinec, loses to Hewitt and Alicia Molik 6-3, 6-1 as Switzerland loses 3-0 to Australia at the Hopman Cup, the international mixed team competition, in Perth, Australia. Vavrinec opens the best-of-three-match series losing to Molik 6-3, 6-4.

2013 – At the Brisbane International, Roger Federer and Rod Laver attend a dinner at the Stamford Plaza in Brisbane organized by the tournament where Australian poet Rupert McCall recites his new poem, *The Masterpiece*. Both "the Rocket" and the "Swiss maestro" are moved by McCall's words, mixed in with smiles, faces of reflection, and appreciation. The poem creates a legendary match, with humility as the victor. Earlier in the day, Federer plays the role of tourist in Brisbane, enjoying the city skyline from Kangaroo Point and visiting the Koala Sanctuary with this family.

December 30

2000 – Roger Federer clinches Switzerland's victory over Thailand at the Hopman Cup defeating Paradorn Srichaphan 6-4, 6-2 after teammate Martina Hingis beats Tamarine Tanasugarn 6-1, 6-1. Federer and Hingis then team to defeat Tanasugarn and Srichaphan 6-0, 6-1.

2011 – Novak Djokovic beats Roger Federer 6-2, 6-1 in the semifinals of the Mubadala World Tennis Championship, an exhibition tournament in Abu Dhabi, United Arab Emirates.

2013 – Roger Federer conducts a pre-event press conference at the Brisbane International and explains to the media the process and timeline of changing to a new 98-inch racquet.

"It's one again that Wilson worked on and adjusted after my comments," Federer says. "They wanted to do some more work on that racquet anyway. They sent me one round of racquets after the U.S. Open. and now another one after the [Barclays ATP] World Tour Finals. I tested again a couple and chose the one I'm playing with now, that I've been practising with two and a half straight weeks in Dubai. I feel very comfortable, more comfortable than I did with the one after Wimbledon, which felt very different but very good as well. This one feels more of an extension that I had before, but it's more futuristic in form, I guess. I'm actually very eager to see how it's going to react in the matches now."

December 31

2002 – Roger Federer struggles with lucky-loser entrant Andrei Stoliarov of Russia in his opening match of the 2003 tennis season, needing one hour and 26 minutes and three sets to register the 6-2, 6-7 (4), 6-4 win at the Qatar Open in Doha. Federer slams 16 aces in the victory.

2013 – Roger Federer and Nicola Mahut pair in doubles at the Brisbane International and upset the No. 1 seeds Julien Rojer and Horia Tecau 7-5, 7-6(5) in the first round. Federer hits one of the most incredible shots of his career during the match, leaping to hit a stretch overhead with excessive spin that lands on the other side of the court like a drop shot just over the net, before spinning back on to Federer's side of the court to win the point. Tweets Christopher Clarey of the *New York Times*, "Thought I'd seen #Federer hit every shot in the book. Until this: an overhead drop shot winner"

2011 – Rafael Nadal beats Roger Federer 6-1, 7-5 to claim third place at the Mubadala World Tennis Championship in Abu Dhabi, United Arab Emirates. After the match, Federer downplays losing to both Novak Djokovic and Nadal in the exhibition tournament. "It's about getting ready and feeling fine out there and enjoying a great atmosphere here and having the chance to play world class players," Federer says. "Trying a few things, see where you are at and see where the other guys are at. Obviously, I could tell Novak and Rafa are playing really well. That is not a surprise to me. I expected them to be in good shape for next year and they proved that to me this weekend."

2010 – Roger Federer defeats Robin Soderling 6-7 (3), 6-3, 6-3 in the semifinals of the World Tennis Championships exhibition tournament in Abu Dhabi, United Arab Emirates. Federer advances to face Rafael Nadal, who defeats Tomas Berdych 6-4, 6-4.

ALSO FROM
NEW CHAPTER PRESS

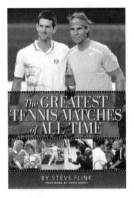

The Greatest Tennis Matches of All Time
By Steve Flink

Author and tennis historian Steve Flink profiles and ranks the greatest tennis matches in the history of the sport. Roger Federer, Billie Jean King, Rafael Nadal, Bjorn Borg, John McEnroe, Martina Navratilova, Rod Laver, Don Budge and Chris Evert are all featured in this book that breaks down, analyzes, and puts into historical context the most memorable matches ever played.

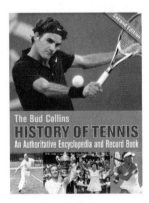

The Bud Collins History of Tennis
By Bud Collins

Compiled by the most famous tennis journalist and historian in the world, this book is the ultimate compilation of historical tennis information, including year-by-year recaps of every tennis season, biographical sketches of every major tennis personality, as well as stats, records, and championship rolls for all the major events.

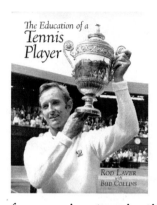

The Education of a Tennis Player

By Rod Laver with Bud Collins

Depicting the monumental achievements of a world-class athlete, this firsthand account documents Rod Laver's historic 1969 Grand Slam sweep of all four major tennis titles. This frank memoir details Laver's childhood, early career, and his most important matches. Each chapter also contains a companion tennis lesson, providing tips on how players of all levels can improve their own game and sharing strategies that garnered unparalleled success on the courts. Fully updated on the 40th anniversary of the author's most prominent triumph, this revised edition contains brand new content, including the story of Laver's courageous recovery from a near-fatal stroke in 1998.

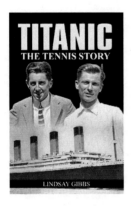

TITANIC: The Tennis Story

By Lindsay Gibbs

A stirring and remarkable story, this novel tells the tale of the intertwined life of Dick Williams and Karl Behr who survived the sinking of the *Titanic* and went on to have Hall of Fame tennis careers. Two years before they faced each other in the quarterfinals of the U.S. Nationals – the modern-day U.S. Open - the two men boarded the infamous ship as strangers. Dick, shy and gangly, was moving to America to pursue a tennis career and attend Harvard. Karl, a dashing tennis veteran, was chasing after Helen, the love of his life. The two men remarkably survived the sinking of the great vessel and met aboard the rescue ship *Carpathia*. But as they reached the shores of the United States, both men did all they could to distance themselves from the disaster. An emotional and touching work, this novel brings one of the most extraordinary sports stories to life in literary form. This real-life account – with an ending seemingly plucked out of a Hollywood screenplay - weaves the themes of love, tragedy, history, sport and perseverance.

www.NewChapterMedia.com